German Unification
and Its Discontents

German Unification
and Its Discontents

Documents from the Peaceful Revolution

RICHARD T. GRAY
and
SABINE WILKE

Editors and Translators

University of Washington Press

Seattle and London

Library of Congress Cataloging-in-Publication Data
German unification and its discontents : documents from the peaceful revolution
    /Richard T. Gray and Sabine Wilke, editors and translators
        p. cm.
    Documents translated from German.
    Includes bibliographical references and index.
    ISBN 0–295–97491–5 (alk. paper)
        1. Germany—History—Unification, 1990—Sources.   2. Germany (East)—
Politics and government—1989–1990—Sources.   3. Germany (West)—Politics and
government—1982–1990—Sources.   4. Opposition (Political science)—Germany
(East)—Sources.   I. Gray, Richard T.   II. Wilke, Sabine, 1957–
DD290.22.G47   1995   95–39753
943.1087'8—dc20   CIP

The paper used in this publication meets the minimum requirements of American National Standard for Information Sciences—Permanence of Paper for Printed Library Materials, ANSI Z39.48-1984. ∞

Photographs following page 136 courtesy German Information Center, New York.

Contents

List of Illustrations

Acknowledgments

The editors would like to thank Bill Hutfilz and Laura Jackson for translating selected documents for this volume. Unless otherwise noted, all other translations are our own. Thanks are due also to Eddie Cox and Sylvia Rieger for proofreading the manuscript and compiling the index. We are grateful to the following publishers and authors for granting us translation rights and permission to reprint: Wolf Biermann for "Das war's. Klappe zu. Der Affe lebt.," first published in *Die Zeit*; Bouvier Verlag for documents from Helmut Herles et al.,*Vom Runden Tisch zum Parlament*; *Deutschland Archiv* 22 (1989) for selected speeches; *Frankfurter Rundschau* for "Nein zum Staatsvertrag"; Goldmann Verlag for documents from Benno Zanetti, *Der Weg zur deutschen Einheit: 9. November–3. Oktober 1990*; Stefan Heym for "Aschermittwoch in der DDR" and "Auf Sand gebaut"; Wilhelm Heyne Verlag for documents from Severin Weiland et al., *9. November: Das Jahr danach* and Michaela Wimmer et al.,*"Wir sind das Volk!": Die DDR im Aufbruch*; Luchterhand Literaturverlag for Martina Krone, "Keine Chancen mehr für uns?"; Rowohlt Verlag for Günter de Bruyn, "Fromme Wünsche, offene Fragen" and documents from Charles Schüttekopf, *"Wir sind das Volk!": Flugschriften, Aufrufe und Texte einer deutschen Revolution*; *Der Spiegel* for Lothar de Maizière's speech at the signing of the Unification Treaty; Steidl Verlag for Günter Grass, "Ein Schnäppchen namens DDR"; and Verlag für internationale Politik for documents from *Europa-Archiv* 45 (1990). All reasonable efforts have been made to establish copyright holders for other materials not in the public domain. Jürgen Habermas's essay "D-Mark Nationalism" was initially published in *New German Critique* 52 (1991): 84-101 under the title "Yet Again: German Identity–A Unified Nation of Angry DM-Burghers?" The editors wish to thank *New German Critique* for permission to reprint this essay in modified form. Some of the longer documents have been excerpted and our deletions are marked by ellipsis.

We would also like to express our gratitude to the "Dokumentationsstelle für unkonventionelle Literatur" at the Landesbibliothek Stuttgart, Germany, for giving us access to many of the flyers and other non-conventional documents from the revolution in East Germany; we thank the director of the "Dokumentationsstelle" for granting us permission to reprint these materials in English translation. We are grateful also to the German Information Center for providing us permission to reproduce the illustrations. The translating and editing of this volume could not have been completed without the generous support of the Royalties Research Fund of the University of Washington.

The published sources from which documents were drawn are listed in the bibliography. The glossary explains German terms, political organizations, acronyms, and other relevant data. The index of persons includes brief biographical facts about each individual.

Introduction
How the East Was Won

For forty years the dream of German unification was the mythos that–invisible and unimaginable, but nonetheless omnipresent– formed the touchstone of West German political life. The West German Basic Law *(Grundgesetz)*, the very constitution on which the Federal Republic of Germany (FRG) was founded in 1949, defined this republic as a kind of transitional state whose structures were to be dissolved or renegotiated at such time in the future when the Germans would face the option of being unified into a single nation. At the same time, however, Article 23 of the Basic Law outlined the provisions according to which its statutes could be extended to parts of the prewar German territory that were not yet consolidated under its aegis. Thus a fundamental ambivalence about the actual process of eventual unification was codified in the West German constitution itself. A practical political precedent for the implementation of Article 23 was established in 1957 when the Saarland, which had been under French control since 1945, joined the Federal Republic of Germany in accordance with the provisions of this statute. Throughout the Cold War, however, it was impossible for anyone in the West to imagine that the territory of the German Democratic Republic (GDR), which appeared to be firmly integrated into the socialist camp, could ever be simply annexed to the FRG without a renegotiation of the Basic Law. When on 9 November 1989 the Berlin Wall was opened and the idea of German unification was suddenly transformed from an impossible dream into a possible political reality, questions about the process of unification divided the defenders of unification in East and West. While West German politicians began posturing for a simple annexation of the GDR according to Article 23, the revolutionary democrats of the GDR who had helped initiate the "peaceful revolution" argued for convening a constitutional congress that would formulate a new constitution for a united Germany.

Throughout the postwar era the significance of German unification extended far beyond the political parameters of the two German states. For the Western allies the notion of German unification assumed the character of a utopian project that would spell the overcoming of the Cold War and the ultimate defeat of communism. Divided Germany became the most palpable symbol of the ideological rift running through the heart of Europe; and for the West the political "island" of West Berlin, which was rescued from the siegelike conditions of the Berlin blockade by an intensive and costly Allied airlift, became a European tinsel town that concretized the economic benefits of capitalism. Thus the "German Question"–the unresolved issues of German nationhood, ideological and military allegiance, and weight and position in European politics–became the focal point for all the central issues of the Cold War.

It is often forgotten that German unification was first broached by Soviet leader Joseph Stalin, who in 1952 addressed a note to the Western allies suggesting that the country be reunified on the basis of free elections held in all of Germany. Stalin's major political condition for unification, however, was an insistence that united Germany permanently embrace political neutrality–a condition that was rejected by the Western powers and the West German populace. It is no coincidence, of course, that almost forty years later, on 1 February 1990, East German leader Hans Modrow formulated a plan for unification that included German neutrality as one of its stipulations (see document 41). The question of German neutrality became fundamental in the discussions about unification, with the West once again opposing a neutral Germany. This time, however, Western intransigence on this question paid off, and neutrality soon became a moot issue.

The rejection of unification by the West in 1952 can be comprehended only in the context of the intense ideological and political tensions of the immediate postwar era. Western Germany was already beginning to experience the "economic miracle" that would mark its recovery from the destruction of World War II and its reemergence as a major European–indeed, world–economic powerhouse. Moreover, under the leadership of Konrad Adenauer, who was West German chancellor from 1949 to 1963, the Federal Republic attained a high degree of internal political stability as well as political integration into the Western bloc. In 1955 the Federal Republic joined the NATO alliance and was granted almost complete sovereignty by the occupying powers. A parallel development, albeit on a smaller scale, took place in East Germany, as the GDR established itself as one of the most politically stable, ideologically faithful, and economically powerful states in the Soviet sphere of influence. Each German state thus succeeded in establishing a relatively secure political identity–defined in part, to be sure, by ideological opposition to the "other" Germany across the border. Symptomatic of such political hostility was the Hallstein Doctrine, which governed the policy of the FRG toward the GDR throughout the 1950s and 1960s. This doctrine formulated the refusal by West Germany's ruling conservative Christian Democratic Union (CDU) to acknowledge the GDR's right to exist as an independent state. The result was that there were no open diplomatic channels between the West German and East German states until the introduction of *Ostpolitik*, a policy of rapprochement with the GDR initiated by West Germany's first Social-Democratic (SPD) chancellor, Willy Brandt, in 1969.

The growing ideological alienation that separated the two states crystallized especially clearly around divergent attitudes toward Germany's Nazi past and the crimes of the Holocaust. Officially, the West Germany of Konrad Adenauer pursued a policy of *Vergangenheitsbewältigung*, "overcoming the past," by attempting to come to terms with the heritage of the Third Reich. This policy included payment of over 100 billion German marks in reparations to individual Jews and to the state of Israel, as well as state sponsorship of scholarship on the Nazi period, largely organized through the Institut für Zeitgeschichte (Institute for Contemporary History) in Berlin. On the other hand, politicians who had been members of the Nazi Party and had actively supported the Hitler regime–Hans Globke and Kurt Georg Kiesinger were prominent figures–played important roles in West German political life. Kiesinger, in fact, rose to the highest office, becoming West German chancellor during the so-called Grand Coalition between the CDU and the SPD from 1966 to 1969. In other words, what in postwar West German society was euphemistically called "coming to terms with the past" was in fact strategic neglect and repression of this past and the sense of guilt it engendered. In East Germany, by contrast, former Nazi politicians were systematically brought to trial and convicted, allowing citizens to develop a certain sense of self-righteousness with regard to their treatment of the Nazi past. At the same time, however, the GDR was able to disavow any moral responsibility for the Nazi atrocities by defining itself as an "antifascist" state that had actively participated in the defeat of Hitler's Third Reich. This attitude was concretized in the GDR's refusal to compensate Jewish victims of fascism or pay reparations to Israel. Thus each German state developed a form of historical revisionism that allowed evasion of the issues of guilt and responsibility for the Nazi crimes. In effect, each was able to accuse the other of perpetuating the fascist heritage: the East pointed the finger at the West because of the role of former Nazi functionaries in FRG political life; the West indicted the East as a state that adopted and continued the totalitarian politics of the Hitler era.

The political estrangement between the FRG and the GDR did not begin to mollify until 1969, when a political reorientation of the West German Liberal Democratic Party (FDP), which had previously supported the CDU but now aligned itself with the SPD, allowed the Social Democrats to occupy the chancellorship for the first time. The administrations of Willy Brandt (1969-74) and Helmut Schmidt (1974-82) radically changed the course of West German policy toward the GDR. Their *Ostpolitik* established official diplomatic relations between the two German states and led to the negotiation of several agreements to regulate such things as economic exchange and travel regulations across the border. The Moscow and Warsaw Treaties of 1970, to which both Germanies were signatories, acknowledged the Oder and Neiße rivers as the definitive western border of Poland and renounced any German claims to territory beyond the borders of the FRG and the GDR. In 1982, again largely due to a reorientation by the Liberal Democrats, the Christian Democrats regained power and named Helmut Kohl chancellor. After the detente of the 1970s, the 1980s were an era of ideological retrenchment in West Germany, guided in part by the policies of then US President Ronald Reagan. One of the most hotly debated political issues of this period was the so-called NATO double-track decision, which deployed on West German soil Cruise and Pershing rockets aimed at the Warsaw Pact nations. Symptomatic of the new conservatism that fashioned West German political and cultural life was the 1986-87 scholarly debate known as *Der Historikerstreit* ("The Historians' Dispute"). This debate was initiated by a group of historians who claimed that the crimes committed by the National Socialists were on the same order as atrocities committed by such regimes as Stalin's Soviet Union or the GDR. Historians Ernst Nolte and Michael Stürmer went so far as to explain the Holocaust, the Nazis' extermination of six million Jews, as modeled on acts of mass destruction perpetrated by Stalin and the Bolsheviks in the 1930s and 1940s. This revisionist historiography, which attempted to minimize the horror of the Nazi Holocaust by comparing it with other political massacres, was met by a wave of protest by West German intellectuals. It was in this climate of increasing ideological retrenchment that the possibility of German unification suddenly burst upon the political scene.

When on 9 November 1989 the leadership of the GDR made the decision to open the Berlin Wall, the most potent symbol of the

Cold War and German political division, the West awoke suddenly to the realization that its utopian dream of an end to the Cold War standoff was on the verge of becoming a reality. In the United States the opening of the Wall was celebrated as a confirmation of the anticommunist, Cold War policies of the postwar years, and especially of the Reagan administration's intransigence on the issue of European disarmament. The self-celebratory character of the American response to the fall of the Iron Curtain was concretized most clearly in the transformation of the Berlin Wall and the Brandenburg Gate into the backdrop for evening news programs. Most Americans experienced German unification and the end of the Cold War as this well-choreographed media event, and it is likely that for many the most vital image of this central occurrence in postwar European and world history will be the picture of news anchors Tom Brokaw or Dan Rather reporting from their makeshift newsrooms in front of the Brandenburg Gate. But to interpret German unification in terms of ideological self-confirmation of the West's Cold War policies is to strip it of its political and historical substance, to reduce it to an ideologically charged image that ignores the conflicts, debates, and political negotiations that constituted the core of the historical event itself.

The present volume offers a detailed documentation of the circumstances and events that shaped the process of German unification, from the grassroots democratic movements that fueled the peaceful revolution in the GDR to the merger of the two German states on 3 October 1990, the "Day of German Unity." Two basic organizational possibilities presented themselves for ordering the documents translated and collected here: grouping the materials (regardless of their date of origin) according to their political positions and thematics, or presenting them in simple chronological order. Although the first option promised both to make the volume easier to use and to lend the documents a certain political coherence, we decided to opt for chronological sequence. This decision was informed by several considerations: first, by our sense that a thematic approach might enforce upon the material a coherence that it never possessed, thereby giving the unwarranted impression that from the outset German unification was staged with political purposiveness and ideological design; second, by our desire to recreate in the organization of the material the actual sequence in which events unfolded, thereby simulating in the reader's encounter with the documents the historical process according to which German unification was ultimately achieved; and third, by our belief that chronological ordering would help throw into relief certain historical moments and events in the logic of unification that are in danger of being obscured or forgotten as the official history of this event is written in a climate of national accomplishment and ideological self-aggrandizement.

It is important to remember that the precise form taken by German unification–namely, the incorporation of the territory of the former GDR into the FRG and the extension in unmodified form of the laws and political structures of the FRG onto the former GDR and its inhabitants–was decidedly not the aim of the revolutionary citizens' movements within East Germany responsible for setting the process of German unification in motion. From the outset, the interest of these groups was introduction of democratic reforms into the socialist structures of the GDR, along the lines proposed for the Soviet Union by Michail Gorbachev in the policies of perestroika and glasnost. The rhetoric of the GDR reformers, which appealed to concepts such as "radical renewal," "revolutionary transformation," "democratization," "openness," and the "constitutional state," was drawn, in fact, directly from the discourse of reform employed by Gorbachev. The juxtaposition of speeches by Erich Honecker and Gorbachev at the celebration of the GDR's fortieth anniversary (documents 8 and 9) brings out particularly well the confrontation between Honecker's hard-line Stalinist rhetoric and Gorbachev's language of reform. This discursive conflict reflects in microcosm the clash between the East German Socialist Unity Party (SED) and the GDR reformers in the first weeks of upheaval. One recognition that the sequential reading of the historical documents brings home is the manner in which the rhetoric of reform was gradually appropriated by mainstream politicians in both East and West. Already the first speeches by Honecker's immediate successor, Egon Krenz (documents 13, 15, and 18), manifested an attempt to pay lip service to the ideas disseminated by the reform movement and to lay claim to their immanent implementation as a strategy for quelling the demonstrations for reform. As we know, Krenz's tactic failed, and his successor, Hans Modrow, was the first SED leader who did not merely adopt the rhetoric of the reformers but actually sought to engage them and their ideas for a political transformation of the GDR state and society. When in the spring of 1990 West German politicians entered into the struggle to win over the GDR populace as a potential new electorate, they, too, appropriated the discourse of reform, the rhetoric of which they employed in a two-fold manner: first, as a way of appealing to GDR citizens and portraying West German political parties as instruments for realizing their program of reforms; second, as a means for discrediting forty years of SED governance and the aberrance of the socialist planned economy. This strategy helped the West Germans undercut the credibility of the then-current GDR government and its leading politicians.

Throughout the early phase of the peaceful revolution, many of the reformers still held out hope for an East German "third path," an individual political course that would steer around the Scylla and Charybdis of the Cold War, rejecting the ideologically tainted political opposition between "democracy" and "Stalinist dictatorship" on the one hand and the choice between a capitalist free market or the socialist planned economy on the other. When German unification was addressed at all in this context, it was conceived in terms of such a "third path," as a rapprochement based on mutual reform in both the GDR and the FRG, a process that would place a future unified Germany outside the political and economic bloc structure characteristic of the Cold War. For many, however, the idea of the "third path" was politically suspect from the outset because it evoked the historical notion of the *Sonderweg* ("special path"), which was associated with conservative German political programs of the early twentieth century. The concept referred to the unique political and cultural status that Germany was said to occupy because of its geographical location in the center of Europe, on the divide between East and West. For many people, it was precisely this belief, understood as an argument about the cultural specificity of the German people, that had led to the distorted nationalism and terror of the Third Reich. However, in contrast to such older notions of a German *Sonderweg*, the "third path" envisioned by the East German reformers made no claims about the cultural individuality of the German people, but merely attempted to address the possibility of a political and economic alternative to the established models in Eastern and Western Europe. Still, the idea of a Germany that independently pursued some political "third path" could not help but call forth fear and opposition from neighbors both to the east and to the west. One of the motivating forces behind the rejection of German neutrality, in fact, was the belief, based on historical experience, that Germany could be effectively controlled only if solidly integrated into a greater European political alliance.

The prospect of a unification process that would require reform of the FRG met with spontaneous resistance in West Germany. As history would have it, the revolutionary cycles in the FRG and the GDR were wholly out of sync, so that the last thing one could expect from Helmut Kohl's West Germany of the 1980s, riding high on an economic boom and the strength of the German mark, was an admission of a need for political and economic reform. As interesting as it is to wonder what might have happened if the FRG of 1989 had been experiencing the social turmoil it faced in the troubled years of the late sixties, this remains a matter of idle speculation. What is clear, however, is that talk of a "third path" was radically cut off by Hans Modrow's plan for German unification presented on 1 February 1990 (document 41). As the documents gathered here bear out, nothing in the previous positions of the Modrow government or the Round Table discussions carried on by the democratic opposition in the GDR gave any indication of a willingness to consider such a speedy merger of the two German states. Modrow's plan appeared as a bolt out of the blue and established overnight new terms in which the ongoing debate over German-German rapprochement was carried out. For the first time, German unification was officially on the political agenda–even though Modrow's plan envisioned only the formation of confederative structures that would pave the way for unification. Unification was the long-range goal that lurked behind Helmut Kohl's ten-point program for overcoming the division of Germany, outlined already at the end of November 1989 (document 26), but Kohl's concrete suggestions were restricted to structures that would further a German-German confederation, and unification was broached only as a wish that would be fulfilled in the distant future. It is unclear why Modrow decided to put unification on the table at the time and in the manner that he did. Most likely he had become aware that the momentum of political events in both East and West Germany, along with rapid deterioration of the East German economy, had already made unification inevitable. He may have thought that positioning himself as the leading spokesperson of unification could serve as a preemptive strike that would allow him to take the political initiative and create a better bargaining position for the GDR and its citizens in the unification negotiations with the FRG. If this was Modrow's aim, it certainly backfired. For just ten days after Modrow announced his plan for unification, Helmut Kohl was in Moscow securing the blessing of Michail Gorbachev for the Germans' right to free self-determination with regard to the question of their unification in a single state (document 42). Three days later, on 13 February 1990, Kohl and Modrow met in Bonn and began to cement plans that would lead to the economic, currency, and social union of the two German states and to ultimate unification. Although Modrow was the first to put the ball of German unification in play, it was Kohl who ultimately ran with it, using the increasing severity of the crisis in the GDR as legitimation for speedy unification. The ball, in fact, was never again in Modrow's court, and bit by bit the gains he had hoped to make by coming forward with a unification plan—in particular, social and economic protection of GDR citizens, establishment of an economic system in which planning and market are interconnected, and, above all, guarantee of military neutrality for a united Germany—were eroded until his plan conformed with the program the West German politicians had in mind for effecting German unification. Ultimately, then, Modrow played into the hands of Kohl, but perhaps the historical momentum had indeed already carried the process so far along that the result, unification according to the terms dictated by West German politicians and economists, had become truly inevitable.

Once unification came to be seen as a politically viable alternative, one that was sanctioned even by the Soviet leadership, the terms of interchange between West and East Germany changed completely. In the West, the strategy of unification was couched in the rhetoric of national solidarity, responsibility, prudence, and, above all, pan-European unity. In the East, the discourse and ideas engendered by the citizens' movements during the peaceful revolution were quickly banished. These idealistic demands, theories, and hopes were supplanted by much more concrete and practical political issues. As a result, arguments about "reform," a "third path," and "radical restructuring" of the GDR came to be overshadowed by concerns about flight of East Germans to the West; economic assistance for the GDR and its citizens; currency union between the FRG and the GDR and the rate at which East German marks would be exchanged for West German marks; and questions of political consolidation and unification. It is significant to note that even the discussions at the East German Round Table, at which the self-ordained opposition to the SED rulers, the diverse citizens' movements and political groupings that emerged from the peaceful revolution, as well as the former bloc parties and political organizations such as the trade unions were represented, also began to focus on these more pragmatic issues, gradually either leaving the rhetoric and demands of revolution behind, or reducing them to mere addenda or second thoughts. The first freely elected prime minister of the GDR, Lothar de Maizière, eventually claimed that the political will of the electorate, as he understood it, gave him a mandate for speedy unification. This appeal to the will of the electorate justified a unification policy that bypassed both parliaments and ultimately prevented the German people from having immediate input into the political process.

It is the fate of all revolutions that the idealism responsible for generating revolt in the first place must at some point revert to sober realism; but usually the ensuing realism and initial idealism at least have something in common. This is scarcely the case for the peaceful revolution in the GDR. The realism it produced degenerated quickly into economic opportunism and the drive for prosperity, no matter what the political price. This was made most evident by the intensity with which the East German opposition clung to the demand for a one-to-one exchange rate of D-marks for GDR-marks as the foundation of an economic and currency union between the FRG and the GDR. All the fervor that once fueled the revolution was eventually channeled into this single demand, and the political questions stirred up by the revolutionary opposition were dispelled by the obsession with and promise of wealth. This reduction of the revolution to a matter of national economy may also help explain the virility and persistence of neo-Nazism and xenophobia in eastern Germany. Since all the idealistic hopes of the revolution were eventually invested in the material expectation of salvation by the D-mark and the West's productive economy, when the anticipated economic miracle failed to arrive with all the speed and force with which it had been conjured up in people's fantasies, their disappointment and frustration sought a convenient avenue for ventilation.

Looking back on this historical process from the perspective afforded by the documents collected here, it appears that two major interventions radically changed the pace and direction of events. One, Modrow's surprise plan for German unification, has already been discussed. The other was the SED's electrifying decision to open the border to West Germany and West Berlin. It is more than a curiosity of the historical process of unification that the two seminal occurrences were initiated by the leadership of the SED, the political group that was invested most heavily in retaining the prerevolutionary status quo. On the one hand, this testifies to the unpredictability of political actions and their repercussions in times of deep-seated turmoil and upheaval; for those moves calculated by the SED to shore up its own position unwittingly became the motors behind unification. On the other hand, however, the fact that unification evolved out of the failed tactics of the SED rather than out of the initiatives and programs of the West German politicians and their parties bears testimony to the West's incapacity to deal creatively with the emerging political realities. To be sure, the SED's decision to open the Wall had been forced upon it by the flight of GDR citizens across the Hungarian border and by the fact that the West German embassies in Eastern bloc countries had become refuges that opened the door to the West. But the SED no doubt hoped that by making concessions on one of the most concrete and vociferously expressed demands of the GDR opposition groups, the issue of free travel, they would be able to blunt the force of the revolt that manifested itself in the growing demonstrations throughout the country. At the same time, the SED leadership certainly realized that opening the border would present the FRG with a political and economic problem that had the potential to shake the very foundations of West German society: dealing with the flood of East German refugees that would stream into the West and demand their fair share of the wealth and prosperity. If this was, in fact, calculated by the East German leadership, then in a sense the fall of the Wall was a brilliant political move, for it permitted the GDR to turn its own internal problems, which had supplied ample grist for the mills of West German propaganda about the failure of state socialism, into a political and economic crisis for the FRG itself. That the West German politicians then began to perceive the refugee problem more as an economic bane than as a propaganda boon was evident in the speech given by Helmut Kohl at Schöneberg City Hall in Berlin just two days after the border was opened (see document 21). On this occasion Kohl not only encouraged the citizens of the GDR to remain in their "traditional homeland," as he euphemistically referred to the GDR, but admonished those who had already fled to the West to return to the GDR and participate in the rebuilding of their country.

This theme continued to appear as a prominent leitmotif in the arguments of West German politicians throughout the rest of the unification debate. The promises of immediate economic assistance for the East that followed shortly after the fall of the Wall should thus be seen as anything but gestures of goodwill on the part of FRG politicians. Indeed, they were conceived as emergency measures to stem the tide of refugees and prevent economic and social disaster in the FRG itself. As it turns out, of course, the promised economic assistance was repeatedly withheld, and the aid really arrived only with the ratification of the first State Treaty creating an economic and currency union. Renegging on the promise of immediate financial aid became one of the trumpcards in the hand of the West German leadership, for it gave them precisely the leverage they needed to sell unification according to Article 23 of the Basic Law as the only acceptable answer to the newly posed German Question. Thus the opening of the border entailed an irreversible and, one might say, perverse logic all its own: most likely intended as a quick fix for East German political stability and as a simultaneous threat to the stability of the West, it ultimately forced the West German politicians to turn to the tactic of speedy unification as the most effective way of keeping the East Germans in the East and thereby ensuring the stability of the West. Implicit in all of this was the unpleasant (and easily repressed) recognition that the economic prosperity of the West Germans was just as dependent on the isolation from the East provided by the Iron Curtain as was the political stability of the East on its isolation from the West. But the East Germans should also have recognized in the "stay put" rhetoric of the West Germans an unwillingness to share the wealth they had accumulated. Whereas the East Germans tended to view unification in terms of a family reunion in which the poorer relatives, long cut off from the prosperous family homestead, would be taken in and rehabilitated, the West Germans were inclined to view it more like a business deal, a sort of corporate merger, arranged such that the parent company could not possibly lose and might even stand to make long-term gains by swallowing up its weaker competitor.

This is the story that emerges from an examination of the arguments, rhetoric, and events of German unification as they are concretized in the documents collected here. Interspersed with the official political positions of the East and West German governments are documents from the opposition groups in the GDR and critical responses to the unification process by intellectuals from East and West Germany. But the story of unification is not complete until one considers the historical failure of the radical opposition, on both sides of the intra-German border, to respond creatively to the provocation of the peaceful revolution in the GDR and develop concrete practical alternatives either to the market economy and achievement orientation of the FRG or to the planned economy and relative unproductivity of the GDR. This story of failure is also elucidated in some of the critical responses to the unification process.

In the West the left-of-center opposition parties, the SPD and the Greens, seemed capable of assuming only extreme positions on the unification issue: they tended to play the role either of claqueurs for the policies of the ruling government coalition or of querulants who could be denounced for placing unreasonable obstacles in the path of unification. The Greens, at least, steered a consistent course of opposition to the terms of unification that were dictated by the Kohl government. The SPD, by contrast, played a much more ambivalent role. Because they held a majority in the West German *Bundesrat*, the upper house of parliament representing the individual *Länder* (federal states), the Social Democrats wielded a powerful political weapon that could be used against Kohl and his policies. The SPD did, in fact, threaten to defeat the first State Treaty in the *Bundesrat* if the Kohl government refused to make certain concessions to ensure the social and economic security of GDR citizens. But the SPD's demands amounted to little more than a fine-tuning of the program established by the CDU and FDP coalition so that, unable to offer any visionary leadership of its own, it essentially fell into step with the Kohl government. The leadership vacuum in the SPD had been a problem since Hans-Jochen Vogel had replaced Helmut Schmidt as head of the party. This situation was aggravated by the fact that the SPD leadership was going through a difficult process of transition, with Oskar Lafontaine, the representative of the younger generation in the SPD, being groomed as the party's candidate for chancellor in the next *Bundestag* elections. Lafontaine and Vogel, however, had vastly divergent opinions about the position the SPD should take with regard to unification, Lafontaine pleading the case for opposition and intransigence, and Vogel inclined to grasp the historical opportunity for a unified German nation. This dispute unleashed a crisis in the party that undercut its authority and power, and it was Vogel's nationalist position that finally won the upper hand. Some members of the extreme left wing of the SPD refused to accept the official policy of the party and expressed their dissatisfaction by refusing to go along with the party majority—an action that is extremely unusual in West German party politics, where *Bundestag* representatives are expected to follow the party line—and casting "no" votes against the State Treaty that created an economic and currency union between the FRG and the GDR (see document 59).

If the West German opposition was in disarray, this was no less true for the opposition parties in the GDR. Having emerged as grassroots organizations, they had very diverse aims and were from the outset more fragmented than they were unified. With the re-establishment of East German branch organizations of the CDU and the SPD, which then drew large followings and were joined by some of the leaders of the peaceful revolution, the GDR political organism began to look more and more like a clone of the FRG. Most important, perhaps, was that the citizens' initiatives and political groupings that had initiated the peaceful revolution were increasingly marginalized, coerced either into joining forces with one of the major parties opposing the SED's successor party, the Party of Democratic Socialism (PDS), or banding together in a futile attempt to assert political influence in the rapidly changing political landscape. Their marginalization was exacerbated, of course, by the fact that as grassroots organizations they lacked the financial assets, the infrastructure, and the party organization to compete against parties such as the East-CDU and East-SPD, who could depend on the financial backing of their sister-parties in West Germany and could rally behind the recognized West German politicians who were their standard-bearers. To make matters worse for any pan-German opposition to the policies of the Kohl government, the East-SPD lent its full support to the movement toward unification, protesting when its ally in the West threatened to undermine the process. All in all, then, the political cards were heavily stacked in favor of the bandwagon drive for unification according to the statutes of Article 23 of the West German Basic Law. The bitter irony of this, of course, was that the only people who refused to join the bandwagon were those opposition groups of the peaceful revolution who were responsible for setting the whole process in motion in the first place.

To the extent that there are regrets among oppositional intellectuals about the course of German unification, these regrets stem from the missed opportunity to try out the "third path" envisioned by the GDR opposition groups. In the post–Cold War world it has become acceptable to declare the socialist experiment, and often even socialism itself, dead. It is important to recognize, however, that the socialism realized in the GDR and Eastern Europe was a socialism defined in large part by its ideological and military confrontation with an inimical West. Might socialism have developed in more positive and successful directions if it had evolved in a friendlier geopolitical environment, one characterized by mutual cooperation rather than blind hostility and competition? This is the question that the activists of the peaceful revolution in the GDR were eager to test in the post-Cold War world that was just beginning to take shape. The realities of German unification, which transpired as an exemplary winning of the East, removed this question, for better or for worse, from the agenda of European politics.

At the time of this writing, four years after German unification, it is still too early to try to assess the long-range repercussions this event will have on German political life. Although the so-called Super Election of 1994 returned Kohl's CDU/FDP coalition to power, its electoral support began to show signs of slippage. One important indication of the 1994 elections was that of dwindling enthusiasm for the extreme right-wing parties that had entered the German political scene in recent years. Part of the reason for this, of course, was that some of these parties' central issues had been preempted by Kohl's post-unification government. The best case in point is the new German law regulating the influx of political-asylum seekers. The right-wing German Republican Party had built its base of supporters primarily by arguing for policies that would stem the tide of immigrants from Eastern Europe and the Third World that was flowing first into Western and then into unified Germany. The position of the Republicans smacked of the "Germany for the Germans" rhetoric that was—and still is—being voiced by German neo-Nazis, a rhetoric that only too easily invoked the National Socialist concept of *Lebensraum*, "living space," that fueled Hitler's war of aggression. But the political wind was taken out of the sails of the Republican Party in July 1993 when the German government, following acrimonious debate among the partners of the ruling coalition, enacted a tough new asylum law that effectively cut the number of asylum seekers by over fifty percent. The poor showing of the Republicans in the 1994 election can be attributed in part to the fact that they had lost their flagship political issue.

The new German asylum law has been interpreted by some as a sign that intolerance toward non-Germans is once again becoming the official policy of a united Germany intent on protecting its wealth and preserving its cultural integrity. Of course, it should not be forgotten that many of the nations of the First World have resorted to stricter immigration laws in the interests of economic protectionism. More significant in the context of united Germany is the question whether the asylum law should be seen as one manifestation of a groundswell of political conservatism that could lead to an alienation and radicalization of the German left in general, but in particular of the supporters of the PDS in the new eastern *Länder*. What is certain is that in the four years since unification, the hopes of many ex-GDR citizens and of the opposition parties in the West that the policies of the united Federal Republic would be "socialized" and reformed by the merger with the once socialist GDR have largely been disappointed.

This increased marginalization of the left-oriented opposition has crystallized in post-unification Germany around two hotly debated issues: the new abortion law and the decision to allow German troops to participate in UN peacekeeping missions. At the time of unification the two German states had vastly different abortion laws. In West Germany abortion was illegal except in cases of medical necessity or social and ethical exigency (e.g., insufficient financial means, genetic problems, rape). In East Germany abortion was legal within the first trimester. In 1992 the legislature of united Germany passed a compromise bill that made abortion legal within the first twelve weeks of pregnancy on the condition that the woman go through pregnancy counseling. But the German supreme court threw out this law in 1993, demanding new legislation that takes into consideration the obligation of the state to protect human life. In the meantime, the court's 183-page ruling set out standards on the abortion issue. This, in turn, triggered a wave of protests by feminist organizations throughout Germany. At present the final form of the abortion statute is still under discussion, but feminists and the left opposition fear a tightening of abortion rights. Regarding the deployment of German troops in UN peacekeeping missions, the German supreme court upheld, against the vocal opposition of the Social Democrats, the law that would make such participation possible. For many Germans, the very idea of German troops on foreign soil invokes memories of the wars of aggression that have disfigured the nation's political past. But the Kohl government could point to the encouragement of its NATO allies, who were anxious to see Germany take a greater economic and political responsibility in the post-Cold War world order, in support of its decision to commit troops to UN missions.

The perception that the Kohl government, under the influence of its conservative faction, has been moving precariously far to the political right has tended to alienate Germany's leftist opposition. One of the greatest dangers, perhaps, is that unified Germany could experience a period of polarization that would radicalize forces on both the right and the left. If such political division were to be added to the economic division between the wealthy "Wessies" and their poorer cousins, the "Ossies" of the former GDR, Germany could find itself entering a period of sociopolitical turmoil and instability. It is obvious today that the psychological wall that separates the citizens of western Germany and their fellow Germans in the east is much stronger and more impenetrable than the concrete wall that once divided them. The question is whether there are any political leaders in united Germany who are willing and able to initiate a peaceful revolution that can tear down this resilient barrier.

Richard T. Gray and Sabine Wilke
Seattle, April 1995

Map of United Germany

Chronology of Significant Events

1989

May 4   The first hole in the Iron Curtain appears when Hungary opens its border with Austria. GDR refugees begin to cross over the so-called "green border" between the GDR and Hungary in order to flee to the West.

May 7   Local elections are held in the GDR; opposition leaders protest alleged manipulations and falsifications of the results.

June 5   *Neues Deutschland* defends the bloodbath at Tiananmen Square in Beijing.

July 7   In the climate of relaxing East-West relations, Michail Gorbachev addresses the European Council.

Aug. – Sept.   East Germans use the border with Hungary as a means for emigrating to the West. By the end of September, 30,000 East Germans have fled their country.

Aug. 8   The Consulate of the FRG in East Berlin is closed because it is swamped with East German refugees. The East German refugees holed up in consulates in East Berlin, Budapest, and Warsaw demand safe passage to the West.

Aug. 13   The Consulate of the FRG in Hungary is closed because it is overflowing with refugees. The physicist Dr. Hans-Jürgen Fischbeck appeals before an assembly of opponents to the East German regime for the founding of an oppositional political party to take part in the *Volkskammer* elections in 1991.

Aug. 19   The largest wave of East German refugees since before the construction of the Berlin Wall: about 900 citizens of the GDR use the "Pan-European Picnic" held at the GDR-Hungarian border as a way to flee to Austria.

Aug. 24   GDR citizens in the embassy of the FRG in Hungary are evacuated by the Red Cross.

Aug. 28   Initiative for the founding of a Social-Democratic Party in East Berlin.

Sept. 4   Representatives of the socialist opposition ratify the appeal "For a Unified Left in the GDR." Police in Leipzig violently disperse civil rights demonstrators.

Sept. 10   The independent opposition group New Forum is founded. The group applies for permission to establish

	local party chapters, but permission is denied by the government on Sept. 20.
Sept. 12	The citizens' initiative Democracy Now is founded.
Sept. 14	The opposition group Democratic Awakening is founded.
Sept. 21	A flier appears calling for the founding of the politcal group New Forum.
Sept. 25	The largest demonstration on GDR soil since the building of the Berlin Wall takes place in Leipzig. About 5,000 demonstrators march through the center of town and hold a sit-in at the main train station. The demonstrators demand reforms and the legalization of the New Forum. The police show restraint.
Oct. 1	West German Foreign Minister Hans-Dietrich Genscher announces from the balcony of the West German embassy in Prague that the East German refugees will be permitted to travel to the FRG.
Oct. 3	Only a few days before the celebrations for the fortieth anniversary of the GDR, demonstrations in the GDR take on a more massive character.
Oct. 4	The first trains with emigrants from the Prague embassy pass through the GDR. In Dresden 5,000 people gather at the train station and some try to board the trains.
Oct. 5	The GDR closes its border with Czechoslovakia.
Oct. 6	Michail Gorbachev arrives in East Berlin.
Oct. 7	The celebrations for the fortieth anniversary of the founding of the German Democratic Republic begin. The Social-Democratic Party of the GDR is founded under the leadership of Ibrahim Böhme.
Oct. 8	Thousands of GDR citizens demonstrate in the streets chanting: "Democracy now or never." Several demonstrators are beaten and detained. Soviet leader Gorbachev appeals to the GDR leadership for change.
Oct. 9	The first "Monday demonstration" is held in Leipzig, in which approximately 70,000 people participate.
Oct. 11	The GDR leadership calls a special meeting to deal with the crisis and demands that Erich Honecker put together a report on the current situation. In this report the SED Politburo speaks for the first time of the necessity of reforms.

Oct. 12   The GDR opposition reacts optimistically to the state-
           ment by the SED Politburo, but points out that all the
           previous governmental and party structures, as well as
           all the functionaries and personnel, have remained the
           same.

Oct. 13   At a meeting with the bloc parties of the GDR
           (Christian Democrats, Liberal Democrats, National
           Democrats, and the Farmers' Party) Honecker promises
           reforms. The New Forum is declared a hostile organiza-
           tion.

Oct. 16   120,000 people, demanding reform and free elections,
           take part in the largest demonstration to date in
           Leipzig. Because of the mass exodus of workers, the eco-
           nomic situation in the GDR is becoming critical.

Oct. 18   Erich Honecker is forced to resign as General Secretary
           of the SED after 18 years of service. He is succeeded by
           Egon Krenz, who promises reforms.

Oct. 19   The *Ministerrat* of the GDR initiates reform. The Sec-
           retary of the Interior is called upon to formulate a new
           law regulating travel by East German citizens outside
           the GDR. The West German government promises eco-
           nomic support, but makes it contingent upon fundamen-
           tal reform.

Oct. 20   The GDR asks those who fled the country earlier in the
           year to return home, promising that they will suffer no
           repercussions and that they will be issued passports to
           allow them to travel legally.

Oct. 24   The *Volkskammer* elects Egon Krenz as head of the
           Staatsrat.

Oct. 25   More than 100,000 people in Dresden participate in
           open discussions.

Oct. 26   The first official meeting between opposition leaders
           and the SED Politburo takes place. In Dresden, hun-
           dreds of thousands of people respond to the call to hold
           open discussions with Hans Modrow, the local party
           leader, and Dresden mayor Wolfgang Berghof.

Oct. 27   The GDR announces a comprehensive amnesty for all
           those who have fled and those arrested during demon-
           strations. The promised new travel regulations are an-
           nounced. As of November 1, every GDR citizen will be
           allowed to travel to the West for up to 30 days.

Oct. 29   Well-known GDR artists, among them Christa Wolf, Stefan Heym, Stephan Hermlin, Ulrich Plenzdorf, Volker Braun, and Daniela Dahn, meet at the Church of the Redeemer in Berlin. The West German CDU General Secretary, Volker Rühe, suggests a 1:1 exchange of GDR-marks for D-marks.

Oct. 30   Mass demonstrations take place in the cities of Leipzig, Halle, Schwerin, and Karl-Marx-Stadt (Chemnitz). The demonstrators demand democracy, free elections, the separation of party and state, the elimination of the power monopoly of the SED, legalization of the New Forum, the dismantling of the Berlin Wall, legalization of civil disobedience, environmental protection, freedom of the press and freedom of thought, a constitutional state, and educational reforms.

Nov. 1   Egon Krenz meets with Michail Gorbachev in Moscow. Krenz stresses that German unification and the demolition of the Berlin Wall are "unrealistic demands" and emphasizes the leadership role of the party.

Nov. 2   Thousands of GDR citizens demonstrate for reform. The wave of refugees continues despite promises of internal reforms in the GDR. The leader of the GDR trade union organization, Harry Tisch, resigns, as do many other officials of the SED regime.

Nov. 3   The situation in the German embassy in Prague has once again become critical. The number of GDR refugees on the grounds of the embassy has risen to 4,000. The Politburo holds an emergency meeting. Egon Krenz announces drastic changes in the GDR, among them the resignations of five further politicians.

Nov. 4   2,000 refugees leave the embassy in Prague for West Germany. Mass demonstrations in East Berlin: one million people demonstrate peacefully for a reformed GDR. Altogether 28 speakers, mainly opposition leaders and artists, offer criticism and demand democratic reforms.

Nov. 5   15,000 GDR citizens emigrate to Bavaria within two days. The West German political parties begin to express their concerns about the refugee situation.

Nov. 6   The first draft of the new travel regulations for East German citizens is published in GDR newspapers. The New Forum reacts skeptically. GDR citizens are crossing from Czechoslovakia into Bavaria at the rate of 200 per hour.

Nov. 7　　The GDR government under Willi Stoph resigns. The East German Green Party is founded in East Berlin. Its members demand a "far-reaching ecological reconstruction of the GDR," as well as political reforms.

Nov. 8　　The entire Politburo resigns. The Central Committee of the GDR elects a new, but smaller Politburo. Hans Modrow emerges as one of the new leaders of the SED. The New Forum is declared legal.

Nov. 9　　Günter Schabowski, a Member of the GDR Politburo, announces the opening of the borders to the FRG and to West Berlin. Thousands of people rush to the border and celebrate until the morning hours. The *Bundestag* interrupts its session in reaction to the decision of the GDR leadership. The Soviet Union salutes the changes in the GDR. In West Germany some politicians begin suggesting that the flood of refugees from the GDR must be halted.

Nov. 10　　The Berlin Wall is broken through in additional places so that more border crossings become available. Berlin citizens assist in the effort. The entire city celebrates. West German Chancellor Helmut Kohl interrupts his visit to Poland to participate in a demonstration at the Schöneberg City Hall in West Berlin. Egon Krenz promises reforms of the sort that will lead, in his words, to a "revolution on German soil." Free elections and new political groups are part of a reform package. More SED leaders step down.

Nov. 11　　Chancellor Kohl and SED party leader Egon Krenz agree to meet in the GDR at the beginning of December.

Nov. 12　　One million GDR citizens use the weekend for trips to the West. Traffic comes to a halt and stores stay open late.

Nov. 13　　The *Volkskammer* elects Hans Modrow to succeed Willi Stoph as GDR Prime Minister. The demonstrations continue despite the new travel regulations and the opening of the Wall. The GDR opposition warns against a sell-out of the GDR.

Nov. 16　　The West German government demands from the GDR the abandonment of its socialist planned economy and the introduction of a social market economy as the precondition for economic aid. The opposition West German Social-Democratic Party denounces this demand. West German President Richard von Weizsäcker advises his fellow West German politicians against offering unsolicited advice for reforming the GDR.

Nov. 17   GDR Prime Minister Modrow presents his new cabinet. The SED retains the most significant posts. Modrow sends a memorandum to the European Community in Brussels expressing his wish for cooperation with the European Common Market.

Nov. 18   The *Volkskammer* initiates the first public debate about the recent events by reporting on the police actions taken against protesters who disrupted the fortieth anniversary celebration of the GDR. The European Community promises far-reaching economic aid with the stipulation of political reforms. The value of the GDR-mark reaches an all-time low. Modrow announces that the national debt of the GDR is higher than had previously been assumed.

Nov. 19   50,000 people demonstrate in Dresden for free elections and an end to the leadership role of the SED. Modrow appeals to the citizens of the GDR not to throw away their hard-earned money by shopping in the West.

Nov. 20   For the first time the GDR press reports openly about the luxurious living conditions of East German political leaders. More than 100,000 people demonstrate in Leipzig for free elections and an end to the SED's monopoly on political power.

Nov. 21   The government of the FRG states its unwillingness to offer the GDR immediate economic aid. Opposition leaders in the GDR react to this decision with severe criticism. The economic situation in the GDR continues to deteriorate.

Nov. 22   The SED leadership proposes round-table discussions with the opposition about free elections and constitutional reform. The opposition demands that elections not be held until later the following year so that the new parties and citizens' initiatives will have time to develop effective political structures.

Nov. 23   West Berlin Mayor Walter Momper warns against a destabilization of the GDR and demands that the FRG offer unconditional economic aid.

Nov. 24   Egon Krenz announces the end of the SED's leadership role. The East German CDU discusses the possibility of a German-German confederation. The leader of the West German Social Democrats, Hans-Jochen Vogel, appeals to the ruling parties of the FRG to suspend all conditions for economic aid to the GDR.

Nov. 25   In an interview with the *Financial Times*, Egon Krenz does not preclude the possibility of a confederation between the two German states, provided that the NATO and Warsaw Pact military alliances are dismantled.

Nov. 28   West German Chancellor Kohl presents his Ten-Point Program for overcoming the division of Germany and of Europe. GDR intellectuals and artists criticize Kohl's plan, calling it arrogant.

Nov. 29   The GDR bloc parties also criticize Kohl's plan, exposing German unification as its hidden agenda. They insist on the continued sovereignty of the GDR. Egon Krenz and Hans Modrow sign the appeal "For Our Country," which envisions the continued existence of the GDR as a socialist alternative to the FRG. Over 10,000 members of the SED and others take to the streets in Leipzig to demonstrate against unification.

Dec. 1   The *Volkskammer* eliminates from the GDR constitution the SED's monopoly on power. The *Volkskammer* apologizes officially for the participation of GDR troops in the occupation of Czechoslovakia in the summer of 1968. The West German Parliament supports Chancellor Kohl's Ten-Point Program.

Dec. 2   In an interview, GDR Prime Minister Hans Modrow agrees with some aspects of Kohl's Ten-Point Program, but he rejects the idea of unification. Thousands of people demonstrate for the resignation of the Politburo and demand that Egon Krenz step down.

Dec. 3   The members of the Central Committee and the Politburo of the SED hand in their resignations. Several former functionaries of the SED are arrested. Several hundred women found the Independent Women's Organization in Berlin and they call for their inclusion at the discussions of the Round Table.

Dec. 4   The West German Social Democrats declare their opposition to an overhasty unification of the two German states.

Dec. 5   The FRG and the GDR reach an agreement stipulating that as of January 1, 1990, West Germans will be able to travel to the East without having to comply with the mandatory exchange law, which required the exchange of 25 D-marks for 25 GDR-marks upon entry to the GDR. West German Chancellor Kohl and East German Prime Minister Modrow agree to meet in Dresden on Dec. 19. More former GDR functionaries are placed under arrest.

Dec. 6   Egon Krenz resigns his post as General Secretary of the SED and head of the government after just 44 days in office.

Dec. 7   The Round Table meetings between the GDR government and the opposition commence.

Dec. 8   The SED holds an extaordinary party congress. Gregor Gysi demands a radical break with Stalinism and with centrally administered socialism.

Dec. 9   Gregor Gysi is elected new leader of the SED. Modrow warns about incipient economic chaos in the GDR. He argues that economic renewal must be the kernel of the renewal of socialism.

Dec. 11   About 200,000 GDR citizens demonstrate for reforms; many of them demand German unity. "We are one people" and "Germany, united Fatherland" begin to be heard more often.

Dec. 12   US Secretary of State James Baker declares that the US will support German reunification within the context of European unification. He promises economic aid for the GDR.

Dec. 13   Kurt Masur, Director of the Leipzig Gewandhaus Orchestra and a prominent spokesperson of the GDR opposition, warns against making radical demands for German unification.

Dec. 15   GDR Prime Minister Hans Modrow demands from the FRG the economic aid West German Chancellor Kohl had previously promised to provide.

Dec. 16   Erich Honecker accepts the blame for the crisis in the GDR.

Dec. 17   The Socialist Unity Party (SED) changes its name to the Party of Democratic Socialism (PDS).

Dec. 18   The Round Table meets for the second time. Opposition leaders question the legitimacy of the Modrow government. In Leipzig, 150,000 people demonstrate in support of German unification.

Dec. 19 West German Chancellor Kohl travels to Dresden and agrees to a set of treaty regulations about economic cooperation between the GDR and the FRG. He is greeted by tens of thousands of GDR citizens who call for German unification.

Dec. 20 Chancellor Kohl speaks with representatives of the GDR opposition. He warns against the destabilization of Europe and admonishes that German unification be approached with prudence.

Dec. 21 French President François Mitterand visits East Berlin and announces that France would have nothing against German unification, if that is what the German people desire.

Dec. 22 The Brandenburg Gate opens up after 28 years. East German Prime Minister Modrow, West German Chancellor Kohl, and the mayors of East and West Berlin celebrate the occasion.

1990

Jan. 3 1,250,000 people demonstrate in East Berlin against neo-fascism.

Jan. 4 The government of the GDR proposes constitutional changes in order to facilitate joint ventures with Western businesses.

Jan. 6 The leader of the PDS, Gregor Gysi, demands the dissolution of the military blocs in Europe.

Jan. 8 The GDR opposition and government parties interrupt their cooperation at the Round Table because of disagreements over the Office for National Security. The opposition seeks to dissolve the Office and presents Modrow with an ultimatum.

Jan. 9 The *Volkskammer* debates a draft proposal to prohibit any form of support of GDR political parties by West German parties in the upcoming election.

Jan. 10 Chancellor Kohl threatens to withhold economic aid if the *Volkskammer* passes a new election law without the approval of the opposition.

Jan. 11 GDR Prime Minister Modrow presents his first state of the nation address, reporting on the first eight weeks of his term. The *Volkskammer* votes to set May 6 as the day for East German elections.

Jan. 15   Prime Minister Modrow appears at the Round Table to offer the opposition direct participation in the negotiations with West German Chancellor Kohl.

Jan. 16   Prime Minister Modrow becomes the first ruler of the GDR to visit West Berlin.

Jan. 18   West German Chancellor Kohl suggests an earlier date than May 6 for elections in the GDR. The opposition parties at the Round Table demand the right to speak before the *Volkskammer* as well as control over the dissolution of the Stasi. The US ambassador to West Germany declares that the United States will accept a unified Germany only on the condition that it is a member of NATO.

Jan. 20   The PDS enters a profound crisis. Several prominent members resign. Party leader Gregor Gysi offers political representation to the opposition.

Jan. 22   The opposition signals its willingness to participate in the Modrow government.

Jan. 25   The East German CDU withdraws its politicians from the Modrow government.

Jan. 26   The opposition demands a greater role for the Round Table in governmental affairs.

Jan. 27   The New Forum demands a referendum on German unification.

Jan. 28   After difficult negotiations, GDR Prime Minister Modrow and the opposition agree on a government that includes all parties. This "government of national responsibility," as it is called, is, for the first time in GDR history, made up of primarily non-communists. The decision is made to hold the *Volkskammer* elections on March 18.

Jan. 29   GDR Prime Minister Modrow explains to the *Volkskammer* the governing principle of the new leadership.

Jan. 30   Modrow speaks with Soviet leader Michail Gorbachev in Moscow; Gorbachev announces that he has no principal objections to German unification.

Feb. 1   Modrow proposes a step-by-step plan for German unification. According to his plan, Germany will become a neutral country. The West German CDU supports his plan, but objects to the idea of German neutrality.

Feb. 2   The PDS distances itself from Modrow's plan. Out of protest against this plan for unification, the United Left decides not to participate in the Modrow government.

Feb. 3   Kohl speaks with Modrow in Davos and promises economic aid for the GDR before the elections.

Feb. 4   Modrow begins to back down from his position on neutrality for a unified Germany and declares that his plan for unification is not contingent on the question of neutrality. The Soviet Union states its willingness to withdraw its troops from the territory of the GDR if US troops and the troops of Great Britain and France agree to withdraw from the territory of the FRG.

Feb. 5   The *Volkskammer* accepts the earlier date of March 18 for elections. The Round Table passes a resolution against the active participation of West German politicians in the election campaign. The East German CDU and SPD do not accept this resolution as binding. Three of the more conservative GDR parties (Democratic Awakening, German Social Union, and the East German CDU) join together to form the "Alliance for Germany." Hundreds of thousands of people demonstrate throughout the GDR for unification.

Feb. 6   The government of the FRG invites the GDR to enter into immediate negotiations about an economic and currency union. US Secretary of State James Baker agrees with West German Foreign Minister Hans-Dietrich Genscher that a unified Germany ought to be a member of NATO but that there should be no NATO troops present on the territory of the former GDR.

Feb. 7   Three of the most important liberal political groups in the GDR, the New Forum, Democracy Now, and the Initiative for Peace and Human Rights, join together to form the "Election Alliance 90."

Feb. 8   The GDR officially declares that the entire German people (not just the German fascists, as GDR propaganda had previously held) were responsible for the Holocaust and announces the willingness of the GDR to offer compensation to the victims of the Holocaust. The economic situation in the GDR continues to deteriorate.

Feb. 10   After conversations with Soviet leader Michail Gorbachev, West German Chancellor Kohl announces that the Soviet Union acknowledges the right of the German people to decide about the timing and course of German unification. The Soviet Union emphasizes that membership of united Germany in NATO is not an option. All four of the major WWII allies (Britain, France, the Soviet Union, and the US) will participate in the process.

Feb. 12   The Round Table accuses the West German government of aggravating the problems in the GDR and destabilizing the country by questioning its credit record. They demand an immediate economic relief package of ten to fifteen billion D-marks.

Feb. 13   East German Prime Minister Modrow and West German Chancellor Kohl meet in Bonn. They agree on the formation of a joint committee to negotiate an economic and currency union. West Germany refuses to provide the GDR with immediate economic assistance.

Feb. 15   The *Bundestag* discusses unification. Chancellor Kohl asserts that German unity has never been so near. The leader of the opposition West German Social Democrats, Hans-Jochen Vogel, agrees with plans for German unity but criticizes the West German government for not supplying the GDR with an immediate economic aid package.

Feb. 19   GDR Prime Minister Modrow criticizes the plan to introduce a German currency union before elections are held in the GDR. He points out that a currency union must be combined with a social package. The participants at the Round Table protest against the annexation of the GDR by the FRG according to Article 23 of the West German Basic Law.

Feb. 20   In a declaration before the *Volkskammer*, Prime Minister Modrow supports immediate negotiations for German unification. Chancellor Kohl campaigns in Erfurt for the East German CDU.

Feb. 24-25 Chancellor Kohl and President Bush meet at Camp David. Both support membership in NATO for a united Germany.

Mar. 1   The "Alliance for Germany" adopts the campaign slogan "Freedom and affluence—never again socialism." The principal plank in their election platform is the annexation of the GDR by the FRG according to Article 23 of the West German Basic Law.

Mar. 6   In a joint declaration, East German Prime Minister Modrow and Soviet leader Gorbachev support the idea of a gradual merger of the two German states, but they warn against the annexation of the GDR by the FRG according to Article 23 of the West German Basic Law. Lothar de Maizière, leader of the East German CDU, speaks out against an unconditional annexation of the GDR by the FRG.

Mar. 7   The *Volkskammer* passes by a wide margin the "Social Charter" proposed by the Round Table in which the social security of all GDR citizens is established as the basis for negotiations with the FRG about unification.

Mar. 8   109,000 "unofficial collaborators" of the former Stasi are dismissed. The leader of the Democratic Awakening, Wolfgang Schnur, resigns his post after it is revealed that he was a long-time collaborator with the Stasi.

Mar. 11   About a thousand people protest in East Berlin against a sell-out of the GDR.

Mar. 12   At its final meeting, the Round Table passes a new draft constitution to be legitimized by a referendum of the entire population. It rejects an extension of the West German Basic Law to the territory of the GDR.

Mar. 13   West German Chancellor Kohl proposes an exchange rate of 1 GDR-mark for 1 D-mark as the basis for an economic union.

Mar. 14   The first of the so-called Two-Plus-Four Talks is held in Bonn, in which officials of the two German governments and representatives of the governments of Britain, France, the Soviet Union, and the US discuss the process of German unification.

Mar. 18   The first free elections in the GDR are held, with a surprising victory of the conservative Alliance for Germany, which garners 48% of the vote. The East German SPD receives only 22% and the PDS 16%, while the League of Free Democrats receives 5%.

Mar. 19   The leader of the East German CDU, Lothar de Maizière, invites the SPD and the League of Free Democrats to join in a coalition government that will be large enough to ensure a two-thirds majority for constitutional changes. The Social Democrats hesitate to accept this offer because they do not want to join in a coalition with the German Social Union (DSU), which is a part of the victorious Alliance for Germany.

Mar. 20   The West German coalition parties (CDU and FDP) agree on a timetable for German unification: they plan an economic, currency, and social union of the two German states for July 1. According to this plan, the GDR will constitute five new *Länder* (federal states) in a unified Germany.

Mar. 23   Lothar de Maizière declares himself a candidate for the office of Prime Minister of the GDR.

Mar. 30   The West German *Bundesbank* recommends an exchange rate of 1 D-mark for 2 GDR-marks for all savings of GDR citizens over 2,000 marks.

April 1   The proposal of the West German *Bundesbank* is rejected by all the parties represented in the *Volkskammer*, who favor an exchange rate of 1 : 1.

April 3   The East German SPD agrees to coalition talks with the CDU.

April 5   The first freely elected *Volkskammer* is constituted in East Berlin. Sabine Bergmann-Pohl is elected President of the *Volkskammer*. Lothar de Maizière is asked to form a government. The Round Table offers its draft constitution to the *Volkskammer*. Hundreds of thousands of people take to the streets in numerous cities of the GDR to protest against the proposed exchange rate of 1 D-mark for 2 GDR-marks for savings of GDR citizens over 2,000 marks.

April 8   Coalition negotiations for the new East German government are completed. The SPD is represented by 7 ministers in a cabinet with a total of 24 posts.

April 12   The so-called "grand coalition" between the CDU and its allies and the SPD takes office in the GDR. All the coalition partners agree to support German unification on the basis of Article 23 of the West German Basic Law, including the formation of *Länder*, the introduction of an economic, currency, and social union on July 1, and an exchange rate of 1 : 1. The *Volkskammer* elects Lothar de Maizière Prime Minister.

April 19   In his governmental policy statement, Lothar de Maizière appeals to the solidarity of West German citizens

with their compatriots in the East. He supports an exchange rate of 1 : 1 for wages and pensions. The parties
of the grand coalition reject the constitution drafted by
the Round Table.

April 23   The West German government offers an exchange rate of
1 : 1 for wages and pensions up to 4,000 marks. For sums
above 4,000 marks they suggest a rate of 1 D-mark for 2
GDR-marks.

April 24   GDR Prime Minister Lothar de Maizière meets with
FRG Chancellor Kohl in Bonn. They agree on July 1 as
the date for the introduction of an economic, currency,
and social union between the two German states.

April 25   Formal negotiations begin between the FRG and the
GDR over the State Treaty that will regulate the
merger of the two German states. The GDR government
argues for a better exchange rate.

April 27   The East German and West German defense ministers
agree on membership of united Germany in NATO, with
the stipulation that no NATO forces will be stationed
on the territory of the former GDR.

April 29   East German Prime Minister de Maizière travels to
Moscow. He rejects the Soviet proposal of a neutral status for united Germany. Michail Gorbachev remains
firm about his opposition to NATO membership for
united Germany.

April 30   Sabine Bergmann-Pohl, President of the GDR *Volkskammer*, and Rita Süssmuth, President of the FRG *Bundestag*, meet in Berlin.

May 1   The East German and West German parliaments hold a
joint session at the Berlin *Reichstag*.

May 2   The exchange rate is set at 1 : 1 for savings up to 2,000
GDR-marks for children up to fourteen, 4,000 GDR-
marks for adults, and 6,000 GDR-marks for senior citizens. For sums above these amounts the rate is 1 D-mark
for 2 GDR-marks.

May 5   The foreign ministers of both German states meet with
their American, Soviet, British, and French counterparts in Bonn for the first high-level meeting of the
Two-Plus-Four Talks. The Soviet Union agrees in principle to unification and is willing to compromise on the
question of united Germany's membership in NATO.

May 6   The first free local elections are held in the GDR. With
           34%, the CDU is still the strongest party, despite a con-
           siderable loss of support in comparison with its showing
           in the national election. The SPD receives 21%, the
           PDS 15%, and the League of Free Democrats 7% of the
           vote.

May 11   The *Volkskammer* debates the details of the State
           Treaty. Prime Minister Lothar de Maizière paints a
           bleak picture of the economic situation in the GDR and
           admonishes GDR citizens not to expect an immediate
           upturn after the introduction of the currency union.

May 13   Each party has a different idea about the date for the
           first all-German elections. Chancellor Kohl suggests
           December 2, the FDP speaks of January 1991, and
           Markus Meckel suggests the spring of 1991. The commit-
           tee of experts negotiating the State Treaty completes
           its recommendations and proposes a draft for a currency,
           economic, and social union on July 1, 1990. The question
           of property rights is left open.

May 14   FRG Chancellor Kohl and GDR Prime Minister de
           Maizière hold talks on the State Treaty. They agree on
           July 1 as the date for the introduction of the currency
           union but cannot agree on the social aspects of this pro-
           cess or on the introduction of structural changes in the
           GDR.

May 15   West German and East German SPD leaders express
           their opposition to the December 2 date for all-German
           elections.

May 16   Chancellor Kohl and the leaders of the West German
           Länder agree on a four-year program to finance German
           unity. They propose the establishment of a "German
           Unity Fund."

May 18   The GDR signs the State Treaty establishing the cur-
           rency, economic, and social union with the FRG. The
           most important item is the introduction of the D-mark
           as the official currency of the GDR and the introduction
           in the GDR of the Western system of a social market
           economy.

May 21   The West German Social Democrats, without whose
           votes the State Treaty will not receive the necessary
           two-thirds majority in the *Bundesrat*, demand that the

Treaty be revised to include more social and ecological measures.

May 27   GDR Foreign Minister Markus Meckel and Defense Minister Rainer Eppelmann express the wish that all-German elections not take place before the end of 1992.

May 28   The East German Social Democrats protest against the intention of the West German Social Democrats to prevent ratification of the State Treaty.

June 2   Right-wing violence breaks out in several East German cities.

June 6   In an interview, GDR Prime Minister de Maizière defends the State Treaty as a reasonable course for introducing a market economy in Eastern Germany.

June 8   The *Volkskammer* discusses the recent increase in xenophobia in the GDR. Excerpts of a separate draft constitution for the GDR, which includes the right to work as well as abortion rights for women, are published. The West German Social Democrats repeat their demand for better social and ecological programs before agreeing to ratify the State Treaty.

June 9   Wolfgang Thierse is elected the new leader for the East German Social Democrats. He appeals to the West German SPD not to scuttle the State Treaty. Chancellor Kohl refuses to amend the State Treaty. The Green Parties in East and West Germany refuse to accept the State Treaty.

June 12   Soviet leader Michail Gorbachev proposes an associate membership of united Germany in both NATO and the Warsaw Pact. The West criticizes this proposal as unrealistic.

June 14   The West German Social Democrats give in to pressures to accept the State Treaty.

June 17   Delegates of the *Bundestag* and the *Volkskammer* join in the celebrations for the so-called "Day of German Unity." The *Volkskammer* discusses a motion about immediate unification with the FRG.

June 19   The West German SPD is successful in bringing about some final revisions in the State Treaty during debate in the *Bundesrat*.

June 20   The *Volkskammer* votes for acceptance of the State Treaty. A second Treaty regulating the details of unification is scheduled to follow. GDR citizens' initiatives present a list of over 200,000 names of people who do not support the State Treaty. Chancellor Kohl appeals to the West Germans to show solidarity with the citizens of the GDR. In a joint declaration of the *Bundestag* and the *Volkskammer*, the existing Polish-German border is officially recognized.

June 22   The West German *Bundesrat* passes the State Treaty. Checkpoint Charlie in Berlin is dismantled. The Two-Plus-Four Talks stall over the question of when united Germany should be granted full sovereignty.

June 24   GDR Prime Minister Lothar de Maizière asserts that Berlin should be the capital of united Germany.

June 25   President of the *Bundestag*, Rita Süssmuth, and President of the *Volkskammer*, Sabine Bergmann-Pohl, pay an official visit to Israel.

June 29   The President of the FRG, Richard von Weizsäcker, voices his support for Berlin as the new capital of united Germany. The West German *Länder* decide to send administrators to the East German state governments to help them develop an efficient administration.

June 30   In a television address, GDR Prime Minister de Maizière calls the State Treaty a bridge for the unification of the two German states. Richard von Weizsäcker's support for Berlin as capital meets with criticism among leading West German politicians.

July 1   The currency, economic, and social union takes effect in the GDR. The D-mark becomes the sole currency throughout all of Germany. Long lines form at banks and post offices in the GDR. People in East Berlin celebrate the currency union with wine, champagne, and fireworks. Initially, every GDR citizen is entitled to withdraw up to 2000 D-marks from his or her account. Prime Minister de Maizière appeals to the citizens of the GDR to embrace the event as a courageous new beginning. West German Chancellor Kohl calls it a "decisive step toward the unity of our fatherland."

July 2   The government coalition in the GDR agrees on December 2, 1990 as the date for the first all-German elections. Local elections in the GDR are planned for October 14, 1990.

July 4   The Bonn coalition begins preparing for all-German elections on Dec. 2. Detlev Rohwedder is confirmed as head of the *Treuhand* organization, the institute established to privatize the socialized industries and state property of the GDR.

July 5   Prime Minister de Maizière appeals to NATO to abandon its military character, renouncing its strategy of "flexible response," which accepts the use of nuclear weapons as a possible military strategy. According to de Maizière, NATO should become a purely political alliance.

July 6   In its "London Declaration" NATO agrees "never and under no circumstances to strike first." The states of the Warsaw Pact are no longer considered enemies. The negotiations for the Unification Treaty get underway in East Berlin.

July 9   GDR citizens can now withdraw unlimited sums of money from their bank accounts.

July 10   The coalition government in the GDR is divided over the question of whether the five-percent clause, valid in the FRG, which prevents parties receiving less than five percent of the total vote from being represented in parliament, should apply to all of Germany, as the SPD suggests, or whether it should only apply to the West, as is the wish of the CDU. They also cannot agree on a date for the annexation of the GDR by the FRG according to Article 23 of the West German Basic Law. De Maizière suggests unification four weeks after the elections, the SPD holds out for a date prior to the all-German elections.

July 11   The GDR citizens' initiatives and the West German Green Party form an election alliance for the upcoming all-German elections.

July 15   A heated discussion begins about the process of German unification. The West German SPD and the FDP continue arguing for the annexation of the GDR before the elections while the CDU sticks to its proposal of treating Eastern and Western Germany as two different electoral zones.

July 16   Chancellor Kohl and Soviet President Gorbachev come to an agreement about Germany's NATO membership:

	the future united Germany can decide freely and independently about its membership in a military alliance.
July 17	The question of the Polish-German border is settled in Paris at one of the Two-Plus-Four meetings. A German-Polish treaty will be presented to the future all-German parliament shortly after unification.
July 18	United Germany will have two different abortion regulations: at least for a transitional period, the liberal abortion laws of the GDR will remain in effect for citizens of East Germany.
July 20	A motion by the League of Free Liberals in the *Volkskammer* for unification of the GDR with the FRG on December 1 is defeated.
July 22	A second motion by the League of Free Liberals for unification on December 1 is defeated.
July 23	The debate about the date for unification threatens to divide the grand coalition in the *Volkskammer*.
July 24	The GDR League of Free Liberals leaves the coalition.
July 25	The CDU and the Social Democrats signal their willingness to compromise on the date of unification and on the five-percent clause.
July 30	The West German ruling coalition parties, CDU and FDP, agree on a compromise according to which smaller parties may form clusters so that an all-German implementation of the five-percent clause will be possible.
Aug. 1	The East German coalition accepts the compromise proposed by the West German coalition parties. The leader of the PDS, Gregor Gysi, calls this agreement a manipulation of the election. The Greens and the "Alliance 90" also voice their strong opposition. The West German ruling coalition parties suggest the fall of 1990 as a possible date for unification.
Aug. 3	The *Volkskammer* presents a draft of the Unification Treaty. Berlin is mentioned as capital, but not as seat of the government. Prime Minister de Maizière proposes October 14 as the date for all-German elections. West German Chancellor Kohl supports this date. The West German SPD opposes this election date, declaring the process by which it was established to be unconstitutional.

Aug. 4   The draft of the Unification Treaty between the FRG and the GDR includes compromises about constitutional changes, legal matters, international obligations, and financial questions. The two German states still fail to reach an agreement in the areas of culture, education, and social and scientific matters.

Aug. 5   The GDR citizens' movements and the Green Party begin negotiating a joint election platform.

Aug. 6   The Bonn government denies that tax increases will be necessary to finance unification. The PDS and other left-wing organizations from East Germany and West Germany agree on a joint election platform.

Aug. 7   West German Chancellor Kohl meets with representatives of the SPD, the parliamentary opposition. The SPD remains firm on the question of the date for all-German elections, insisting on December 2.

Aug. 8   The *Volkskammer* demands annexation of the GDR by the FRG on October 14, with all-German elections being held on the same date.

Aug. 9   The West German government agrees to hold all-German elections on Dec. 2 after the SPD threatens to defeat the constitutional amendment necessary to set an earlier election date. GDR Prime Minister de Maizière meets with Helmut Kohl in Bonn. He argues for unification on October 14.

Aug. 12   In face of the worsening economic situation in East Germany, leading GDR Social Democrats renew their demand for a speedy unification.

Aug. 13   Politicians from both German states commemorate the building of the Berlin Wall twenty-nine years ago on this date. The GDR coalition partners finally agree to a compromise on the Unification Treaty.

Aug. 15   GDR Prime Minister de Maizière fires his Ministers of Finance and of Agriculture and accepts the resignation of the Minister of the Economy and the Attorney General, blaming them for the economic crisis in the GDR. The mayors of East and West Berlin lobby for Berlin as the parliamentary seat of united Germany.

Aug. 16   The East German SPD and the League of Free Liberals threaten to vote against the Unification Treaty. De Maizière continues to negotiate with Bonn. The East German SPD leaves the ruling coalition.

Aug. 17   The East German SPD announces several conditions for accepting the Unification Treaty, among them better financial support of the GDR *Länder*. Chancellor Kohl appeals to the parties in the GDR to ratify the Unification Treaty. The parties in Bonn prepare for early unification on October 14.

Aug. 19   Although the SPD has left the ruling coalition in the GDR, its representatives do not want to vote against the Unification Treaty. They demand revisions, however.

Aug. 20   GDR Foreign Minister Markus Meckel resigns. Lothar de Maizière assumes this post in addition to that of Prime Minister. The West German government refuses to make changes in the Unification Treaty. The East German Social Democrats continue to call for early unification. De Maizière emphasizes that he is still striving for unification on October 14.

Aug. 21   The GDR Social Democrats refuse to support unification on October 14. They demand that unification take place even earlier, on September 15. The West German government and the West German *Länder* struggle over the questions of taxation as set forth in the Unification Treaty. Detlev Rohwedder assumes his duties as chairman of the *Treuhand* organization.

Aug. 23   After weeks of heated debate, the *Volkskammer* accepts October 3 as the date for German unification. All-German elections will take place on December 2. The fight over abortion rights continues.

Aug. 29   The West German government and the West German *Länder* reach a compromise about the distribution of taxes in united Germany.

Aug. 30   The West German government and the West German opposition SPD finally arrive at a compromise on the final version of the Unification Treaty. The abortion laws presently binding in the GDR will remain in force on the territory of the GDR for a transitional period of two years.

Aug. 31   The two negotiators of the Unification Treaty, Wolfgang Schäuble and Günther Krause, sign the Treaty in East Berlin.

Sept. 2   The leader of the West German SPD, Oskar Lafontaine, renews his demand that German unification be financed through higher taxes.

Sept. 4   The former central office of the Stasi in East Berlin is occupied by a group of civil rights leaders who demand information about their personal files. They protest the plan to turn the Stasi files over to the government of the FRG. The last series of the Two-Plus-Four Talks begin.

Sept. 5   West German Chancellor Kohl decides to increase his cabinet after unification by four posts in order to accommodate leading GDR politicians. By this date, the number of people unemployed in the GDR has risen to nearly two million.

Sept. 6   The *Volkskammer* postpones its debate on the Unification Treaty. Prime Minister de Maizière promises more negotiations about the Stasi files. The occupation of the Stasi central office in East Berlin continues.

Sept. 7   The Two-Plus-Four Talks about German unity are concluded.

Sept. 10   Bonn and Moscow reach a compromise about the financing of Soviet troops in the GDR. Bonn will pay the Soviet Union a sum of 12 billion D-marks to assist in the resettling of the Soviet troops.

Sept. 12   In Moscow, the foreign ministers of the FRG, the GDR, and the four allied powers (Britain, France, the Soviet Union, and the US) sign the treaty that gives Germany full sovereignty. This will go into effect on October 3. Soviet troops will remain on the territory of the GDR until 1994. The West German government calls the signing of this treaty the official end of the postwar era.

Sept. 13   The foreign ministers of Germany and the Soviet Union sign a general treaty, which includes a clause stating that Germans and Soviets will never go to war with each other again. The treaty also assures the rights of ethnic minorities in both countries.

Sept. 15   Several members of the *Volkskammer* are accused of cooperation with the Stasi. The two negotiators of the Unification Treaty, Schäuble and Krause, come to an agreement about the treatment of the Stasi files: only regional representatives of the *Länder* and a special investigator elected by the *Volkskammer* and accepted by the *Bundestag* will have access to the files.

Sept. 18   The negotiations for the Unification Treaty are completed. The Stasi files will remain on the territory of the GDR. People will only have access to them if it can be assured that the interests of other parties will not be violated. The demonstrators occupying the Stasi central office want to go on with their hunger strike until unconditional access to their files is granted. West German Chancellor Kohl and French President Mittérand agree to reduce the number of French troops in Germany by 50% within the next two years.

Sept. 20   The *Volkskammer* and the *Bundestag* ratify the Unification Treaty.

Sept. 21   The *Bundesrat* votes unanimously to ratify the Unification Treaty.

Sept. 24   The GDR officially leaves the Warsaw Pact.

Sept. 26   The GDR *Ministerrat* holds its last meeting. Prime Minister de Maizière declares that the GDR government has fulfilled its task of bringing about unity in the speediest and most effective manner.

Sept. 28   The demonstrators occupying the former Stasi central office end their hunger strike.

Sept. 29   The West German Supreme Court declares the all-German election unconstitutional in the planned format and requires separate election rules for East Germany and West Germany. More than 10,000 women demonstrate for abortion rights and for their economic independence.

Oct. 1   The four allied powers sign a declaration in New York that grants full sovereignty to Germany. The West German and East German CDU merge at a joint party congress held in Hamburg.

Oct. 2   The *Volkskammer* holds its last meeting. The celebrations for the Day of German Unity begin.

Oct. 3   The Day of German Unity. At midnight the GDR ceases to exist and becomes part of the FRG. Hundreds of thousands of people celebrate in the major cities. Right-wing and left-wing extremists battle with the police.

Dec. 2   The first all-German elections are held. Helmut Kohl's CDU (with its sister party the CSU) remains the strongest party with 43.8% of the votes, 319 seats in the *Bundestag*. The CDU's coalition partner, the FDP, receives 11% or 49 seats, its best electoral showing since 1961. The CDU and FDP thus consitute a majority in the *Bundestag* and can continue their ruling coalition. The SPD receives only 33.5% of the vote (239 seats), its worst results since 1957. The Green Party receives only 3.9% in Western Germany, 5.9% in Eastern Germany. Because they clear the 5% hurdle for parliamentary representation in the East, they receive 8 mandates in the newly constituted *Bundestag*. The PDS, the successor party to the East German SED, receives 9.9% of the votes and holds 17 seats in the *Bundestag*. The right-wing Republican Party receives only 2.1% and does not gain representation in the *Bundestag*.

German Unification

and Its Discontents

"Böhlen Platform": Communiqué after a Meeting of Representatives of Diverse Socialist Reform Groups of the GDR (September 4, 1989)

For a Unified Left in the GDR!
An Appeal

In light of the persistent economic stagnation and the aggravation of the political crisis in our country, we would like to direct this appeal to all political forces in the GDR that support a democratic and free socialism. A left-oriented, alternative concept for a revolutionary turn becomes more urgent with each passing day!

We are well aware of the difficult preconditions: the discrediting of the socialist project by the rulers here, who let this project devolve into the distorted image of a workers' movement with particular battle aims, has produced more disillusionment and passivity among the majority of the population than it has courageous and problem-oriented thought and actions. And yet, there are not only the waves of emigrants from the GDR, but also more and more people who want to remain here and effect changes in the existing conditions. In this context it is more important than ever that we produce a wide consensus among those on the left in our country and that we develop a realistic, politically feasible, and effective social program for a socialist reconstruction of the GDR.

There are several reasons for this:

First of all, the restructuring in the Soviet Union demonstrates that far-reaching reforms within "really-existing socialism" are not only necessary, but also possible. On the other hand, the dangerous political upheavals that are occurring in the wake of these social changes in the Soviet Union and Poland, changes that began far too late, send a clear message. . . . We believe that the GDR in particular stands at the threshold of a historical opportunity for the radical renewal of the socialist concept of society. If this renewal is postponed, this will have consequences that quite possibly will cut off for years to come–and not only in this country–the chance for a society that is socially just and that guarantees the free development of each of its members.

The external conditions for a radical renewal are complicated enough: in modern international capitalism the disappointment of the working class about the ineffectiveness of the social-democratic welfare state is fostering a continued neo-conservative turn to the right. The trade unions have their backs against the wall. The decreasing influence of West European communist parties and the process of their fast-paced social-democratization fully deserve to be called "dramatic." The internationalism of communist mass parties has *de facto* ceased to exist, and this fact is disguised behind a still functioning, but nevertheless deplorable social-democratic internationalism. The fascination with the encouraging rise of the CPSU out of the ghetto of stagnation, Stalinism, and the arrogance of power increasingly gives way to the concern that the newly developing centrifugal forces could destroy more than just the impediments to a truly socialist development. The economic reorganization in the reforming socialist countries is either failing to produce any results or is utilizing questionable methods. The deficits of a radical renewal of theoretical thought on a Marxist foundation are catastrophic in light of the present challenges.

And yet there is a chance. A powerful turn in the direction of socialism would today no longer be subject to military intervention on the part of "well-meaning brother countries."[1] Because of the desolate economic situation, political intervention on the part of the West under the guise of "economic cooperation" is much more likely.

The decisive question remains the social base, the political maturity, and the programmatic earnestness of those forces in our country that side with socialism. For us this means that we must regain this foundation under the present conditions in the GDR. And here the preconditions are undoubtedly more favorable than they are in other "really-existing socialist" countries—in spite of the continued political repression, especially of left-oriented forces, in the GDR. The Left in this country cannot afford to be factionalized. We have to be the driving force behind a "coalition of reason" that rests on the manifoldness of all those political and social forces in the GDR that believe in socialism; but above and beyond this we must offer a new socialist perspective to all the existing social and political factions. In this sense a unified Left has to develop within a short span of time, on the basis of free, equal, open, and public discussions, a conceptual program for political and economic restructuring whose realization will be able to draw on wide social acceptance. No one who desires to participate in this process of renewal, not even a member of the SED, should be excluded. On the other hand, the most recent experiences demonstrate especially well where an unprincipled conceptual relativism with regard to society can lead. We are decidedly against "replacing" political-administrative re-

pression with capitalist exploitation. The Left must come together on the basis of:
  –social ownership of the means of production as the predominant and prospective basis of socialist society;
  –an increase in the self-determination of the producers in order to realize the real socialization of all economic activity;
  –the determined realization of the principle of social security and justice for all members of society;
  –political democracy, legal justice, the consistent realization of inalienable human rights, and the free development of every individual;
  –the ecological reorganization of industrial society.
The time is more than ripe for an open discussion of the questions that arise in this connection. The dialogue among the forces of a Left that is unifying on such a basis can and should take place publicly, despite the fact that under current conditions we still face the threat of repercussions in the workplace and will be subjected to the political pressure exerted upon politically nonconformist thought. The organizational merger of a unified Left must be preceded by the process of dialogue described here. . . .

NOTES

Source: Schüddekopf, 18-22.

1. Socialist countries used to refer to each other as "brother countries." Here this designation is used ironically to refer to the Soviet military interventions, supported politically and militarily by the GDR regime, that crushed democratic reform movements in Hungary in 1956 and Czechoslovakia in 1968.

2
"New Beginning '89": Call for the Founding of the Political Grouping "New Forum" in the GDR (September 10, 1989)

In our country the communication between state and society is obviously troubled. Evidence of this is provided by the widespread dissatisfaction that has led people to retreat into a private niche or to emigrate in large numbers. In other areas of the world such massive flights are caused by deprivation, hunger, and violence. This is decidedly not the case in our country.

The troubled relation between state and society paralyzes the creative potential of our society and hinders the solution of the immanent local and global tasks with which we are faced. We are dissipating our energy in ill-humored passivity even though we have more important things to do for our lives, for our country, and for humanity.

In the political and the economic spheres, the balancing of interests among various groups and levels of society is functioning improperly. Communication about the situation and about competing interests is impeded. In private everyone states his or her diagnosis frankly and indicates those measures that are most important to him or her. But people's wishes and goals are very different and are not being rationally weighed against one another and examined in light of their feasibility. On the one hand, we would like to have an expanded range of consumer goods and better distribution; on the other hand, we see the social and ecological cost of these things and plead for a rejection of unhindered growth. We want some leeway for economic initiatives, but do not want to degenerate into an elbow-society. We want to preserve what has proven to be workable and yet still create room for innovation, so that we might live more economically and pose a lesser threat to nature. We want order, but we do not want to be treated in a patronizing manner. We want free, self-confident human beings who nevertheless act with regard to society as a whole. We want to be protected from violence without having to tolerate a state full of watchdogs and informers. Loafers and loudmouths must be driven out of their cushy jobs, but we don't want to disadvantage the socially weak and the defenseless. We want an effective health care system for everyone; but no one should be able to call in sick at the expense of others. We want to participate in export and world trade, but we want to become neither the debtor nor the servant of the leading industrial nations, nor the exploiter and creditor of economically weaker countries.

In order to recognize all these contradictions, to hear and pass judgment on opinions and arguments about them, to distinguish between general and particular interests, we need a democratic dialogue on the tasks of the state, of the economy, and of culture. The entire country needs to reflect on and discuss these questions in public. Whether or not we will find ways out of the present crisis in the near future will depend on our willingness and desire to do this. Given the current stage of our social development it is important that:

–a greater number of people take part in the process of social reform;

–the various individuals and groups find a way to act in concert.

That is the reason why we have joined together to form a political platform for the entire GDR that will make it possible for people from all professions, walks of life, parties, and groups to participate in discussing and finding solutions for the crucial social problems in this country. For this comprehensive initiative we have chosen the name "New Forum."

We will give the activity of the New Forum a legal basis. In doing this we refer to Article 29 of the GDR constitution, which guarantees the right to realize our political interests on the basis of common actions in a political organization. We will register the founding of this association with the responsible agencies of the GDR, in accordance with the decree of November 11, 1975, on the "Founding and Activities of Associations."

All the aims to which the New Forum wishes to give voice are based on the desire for justice, democracy, peace, and the protection and preservation of nature. This is the impulse that we want to see brought to life in all spheres in the coming restructuring of our society.

We appeal to all citizens of the GDR who want to take part in the restructuring of our society to become members of the New Forum. The time is ripe.

NOTES

Source: Zanetti, 193-94.

3
"A Call for Intervention in Our Own Affairs": Flyer of the Citizens' Movement "Democracy Now" (September 12, 1989)

Dear friends, fellow citizens, and fellow individuals affected by the recent events!

Our country is living in a state of internal turmoil. Some people are chafing under the existing conditions, others have simply resigned themselves to them. Throughout the country one can observe a significant decline in public approval of the conditions that have historically developed in the GDR. Many are scarcely capable of affirming their presence here. Many are leaving the country because accommodation has its limits.

Only a few years ago "really-existing" state socialism was still considered the only possible model of socialism. Its characteristics are the power monopoly of a centralized state party, state control over the means of production, the penetration and uniformization of society by the state, and the patronization of the citizenry. Despite its indisputable achievements with regard to social security and justice, it is obvious today that the era of state socialism is coming to an end. Socialism needs a peaceful, democratic renewal.

Introduced and supported by Gorbachev's initiative, the Soviet Union, Hungary, and Poland are moving along the road of democratic restructuring. Enormous economic, social, ecological, and ethnic problems stand in the way and could put an end to this process of restructuring, with disastrous consequences for the entire world. Everything the socialist worker's movement has struggled to achieve in the areas of social justice and communal solidarity is at stake. Socialism must now find its authentic, democratic shape if it is not to be lost to history. It must not be lost, because in its search for survivable forms of human coexistence our endangered humanity needs alternatives to Western consumer society, whose prosperity is paid for by the rest of the world.

Contrary to all the attempts to whitewash matters, the signs of the political, economic, and ecological crisis of state socialism are unmistakably visible everywhere, even "in the colors of the GDR." But there are no indications that the leadership of the SED is ready to change its way of thinking. It seems as if they are banking on a failure of the reforms in the Soviet Union. But it is necessary that we help realize this democratic restructuring.

The political crisis of the socialist system in the GDR became particularly apparent on the occasion of the local elections of May 7, 1989. The doctrine of the "moral-political unity of party, state, and people," which was supposed to justify the power monopoly independent of elections, could only be preserved by a falsification of the election results.[1] Ten to twenty per cent of the inhabitants of larger cities openly refused to support the candidates of the National Front. This number would no doubt have been much higher if balloting were done in secret.

Not very many people still believe themselves to be represented by the National Front. They have no political representation in society. The demand of many citizens for a democratization of the relationship between state and society can still not be publicly voiced in the GDR. For this reason we call for a

Citizens' movement "Democracy Now"

We turn to all those individuals who are affected by the crisis in our country. We invite all initiative groups with similar concerns to join with us. We are hoping in particular for an alliance of Christians and critical Marxists. Let us reflect together on our future, on a society of solidarity in which:

–social justice, freedom, and the value of the human individual are guaranteed to all;

–social consensus is sought in public dialogue and realized through the just balancing of all the different interests;

–the responsible and imaginative work of citizens creates a vital pluralism in our community;

–a just and secure political order ensures internal peace;

–the economy and ecology are brought into harmony;

–prosperity is no longer increased at the expense of poorer countries;

–the fulfillment of life can be sought and found more than previously in communal actions and creative activity for the common good.

We invite all those who want to take part to enter into a dialogue about the principles and concepts of a democratic restructuring of our country. In January or February 1990 we would like to call a meeting of representatives of those who want to take part. At this meeting a program outlining general principles should be established and speakers elected who represent this program in the dialogue among all social forces, something that is urgently needed.

We also hope for the possibility of assembling our own list of candidates for the upcoming *Volkskammer* elections.

As a first unfinished, incomplete, and provisional contribution to this dialogue, we attach a set of "Theses for a Democratic Reconstruction of the GDR." Please give us your opinions and your critiques. We ask you to make suggestions for changes, additions, and elaborations. Please also write to us if you want to support this appeal, and let us know if you want to support our organization.

Let us join together and jointly re-establish hope in our country! Please copy and circulate.

Theses for a Democratic Restructuring of the GDR

The goal of our suggestions is to secure the domestic peace of our country and thereby to serve international peace as well. We want to help form a society of solidarity and to democratize all areas of life. At the same time, we must enter into a new form of partnership with our natural environment.

We want to see the socialist revolution, which bogged down at the stage of state socialism, carried further and thereby given a role in the future. Instead of a tutelary state ruled by a party that set itself up, without any societal sanction, to be the director and schoolmaster of the people, we want a state that is founded on the fundamental consensus of society, a state that is accountable to society and thus becomes a public matter (*res publica*) of free-thinking citizens. Proven social accomplishments should not be put at risk by any program of reform.

As Germans we have a special responsibility. It demands that the relationship of the German states be freed on both sides from ideological prejudices and shaped in the spirit and practice of honest neighborliness on equal terms. We invite the Germans in the Federal Republic to work toward a restructuring of their society that could make possible a new unity of the German people in the common house of the European peoples. For the sake of unity, both German states should undertake reforms that will bring them closer together.

History has imposed upon us Germans a special obligation to work for peace. We ought to meet this obligation by reducing the defensive potential of the National People's Army and through the introduction of a social peace corps as an alternative to military service.[2]

NOTES

Source: Schüddekopf, 32-38.

1. The SED's claim to leadership on all levels of society as well as its power monopoly were ideologically justified by this appeal to the moral-political unity of the party, the state, and the people.

2. This appeal concludes with brief expositions of three directions for reform of the GDR: 1) From Authoritarian State to Republic; 2) From State to Social Control of the Means of Production; 3) From Exploitation and Pollution of the Environment to a Lasting Coexistence with Nature.

4
"Call for an Initiative Group 'Social-Democratic Party' in the GDR" (September 26, 1989)

Things cannot go on like this!
Many of us are waiting for something to change.
But that is not enough!

We want to do our part.
The necessary democratization of the GDR has as its prerequisite the principal challenge to the ruling party's claim to all truth and power.
We need an open intellectual discussion about the state of our country and its future course.
For that to happen we need efforts toward the development of programs and citizens who bring with them or are willing to acquire the necessary competence for such efforts.
We, the undersigned, believe that the founding of a *Social-Democratic Party* is important for the future course of our society.

Our aim:
an ecologically oriented social democracy.
This necessitates the clear separation of state and society, as well as:
   –the enabling, support, and protection of the fundamental social, cultural, and political rights of our citizens and the assumption of the responsibilities attendant upon those rights;
   –the guaranteed protection of our natural environment and the safeguarding of natural resources and living species for coming generations.
We appeal to all those who support the following indispensable programmatic statements to form local groups:
   –constitutional state and strict separation of powers;
   –parliamentary democracy and party pluralism;
   –relative (financial, economic, cultural) independence of regions (federal states), counties, cities, and local communities;
   –social market economy with a strict prohibition of monopolies to guard against an undemocratic concentration of economic power;
   –democratization of economic structures;
   –free trade unions and the right to strike.

We seek to establish joint and binding forms of organization with all those who agree with these fundamental principles.

Those who are not in agreement with us should make themselves known and determine their own democratic perspective.

We seek an alliance with all those who want to work toward a fundamental democratization of our country.

Martin Gutzeit, Arndt Noack, Markus Meckel, Ibrahim Böhme

NOTES

Source: Schüddekopf, 41-42.

5
Joint Declaration of Oppositional Groups in the GDR
(October 4, 1990)

On October 4 representatives of:
> the citizens' movement Democracy Now,
> Democratic Awakening,
> the Group of Democratic Socialists,
> the Initiative for Peace and Human Rights,
> the Initiative Group Social-Democratic Party of the GDR,
> the New Forum,
> as well as representatives of peace circles,

came together to discuss the possibilities for joint political actions.

We welcome the emerging variety of initiatives as a sign of change and of growing courage to stand up publicly for one's own political positions.

We are united in the will to a democratic restructuring of state and society. What is at stake is the end to a situation in which the citizens of this society do not have the possibility of exercising their political rights in the manner set forth in the human rights convention of the United Nations and the CSCE Documents.

We declare our solidarity with all those who are being persecuted for acting in accordance with these aims. We support the release of all who have been incarcerated, the rescinding of all sentences, and the suspension of all judicial inquiries.

We deem it to be of primary importance that we begin a discussion in our country about the minimal conditions that would have to be observed to make possible a democratic election.

This election must facilitate different political decisions. It must be secret, which means that voters would be required to use an election booth. It must be free, which means that no one should be put under pressure to vote a certain way.

The next elections should be held under UN supervision. We want to cooperate and examine the extent to which we can realize an election alliance and put forward joint candidates.

To transform our country politically we need the participation and criticism of all. We call on all citizens of the GDR to take a hand in this democratic renewal.

Angelika Barbe (Initiative Group SDP); Mariannne Birthler (Initiative for Freedom and Human Rights); Ibrahim M. Böhme (Initiative Group SDP); Rainer Eppelmann (Democratic Awakening); Martin Gutzeit (Initiative Group SDP); Barbara Hähnchen (Peace Circle of Pankow); Heinz Küchler (Democracy Now); Kathrin Menge (New Forum); Rudi Pahnke (Democratic Awakening); Sebastian Pflugbeil (New Forum); Gerd Poppe (Initiative for Freedom and Human Rights); Ulrike Poppe (Democracy Now); Werner Schulz (Peace Circle of Pankow); Dr. Wolfgang Ullmann (Democracy Now); Reinhard Weidauer (Democratic Awakening); and a representative of the Group of Democratic Socialists.

NOTES

Source: *Aufbrüche*, 18.

6
"I'm Staying": Essay by the GDR Historian Karlheinz Blaschke in Response to the Fortieth Anniversary of the GDR (October 5, 1989)

These last few weeks before the fortieth anniversary of the GDR have thrown light on this German state in a manner that only poorly suits the cheerful atmosphere that normally precedes a day of festivities. In addition to the ever increasing number of official applications by GDR citizens to leave the country–the exact number has never been released–there were the hundreds of refugees inside the embassies of the Federal Republic and the dramatically increasing numbers of those fleeing via Hungary. Behind these events there stood and stand personal decisions by people who could no longer endure living under the existing circumstances and who therefore made the decision to leave their country, their family, their property, and their place of work after careful consideration of all the difficulties and risks. Those who have experienced and suffered under these conditions will have understanding for the fact that tens of thousands of people are trying to solve on an individual level a problem that is in truth a general societal problem.

. . . Much has been written about the several thousand, indeed, tens of thousands of GDR inhabitants who have fled, whereas the fact that sixteen million have stayed has hardly been mentioned. We sixteen million–by no means only communists–also suffer under the conditions in our country; but we live in the hope that something will change and with the feeling that we belong together and that we need each other. We are a community forged by fate and mutual suffering, just like the passengers of a ship distressed at sea. Everyone who leaves drains the energies that could bring about rescue. . . .

Without doubt, staying in the GDR necessitates both the willingness to reject many attractive offers by the West and a general attitude of willingness to help others. . . . The majority of people are staying in the country. These are not only older or elderly people; young people, too, are organizing their lives here in such a way that they see in them a meaningful future, and by no means is everyone who builds his or her house with unspeakable difficulties and starts an independent professional existence an unshakable communist. These people may have very different reasons for the conscious decision to stay, the bond with their family and the nature of their value system play a role. . . .

The population of the GDR is overburdened with the heavy load of a rigid bureaucracy that strangles many creative initiatives, with functionaries in leading positions who are unqualified and who shy away from all responsibility. Our workers are no less industrious, our engineers and scientists no less capable and intelligent than those in the West; but their willingness to give their best is impeded by the lack of understanding they confront at every turn. . . .

Everyone in the GDR should feel called upon to stay in this country. It is here that we have our task, it is here that we are needed, it is here that we must prove ourselves and invest our energies so that everyone can lead a life that is worth living. . . . Let's stay here out of love for our homeland, for our country and its people, its culture and its historical traditions, which must have a future!

NOTES

Source: Wimmer, 54-56.

7

Statement by the "New Forum" on the Occasion of the Fortieth Anniversary of the GDR (October 6, 1989)

Appeal to all members of the Socialist Unity Party

The operations of the New Forum are as new to our society as they are vitally important. Ten thousand signatures from all levels of society already prove that action for a common cause and a sense of responsibility have not perished in the stagnation of our societal existence. Not only has the crisis situation in our society become unbearable, but the prohibition on public discussion of the social conditions of our existence has also become indefensible.

These ten thousand signatures represent anything but a hostile action against the state—indeed, they are an act of civic responsibility. We protest against the government's attempts to portray us as enemies of socialism. The New Forum is a platform for new ways of thinking. This is no more hostile to socialism in the GDR than it is in the Soviet Union. We may some day be able to dispense with the New Forum—today it is indispensable. We will hold up our democratic actions as foils against all attempts to side-step societal dialogue by means of criminalization, exclusion, and intimidation.

The socialism that the government so sanctimoniously considers to be endangered cannot be threatened by a popular movement. Citizens' initiatives do not threaten social life; on the contrary, they help develop it. It seems rather that the inactivity of the SED is threatening the existence of socialism on German soil. We appeal expressly to the two million members of the SED: you constitute the largest and most important political body in our country. You have at your disposal an enormous amount of professional knowledge and leadership experience that is urgently needed for the renewal of our society. You lay claim to the leadership role—excercise it! Initiate discussions among your own ranks, lead the entire party onto a constructive course! In the last few weeks many resolutions were sent to the Central Committee from grassroots organizations. Do the members of the Central Committee at least know the number and the content of these resolutions? Were they taken under advisement? Are they being implemented? If in a socialist society even the leadership party with two million people is denied the possibility of internal discussion and cooperation, then it is unavoidable that this will result in agonizing and unbearable tensions. The discussion in which the SED itself has to engage is an important part of the entire societal discussion that our country needs.

We call for active and responsible behavior from all citizens of the GDR. Precisely the resignation that has penetrated deep into all sectors of society and the suspicious helplessness of the political leadership demand the revitalization of the democratic activity of all citizens in all existing structures over the coming months.

NOTES

Source: Schüddekopf, 69-70.

8

"Great Things Were Accomplished by the People and for the People": Erich Honecker's Speech on the Occasion of the Fortieth Anniversary of the GDR (October 7, 1989)

. . . Today our republic belongs among the ten most productive industrial nations in the world, among the two dozen or so countries with the highest standard of living. And we should not forget that our wealth does not bubble up out of the earth, nor was it achieved at the expense of others. The GDR is the work of millions, of several generations who built up their workers' and farmers' state through hard work, a state with modern industry and agriculture, with a socialist educational system, a state in which science and culture thrive. Finally–the GDR, a world nation in the area of sports. We accomplished all this with our hands and our heads, under the leadership of the working-class party. Nothing, truly nothing came easy or was given to us on a silver platter. In addition, we not only had to remove more rubble than those who live west of the Elbe and Werra rivers, but also the stones with which those living there tried to block our path.[1] Today the GDR is an outpost of peace and socialism in Europe. Never overlooking this is what protects us, but it ought also to protect our enemies from misjudging us. . . .

Especially at a time when influential forces in the FRG want to seize the opportunity to wipe out the results of the Second World War and the postwar developments by means of a coup, they must again learn that these conditions cannot be changed, that the GDR will continue to stand firm as the breakwater for the waves of neo-Nazism and chauvinism at the western border of socialism in Europe. The firm anchoring of the GDR in the Warsaw Pact cannot be shaken.

If the enemy is presently spreading lies about the GDR to a hitherto unknown extent, then this is no accident. The forty-year existence of the GDR also amounts to the forty-year defeat of German imperialism and militarism. Socialism on German soil is so unbearable to them precisely because the once exploited masses here give concrete proof that they are capable of determining their fate themselves without capitalists.

Forty years of the GDR–these were forty years of heroic work, forty years of successful struggle for the rise of our socialist republic, for the good of the people. And we will continue down that road. What is important is that the leading party in our society, the German Socialist Unity Party, further strengthen its own ranks in preparation for its twelfth party congress, that it link even more closely with the working class, the communal farmers, the intelligentsia, the entire people. We will continue to act according to Karl Marx's insight that it is not only a matter of interpreting the world, but of changing it.[2] We will continue to change our republic in the colors of the GDR through our policy of continuity and renewal within the context of the community of socialist countries. Our aims are laid down in the platform of our party. It is a matter of continuing to form a developed socialist society.

It goes without saying that this is not a project that can be successfully finished within a short time and according to already existing recipes, without constantly searching for the most effective solutions on a case-by-case basis. It is a question, rather, of a historical, a long-term process of far-reaching transformations and reforms in all areas. This is why socialism, as a real alternative to capitalism, constantly attains a higher level, this is why its advantages have a more lasting effect upon people's lives. By means of their active participation in all societal affairs, according to the principle of "share in the work, share in the planning, and share in the government," they are the masters of their present and their future. One thing is clear, we still adhere to the motto coined in the founding years of the GDR: Always forward, never backward. . . .

In forty years we have developed an economy with a modern infrastructure and great productivity. It is characterized by dynamism and growing effectiveness. In 1989 our gross national product will be 279 million marks, eleven times that of 1949. Work productivity rose ten-and-one-half times. In industry alone our productivity increased eighteen fold during this same period of time. There is as much construction now each month as there was during the entire year of 1949. Our agricultural harvest has nearly doubled, and the production of cattle has risen by a factor of eight. The daily sales of industrial goods for our population is thirteen-and-a-half times greater today than it was forty years ago. . . .

Meanwhile, an ever greater part of our economic growth comes from high technology. We have every reason to be proud of the fact that our republic managed to develop its own productive microelectronic industry, one that today produces internationally recognized results. The success of our electronics specialists in Jena and Dresden, in Erfurt and other places has, moreover, broken through Western embargoes. We will now speed up this development and with the help of this key industry advance into ever greater realms of production. Moving from such points of departure, our economy is capable of increasing production faster, in some areas by three hundred to seven hundred percent, and of injecting microelectronics into our daily lives. Consumer goods and services will go far beyond the present level and increase the national prosperity.

Modern technologies strengthen our economic potential and, at the same time, offer an interesting field of creative work and personal development for many of our workers. This is especially true of our younger generation. Isn't it one of the greatest achievements of our republic that without exception all our young people have a future, that they do not stand around on the streets, remain without an education, that they are not dependent on drugs, or that they do not just vegetate without a roof over their heads? "The trust and responsibility of our youth," that is our world, the better world. Anyone who strives for a meaningful life will recognize the underhanded magic that shines from across the border for what it really is. . . . The scientific-technological revolution transpires here in conjunction with social security; it is, to quote Karl Marx, one of the wellsprings of societal wealth.

One of the most obvious examples for this is our low-cost housing program, with the help of which we will have solved the housing question as a social problem by the end of 1990. Including the year 1989, we will have built or modernized 3,270,000 apartments. But there is more. If in 1949 the GDR had room for 5,000 children in daycare, today there is room for 365,000. There are more than 890,000 kindergarten spaces, enough to take care of all the children whose parents wish to take advantage of this. Since the seventh party congress alone, 55,000 classrooms were built in our schools. 71 per cent of all schools now have their own gymnasium. We also built no small number of nursing homes. Many department stores improved their shopping conditions. New health clinics were built. The old and renowned Berlin Charité was rebuilt and expanded. In every district new district hospitals were built. Since 1971, 120 indoor swimming pools were built. All this improved the quality of life and changed the face of our cities and towns.

The year-long maternity leave, the interest-free loan for married couples, and other important forms of assistance for young families, which have been part of everyday life in the GDR for a long time, are among the fruits of this policy. In 1959 we began to introduce mandatory education for the first ten grades. Today the ten-grade model of general education in polytechnical high schools is a normal part of the development of our children. For our retirees, the sixth increase in social security payments since the seventh party congress will go into effect in December of this year.

This is the way we set our priorities in social policy, as befits the character of our workers' and farmers' state. We concentrated our means on the satisfaction of fundamental human needs. To be sure, one cannot solve all problems simultaneously, since, as we all know, you can spend each mark only once. But with our increased achievements, our possibilities, too, will grow.

We would not have been able to cope with the stormy development of our productive forces if we had not initiated a far-reaching transformation in our planned economy itself. Fresh in our memory is the not so easy process by which the state-owned businesses were created and perfected. The combination of science, production, and market in these strong economic units has proven successful. Many businesses are successfully competing in world markets, a position, of course, that must be reasserted with each passing day. That is why there is no reason to stop and take a breather; on the contrary, we must strengthen our work in this area.

The state-owned businesses have attained a maturity that allows us to realize step by step a new quality of leadership, planning, and economic accounting. Autonomous production of resources–

that is a key phrase for changes no less far-reaching than those of
the past five years. We are opening up a wide space for responsibility and individual initiative on the solid ground of a balanced
plan. The influence of the individual worker, as well as of the collective and the trade unions, will be increased in the factories. The
principle of merit will take root more effectively, so that good
work will be rewarded all the more. All of this will tighten the relationship between the individual and state property, including
the rights and duties associated with it. We see the socialist
planned economy as a living organism that can never be viewed as
finished and perfected. . . .

All in all, the sum of these forty years of the GDR amount to
this: Great things were accomplished by the work of the people
and for the people. In the future, as well, no lesser efforts will be
necessary. New problems demand new solutions, and we will find an
answer to every question. We will find it in conjunction with the
people for our progress along the road to socialism in the German
Democratic Republic. . . .

NOTES

Source: *Deutschland-Archiv*, 22 (1989), 1431-33.

1. The Elbe and the Werra are two rivers that formed the former border
between the GDR and the FRG.
2. In his "Theses on Feuerbach," the German social philosopher Karl
Marx had criticized traditional philosophers by arguing that they had "only
interpreted the world in various ways," whereas the true charge of philosophy would be "to *change* it."

9
"We Are United by the Ideals of Socialism and Peace": Michail Gorbachev's Speech on the Occasion of the Fortieth Anniversary of the GDR (October 7, 1989)

We have no doubt that the German Socialist Unity Party, with
its intellectual potential, its rich experiences, and its political authority, is capable, in cooperation with all societal forces, of finding answers to those questions that have been placed on the agenda
by the development of the republic and are moving its citizens. In
essence it is a question of developing those possibilities that are
inherent in our socialist system–the system of the workers, the rule
of the people.

The Soviet Union is sincerely interested in the fact that the German Democratic Republic continues to become strong, to grow, and to develop! . . . I would like in particular to mention the following. For the socialist world, as well as for today's civilization in general, the growing variety of forms for organizing production, of social structures, and of political institutions is characteristic. It confirms Lenin's thesis that each and every nation will discover its own peculiar nature in this or that form of democracy, and at this or that pace of socialist transformation.

The attempts to unify and standardize in matters of societal development, on the one hand the imitation, on the other hand the forced imposition of any binding patterns whatsoever, belong to the past.[1] The range of creative possibilities is growing, the idea of socialism itself is acquiring an incomparably richer content. The choice of its forms of development is a sovereign decision of every nation. But the greater the variety and specific nature of these forms, the greater the need to exchange our experiences and discuss theoretical and practical problems. And, of course, the need to act in concert. To put it differently, this manifoldness is not only no obstacle, but, on the contrary, a further weighty argument for the development of cooperation. . . .

The fiftieth anniversary of the beginning of World War II was the occasion for lively discussions and debates, for the search of history for answers to questions with which the present confronts us. Unfortunately, it also happens that we examine history for only those answers that we would like to hear. I am referring to attempts to place the blame for the division of Europe into two opposing military blocs on the Soviet Union and its allies. We are constantly challenged to undertake measures for the removal of this division. We have already heard such demands as: the Soviet Union should remove the Berlin Wall, and only then could one have faith in its peaceful motives. And in the FRG we have of late heard voices that demand the restitution of Germany in the borders of 1937, and even Polish Silesia has been mentioned.[2]

It seems as if the reforms in the Soviet Union and other socialist countries have seduced some politicians into laying claim once more to their old demands. They have even gone so far as to offer a questionable interpretation of the Soviet-German Declaration signed this past June in Bonn. These questions have an extraordinary significance for the future of the European nations, for world peace. That is why we need full clarity. Above all, our Western partners should keep in mind that all questions concerning the GDR are decided in Berlin, not in Moscow. The GDR is a sovereign state, it autonomously enacts measures with regard for the various tasks necessary for the protection of its interests and issues in keeping with its domestic and foreign policies. . . .

Now to the order that emerged in Europe. We do not idealize it. But the main thing is that until now it was precisely the acceptance of the postwar realities that secured peace in Europe. What is more, out of this order grew the Helsinki process, the continuation of which promises further positive changes in the entire European situation and gives us prospects for the construction of a house that will encompass all of Europe. In a word, the existing realities on the continent, including the borders of sovereign states as key components, do not present an obstacle to the progression of international relations. Every time the West set stock in changing the postwar map of Europe, this led to renewed tensions in the international climate, an increase in the danger of nuclear conflict, and in no way contributed to the solution of the pressing problems tied to human interests. And vice versa, the achievement of a realistic course brought great positive results both for the general health of the European climate as well as for the improvement of relations between the two German states and the deepening of contacts among people. . . .

There is, in fact, nothing more important than the following two fundamental truths which humanity began to understand in the twentieth century after making great sacrifices.

First: In the nuclear age, as humanity stands before the duty to fight for survival, the most burning problems of the present day can only be solved through common efforts and in a peaceful manner, through political means. There is no other way; a different way would be deadly for us all.

Second: History has its own laws, its own tempo, its own rhythm, all of which are determined by the maturation of objective and subjective factors of development. To ignore this means to create new problems.

Comrades!

We are aware of the great interest with which you in the GDR follow our affairs, the radical transformations taking place in the Soviet Union. This transformation is an extremely difficult task, one that demands the greatest exertion of all our physical, intellectual, and moral energy from both the party and the people. But for us it is a matter of survival, and—we are firmly convinced of this—it will lead our country to new successes and will unfold the rich potential of socialism in an incomparable way. Democratization, openness, a socialist constitutional state, the free development of all its ethnic groups and their equal participation in matters that concern the entire country, dignified living conditions for the entire population and guaranteed rights for everyone, extensive possibilities for the creative potential of every human being–this is what we strive for, and we are guided by these aims.

Our party and our nation are firmly resolved to bring to a successful conclusion those reforms that will radically renew Soviet society. . . .

NOTES

Source: *Deutschland-Archiv*, 22 (1989): 1434-35.

1. Gorbachev is hinting at the fact that at the time of his speech to the East German populace on the occasion of the fortieth anniversary of the GDR, the Soviet Union no longer considers the Eastern European states "satellites" that must imitate its own policies, and that, moreover, the Soviet Union is neither prepared nor willing to intervene on behalf of the GDR regime, as it did in Hungary in 1956 and Czechoslovakia in 1968, in the case of political unrest.

2. The phrase "the restitution of Germany in the borders of 1937" refers to the geographic expansion of Germany undertaken by Adolf Hitler before the annexation of those parts of Europe–i.e., Czechoslovakia, Austria, and parts of Poland–that had a strong German cultural tradition. Germany in the borders of 1937 includes not only the the area covered by the FRG and the GDR, but also parts of present-day Poland.

10
Flyer to Welcome East German Emigrants at the Border Crossing in Passau (Early October 1989)

Instructions for Germans from the GDR

Welcome!

After days of insecurity you have reached your destination!

The federal government, the *Länder* and districts, as well as the churches, relief organizations, and social associations have made provisions as best they could to welcome you and integrate you into the Federal Republic of Germany. You will soon find a new home here. But not everything is successful in the first few days. In order to make your arrival easier we ask that you pay attention to the following instructions:

1. If you have the possibility of finding *housing* with relatives, friends, or acquaintances, please fill out the attached certificate and submit it to one of the easily recognizable *entrance offices* immediately upon your arrival in the Federal Republic of Germany.

At this office you will receive from the Red Cross a sum of money from the Friedland Relief Fund.[1]

Furthermore, you will get an application form for entrance procedures. Please send it from your new place of residence to the immigration office in Gießen. From there you will receive your entrance document and transitional financial assistance from the government of the Federal Republic.

The entrance office guarantees your immediate transport to the destination of your choice. Once there, you should immediately contact the unemployment office.

2. If you have *no possibility for housing* in the Federal Republic of Germany, you will first be accepted at one of the following shelters:

–Freilassing
–Trostberg near Altötting
–Passau
–Tiefenbach near Passau
–Vilshofen
–Hengersberg near Deggendorf
–Schöppingen near Münster.

You will only stay in the provisional shelter for a very short time and soon travel on to one of the West German Länder.

3. Should the shelter be overcrowded, you will be moved to another camp. From there you will immediately receive further information about travel to the *Länder*.

4. If you are traveling with your *own car*, please drive up to the posted entrance office. There you will receive gas for your continued journey.

It is necessary for you to have minimum insurance for your vehicle as soon as possible, by the latest within ten days after your entry into the Federal Republic of Germany. If you are involved in an accident before you have insurance within the first ten days after your entry, you can write to HUK-Insurance, Glockengießerwall 1, 2000 Hamburg 1.

5. For further information, the police, the Federal Border Patrol, the Red Cross, the Technical Relief Organization, the Automobile Club, and the staff in the entrance offices will be available.

Issued by the Interior Ministry of the Federal Republic of Germany

NOTES

Source: *Aufbrüche*, 152-53.

1. Friedland is a small community in the vicinity of Göttingen near the former border to the GDR; traditionally it has served as one of the camps for East German refugees and its relief fund is targeted specifically for such purposes.

11
Declaration by Participants at a Meeting of the "United Left" in Böhlen near Leipzig (October 13, 1989)

The events of the last weeks have changed the situation in our country. Many people are asking themselves if an upheaval has truly begun and what can be done. What has happened?

While the wave of people who fled this country was reaching its peak, the political leadership continued to treat the citizens of our country like human trash: ten thousand citizens who fled were condemned as deserters who were manipulated by the Western media and by Cold War warriors, deserters whose absence should not be lamented. More circumspect opinions were buried under this intensive barrage. On the other hand, central concerns of the population continued to be ignored, demands for democratization were disparaged, and participants in public demonstrations were initially all characterized as anti-socialist rowdies and agitators. The credibility of ritualized statements of loyalty to the security organizations and the SED leadership or horror stories in the manner of tabloid journalism reached a new low after October 7.[1] The blunt weapon of the empty phrase or the persuasiveness of the nightstick remained the only "arguments" employed by the rulers in their dialogue with the people.

And yet the flood of protests, even from among the rank and file of the labor unions, the party groups, and more and more professional organizations, could no longer be met with silence when at the same time tens of thousands were taking part in peaceful demonstrations and disparagement or intimidation became increasingly ineffective. Finally, an objective interaction with our problems and conflicts could be ascertained on various levels, but the picture is still shaped by old patterns. Hopeful signs given by a few people in state offices or by individual functionaries of various parties and mass organizations, which signaled at least an openness for dialogue, were in danger of being extinguished by the massive press campaign against rowdies and paid counter-revolutionaries. The government is less and less able to adhere to its position that the departure of tens of thousands of people can be attributed mainly to the subversive activities of Cold War warriors in the West. And more and more it proved to be ineffective to constantly deny, increasingly turning a blind eye to reality, that there were internal causes and to react with cynicism to this incredible loss of people and hope. The scorn with which until now the needs of the majority of those citizens who are resolved to stay in the GDR were swept aside is now causing more and more damage to those in power. A growing number of members and functionaries of the SED sees matters this way, as demonstrated by their public appeals for dialogue. The lie that the ultimate aim of those people in our country who are pressing for reforms is the destruction of socialism in the GDR comes into ever greater contrast with the demands of those people who are demanding reform precisely because they finally want to build socialism in the GDR! With the imputation that an opposition manipulated by the West is striving for the re-establishment of capitalism, the political leaders presume to defend a socialism that neither deserves this name nor is supported in its present form by the population. The struggle to attain socialism is yet to be won! Not just some day, but today we are called upon to make socialism possible by taking our affairs into our own hands and putting an end to the fateful political stagnation of the past.

When on October 11 the leadership of the SED called upon the Politburo of the SED to initiate a societal dialogue about all the problems this country is facing, it admitted the need for action it had previously denied and indirectly put into question the effectiveness of its former policies.[2] Let's not take the attitude toward dialogue of the party leaders, who are responsible for the present situation, as the yardstick for our actions, but rather our own willingness for radical change in the name of socialism and democracy! Right now all citizens, including the members of the SED, are not only increasingly summoned, but also capable of committing themselves to such a course.

We can no longer take the irresponsibility of the powerful in this country as the yardstick for everything we do. It is not the offer of dialogue in the declaration of the Politburo from October 11 that is the basis for our actions, but rather the pressure originating in the severe contradictions and the challenge to everyone in this country to finally change things on their own. We should not have any illusions about the situation that has developed and those who are responsible for it: it is not only the prospects for socialism in the GDR that are at stake; the preservation and development of such significant social accomplishments as the eradication of unemployment, free medical care for all citizens, social security, or equal educational opportunities for proletarian children are also at risk if we do not put a stop to this stagnation soon. We must also fear that in their disappointment, more and more people will distance themselves not only from the government and the SED but from the socialist path in general. 100,000 people have already left the GDR this year alone, and the flood shows no signs of ebbing. The "proven" method of walling in even more thoroughly those who stay behind and, in addition, of surrounding with security agents those people who publicly voice their protest and their willingness to stay has only increased people's rage, and it contains the danger of escalation. The continuation of this bankrupt course also endangers everything of which the GDR can justifiably be proud.

While before 1961 already two-and-a-half million people turned their backs on the GDR, today every one-sided attribution of responsibility to the West is as helpless as it is ridiculous in the face of the mass exodus of tens of thousands of primarily younger citizens who spent their entire lives in the walled-in sterility of GDR socialism. In fact, to reproach the enemies of socialism abroad for behaving like enemies of socialism reveals itself to be nothing but a wretched diversion. . . .

What can be done?

If we are to put an end to the continuation of the failed course pursued by the political leadership and hence to the threat to the prospects for socialism in our country, the struggle should not only concentrate on the fight for the uncensored word. This important process was initiated by the "New Forum" and other citizens' initiatives. But if we are to prevent the costs of the previous failed course from being passed off on the population, if we are to enforce a fundamental change in development, a breakthrough in the direction of democratization and socialist freedom, then this has to be accomplished by the workers in the factories–especially since they always had to bear the primary burden that resulted from every failed policy. The broad dissatisfaction in the factories has to be expressed, and the will to change that is evident there must seek out and find its channels. Let's stop doing nothing but complaining and let's begin joining ranks in the factories! We need the commitment of the workers for the creation of independent committees and commissions to focus the interests of the workers and employees and transform them into initiatives. These independent committees and commissions, which should be formed immediately, could deal with the founding of independent advisory boards and the democratization of the labor unions. For this process all opportunities that are available inside or outside of the bureaucratized labor unions can be utilized in order to expand the control of the workers over their own affairs.

We appeal to all socialists in the factories, cooperatives, in the independent groups and in the SED, among the artists and the intelligentsia, to approach one another, to put aside what separates them and search for common solutions with the aim of realizing socialist freedom and democracy. We suggest that the following immediate measures be adopted for a speedy solution to the most important social problems that have accrued and for overcoming the present social crisis.

Immediate Measures to Be Taken to Prepare the Country for a Road to Socialist Democracy and Freedom

1. The resignation of the Politburo of the SED and the government on the grounds that they bear primary responsibility for the catastrophic mass exodus of our youth and the people's complete loss of confidence.
2. The formation of a new political leadership and a temporally limited transitional government, composed of reform-minded forces for the realization of the following measures:
   a) the immediate democratization of the press and the end of press censorship;
   b) the legalization of the "New Forum" and all other groups committed to socialist democracy and freedom, as well as the initiation of a dialogue between equal partners about all the social problems that need to be solved;
   c) the granting of free and public discussion in all societal organizations and parties;

d) the publication of all data and information about the actual
state of the economy and of society. This pertains particularly to:
–the state of the state finances;
–the true state and the actual results of our economy, including
* foreign trade (especially the trade and budget balance)
* the figures for military spending and internal security
* the costs and cost structure of the state and party apparatus;
–the social structure, including the employees of the state,
the party, and the economic apparatus (among them also
the police apparatus);
–the distribution of income among the population (including
the incomes of the nomenclature cadre and their supplementary income, additional revenues and privileges, as
well as their personal rights of usufruct);
–information about the state of the environment;
–the state of the health care system and of medical services;
–the relative health of the population and their life ex-
pectancy according to regions and in comparison with
other countries;
–the extent of the present desire among the populace to
leave the country (the publication of the number of appli-
cants for passports and of those who have left, as well as
their social and professional profile, divided according
to regions);
e) the initiation of a public discussion about the aims and means
of a radical democratization of the political, economic, and
cultural life of our society;
f) thirty-day travel permits for all citizens for all countries
(with the exception of the restrictions, common to all nations,
for reasons of national security), with the availability of
foreign currency in the amount of 500 D-marks per person per
year;
g) the offer to all former GDR citizens who left the country and
were de-naturalized that they will be allowed to return;
h) the summoning within three months time of a governmen-
tally independent congress composed of democratically and
secretly elected delegates of the factory personnel for the
purpose of:

–talks about the economic and political situation in the
  GDR;
–working up measures for the implementation of a radical
  democratization of all areas of society, including the labor unions;
–working up measures for securing the standard of living
  and the social achievements of the nation;
–the election of independent reformers as democratically
  legitimate representatives, responsible to the congress in
  a broad government of reform.

3. The formation of a broad coalition ruled by reason and realism for
the implementation of a radical constitutional and social reform in
the spirit of socialist democracy and freedom.

The expression of such a coalition ruled by reason must be the
formation of a consistent reform government on the basis of anti-
Stalinism and anti-capitalism. This government should be composed, on the one hand, of representatives of the reform wing of the
party and state apparatus who have gained credibility through
their actions, and, on the other hand, of democratically elected
representatives of the congress of factory delegates.

Immediate Measures to Be Taken by a Reform Government

The self-evident presupposition of a governmental coalition for socialist freedom and democracy in the GDR is trust in our adherence
to alliances and treaties with foreign countries. Above all the alliance among a democratized Soviet Union, a democratized Poland,
and a democratized GDR, and especially the acknowledgment of
existing borders, is of crucial importance for each of these countries.

The mandate of such a reform government must advance the following issues:

1. The comprehensive preparation and implementation of a radical
constitutional and social reform in the spirit of free and democratic
socialism on the basis of:
–socialization of the means of production as the primary and
  prospective foundation of socialization along socialist lines;
–the expansion of the producers' self-determination in order to
  realize the actual socialization of all economic activity;
–the consistent realization of the principle of social security
  and justice for all members of society;
–the ecological transformation of industrial society;

–political democracy, a constitutional state, the consistent realization of inalienable human rights, and the free development of every individual member of society.

2. The implementation of consistent economic reforms by establishing the self-administration of the workers as the primary mode for the further development of state-owned property.

3. The development of a program of economic, technical, and ecological modernization, while preserving social justice and without unemployment.

4. The implementation of economic reforms and modernization as a complex program, while preserving social security, justice, and without unemployment.

5. GDR initiatives for the development and implementation of a reform program for COMECON as well as for the organization of the Warsaw Pact according to the principles of a democratic and free socialism.

6. The start of negotiations with the Federal Republic of Germany about the long-term shape of a basic treaty according to the principle of "Two states–one nation," with the aim of:

    a) mutual constitutional recognition;

    b) the development of relations in consideration of the special case of the existence of two sovereign states of contrary socioeconomic character on the ground of one nation, and further expansion of all aspects of common national ties;

    c) the development of a binding framework for the recognition of responsibilities incumbent upon the entire German nation–especially for peace–while protecting the sovereignty of both German states.

7. A guarantee for the free and independent development of West Berlin on the basis of the Four-Powers Agreement and completion of a treaty among the GDR, the FRG, and West Berlin.

8. The elaboration of a program for the development of both parts of Berlin into the political, economic, and cultural link between East and West.

9. The investigation of Stalinist crimes in the GDR and their rigorous prosecution, as well as the rehabilitation and remuneration of all their victims.

10. The condemnation of the illegal and unconstitutional invasion of

Czechoslovakia in August of 1968 by the GDR's National People's Army, and a formal apology to the peoples of Czechoslovakia.[3]

NOTES

Source: Schüddekopf, 125-35.

1. In socialist countries such statements of loyalty to the security organizations and the leadership of the Communist Party had a strictly ritualistic character and hence were viewed as essentially meaningless.

2. On October 11 the SED leadership called a special meeting of the Politburo to deal with the crisis and demanded that Erich Honecker put together a report on the current situation. In this report the Politburo spoke for the first time of the necessity of reforms and of a social dialogue on the problems confronting the GDR.

3. The GDR's National People's Army joined the Soviet Troops in 1968 to put an end to the Prague Spring.

12
Erich Honecker's Resignation Speech (October 18, 1989)

Dear comrades!

After careful consideration and after the results of yesterday's session in the Politburo, I have made the following decision: due to my illness and after the successful operation my health no longer allows the commitment of strength and energy demanded by the developments of our party and our people today and in the future.[1] I am therefore asking the Central Committee of the SED to relieve me of my duties as the General Secretary of the Central Committee of the SED, as Chairman of the *Staatsrat* of the GDR, and as Chairman of the National Defense Council of the GDR. Comrade Egon Krenz, who is capable and willing to act in accordance with the responsibility and the enormous work demanded by the situation, by the interests of the party and the people, and by the preparations for the twelfth party congress, which touch all areas of society, should be recommended to the Central Committee and the Parliament as my successor.

Dear comrades! I dedicated my entire conscious life, in unshakable loyalty, to the revolutionary cause of the working class and to our Marxist-Leninist world-view, to the establishment of socialism on German soil. I consider the founding and successful development of the socialist German Democratic Republic, whose balance sheet we drew up together at its fortieth anniversary, to be the crowning accomplishment of our party's struggle and my own activities as a communist. I thank the Politburo, the Central Committee, my comrades during the difficult time of antifascist resistance, the members of the party, and all citizens of our country for decades of communal and fruitful cooperation for the good of the people. I will be available to my party in the future with my experience and my advice. I wish our party and its leadership the further strengthening of its unity and unanimity, and wish the Central Committee continued success.

NOTES

Source: Schüddekopf, 125-35.

1. Erich Honecker was suffering from cancer of the liver; he underwent surgery on 10 January 1990 to remove a cancerous tumor from one of his kidneys.

13
Egon Krenz's Television Address After Assuming the Post of General Secretary of the SED (October 18, 1989)

If you ask me what occupies my thoughts at this hour, I have only one answer: it is the thought of working together intensively. Talking and quarrelling with each other is important. Communicating with each other is necessary. But working with each other, planing our future, and governing rationally remains the decisive thing. This is the only way in which we can fulfill the high expectations our party members and all the citizens of our country have placed in the twelfth party congress and the shaping of our future.

. . . What is certain is that in the past months we did not assess the essence of the social development in our country realistically enough, and that we failed to draw the proper conclusions soon enough. Starting with today's conference we will introduce a radical turn, above all we will reassume the political and ideological offensive. . . . We are asking everyone to work with us, to plan with us, and to govern with us. Let us take on together those things that must be taken on. . . . Our program is the development of socialist society, its continued renewal. There is no standstill, there can be no standstill. Socialism is not a completed social order, it is a revolutionary social order. The contradiction between what has been achieved and what has not yet been achieved, between ideal and reality, demands constant renewal, which can only have one mean-ing: the well-being of human beings in peace!

In the last few months everyone has noticed: we are experienc-ing the intensification of contradictions that resulted from the real-ization of our party program and the resolutions of our eleventh party congress. The problems in our economy, in both domestic trade and in international markets, have increased. Many unsolved ques-tions related to supplying the population with necessary goods and quality products have piled up. Inconsistencies in the implementa-tion of the merit principle increased. Salary policies, subventions, and social benefits are subjects of lively debate. We are worried about the preservation of our natural environment. . . .

We cannot overlook the fact that the traditional strength of our party, its relationship of trust with the people, has been dam-aged. We are drawing self-critical conclusions from this to aid us in our work. At the same time, we do not fail to see that the enemies of socialism–external as well as internal–are increasingly attempting to turn this situation to their advantage. They smell the air of a new day and are setting about–without the risk of open aggression–trying to "reform" the GDR back into capitalist conditions. More than one hundred thousand people–among them many young peo-ple–have left our country. That is a further symptom of the compli-cated situation that has arisen. We feel their emigration to be a great blood-letting. Each of us can sympathize with the tears of many a mother and father. We suffered many human losses, we suf-fered political and economic losses. This wound will cause us pain for a long time. But many of the statements made in front of Western television cameras by those who left have offended the dignity and pride of their parents, friends, colleagues, and many of us. However, that does not absolve any of us from the duty of searching in ourselves and in our environment for reasons why so many people are turning their backs on us. Only if we frankly face the causes that developed in our society will we be able to give those who even right now are still thinking about leaving an impetus to re-think their decision. We need them.

. . . Our society has enough democratic forums in which people from different levels of the population can express the most diverse interests with regard to a socialism that is worth living. The broad evolution of socialist democracy in the GDR, however, should not be mistaken for a license for irresponsible action, or worse, be mis-used for violent and destructive acts. There can be only one answer to such actions: the safeguarding of peace and order, of the peaceful work of our citizens, the protection of values that all of us created and for which all of us have to pay. Anyone who turns against the foundations of our social order has to answer the question whether he or she wants a different social system than the one the great majority of our people wants. One thing is clear to us: socialism on German soil is not an issue open to discussion!

. . . We acknowledge our duty to maintain peace. That is why we continue to follow the politics of dialogue, so that reason and realism will prevail. We do not see any rational alternative to peaceful coexistence, disarmament, detente, and cooperation between East and West. With the aim of furthering the common responsibility of both German states for a peaceful, regulated, and equal coexistence of two distinct social orders, we are prepared to test paths and possibilities for the long-term shaping of closer relations, regulated by treaties, between the GDR and the FRG. We are also prepared to develop cooperative and permanent forms of economic, ecological, political, cultural, humanitarian, and touristic cooperation.

If the government of the Federal Republic of Germany wants to make a contribution to all of this, it ought to fully acknowledge GDR citizenship on the basis of unambiguous international regulations and legislation, renounce every form of state-sponsored manipulation of the citizens of this country, and constructively support the development of contacts between the East German *Volkskammer* and the West German *Bundestag*, regular consultations between parties and trade unions and leading economic organs and other state institutions. . . . The Politburo made the suggestion to the government of the GDR that it prepare legislation regulating travel of GDR citizens to foreign countries. We assume that this draft will be discussed and ratified by the parliament after a public hearing. In this same context the temporary measures regulating travel to socialist brother countries could be lifted or modified. But truth demands that we state with all clarity that the refusal of the FRG to respect, without any qualifications, GDR citizenship remains a very serious obstacle that stands in the way of the realization of the planned steps for travel to the FRG, to West Berlin, and to other capitalist countries. To insist on clinging to the so-called "responsibility to care for all Germans"–no matter how much one squirms–is part of the fundamental revanchist conception of the FRG that contradicts international law and the Basic Treaty [regulating relations between the GDR and the FRG].[1] . . . In our German Democratic Republic there will be no other form of socialism than the one that all of us create and defend together. Everything is in our power, everything depends on our community, everything depends on the unity and solidarity of our party.

NOTES

Source: Wimmer, 84-87.

1. The Federal Republic of Germany adopted a doctrine that declared its responsibility to care for all Germans, regardless of where they live. In practice this meant that refugees from the GDR could claim West German citizenship and were entitled to the entire range of social benefits upon emigrating to the West.

14
Preliminary Statement of Principles and Discussion Paper of the Reform Group "Democratic Awakening" (October 30, 1989)

The Party "Democratic Awakening": Social, Ecological

Resolution of October 30, 1989

1. The participants eligible to vote agreed to the statement of principles resolved on October 30, 1989 and to the preliminary statute.

In observation of the rights set down in Articles 27 and 29 of the constitution of the GDR, each citizen who agrees to the statement of principles is supposed to be able to participate in the shaping of GDR society by means of the objective and constructive expression of opinions, and to freely decide to become a member of this party, which primarily defines its aim as supporting the participation of citizens in the ecological, political, cultural, social, and economic organization of GDR society.

2. For the duration of preparations for the final founding of the party by May 1, 1990 at the latest, the eligible participants elected a preliminary steering committee consisting of ten members:

Chair:	Wolfgang Schnur, attorney
1. Vice Chair:	Brigitta Kögler, attorney
2. Vice Chair:	Erhart Neubert, sociologist
Treasurer:	Christiane Ziller, musical dramaturgist
Spokesperson:	Rainer Eppelmann, minister
Members:	Edelbert Richter, professor
	Rudi Pahnke, minister

Herbert Wirzewski, locksmith
Günther Nooke, physicist
Dr. Fred Ebeling, engineer

The tasks of the steering committee are defined in paragraph 4 of the preliminary statute for the founding of the party.

3. Until another meeting of all delegates or members can be called, the steering committee has been charged with preparing a document regulating election procedures, the standing order, and financial and membership guidelines, as well as with attending to the legal questions regarding the registration and founding of the party.

4. The steering committee is charged with naming responsible representatives for the following areas:

Brigitta Kögler:
–civil and human rights
–legal and legislative policies

Günther Nooke:
–environmental protection
–social and health care policy

Christiane Ziller:
–policy toward women, families, and children
–culture and education
–organization and leadership of the party

Rudi Pahnke:
–policy toward youth
–cooperation with citizens' initiatives and other democratic political movements and parties

Wolfgang Schnur:
–questions of disarmament, peace, and military service

Wolfgang Schnur and Rainer Eppelmann:
–problems of the two-thirds world
–international cooperation and foreign policy

Rainer Eppelmann:
–public relations, media coverage, and editorship of a newspaper

Dr. Fred Ebeling:
–fiscal and economic policy
–science and technology

Dr. Fred Ebeling and Herbert Wirzewski:
–labor and trade-union policies

Edelbert Richter and Erhart Neubert:
–establishment of a platform commission

Preliminary Statement of Principles

The society of the GDR is in a moral, social, economic, ecological, and political crisis. The symptoms of this development can no longer be repressed. Citizens are still being patronized.

There are no sufficient political structures for the public formation of the will of the citizens.

Since a dialogue requires equal partners, our society can only become democratic when other political units besides the Socialist Unity Party can be constituted.

We understand our initiative as an attempt to do precisely that. The critical attitude of Democratic Awakening (DA) toward really-existing socialism does not mean that we reject the vision of a socialist social order. We are participating in the debate about how to conceive socialism.

DA is a political association that wishes to develop into a party. It operates within the framework of democratic constitutional principles.

Our aim is a democratic awakening for a productive industrial society with ecological and social aims.

A renewed democratic republic requires:
1. *The separation of state and political parties*
The state rests on a democratic constitution and on values developed out of public debate. It does not rest on a single party's claim to truth. State institutions are subject to public control and are ideologically neutral.
2. *The development of a free public sphere and unobstructed access to it*
Society controls and evaluates the directions of its development by means of constant public debate. It is here that social contradictions are revealed. This requires the dissolution of the state's monopoly on information and the media. We are for free media, accessible to all. Every citizen has the right to request information about all the political and societal activities of the government.
3. *Free formation of the will of the people and the public expression of that will through political means*
We are for a multi-party system on the basis of substantive alternatives. Every legal party can take over the control of the government according to the principle of majority rule. We strive for a

situation in which mass organizations do not have a seat in parliament.

4. *The separation of state and society, and societal control over the state*

The executive and the legislative organs that control the state must be separate. The independent administrative and constitutional jurisdiction protects the basic rights of citizens from the power of the state.

5. *The socialization of the means of production*

Socialized property is a misleading term for the state property that currently exists in the GDR, which should be abolished. State property should be limited to major industries, publicly controlled, and tied to employee participation in management or self-administration. Smaller industries and service industries can be organized as cooperatives or can be privately owned. We reject monopolized forms of property.

6. *Limitation of the economic plan to fundamental tendencies of the economic development and role of the market*

The economic plan establishes a general framework for economic action. Free-market principles become effective for furthering the self-responsibility of all. The state has the duty to protect those who are socially weak and to reduce the threat to our environment.

7. *Economic effectiveness and social justice*

The balance between the concerns of economic effectiveness and of social justice is brought about by society itself. That is why we demand free and independent labor unions and the representation of other interest groups. An effective protection of minorities must be guaranteed by legal means as must be the establishment of variable public funding sources.

8. *The ecological reorganization of industrial society*

Ecological factors must be increasingly included in the cost analysis of industries. By means of taxation and legal regulations, our long-term goal is that the most environmentally sound mode of production will also be the most economical mode. The development and utilization of renewable energy sources is furthered by an extensive competition that makes particular use of market forces. The collective and private initiatives that would presumably evolve as a response to the urgency of ecological transformation will be the decisive motor driving these developments. Adhering to the principle of public formation of the will of the people, they are at the same time co-initiators of a change in the pattern of needs.

9. Direction of foreign policy

The political demands and practical aims of DA are grounded in the great hope for the construction of a common European house, a peaceful European order, and a world that is more just. We value highly the particular relationship to the Federal Republic of Germany, founded on the unity of German history and culture. The DA also gives consideration to the attachments between friends and families of millions of citizens separated by the German-German border. We are working under the assumption that there will be two German states. We support an active rapprochement of the two German states within the framework of a peaceful European order.

NOTES

Source: Schüddekopf, 161-65.

15

Egon Krenz's Television and Radio Address to the Citizens of the GDR (November 3, 1989)

. . . I am turning in this critical time to all citizens of the German Democratic Republic and all members of the Socialist Unity Party.

We are fully justified in claiming that with the ninth meeting of the Central Committee of the SED a new stage has begun in the development of our socialist fatherland. The political turn that we initiated has meanwhile affected all areas of our society. Above all, millions of people have been touched and moved by it. They are–and we all are–working toward the renewal of societal life with the aim of reshaping socialism so as to make it more livable for every citizen of our country. This new beginning, this awakening of our people, is accompanied by many conversations, discussions, debates, demonstrations, and other expressions of intent. All these forms fall under the category of dialogue. It is only natural that in this process many questions are being asked. Indeed, there are more questions than can be answered today. In these processes, characterized by a hitherto unknown political dynamic, a certain amount of unrest and anxiety among the citizens cannot be overlooked and overheard. They have concerns about the unshakability of the socialist foundations of our society and about their unquestioned socialist future.

In my function as General Secretary of the party of the working class and head of state of our country, I assure you all: we will not allow the forty-year history of our German Democratic Republic, the great achievements of our workers and farmers, our scientists and artists, our women and youth, our soldiers and our security police, which taken together are the foundation of our republic, to be belittled. The renewal of our socialist society that is so urgently needed is only possible on the foundations of that which we all created together. At the same time, we will never forget that the peace and security of every citizen on our continent is dependent on the stability of a socialist GDR, located at this sensitive place in the world where socialism and capitalism meet. Our Warsaw Pact allies look to and rely upon us.

In my speech at the ninth meeting of the Central Committee, I spoke of the huge mountain of work that awaits us. I can only say that life is taking us literally. Anyone who wants change cannot preserve his or her energy. The very first results of our work are now in. Perhaps they have not come quickly enough and for some people they may not go far enough. But they make one thing perfectly clear: we are moving ceaselessly forward. We are about to develop new things in politics, in our economy, in our common social life, in the democratic development of our state. There is no turning back. The evidence for this is, among other things, the draft of the new law regulating travel, which will be made public soon, the more precise formulation of paragraph 213 of our criminal code, the convening of a federal commission for the drafting of media legislation, a decree for the publication of environmental data, and, last but not least, the amnesty ratified by the *Staatsrat* of the GDR.[1]

. . . We want full sovereignty for the people of the GDR. With this in mind we are striving for a reform of the political system. The free-thinking citizen, his or her right to free development and to democratic participation in all the affairs of society and state, are the centerpiece of our policies. Our concern is the rich political culture of socialist society. That means comprehensive and true information, diversity of opinion and difference of opinion, tolerance for those with different views, and honest struggle for common solutions.

We suggest the establishment of a constitutional court charged with assuring compliance with the constitution. Administrative reform is unavoidable. We also need a law regulating political organizations. We take the critique of excessive representation and of special privileges to be justified. Such practices, which accord neither with our socialist morality nor with the principle of merit, must stop. Constitutionality requires that we protect the civil order, take action against lawbreakers and perpetrators of violent crimes, protect citizens and their property from them. Our nation needs security organizations in order to secure its task of restructuring. That includes the demand for their lawful behavior in every regard.

We are in favor of a civilian alternative to military service.

We take very seriously the citizens' dissatisfaction with numerous flaws in the provision of goods, with the insufficient continuity of production, and with excessive bureaucratic structures. The Central Committee will occupy itself with immediate measures for the improvement of everyday life. At the same time, the situation demands a fundamental change in our economic policy in conjunction with comprehensive economic reform.

We also need a reform of our educational system, from general education to vocational and university training. At the center stands the training of young people who are knowledgeable and capable, and who as active citizens realize with energy, skill, and sincerity their ideas about life and work under socialism.

We see the renewal of our socialist society above all as a great spiritual renewal. We have instituted in the life of our party, in its structures and party statutes, guarantees that make this renewal irreversible. We need a democratization of cadre politics and term limits for elected officials. Leadership by the party means developing political concepts–such as this program for action–and making the members and organizations in the representational bodies, in the government, in the councils and other organs of state and economy capable of implementing them. We want a strong SED, closely connected with the people, that is ready to act and is permeated by a new democratic self-awareness. . . .

Dear citizens of the German Democratic Republic!

In the coming days we have to accomplish three things. We must secure bread for our people and the material foundation of society in daily, strenuous, and uninterrupted work. At the same time, we have to take measures for formulating and passing the first decrees and legislation in order to give our lives those characteristics of renewal that are possible and realistic today. We also must conceptually establish the framework for the reforms that will determine the immediate and more distant socialist future of the GDR. For this we need dialogue. We are engaging in it under the motto of "more democracy for more socialism and a better form of socialism."

Some degree of impatience is noticeable at present. That is understandable and can even serve our aims. But it also contains certain dangers. Problems that have developed and accumulated over the years to form a tangle of serious contradictions and crises cannot be corrected within a few days or even a few weeks. To proceed without circumspection and overhastily would eventually do more harm than good. That is why we need to examine and consider thoroughly what steps really need to be taken and in what order.

In the factories and cooperatives, among scientists and artists, in all parties and organizations, in the churches, in the other religious communities, even in newly founded movements, people are searching for solutions, for the best path for our country. We welcome and will listen to every proposal, every idea that perfects the humanist essence of socialism. But there are also false voices that can be heard in our country, and in particular demagogic advice from across the border that does not further the process of renewal, but instead wants to stall it at the outset, falsify and destroy it. This includes the disparagement of people who hold responsible positions in the social order. We stand at the side of those who have always loyally done their duty for our people. I appeal to all citizens of our republic to stand together more firmly these days and to do everything, everything in their power for our common homeland, the German Democratic Republic.

I appeal once more to those citizens who are considering leaving the GDR: have faith in our politics of renewal! Your place, dear fellow citizens, is here. We need you. If you should nevertheless decide to do otherwise, apply trustingly to the appropriate agencies of the GDR. That is the shorter and better way.

I also want to take the opportunity of addressing the comrades of my party, the Socialist Unity Party of Germany. In this tense and eventful time, it is above all we communists and our party, which has already weathered many storms and struggles, that are challenged. It is incumbent upon every individual member to win back the trust of the citizens of our country. Every sympathetic, open word in the context of workers' collectives and families is important, as are our actions at the workplace, in the factories, in the fields, in the construction offices, and wherever we work diligently for our country and its citizens. My appeal is directed to all citizens, asking them to stand together in order to preserve those values we created over decades. Together we also want to tackle all that is new. This is the only way in which we will be able to introduce, step by step, a new order into our society.

In this spirit let us go to work decisively and above all prudently to solve in strenuous labor the many problems that stand before us. Let's wish ourselves for these endeavors success, creative energy, and health!

NOTES

Source: *Deutschland-Archiv*, 22 (1989): 1437-40.

1. Paragraph 213 of the GDR criminal code refers to "illegal border crossing" and appears in the context of chapter eight of the GDR criminal code regulating "offenses against the political order in the GDR."

16
Call for the Founding of a Green Party in the GDR
(Early November 1989)

For a renewal of our society the transformation of our destroyed environment is of decisive importance. But it is not only our environment that is already contaminated, but to a much greater extent our consciousness, namely, by the utopia that constantly increasing prosperity and–as its precondition–permanent economic growth can be made the goal of social development. This kind of utopia leaves us with the impression that human beings can do as they please within the earth's ecosystem. It even gets inflated into the militant claim that they can subjugate the earth.

Related to this is the idea that productivity and its rewards are the central yardsticks for the evaluation of human existence. This assumption, in all its arrogance, pushes the weak to the margins of their possible existence. Indeed, it increasingly pushes them over the edge. It makes little difference whether they die alone and undignified in a nursing home, whether they are shoveled into mass graves in the Third World, or even whether they are exhibited in a museum of extinct species of plants and animals. It is consistent with our contaminated consciousness that, for the first time in the history of the earth, we have initiated the extinction of all life. Thus we act only out of a drive for self-preservation when we, who share the responsibility for this, seek to put an end to this process and this way of thinking. For that reason we hope to lend political strength to our ecological world-view in the GDR by founding a Green Party, by adopting this world-view without compromise as the point of departure for all our efforts.

As an initiative group we have formulated the following call for the founding of a Green Party in the GDR. The Green Party in the GDR stands on the side of all those forces fighting for democracy and freedom in our country through far-reaching reforms.

The Green Party is ecological, feminist, and non-violent.

The particular aims of the Green Party are:

The rigorous ecological restructuring of our country based on a radical rejection of environmentally destructive and wasteful growth, as well as of the Stalinist attitude toward human beings, the economy, and the environment. There is a need for urgent action in the ecologically catastrophic areas of Leipzig, Bitterfeld, Halle, Dresden, Karl-Marx-Stadt, and Cottbus, as well as for the preservation of many historical districts, cultural landscapes, and castles–in Mecklenburg, for example.

The permanent securing of peace by means of general and complete demilitarization. The dismantling of military alliances, the reduction of the National People's Army to the minimum necessary for defense, and the abolishment of the restricted military zones are urgent needs for the preservation of peace and the environment.

We reject violence, national chauvinism, and racism, and we believe in absolute anti-fascism.

Unlimited equal rights for all women and men on all economic and political levels, from the local representatives to the composition of the *Staatsrat*–all of which still have the character of primarily patriarchal institutions. In this context, the woman as mother should be afforded a privileged position.

Nature must be protected for its own sake from the unhindered development of human beings. This is the only way in which it can be the foundation of human community and culture. In the case of every economic pursuit we therefore need to ask: where does this lead, for whom, and why?

Above all, we want to prevent the present movement of renewal in our country from producing, under the pressure of an unreasonable, short-sighted, material need to catch up, a society of elbow-freedom, wastefulness, and with a throw-away mentality.

We consider the ecological orientation of all levels of education to be urgent; for example, the introduction of environmental and peace studies.

Acting on the basis of the constitution of the GDR, we will work for constitutional reform.

We are working under the presupposition that the activity of the Green Party in the GDR will not be subjected to any impediments by the state.

We will cooperate–nationally as well as internationally–with all citizens, organizations, and groups on projects that support our ideas, even only partially. As part of the European Green movement we will use our influence for juster distribution mechanisms that will also guarantee permanent development to the people of the Third World and help prevent the breakdown of the global ecosystem. We demand partnerships across national borders for the joint ecological reconstruction of environmental crisis areas.

Trusting in the fundamental political turn in our country, we call upon all interested inhabitants, regardless of their worldview, religion, or nationality. Establish grassroots organizations of the Green Party of the GDR on local and regional levels as an expression of your concerns about the catastrophic development of our environment and of your responsibility to our children and unborn generations. Elect speakers to work out proposals for the platform and the grassroots-democratic organizational structure. Suggest alternative concepts on the basis of problems and questions relevant to your community, city, region, and the entire GDR. Make creative and practical proposals for the ecological restructuring of our society.

Begin with actions!

The first delegate assembly, which will determine, among other things, a platform, the structure, and the personnel issues of the Green Party in the GDR, will take place early in 1990 at one of the locales in the GDR where the environmental destruction has been greatest.

For a societal turn that is green!

The Green Party

NOTES

Source: Schüddekopf, 186-88.

17
Speeches at the Protest Demonstration on Alexanderplatz in East Berlin (November 4, 1989)

Speech by Christoph Hein

Dear fellow citizens who have begun to think for yourselves:

There is a lot for us to do and little time in which to do it. The structures of this society must be changed if it is to become democratic and socialist, and there is no alternative to this. We must also speak about dirty hands, about dirty vests, ossification, corruption, misuse of power, theft of public property. All this has to be cleared up and this clearing-up must also occur in the places of government; it ought to begin there. Let's be careful not to confuse the euphoria of these days with the changes that will have to be made. The enthusiasm and the demonstrations are helpful and necessary, but they are no substitute for work. Let's not be deceived by our own enthusiasm! We haven't made it yet: we have not yet reached safe harbor. And there are still enough forces that do not wish change, that fear, and have something to fear from, a new society. I would like to remind all of us of an old man, one who now is probably quite lonely. I am speaking of Erich Honecker. This man had a dream. And he was ready to go to prison for this dream.[1] Then he had the chance to realize his dream. It was not a good chance, because defeated fascism and overpowerful Stalinism helped bring it about. A society was established that had little to do with socialism. This society was and is characterized by bureaucracy, demagoguery, surveillance, misuse of power, patronization, and even criminality. A structure was created to which many good, intelligent, and honest people had to subjugate themselves if they did not want to leave the country. And no one knew any longer how to work against this structure, how to break it up. And I believe that even for this old man our society is by no means the fulfillment of his dreams. Even he, who stood at the head of this state and was particularly responsible for it and its successes, but also for its failures, omissions, and crimes, even he was impotent in face of these ossified structures. I bring up this old man only so as to admonish us not to establish structures today to which we will be helplessly subjugated some day. Let us create a democratic society, on a constitutional foundation, whose justice remains open to challenge! A socialism that does not make a mockery of this word. A society that is appropriate to human beings and does not subjugate them to structures. That will create a lot of work for all of us, a lot of detailed work, as well, worse than knitting. And one more thing. Many people, as we all know, are willing to take credit for success. Apparently many people believe that the changes in the GDR have already been successful, since many people have shown up, strange people, some in high political places, who want to take credit for these successes. But I think that our memory is not so bad that we do not know who it was who started to break up the all-powerful structures, who put an end to the slumber of reason. It was the reason of the streets, the demonstrations of the people. Without these demonstrations the government would not have been changed, the work that is only just starting would not have begun. And Leipzig is the first place that deserves to be mentioned. The mayor of our city should propose to the *Staatsrat* of the *Volkskammer*, in the name of all citizens of Berlin, since we are all standing here together right now, that Leipzig be called the city of heroes of the GDR. We have grown accustomed to the long name "Berlin, capital city of the GDR."[2] I believe that it will be easier to get used to a street sign that says "Leipzig, the city of heroes of the GDR." This name will express our thanks, it will help us make the reforms irreversible, it will remind us of our past failings and mistakes, and it will remind the government of the reason of the streets, which always remained alert and is now raising its voice.

Speech by Stefan Heym

Dear friends, fellow citizens:

It's as if someone had thrown open the windows after all those years of stagnation, of intellectual, economic, political stagnation, after all those years of dullness and staleness and bureaucratic arbitrariness, of official blindness and deafness. What a change! Less than four weeks ago: the nicely built platform just around the corner, with the parade, as ordered, before our illustrious dignitaries.[3] And today: you, who gathered out of your own free will, for freedom and democracy and for a socialism that is worthy of the name.

During the time which is now hopefully over, how often people came to me with their complaints. One had experienced injustice, another was oppressed and harassed, and all of them were frustrated. And I said, then go out and do something. And they said, with resignation, that they couldn't do anything. And that went on and on in our republic, until it couldn't go on any longer, until so much indignation had built up in this state, and so much anger in people's lives, that part of them ran away. But the others, the majority, declared, on the streets and publicly: That's enough! It's time for change! We are the people!

One man wrote to me–and he is right: In these last weeks, we overcame our speechlessness and now we are about to begin to stand tall, and that, my friends, in Germany, where until now all revolutions have failed and where people always bowed to authority, under the emperor, under the Nazis, and later on, as well.

But to speak, to speak freely, to walk, to stand tall, that is not enough. Let us also learn how to govern. Power does not belong in the hands of a single person, of a few, of an apparatus, or of a party. Everyone, everyone has to partake of this power. And whoever exercises power and wherever it is exercised, they must be subject to the control of the citizens. For power corrupts, and absolute power, as we can still see today, corrupts absolutely. Socialism–not the Stalinist kind, the real kind–the kind that we finally want to erect, for our sake and for the sake of Germany, this socialism is not conceivable without democracy. But democracy, a Greek word, means the governance of the people. Friends, citizens, let us exercise this form of governance.

Speech by Christa Wolf

Dear fellow citizens:

Every revolutionary movement also liberates language. What up to that point had been so hard to express, now suddenly passes our lips. We are amazed at what we had apparently thought for a long time and now call out to each other. "Democracy – now or never!," and what we mean is governance by the people. We remember those beginnings in our history that got bogged down or were brutally suppressed, and we do not want to pass up the opportunity inherent in this crisis, since it awakens all our productive energies. I have some difficulties with the phrase "turn." It makes me think of a sailboat, with the captain is yelling: "Prepare to make a turn!," because the wind has turned and is blowing in his face, and the crew ducks when the boom sweeps across the deck. But is this the correct image? Is it still valid in this situation that changes every day?

I would speak of a "revolutionary renewal." Revolutions start from below, below and above exchange places in the value system, and this change sets a socialist society standing on its head back on its feet. Great social movements are underway. We never talked as much in our country as during these past few weeks, never with such passion, with so much scorn and sadness, and yet with so much hope, as well. We want to make use of every day. We do not sleep, or sleep very little. We make friends with people we did not know before, and we fight in a hurtful way with others we thought we knew. That is what we now call "dialogue." We demanded it. Now we are almost sick of the word. And yet we have not really understood what it means. We stare suspiciously at many a suddenly outstretched hand, into many a face that was previously so blank. It is good to be suspicious, it is better to be in control. We are turning around old slogans that oppressed and injured us and are returning them to sender. We fear being used. And we fear declining an honest offer. Our entire country exists in this tension. We know, we have to practice the art of not letting this tension devolve into confrontation. These weeks, these possibilities are given to us just once—through us ourselves.

We watch with astonishment the chameleons, what in the vernacular are called *Wendehälse*, "turn-necks," those who, according to the dictionary, "can adapt quickly and easily to a new situation, behave skillfully in it, and know how to make use of it for their own good." I believe that they in particular are responsible for undermining the credibility of the new politics. Apparently we have not come so far as to be able to view them with humor, although this is something we are successful at in other instances. "Running-board riders step back!," I read on some banners, and I hear some demonstrators call out to the police: "Take off your uniforms and join in with us!" A generous offer, I must say. We even think in economic terms: "Constitutional security saves us the cost of state security forces." And we are prepared to do without existential necessities: "Citizens, turn off the boob-tubes and get moving with us!" And today I saw a truly unbelievable phrase on a banner: "No privileges any more for us Berliners." Indeed, language is liberating itself from the official, newspaper German in which it was wrapped, and it is remembering the words that express feelings. One of them is dream. So let's dream, with our reason wide awake: "Imagine there were socialism and nobody ran away." But we still see the pictures of those who are running away and we ask ourselves: "What should we do?," and in the form of an echo hear the answer: "What should we do?" That begins now, when the demands become rights, and therefore duties: investigative committees, constitutional court, administrative reform.

Much to do, and all that after work, and on top of that still read the newspapers. We will no longer have time for ceremonial parades and prescribed demonstrations. This is a demonstration, officially approved, nonviolent. If it stays like this to the very end we will know more about what we can do, and then we will insist on it. "A proposal for the First of May: Our leadership parades before the people."[4] (None of this is my invention, none of this is mine. That is all the literary talent of the people.) An incredible change, the people of the GDR, always faithful to the state, take to the streets in order to recognize themselves as a people. And for me this is the most important phrase of the last weeks, the thousandfold call: "We are the people!" A simple statement, and we should never forget it.

Speech by Friedrich Schorlemmer

I will speak about solidarity and tolerance. In the fall of 1989 we rose up out of ruins and turned toward a new future. Now it is worthwhile being here, it's getting exciting, stay here. We now literally need everyone. It is true, our country is ruined. Pretty much ruined. It is true, we have lived a dull, oppressed, dependent existence—for so many years. We came here today more open, standing taller, more self-aware. We are finding ourselves. We are ceasing to be objects and becoming subjects of political action. We can be proud.

If yesterday we were still living in the sticky air of stagnation that made it hard to breathe, today we are experiencing changes that take our breath away. Military training is being abolished, civil duty is being introduced. Suddenly it has become exciting to read our newspapers. Mirrors that reflected distorted images have turned into non-distorting mirrors. Why did we have to wait so long for this?! Is all of this only a dream from which we will awaken with disappointment? Or are we all in the middle of a real and permanent democratic awakening? I believe that we now need tolerance and critical solidarity with each other. And not the endless proliferation of understandable emotions.

We need a coalition of reason that cuts across the previous parties as well as the new movements. But that also means that the new movements—all of them—have to be legalized.

The changes cannot be overlooked, but they are still reversible. If up to now those in positions of power had not heard, but at best ignored, the signals of our social crisis, dramatic contradictions have now forced them to come down off their high horses and begin a dialogue among equal partners. And I have experienced how much they now have to listen to. And we will no longer be able to tolerate many of them in their offices. And I would like to express my respect for those who voluntarily step down. The dialogue that has now begun, however, should not be restricted to blowing off steam, otherwise it will degenerate and become the great blathering of the people, until winter sets in and everything goes back to the way it was before. We need further noticeable results from this dialogue. Dialogue must become the normal mode of communication between the people and the government. It should not be an emergency measure in a crisis situation. Anyone who yesterday displayed the sharp claw of power and today holds out the gentle paw of dialogue should not be surprised to discover that many are afraid that the claw is hidden underneath.

Anyone who yesterday was still convinced that the Chinese solution was the correct one, must declare today–and with genuine commitment–that this is not an option for the GDR, otherwise the fear will remain.[5] We now need a democratic structure from top to bottom. The government has to listen to the people and not the people to the government. We will no longer let ourselves be patronized. An atmosphere of trust can only evolve in our country if the greatest internal security risk, the state security force, is radically dismantled and controlled by the people. We allowed it to exist for forty years, now we no longer can nor should tolerate or pay for this huge anxiety apparatus.

Mistakes should now not simply be corrected quickly, they should be recognized as mistakes. But, dear friends, dear fellow citizens throughout the country, let's not dig new trenches, let's give everybody the chance to make their own turn, even if not all of them can remain in their old positions. But please–no thoughts of revenge. Where it is a case of personal responsibility or guilt, we must remain strictly within the law. Let us not tolerate anywhere voices and sentiments of vengeance. And to those of us from the new democratic movements I would like to say: let's not put new intolerance in the place of old intolerance. Let us be tolerant and just to the old and new political opponents and a changing SED.

Let us keep in mind what fears were assuaged by the new leader and what new movements have begun with him. In my opinion, we neither want, nor are we able, to rebuild our country without the SED. But it does not have to have the leadership role.

Tolerance grows out of the recognition that we, too, err, and that new errors are added to old ones. But to make sure that nobody can ever again pass off errors as the truth without being challenged, we need that total democracy that is not based on the indisputable claim to truth and leadership role of a single group. Never again. Therefore: democracy now or never. Without the active solidarity of all democratic forces, we will not succeed in building a sustainable democracy; the fragmentation of democratic forces is always the hour of the dictators. We will still have to pass through low ground, we will not distinguish ourselves with remarkable prosperity. But maybe with more friendliness and warmth.

Coming from Wittenberg, I would like to call to mind to those who govern and those who are governed–in other words, to all of us–a remark made by Martin Luther: Let the minds clash, but keep the fists in check.[6]

NOTES

Source: Zanetti, 202-06 (Hein, Heym, Wolf); Schüddekopf, 211-13 (Schorlemmer).

1. Erich Honecker was interned in a concentration camp during the Nazi era for his socialist beliefs.
2. This was the official designation of East Berlin, a title that deliberately defied the Four-Powers Agreement to divide Berlin into four different sectors.
3. The platform Heym is referring to is the platform built for the celebrations of the fortieth anniversary of the GDR in October 1989.
4. Labor Day in Europe is celebrated on the first of May.
5. The "Chinese solution" refers to the crack-down in Beijing's Tiananmen Square.
6. Wittenberg is the town in Thuringia where Martin Luther posted his 95 Theses in 1517 and unleashed the Reformation.

18
Egon Krenz's Speech Before the Central Committee on the Occasion of the Restructuring of the Politburo (November 8, 1989)

Dear comrades!

Our tenth plenary session has the task:

1. of critically and self-critically analyzing by means of the collective exchange of ideas and opinions the current situation in our so-

ciety from the perspective of our party and drawing conclusions
for the political and organizational work of the SED;
2. of laying the groundwork for preparing our twelfth party congress
   and presenting the comrades of our party and the citizens of our
   country with a plan of action containing our ideas for the revolutionary renewal of socialism in the GDR;
3. of carrying on open and objective discussions and doing everything
   that serves the unity and solidarity of our party, strengthens the
   tie between a collective leadership and the party members, and
   creates irreversible guarantees that errors like those made in the
   past will never happen again.

   . . . The situation in the GDR is tense and very contradictory.
The atmosphere is characterized by a hitherto unknown revolutionary mood. It first expressed itself at the grassroots level, among
the people, the citizens, and the basic organizations of our party. A
people's movement evolved and it manifests itself in many forms–in
confident demonstrations as well as in many-voiced dialogue.

   . . . All of us are experiencing a debate among our people that
was previously unknown. What it manifests is the unforeseen, original, and engaged will to debate about a livable form of socialism.
In this dialogue many elementary demands were formulated. They
appear in our action plan. There are also some illusory ideas and–no
one can and should fail to hear this–even antisocialist conceptions.
That is cause for unease for many of our citizens who must experience every day the lack of restraint with which the enemies of socialism are interfering in the internal affairs of the people of the
GDR and trying to exploit its legitimate demands in order to do
away with socialism and thereby do away with everything that
was created by the working class, the cooperative farmers, and all
other citizens, everything good that was created by the people as a
whole. For this reason our society must remain alert. No one should
carelessly put at risk the singular and unmistakable achievement
that evolved in the forty years of the GDR.

   . . . The question that is on everybody's mind is: What led to the
current condition of our society?

   Our party has invested great intellectual efforts in order to assert its leadership claim. And many comrades have supported this
claim with their hard work. And yet, comrades, a fundamental
shortcoming of our system as it existed up to now was the relation
between party and state, the fact that the party ultimately and to
a high degree tried to fulfill this claim administratively.

The future political system of socialism has to be constituted in such a way that the party manifests its leadership claim by making the greatest possible demands upon itself–by means of a democratically and scientifically supported head start on solutions for pertinent problems, by means of a persuasive cooperation with society, by means of a willingness to learn from the dialogue with all social forces, by means of the hard work of every party organization and every comrade.

The fact is, the problems and questions that are being publicly discussed today did not appear overnight nor even just last summer. The thorough analysis of the development of the GDR since the eighth party congress of the SED will lead us to many new insights. Today we know, for example, that the plan of the eleventh party congress of the SED was not based on a realistic assessment of the situation. It becomes clear from the insights provided by current analyses that at that time the formulation of economic tasks did not derive from reality but from subjective wishful thinking. And on top of that, we did not draw the right conclusions from the significant international developments–those that occurred mainly in the Soviet Union, but also in other socialist countries. The leadership of our party distanced itself from our best friends. Unavoidable developmental processes of modern socialism that had been manifesting themselves for years were understood only superficially, not in their general validity. The full significance of a number of new processes in the development of the productive forces and in world-economic and world-political trends were not understood broadly enough as fundamental decisions that would shape our future.

Negative manifestations resulting from unsolved objective problems of development, but also deriving to an increasing extent from subjective errors in judgment, had increased in many areas.

. . . Instead of addressing problems immediately and directly, we relied on the hope of being able to solve them some day when we would have better conditions. Instead of taking our comrades and all citizens into our confidence and winning them over for a solution based on engaged cooperation, we tried to conjure up an image of the GDR that corresponded less and less with the daily experiences of the people. Conflicts were repressed and necessary answers frequently replaced by administrative measures.

It is also a fact that the existing manifold forms of democracy lag behind the interests and needs of our citizens to have a say in matters. We underestimated the political maturity of our citizens and their willingness to participate in and shape our society with their unmistakable and self-assured individuality. Bureaucratic behavior and heartlessness in dealing with citizens grew on this soil. The disrespect for individuality and for competence in professional and social activities not infrequently led to ignorance concerning the intellectual potential of our people, and this stifled creativity.

It is also a fact, finally, that our economic policy lagged behind reality. New demands on our economy, as well as growing problems in international trade such as the increase in oil prices, the shortage and higher prices of raw materials, were not answered with necessary changes in our economy. Large investments that did not contribute enough to the growth of our gross national product claimed significant amounts of material and financial resources.

. . . All of this had serious consequences for the atmosphere in our country. The dissatisfaction among the population increased. Unrest and insecurity spread.

. . . Those citizens who left the GDR were—with some exceptions—neither opponents of socialism nor criminals. They were citizens who saw no possibilities for the full development of their personalities, for the satisfaction of their individual needs and interests here, and no doubt egoism played a role. They were for the most part people who grew up in our society and whose departure we regret. It tore major holes in the fabric of our society and in our economy.

. . . In many places forms of democratic participation of the citizenry in decision-making are developing out of what first started as spontaneous discussions, and these will clearly take on a permanent quality. The Politburo of the Central Committee believes that new citizens' movements that want to act on the basis of the constitution of the GDR should be legalized.

The many-layered development in the GDR is increasingly reflected in our mass media, in which even after such a short time changes for the better and a new, refreshing spirit cannot be overlooked. We see the responsibility of the journalists to the entire people in furthering the renewal that has been called forth with personal engagement and circumspection, with professional knowledge and farsightedness, and hope that they will not diminish their great social task in the eyes of the public by turning to sensationalism. The open, knowledgeable discussion of social problems and possible solutions has begun. That is good, and we must support this.

. . . A lack of a sense of reality made itself evident in the over-estimation of achieved results, in the portrayal of things we were striving for as things we had already accomplished, in the repression or even negation of things left undone, lacks, and errors. This was apparent to all, especially in the media, which were governed by such behavior. The political culture degenerated. In our society self-criticism was completely out of fashion. Criticism of negative symptoms, in the belief that we should not provide any ammunition to the enemy, was left increasingly to the Western media for their fight against socialism in the GDR. This was compounded by cautious to negative, partly dogmatic, partly arrogant tendencies toward the developments in the Soviet Union, which did not do service to our close alliance with the CPSU and which led to the elimination of the newspaper "Sputnik" from the mail-order newspaper list in the GDR, an action to which many of our citizens responded with a lack of understanding and protest. All this had the effect of stifling initiatives, blocking the willingness to overcome problems jointly. . . . The socialism we are talking about can only be the work of the masses of people themselves. . . . With the elaboration of our social strategy we do not need to start from scratch. Among the fundamental principles for the renewal of our socialist society in the GDR are the political power of workers and farmers, societal ownership of the primary means of production, the responsibility of our party in society, and the alliance of all the democratic forces in our country. Anyone who questions these fundamental principles should seriously reflect: Does he or she want social chaos, does he or she want destabilization at the sensitive line separating socialism from capitalism, does he or she want jobs to be threatened, does he or she want social insecurity instead of social security for all?

. . . The individuality of human beings must consistently be regarded as the societal driving force and source of innovation and be utilized in the interest of the individual and society. Respect for and the development of individuality are necessary for the quality of life in socialism and for the development of a positive attitude toward life. In the future we must above all understand societal freedom as the democratic search for variants and the determination of the most favorable possibilities for further progress. The insight into what is socially necessary, which is indispensable for freedom, must itself be free. For this we must create and guarantee the relevant political preconditions.

Socialist society can only be a democratic society. Despite everything that has been accomplished, we clearly recognize today that the democratic power potential of the workers and farmers and the socialist conditions of production were only realized in an insufficient manner. Dialogue, the struggle for the best possible decisions, freedom of opinions, a high degree of morality and justice, clear responsibilities and effective control mechanisms, conditions for competent and quick decisions have to become essential features of socialist democracy. Only in this way can we persuasively reaffirm the alternative to bourgeois democracy, to the dominance of the special interests of capital, to the corruptibility of politics, to the commercialization of the media, to the scandalous lack of human rights, and to the violation of generally recognized human moral values. . . . We cannot ignore that there is not an insignificant number of households whose monthly income is below average. For them the standard of living must under no circumstances decrease when state subsidies for basic goods and state fees are applied in different ways. . . . The present economic problems and contradictions in the economy of the GDR are not proof of the failure of a planned economy. But they are proof that no economy can tolerate subjectivism, voluntarism, the waste and violation of the conditions of economic balance without suffering, and that in the phrase "democratic centralism" the stress should not be placed only on the last word.

. . . In our trade with nonsocialist countries we hold fast to the principle of reciprocal advantage. Our hand is still extended for further development and the deepening of constructive cooperation with capitalist countries, among them the FRG, as well. Above all, in the interest of productive accumulation we are willing to examine all forms of cooperation with concerns and businesses in the FRG and other capitalist countries. The GDR is willing to cooperate with concerns and businesses in capitalist countries, exchange licenses and technologies, sign lease contracts, and further develop joint ventures.

We are also for the development of economic cooperation with the FRG on major projects in the areas of energy, the environment, chemistry, and other branches that will be useful for both partners.

. . . In other words, we will proceed in such a way that the stability of our economy increases, ecological standards are strictly observed, the social security of the people is preserved, and their interest in high quality work is increased. Everywhere we must create conditions in which the diligence and initiative of our workers can bring the best possible results. At the same time, far-reaching and significant economic restructuring will be conscientiously worked out and persistently set into action. For that we urgently need the advice and the professional knowledge of the many intelligent and experienced economists in our country.

. . . Today we have to admit that the existing political power structures do not function in a sufficiently democratic way. In practice the development of socialist democracy was reduced to the principle of democratic centralism, and that concentrated only on one of its aspects–central state planning and guidance of society.

. . . At this point, dear comrades, a further observation seems necessary: some people have fallen into a state of transfiguration and act as if the GDR were the only state in the world in which there still is a police force as well as defense and security organizations. It should require no further clarification if I state that it is in the interest of all the citizens of our country that in all confrontations among divergent political opinions, the orderly rhythm of life in our society, the peaceful coexistence of all citizens, uninterrupted work, and, finally, the fundamental constitutional principles of our state remain guaranteed. State security and civil order are fundamental conditions for the renewal of our society. . . .

NOTES

Source: Wimmer, 113-20.

19

Resolution of the *Ministerrat* of the GDR Regarding the Opening of the Border to the Federal Republic of Germany and West Berlin (November 9, 1989)

1. Personal travel to foreign countries can be applied for without the presentation of supporting evidence (a reason for travel and information about relatives). Approvals will be given within a short span of time. Reasons for denial are stated only in exceptional cases.

2. The passport and registration divisions of the district offices of the People's Police in the GDR have been ordered to grant permanent exit visas immediately, without the presentation of supporting evidence. An application for a permanent exit visa can still be made as previously at the Offices for Internal Affairs (of the local district councils or city councils).

3. Permanent exit can take place at all GDR border crossings to the FRG or West Berlin.

4. The temporary granting of approval through diplomatic offices of the GDR in foreign countries or permanent exit with a GDR identity card via a third country are no longer in force.

NOTES

Source: Wimmer, 121-24.

20
Walter Momper's Acceptance Speech upon his Election as President of the West German *Bundesrat* (November 10, 1989)

I would like to begin my acceptance speech with an unusual confession. I did not sleep tonight–and neither did many of you, I am sure.

Anyone who experienced this night in Berlin or followed the events on television will never forget the ninth of November, 1989. Last night the German nation was the happiest nation in the world. It was the day of reunion between people from both parts of Berlin. It was the night in which the Wall lost its divisive character. The people of the GDR fought for this freedom on the streets–and yesterday they celebrated this freedom for the first time–together with the people of West Berlin on the Kurfürstendamm and on Alexanderplatz.

For 28 years–since the thirteenth of August, 1961–we have longed and hoped for this hour to come.[1] For 28 years people have been shot at the Wall or have died there, just because they wanted to cross the border. Now, in this hour of joy, let us remember the victims.

Heavy burdens and great problems will fall upon all the *Länder* of the Federal Republic, we are well aware of that. But if we never forget what suffering this Wall caused and if we always remember the happy faces and the joy of yesterday evening, then we will master this challenge together and live up to our responsibilities as state governments. . . .

NOTES

Source: Zanetti, 210.

1. The erection of the Berlin Wall was begun on 13 August 1961.

21
Speeches at the Schöneberg City Hall in West Berlin
(November 10, 1989)

Speech by Willy Brandt

This is a beautiful day after a long journey. But we have only arrived at an intermediate station. We have not yet reached the end of the road. There is a lot ahead of us.

The fact that Berliners, and Germans in general, belong together manifests itself in a moving, exciting way, and it is most moving when divided families unexpectedly and full of tears finally come together again. I was also touched by the image of the policeman on our side who went across to his colleague and said: "After having watched each other from a distance for so many weeks, maybe months, I would like to shake your hand." That is the right way to approach what is coming: to reach out to each other, to be resentful only where it is absolutely necessary. And, wherever possible, to overcome bitterness. I also felt that this afternoon at the Brandenburg Gate.

As mayor [of Berlin] in the difficult years of 1957 to 1966, that is, during the time in which the Wall was built, and as someone who in the Federal Republic and for the Federal Republic had something to do with decreasing tensions in Europe and with the struggle for the greatest possible amount of essential relations and human contact, my wholehearted greetings go to the Berliners in all parts of the city, as well as to my fellow countrymen and countrywomen all over Germany.[1]

A lot will depend on whether we–we Germans on both sides–prove ourselves equal to the historical situation. The rapprochement of us Germans, that is what is important. This rapprochement of Germans has become reality in a different way than most of us expected. And nobody should now act as if they know exactly how the people in both countries will form a new relationship with each other. That they will form a new relationship with each other, that they will come together in freedom and be able to develop, that is what matters.

And it is certain that nothing in the other part of Germany will be as it was before. The winds of change, which have been sweeping across Europe for quite some time, could not pass Germany by. I was always convinced that this division reinforced by concrete, this division by means of barbed wire and a death strip, swam against the tide of history. And I wrote it down again this summer: Berlin will live and the Wall will fall. By the way, a piece of that horrible construction, a piece of it can remain, as far as I'm concerned, as a reminder of a historical monstrosity. Just as at the end of the war after forceful discussions we in our city consciously decided to leave the ruins of the *Gedächtniskirche*.[2]

Those who today are still quite young and those who will come after us will not always have an easy time understanding the historical context in which we are embedded. For that reason I want to say not only that before the division ends–I spoke out against it angrily, but also with a feeling of helplessness, in 1961–we have many things to accomplish, but I also want to remind us of the fact that all this did not just start on the thirteenth of August, 1961. The German misery started with the terroristic Nazi-regime and the war it unleashed. That terrible war that transformed Berlin, like so many other German and non-German cities, into mountains of rubble. The division of Europe, Germany, and Berlin grew out of the war and the inability of the victorious allies to come to an agreement. Now what belongs together is growing together again. Now we are experiencing, and I thank God that I have lived to see it, how the two parts of Europe are growing together again.

I am certain that the president of the United States and the leader of the Soviet Union will know how to appreciate what is happening here when they meet soon on a ship in the Mediterranean.[3] And I am certain that our French and British friends–beside the Americans, proven protective powers in difficult years–will know how to assess with us the importance of this process of transformation, of a new beginning. I know that our neighbors in Eastern Europe understand what motivates us and that it fits into the new thinking and acting that is taking hold of the Central and Eastern Europeans themselves. The guarantee that we can offer to our neighbors and also to the great powers of this world is that we do not strive for a solution of our problems that is not in accordance with our obligations for peace and toward Europe. We are guided by the common conviction that the European Community must be developed further and that the fragmentation of our continent must be gradually but definitively overcome.

Back then, in August 1961, we not only demanded with legitimate anger: the Wall must disappear. We also had to tell ourselves: Berlin has to continue living in spite of the Wall. We reconstructed the city–with the help of the federal government, which we also should not forget. Others who came after us contributed important things to the reconstruction. But here in Berlin, in addition to all the tasks of the inner city, to the construction of housing, to cultural and economic reconstruction, we were charged with the job of keeping open the path to Germany. We thought intensively about how we could work against the especially brutal effects of division–even when the situation seemed hopeless. How despite the division we could preserve and foster German and European unity. Of course, there was not always immediate agreement about how this could best be accomplished.

The date December 18, 1963 has particularly imprinted itself upon my memory. Not only because this was my birthday, but because that was the day on which, thanks to the day visas–that was all we could achieve then–hundreds of thousands went to the other side, not only to be with their relatives in East Berlin, but also to be with those who lived in "the Zone," as the East was referred to in the West. All that was far from sufficient, and it remained terribly fragile. But we did not let ourselves be discouraged from taking even the smallest step to enhance contact between people and not let the cohesion of the nation die.

After this it took almost a decade before the changes that were possible then could be achieved by means of a Transit Treaty and a Basic Treaty. A large number of treaties and agreements followed. It is still correct that, even for national reasons, we could not afford to let a vacuum develop.

It was also correct to ease and improve the external conditions for a divided Germany and the people who lived in it whenever we had the chance. That was the purpose of our treaty policies. That was the purpose of our support for the European conference in Helsinki, which had a difficult start, but was entrusted with human rights, cooperation, and with the dismantling of the excessive armaments in Europe. And this slow movement toward stability, toward decreasing instead of increasing armaments, is now paying off. This movement is underway, it contributed in essential ways to the fact that today we are working within an improved framework. And I add to this: If I understand my fellow countrymen and countrywomen in the other part of Germany correctly, they agree with me, and, I think, with all of us on this. No one wants to have difficulties with the Soviet troops who are still stationed on German soil. They will not remain there forever. The military presence will change. We want peaceful solutions, especially in our relations with the superpower to the East.

Let me say this, too: in addition to the fact that there are signs of hope in the Soviet Union as well, and that there are democratic movements in Poland and Hungary–they will follow in other countries–a new factor of singular quality has to be taken into account. And this has happened because our fellow countrymen and countrywomen in the GDR and in East Berlin took their future into their own hands, so that the entire world could hear them. The people themselves spoke, demanded changes, and, last but not least, the right of truthful information and of free movement and the freedom of organized assembly. I believe that the popular movement in the other part of Germany can only attain fulfillment in truly free elections. And I also believe that it could be a rewarding task to participate in the work of renewal here and now, and not merely to leave it to those who are left behind.

Let me reiterate: nothing will ever be the same as it was. That also means that we in the West will no longer be judged by the more or less beautiful slogans of yesterday, but by what we are willing to do and contribute, intellectually and materially, today or tomorrow. I hope that, where intellectual matters are concerned, the cupboards are not bare. I also hope that the pocketbooks still have something to contribute. And I hope that our engagement calendars have room for what is now called for. What will now be put to the test is not the readiness for moralizing, but for shows of solidarity, for balance, for a new beginning. What matters now is that we move closer together, that we keep a clear head and do our best to do what is in keeping both with our German interests and with our responsibilities toward Europe.

Speech by Helmut Kohl

Dear Berliners, dear fellow countrymen and countrywomen in the GDR and in the Federal Republic of Germany:

Here on this square, in front of the Schöneberg City Hall, Berliners have gathered for over forty years to demonstrate for peace and for the freedom of this city. They came in order to give expression again and again to the message of peace, the message of good will, the message of willingness to cooperate.

Today is a great day in the history of this city, and today is a great day in German history. We all worked for this day. We longed for it to come. We see the pictures of the Brandenburg Gate–pictures of every place where during these hours people from the GDR can come to us and the citizens of this city as well as the citizens of our Federal Republic of Germany can go to the other part of Germany: without controls, without state violence, following their own free will. In this hour and at this place we should also remember those who lost their lives at the Wall. We should do this at a time when this Wall is finally falling.

Ladies and gentlemen, dear Berliners, all of us now face a great test. These days we repeatedly heard from our fellow countrymen and countrywomen in the GDR, in East Berlin, in Leipzig and Dresden, and many other cities, a message of prudence–a message which says that in this happy but, at the same time, difficult hour in the history of our country it is important to remain prudent and act wisely. To act wisely means not to follow radical slogans and voices. To act wisely now means to see all the dimensions of the geopolitical, European, and German development. Anyone like us who, since we have just returned here from Warsaw, was able to experience what the reform process in Hungary and Poland made possible, knows that we now have to find a way, step by step and with circumspection, into a common future. For it is a matter of our *common* future, it is a matter of freedom, above all for our fellow countrymen and countrywomen in the GDR, in all areas of their lives.

The people of the GDR have a right to the free expression of opinions, to a truly free press, to the free formation of labor unions, to the free founding of parties and, of course, according to the United Nations Charter and basic human rights, to free, equal, and secret elections. Our fellow countrymen and countrywomen are in the process of fighting for these freedoms, and in this they have our full support. I also appeal from this side–as I did on Wednesday in the West German parliament–to those in responsible positions in the GDR: renounce your power monopoly now! Join in that spirit of reform that today, in Hungary, in Poland, is securing the future of these people! Free the way for the rule *of* the people, *by* the people, and *for* the people.

I state here once again in the name of the Federal Republic of Germany that we are willing to support this process to whatever extent that is possible for us. We naturally support, out of a sense of moral responsibility for the unity of our German nation, a GDR that progresses in reforms with the goal of freedom, of concrete assistance for people in all areas of society. If these reforms are instituted and if the GDR progresses along this path, then our fellow countrymen and countrywomen who are now thinking about leaving the GDR will remain in their traditional homeland. They want to find their happiness at home. And many of those who in these days found their way to us will be willing to participate in the restructuring of their proper homeland. We, the citizens of the Federal Republic of Germany, want to support them in this with all our hearts. No one can stand to one side. The images of these weeks and days show us our duty. And in this spirit I say to all of you in the GDR: You do not stand alone! We stand at your side! We are and remain one nation, and we belong together!

We are thankful that our friends and partners in the world are helping us follow this path, that they support us, that they show their solidarity with us. We thank our American, British, and French friends for their support and solidarity, which was essential for the freedom of the free part of Berlin in the last decades. Without their steadfastness we would not have experienced this day in this way. Our respect belongs to General Secretary Michail Gorbachev, who together with us in the Bonn Declaration of June 13 explicitly acknowledged every nation's right to free self-determination.

Berliners, the spirit of freedom is taking hold of all of Europe: Poland, Hungary, and now the GDR. The right to self-determination is a basic right of every human being and every nation. We demand this right for everyone in Europe. We demand it for all Germans. I appeal at this hour to all our fellow countrymen and countrywomen: we now want to be one at heart, to shape the future together in solidarity, to stand together now and collectively provide help to those who need help. We want to follow this path with a warm heart and with cool reason.

It is a matter of Germany, it is a matter of unity and justice and freedom. Long live a free German fatherland! Long live a free united Europe!

Speech by Hans-Dietrich Genscher

Berliners from East and West, fellow German citizens from East and West:

My particularly hearty greetings in this hour go to the people in my homeland who have provided an example of the Germans' will to freedom.[4] In these days the Germans in the GDR are shaping the history of German and European freedom. What began in Budapest, what continued in Warsaw, what is finding voice in Moscow, is now also happening in the GDR. Germans are involved when it is a matter of freedom. The dignity, circumspection, and maturity with which the people of the GDR are standing up for their claim to freedom does honor to our entire nation. It must be a model for our behavior in this hour. Of us, too, the same dignity, the same respect, and the same circumspection are required. We don't want to replace the patronization in the GDR with unsolicited advice from us.

In the streets of Berlin during these hours it is being proven that forty years of separation did not make two nations out of one German nation. There is no capitalist, there is no socialist nation, there is only one German nation that has pledged to uphold freedom and peace. In this hour we expect that the first important step made by the leadership of the GDR will be followed by further decisive steps that adhere to the will of the people. The freedom of movement and the freedom to travel now have to be followed by freedom of speech and free elections. It is our responsibility in this hour to support, not only with words but also with the willingness for help when it is requested, the difficult course our fellow citizens in the GDR are taking with regard to the development of their society as they wish it to be, to support their order as they wish it to be. On our side, too, words must be followed by deeds, just as we demanded them from our neighbors to the east.

Dear fellow citizens, in these hours the world is watching our country and this city. Our fellow citizens in the GDR have placed the fate of the Germans at the top of the agenda of international politics. Many of our neighbors are asking us what we Germans want. They are asking the question about the Germans' future. I would like to tell them that the Germans first of all want to live in peace with all their neighbors and that they want to live in freedom. No nation in the world, no nation in Europe has to fear for itself if the gates between West and East are now opening, if freedom and democracy are realized in the GDR. Germans living in freedom, Germans living in democracy have never posed a threat to other nations. And therefore, dear fellow citizens, we say to all our neighbors in West and East: we will stand by what we have chosen. We chose to belong to the community of Western democracies. It was a long road that brought us to this hour. It was the Moscow and Warsaw Treaties, the treaty with Czechoslovakia, the Basic Treaty with the GDR, the Helsinki Final Act. It was a patient struggle for peace, for human rights and freedom. We are continuing down this road. We stand by the treaties we signed. Even today we stood in Warsaw and said to our Polish neighbors: part and parcel of the secure future of our European neighbors is the knowledge of the Polish people that we Germans will never again put in question the existing border between Germans and Poles.

We declare our will to the members of the Warsaw Pact, to those countries that are already on the way to democracy and to those in which this road has yet to be taken: we will not unilaterally abuse any problematic period that may arise in those countries, nor any difficulties that will develop during the course of restructuring. We do not wish any unilateral advantages; we wish only that reform, freedom, and democracy will be possible there, as well. We want this development to be able to take place within a stable framework. For this it is necessary that we pursue more intensively the people's longing for armament control and disarmament. My dear fellow citizens, the negotiations on disarmament must keep pace with the political and human development that is taking place here in Europe.

Dear fellow citizens, what we are experiencing in these weeks is Europe's self-reflection on its most noble virtues, on its great culture, to which all the nations of Europe have made great contributions. To these nations we say: the great goal of us Germans today is that everywhere in Germany we will be able to shape our lives in such a way that our neighbors will view our happiness as their happiness and as a guarantee of a secure future. On a long road we have reached an important way-station. We will have to continue on this road with the same rationality, responsibility, and circumspection, in cooperation with those countries that are our allies and with which we are allied in the European Community, and with ties to our neighbors to the East with whom we signed treaties that made all of this possible.

Dear fellow citizens, when the bell of freedom tolls in all of Europe, then we can say: Germans have taken part in this effort and we were part of it. I greet all our fellow citizens, I greet all Europeans, I greet all those who made this possible.

Thank you.

NOTES

Source: Zanetti, 211-24.

1. Willy Brandt served as Chancellor of the Federal Republic of Germany from 1969 to 1974, and his *Ostpolitik*, or Eastern Policy, was largely responsible for the rapprochement between the FRG and the GDR that resulted in the Basic Treaty between the two Germanies. For these efforts,

which contributed to detente in Europe, Brandt was awarded the Nobel Peace Prize.

2. The "Kaiser-Wilhelm Gedächtniskirche" is a church in the center of West Berlin that was built between 1891 and 1895 in the style of Wilhelminian architechture; the church was partially destroyed in World War II and was left a ruin to serve as a memorial to the victims of the war.

3. Brandt is alluding to the meeting between Presidents Bush and Gorbachev on December 2 and 3, 1989; at this informal summit the two world leaders agreed to step up the pace of negotiations on the reduction of conventional forces and strategic nuclear arms; Gorbachev virtually proclaimed the end of the Cold War.

4. Hans-Dietrich Genscher was born in Halle, GDR.

22
"The Wall Has Fallen": Statement by the "New Forum" Regarding the Opening of the Border (November 12, 1989)

The Wall has Fallen

We have waited for this day for almost thirty years! Wall-sick, we shook the iron bars of our cage. Our youth grew up with the dream of some day becoming free and experiencing the world. That dream can now be fulfilled. It is a day of celebration for us all!

Our daily routine will return. The open border will make the political chaos and the desolate economic situation left behind by the deposed politbureaucracy blatantly apparent. Anyone who was around in 1961 is familiar with the consequences that now threaten us: the chase after the D-mark–overvalued by a distorted pricing system–which will become the primary currency for services, for repairs, and scarce commodities; the sell-out of our values and goods to Western entrepreneurs (directly or indirectly); border-crossers, black market, and currency smuggling (especially in Berlin). Our recreation areas will be flooded by West-mark tourism, just as, no doubt, our sanatoriums and specialized hospitals will be flooded by West-mark patients. Our money, which shrinks in the process of exchange, will return, seek out subsidized goods, and heat up inflation. All that is a threat to the socially weaker half of the population, while the West-mark sharks will swim at the top and get richer by the minute.

We do not want to create panic. We also do not want to resist the urgently needed economic cooperation with the West. We are not calling for laws and prohibitions, since these would not work anyway. But we are appealing to everyone not to take the threatening crisis lying down.

Citizens of the GDR!

The spontaneous and fearless demonstrations of your will initiated a peaceful revolution in the entire country, overturned the Politburo, and broke through the Wall.

Do not let yourselves be diverted from the demands for a political restructuring of society! No one discussed with you either the building of the Wall or its opening, do not let anyone thrust a reorganizational concept upon you that turns us into the hinterland and a cheap labor market for the West! Pay close attention to who profits from the newly emerging enterprises and business deals and how high the social costs are. Do not sell the country down the drain and sell yourselves as slaves-for-hire!

We will remain poor for a longer period of time, but we don't want a society in which profiteers and elbow-types draw the cream off the top. You are the heroes of a political revolution, do not let yourselves be appeased by travel visas and consumer-good fixes that will only drive up your debt!

Demand the implementation of political reforms and the development of a socially acceptable economic concept. Demand free elections for genuine representatives of the people who have no prescribed leadership role, demand a constitutional court, demand freedom of speech and freedom of the press, a reform of the legal system, an educational reform, independent labor unions; demand the immediate, unconditional release of all facts about the true economic situation. Do not let the politbureaucracy shirk its responsibility and leave you holding the bag!

November 12, 1989

For the initiative group "New Forum": Jens Reich, Sebastian Pflugbeil, Bärbel Bohley, Reinhard Schult, Eberhard Seidel, Jutta Seidel.

NOTES

Source: "Die Mauer ist gefallen," flyer.

23
Hans Modrow's Government Policy Statement Before the GDR
Volkskammer (November 17, 1989)

Mr. President, honorable representatives!

On November 13 you elected me chair of the *Ministerrat* and instructed me to form the government of the GDR. I thank you for this trust and ask that you support the new government in every possible way. The government that I will propose to you, after having previously consulted with the participating political parties–the SED, CDU [Christian Democratic Union], GFP [German Farmer's Party], LDPG [Liberal Democratic Party of Germany], NDPG [National Democratic Party of Germany]–is a coalition government of a newly conceived, creative political alliance. This is also demonstrated by the position papers of these parties. This alliance will do everything in its power to ensure that the incipient democratic renewal of civil life in its entirety will spread and set deep roots. It will do everything to ensure that the urgently needed stabilization of our economy is accomplished and that there is a real increase in the gross national product. For this all parties and organizations represented in the National Front, as well as the churches and the different interest groups, should submit their opinions, their advice. This applies also to the Sorbian citizens of our country.

This democratic renewal, a many-sided, even contradictory and angry process, was begun by hundreds of thousands of our people who honestly came out of their shells and took to the streets. The will for the renewal of socialist society and their state took hold of millions of citizens and thus became a political force; political parties and social groups stepped forward with assurance. This government wants to pledge itself to the people of the GDR, who want a good form of socialism.

But that means more than work for everyone and a secure life for everyone and being able to shop well, although these already mean a lot. A better socialism–that must mean chances for all of us to create for ourselves a life that is manifold and meaningful, that allows individuality to thrive and makes comradery in the collective possible, instead of a situation in which one person is the other person's devil. Individuality, I believe, is what we have to pay attention to here. Political and ideological tolerance is an irrevocable part of that. Such a socialism, which can only develop into a productive society through the work of its citizens, should be capable of guaranteeing social securities to all of its citizens according to the degree of its economic successes.

We therefore ask all citizens to support this government. From those who are willing, we need an advance on trust, and I know that with this I am already asking a lot. That is why I want to state at the outset: this government only wants to promise what it can deliver. It therefore wants to appeal to all workers to work as successfully as possible, quickly and more efficiently, every hour and for every mark paid. Our task is to create the framework that will make this possible.

We acknowledge the achievements of the workers in previous decades. The will to preserve what was created with hard work, not to give up anything, not to send up in smoke the effort of all these difficult years, has been expressed over and over again in these days. On the contrary—we want to utilize and make more productive this substance, this great property of the people in industry as well as in other economic areas. To lead the GDR economy out of this crisis, to provide stability and give impulses for growth is now the most important task of the government, and we will set about this task competently. We are responsible to the *Volkskammer* and we will have to account to it for our progress. We understand this as accountability to the people. Everyone who wants to help us accomplish this task is welcome. Everyone who is aware of the vital worth of a functioning economy—and who is not aware of this—should demonstrate this awareness with deeds. Only an economically strong state can do a lot for its citizens. Only an economically potent state can attain ecological progress. Only by means of economic efficiency can our standard of living first be kept stable and—once we have achieved what is necessary—even be increased.

These apparent truisms are basic pillars of our governmental policies, because we take the economy and democracy very seriously. This is a clear rejection of the former limits of the work of government, of previous patronization, of the arbitrary steering of the economy to its detriment by the former member of the Politburo of the Central Committee of the SED, Günter Mittag. Following a proposal made by several parties, the parliament passed a motion to examine the misuse of office and power during the time of the former (so-called) party and state leadership. I welcome this motion. We have to send clear signals in such matters. . . .
Honored Representatives!

These days all of us are experiencing a fascinating, truly moving process: the majority of our citizens have become politicized in the best sense of the word, they exhibit a wakeful or awakening political consciousness and self-consciousness. Hundreds of thousands, even millions have set out to enjoy the new possibilities for travel, to visit relatives or friends in the FRG and in West Berlin, or simply to look around there–and the overwhelming majority come as a matter of course back to their homeland, animated, often also motivated to stay, live, and work in the GDR. Anyone who does not view this opening of the borders–a historical event that is being watched by the entire world–as irrefutable proof for the irreversible transformation of politics and life in the socialist GDR is either blind or malicious.

What was brought about in terms of democratic and, in the best sense of the word, popular changes here since October 7, 1989, is irreversible–the people would sweep aside anyone who dared to seek a return to the former circumstances. Therefore one ought–where this is still the case–to stop demanding further steps, demanding further advances from the GDR.

We see two problems simultaneously. First, the partial absence of many workers from their workplace. They are utilizing the freedom to travel without recognizing the necessity of constantly and reliably creating the material foundations of our country. An initial excess is understandable. Loss of work, which maximizes the economic problems and thus concerns us all, however, is something we cannot afford. . . .

Second, the opening of the borders of the GDR cannot be permitted to lead to an economic and financial blood-letting with long-term effects. It is still too early for the necessary thorough analysis of the transformations begun on November 9. But let me stress: the stability of the GDR is a necessary condition for the stability of Central Europe, even of Europe in general, and that is why it is in the well-conceived best interests of all the neighbors of the GDR, at the very least, not only to observe the changes taking place in our country well-meaningly, but also to support them politically and economically. In this connection I welcome the upcoming meeting of the president of the *Staatsrat*, Egon Krenz, with Chancellor Helmut Kohl, and add: in all questions that lie within its jurisdiction, and that will now be the entire jurisdiction, the government of the GDR is ready to negotiate. . . .

Ladies and gentlemen!

Our governmental program contains reforms like those proposed, demanded, and outlined by the parties and other social forces, as well as by many citizens.

At this point I would like to restrict myself to pointing out known needs and to stressing the principle that, in agreement with all political forces in the country, we want to proceed step by step, quickly but not over-hastily, after proper analyses and discussions, and that means public discussions. I cite as the most important points:

First, reforms of the political system, tied to legislative steps to strengthen the principle of constitutionality and constitutional security. That includes, in particular, an election law as well as a law determining the function of the *Ministerrat* and a law governing the media. Proposals for the transformation of criminal law can follow shortly thereafter. The law regulating travel, sometimes also called a passport law, should be presented after being discussed.

Second, we need an economic reform that must have as its aim an increase in the individual responsibility of economic units in order to significantly increase the effectiveness of their operation, a reduction in central leadership and planning to the amount that is reasonably necessary, as well as–and this may be the most difficult task–the increasing introduction of the principle of rewarding productivity. . . .

Third, we need an educational reform. Apart from scholarly concepts already available, the best pedagogical practitioners in our country, it seems to me, have already instituted in their areas of specialization more than just that initial reform, which calls upon the students: Do not be afraid to express your own opinions!

Fourth, we need a long-term program, re-evaluated on a yearly basis, which should aim at bringing economic and ecological issues into greater harmony–and let me add that the GDR is not as bad in that respect as unnecessary secrecy has made it seem. In the future, no one should be allowed to cancel or obstruct planned measures for the protection of the environment. We urgently need a new energy concept that leads to a reduction in the use of fossil fuels and in the use of energy in general.

Fifth, an administrative reform with the aim of democratizing state leadership and administration, making their work more transparent, but also significantly reducing the administration's budget and personnel. It goes without saying that subsequent to this we have to guard against an increase in administration. Through this measure, members of the state apparatus will be freed up for other tasks. They will be employed, under full protection of the labor laws, according to their qualifications and, if possible, according to their inclinations, a process that cannot be begun and completed in a matter of months. This also applies to the reduction of administrative personnel in industry as well as in organizations and institutions. We should consider charging a government commission with this task. The workers who up to now have completed their tasks with diligence and prudence should be supported in such a way that they can begin an appropriate job, and, as we well know, there is no dearth of rewarding work to be done in the GDR. . . .

In connection with the new travel regulations, it is necessary to take measures for the protection of our currency and to effectively prevent speculation with money and goods. We have put together a committee with the short-term task of preparing relevant proposals to be considered by the *Ministerrat*.

As guidelines for this committee, we determined that they should prepare proposals and measures of a sort that will not have negative effects on the citizens of the GDR, but will exclusively prevent the speculative abuse of existing price and currency differences. . . .

Cooperation with the Soviet Union is a decisive guarantee for the further development of our economy. We therefore need to direct our undivided attention to trade and cooperation with the USSR, beginning by adhering to existing treaties.

The GDR is striving to expand and deepen the trade relations with socialist countries, while protecting reciprocal economic interests, and we will have to adjust to new conditions that emerge from the economic reforms. In trade with non-socialist countries we hold to the principle of mutual advantage. We are interested in expanding our export and import markets as well as increasing cooperation with capitalist firms. The GDR is open to proposals by capitalist partners, which previously were treated unfavorably or fell on deaf ears. Joint ventures, investment sharing, transfer of profit, pilot projects in environmental protection are no longer foreign words to us. That means that in the interest of maximizing the productivity of our economy, the government of the GDR is willing to support cooperation with business in Western industrial countries, so that more and better products will be available on our international and domestic markets; and we know that this result has to be in the interest of both parties. We are counting on constructive cooperation in order to utilize even in the short-term all the potential of our foreign trade activities. We will improve the conditions for contacts and information on all levels–from the factories to the organizations that steer the economy. . . .

Without a doubt, housing and urban planning have to be viewed as an essential task of the government, one we will have to implement practically in direct contact with the citizens of our country. We ought to follow the suggestion to form a governmental committee for social planning and urban development and charge it with working out proposals for effective steps in this area. Ideas by architects and urban planners are already at our disposal. We should use them. . . .

From the position papers of all parties in our coalition one can discern the agreement that economic reform does not mean doing away with economic planning. In economic reform the new government should, however, be guided just as clearly by the idea of making the market, with its relationship of commodity and money, an organic part of a socialist planned economy.

Neither planning without market, nor a market economy without planning. Life demands that we pursue a socialist economic system in which planning and the market are interconnected in such a way that in all sectors of our economy we can produce effectively for the needs of our citizens, for the economy, and for a profitable foreign trade without central planning. That will put our socialist society on a firmer footing and bring in the necessary revenues for the state budget. . . .

Economic reform hence means reshaping the economic structure from top to bottom. That means a new character and a new role for central planning. It should concentrate on balanced economic proportions and networks, an efficient economic structure for production with increasing division of labor, and the development of long-term strategies for an economic and social development that meets ecological requirements. . . .

NOTES

Source: Zanetti, 235-50.

24
" 'We Must Not Falsify Once More.' What Preceded and What Followed the Events of October 9 in Leipzig": Speech by Kurt Masur, Director of the Leipzig Gewandhaus Orchestra (November 1989)

It really began with the first prayers for peace. That is already some time ago. Here in Leipzig in the Church of St. Nicholas we held prayers for peace with an ever greater participation of Christians. And after a while we were joined by other groups, who, because of the public discussions, because of the open atmosphere, were simply attracted by the fact that one could speak freely here. Actually a completely normal process; others then came to the church, of course, who in principle did not want to have anything to do with the church but who merely wanted to be able to express their thoughts. After a while it came about that the police began watching the scene, and that more and more policemen were put in place for security. I remember that around May or June every Monday night at about the same time four or five vans with policemen were always waiting to receive those who came out of the church. All of us observed this escalation because we simply found the sheer amount of police presence inappropriate. This then developed into a sort of protest demonstration which, I think, ended in part with the arrest of some individuals. The escalation and confrontation at the Church of St. Nicholas grew worse and worse. All of us were affected by the atmosphere created by the wave of emigration of many young people to the Federal Republic. And we thought that our fortieth anniversary was celebrated in an inappropriate way. For us it was the anniversary of a quarreling family. All this led to tensions among the people, which then led to the first escalation and to violence between the police and the populace. In Berlin there was another of those confrontations, I believe even worse on the seventh of October than on the eighth. And we knew that on the following Monday, that was the ninth of October, a demonstration would certainly take place here in Leipzig in which violence could play a major role. On that day there were concerts scheduled here in the Gewandhaus, and we were very upset. In the early afternoon I called Dr. Meyer; he took immediate action, notified the other men and asked whether we could have a meeting. We then met in my apartment and discussed what we should do. We met again roughly 45 minutes before the demonstration was supposed to start. We had agreed on having a proclamation read on the Leipzig radio station, in the radio station itself, and in the city forum, as well as during the peace prayers that were held in four different churches that evening. The demonstration had swollen to roughly 70,000 people. . . .

Everything was a question of minutes. Here the district leadership saw to it that the security forces were informed by their commander to withdraw and, if possible, not be so visible that it might provoke the crowd in any way. If being courageous means learning to overcome fear, then that was the case on that evening. The responsibility we assumed went well beyond our authority. It was almost incredible for us all that not a single incident, not a single arrest, no violent act occurred. That then became the paradigm for the entire country.

Even today those who are responsible have a hard time admitting that the security forces were ordered to suppress this so-called counterrevolution. That was clear. I say this as someone without affiliation with any party. I can afford to. No one will admit it, and we did not check up on it. But we know that at some places water cannons, at other places tear gas were ready to be used. And if the security forces had guns, they probably also had ammunition. The GDR avoided by a hairsbreadth having a civil war.

During mass there was a demonstration with the cry "We want out," which was violently dispersed. On October 9 I was fascinated, moved, and shocked when the demonstrators shouted: "We are the people," "We are staying here." That really marked the transformation, the acknowledgment that we want to rebuild our homeland here, but not the way you always told us to, and not the way you always lectured us on how it ought to be.

But euphemistic terms are still used, things are not expressed sincerely, we are already searching for words once more–I am already disturbed by that again. Unrest is now the first civic duty. We have to remain in unrest and impatient. The government offices are still occupied by the same administrators, in the political councils we still have the same lazy people who for ten or twenty years took all their orders from above, who constantly nodded their heads in approval. And that is true from top to bottom. And if we do not implement changes from the bottom up, they will be meaningless.

Resigning from a post does not yet mean very much. But I am not in favor of great show trials against people who for some time may have honestly done their duty in the conviction that they were doing the right thing. But everywhere that provable criminal deeds

have been committed–acts against the socialist idea, I would say–
we have to uncover them so that in the future errors of this sort do
not occur. The cause of the tensions between the people and the government lies almost exclusively in the state apparatus, whereas
prior to the ninth of October our government always declared that
in particular the Western media or some foreign powers were stirring up our people. Our people have shown that they can distinguish perfectly between what they do or do not want, that they are
mature. They want to stay here. They want to build something
other than a society in which egoism has developed to such an extent that it plays the leading role. . . .

We were all trained for a long time in the art of opportunism.
We have even already become an affluent society, let's not deny
that. We may not have enough cars, but we live well, and that
makes people lazy. For this reason, I was especially moved by the
quality of this activity among the people, since not one of them
demonstrated for more money or for better living conditions. Only
ideal questions were at issue. What was at issue was a form of freedom that limited us, that seduced our youth into the schizophrenic
habit of not speaking the truth. The entire situation in our country
today makes it necessary that none of us be motivated by hate. I
personally also have very hard and difficult times behind me in
this country. That also shaped my alertness. I will not give up as
long as I can be active here fighting for everything written about in
the papers, even for the SED's action plan, which really includes
all the points the people on the street were demanding, that is the
separation of state and party, church and youth organizations, that
is the creation of freely elected assemblies, of a true representation
of the people, that is everything that frees up the energy of our
people so that we can be creative again. Our people were no longer
able to be creative. In the last few years I did not see as many
bright eyes in the streets as I have seen lately. That makes one
happy. We should not fall into a state of self-satisfaction again,
into the belief that this does not concern us, that someone else will
go ahead and do it. For us this Gewandhaus provides proof. Sometimes there were school groups who visited here and let slip little
bits of children's wisdom: This is like in the Intershop. No, this is
applied socialism, because we ourselves take it into our own hands,
because we remained alert. We have to use our freedom in such a
way that we think creatively about what we want to do. These are
questions of individual responsibility that all of us have to learn
all over again.

The cultural need that was cultivated here emerged over a period of years. I wrote a personal letter to Erich Honecker after he resigned in which I personally wished that he could overcome his disappointment, and I thanked him for the decision to have this Gewandhaus, the Dresden Semper Opera, and the theater built. That, too, was a lonely decision. He went against all reason in making that decision, for already at that time we were so much in debt that we could not afford all of this. What impressed me most in the past weeks was that the people in our country displayed a knowledge, an honesty, a capacity to articulate themselves of which many of them would not previously have thought themselves capable. I could never have imagined that the first event here in the Gewandhaus could lead to such results. As a premise I said as the master of this house: I guarantee to everyone here that no one who expresses his or her opinion will come to any harm. And if so, then you would have to write to me from prison. One can still notice today that this old fear is still present beneath the surface. But self-assurance, the fact that we are standing tall, can no longer be eliminated. That is the greatest hope that I have. The people here have discovered themselves, and they discovered that they can develop capabilities that reach far beyond what they previously knew themselves to be capable of. That will all cause us to struggle constantly for this country, for a socialism created so that human beings can feel comfortable living in it. That should remain our aim.

NOTES

Source: Zanetti, 251-55.

25
Call for an Autonomous GDR (November 26, 1989)

Our country is bogged down in a deep crisis. We do not want to and can no longer live the way we did up to now. The leadership of one party assumed the domination of the people and its representatives, imbuing all areas of life with structures marked by Stalinism. Without violence, through mass demonstrations, the people forced the process of revolutionary renewal, which is taking place at breathtaking speed. We only have a little time left to have an influence on the different possibilities that offer themselves as ways out of this crisis.

Either we can insist on the autonomy of the German Democratic Republic and try, with all our might and in cooperation with those states and interest groups that are willing, to develop a society of solidarity in our country in which peace, social justice, the freedom of the individual, and the protection of the environment are guaranteed.

Or we must put up with the beginning of the sell-out of our material and moral values, caused by the strong economic compulsions and the unreasonable conditions that influential circles in the Federal Republic have attached to their assistance for the GDR, which will culminate sooner or later in the annexation of the German Democratic Republic by the Federal Republic of Germany.

Let us take the first path. We still have the chance of developing, in a relationship of equals with all European states, a socialist alternative to the Federal Republic. We can still reflect on our antifascist and humanistic ideals which served as the basis long ago. We call on all citizens who share our hope and our concern to join this appeal by appending their signatures.

Berlin. November 26, 1989

Among those who signed were: Frank Beier, theater director; Götz Berger, lawyer; Volker Braun, writer; Tamara Danz, rock singer; Sieghard Gille, painter; Stefan Heym, writer; Uwe Jahn, engineer; Dieter Klein, sociologist; Günter Krusche, general superintendent; Sebastian Pflugbeil, physicist; Ulrike Poppe, housewife; Friedrich Schorlemmer, minister; Konrad Weiß, filmmaker; Christa Wolf, writer.

NOTES

Source: Schüddekopf, 240-41.

26

Helmut Kohl's Ten-Point Plan for Overcoming the Division of Germany and Europe: Speech before the *Bundestag* (November 28, 1989)

. . . Ladies and gentlemen, opportunities are opening up for overcoming the division of Europe and hence of our fatherland, as well. The Germans, who are coming together in the spirit of freedom, will never pose a threat. Rather they will be–and I am convinced of this–an asset to a Europe that is growing ever closer together. The awakening we are experiencing today must first of all be credited to the people who demonstrated their will to freedom in such an impressive way. But it is also the result of political developments that took place over the last few years. Ladies and gentlemen, we in the Federal Republic also contributed substantially to that with our policies. . . .

The road to German unity, as we all know, cannot be planned in the abstract or with an engagement calendar in hand. Abstract models may have a polemic utility, but they do not take us any further. But we can, as long as we want to, prepare the stages today that will lead to this aim. I would like to elucidate these stages in the form of a ten-point plan.

First: Immediate measures are necessary as a result of the events of recent weeks, especially the wave of emigrants and the huge increases in the number of travelers. The Federal Government is willing to provide immediate concrete aid where it is presently needed. We will send humanitarian assistance and medical supplies as long as this is wanted and considered useful.

We also know that the welcome money paid out to each visitor from the GDR once a year is no solution to the problem of travel costs. Ultimately the GDR will have to provide its citizens who travel with the necessary foreign currency. But for a transitional period we are willing to pay a certain amount into a foreign currency fund. Necessary preconditions for this, however, are that persons traveling into the GDR are no longer required to exchange a set amount of money, that entry into the country is significantly eased, and that the GDR makes its own substantial contribution to such a fund. Our aim, if possible, is an unobstructed flow of traffic in both directions.

Second: The Federal Government will continue as previously its cooperation with the GDR in all areas that are advantageous to people on both sides. This is true especially for economic, scientific-technological, and cultural cooperation. An intensification of our cooperation in the area of environmental protection is particularly important. In this area we could decide on new projects in a very short time, regardless of how things develop. The same is true for–and the West German Postmaster General has initiated the relevant round of talks–an immediate and comprehensive improvement in the telephone lines to the GDR and the telephone network within the GDR. . . .

Third: I have made the offer to significantly expand our assistance and cooperation if a fundamental transformation of the political and economic system in the GDR is firmly decided and irreversibly implemented. "Irreversible" means for us, and above all for me, that the GDR state leadership come to an agreement with the opposition groups regarding constitutional change and a new election law. We support the demand for free, equal, and secret elections in the GDR with the participation of independent–and that, of course, also means non-socialist–parties. The power monopoly of the SED has to be abolished. The demanded introduction of a constitutional system above all means the abolition of political crimes and, consequently, the immediate release of all political prisoners.

Mr. President, ladies and gentlemen, economic aid can only be effective if fundamental reforms of the economic system are implemented. This is clear from our experiences with all COMECON states–it has nothing to do with a desire on our parts to proselytize. The centrally planned economy must be dismantled. We do not want to stabilize conditions that have become untenable. We know that economic improvement can only come if the GDR opens itself up to Western investments, if it creates the conditions for a market economy and makes private initiatives possible. I don't understand those who accuse us of patronization in this regard. . . .

Fourth: President Modrow spoke in his government policy statement about a "contractual community." We are willing to take up this idea. The closeness and the special character of relations between the two German states necessitate an even closer network of agreements in all areas and on all levels.

This cooperation will increasingly require common institutions. Already existing commissions could take on new tasks, additional ones could be formed. I am thinking in particular of the areas of commerce, transportation, environmental protection, science and technology, health care, and culture. I do not need to emphasize that in all that now needs to happen, Berlin must be fully integrated. That was, is, and remains our policy.

Fifth: But we are also willing to go a decisive step further, namely, to develop confederative structures between both German states with the aim of creating a federation, that means an organization of federal states, in Germany. But that necessarily presupposes a democratically legitimate government in the GDR.

After free elections in the near future, we can imagine the following institutions:

–a joint governmental committee for permanent consultation and political agreement;
–joint special committees;
–a joint parliamentary committee;

–and many other things in the light of these new developments.
. . .

What a unified Germany will eventually look like, nobody knows. I am certain, however, *that* unity is coming soon, if the people of Germany desire it.

Sixth: The development of intra-German relations remains embedded in the pan-European process, and that always means in East-West relations. The future architecture of Germany must conform to the future architecture of pan-Europe. In this regard, the West has set the pace with its concept of a permanent and just peaceful order in Europe.

In our joint declaration of June of this year, Soviet General Secretary Gorbachev and I spoke of the structural elements for a "common European house." Let me mention the following by way of example:

–Unqualified respect for the integrity and security of each state. Each state has the right to freely choose its own political and social system.

–Unqualified respect for the principles and rules of international law, especially respect for every nation's right to self-determination.

–The realization of human rights.

–Respect for and maintenance of the ancestral cultures of the nations of Europe.

With all of these points, which General Secretary Gorbachev and I have set down, we aim to follow Europe's long-standing traditions and do our part to overcome the division of Europe.

Seventh: The attraction and aura of the European Community are and remain a decisive constant of pan-European developments. We want to and must strengthen them further.

The European Community is now called upon to approach the reform-minded states of Central, Eastern, and Southeastern Europe with openness and flexibility. The state and government leaders of the EC member states decided this a short time ago at their meeting in Paris. The GDR is, of course, included in this. The Federal Government therefore approves the speedy ratification of a trade and cooperation agreement with the GDR, which would give the GDR wider access to the Common Market. . . .

Eighth: The CSCE process is a key element of this pan-European architecture. We want to promote it by utilizing the upcoming forums:

–the human rights conferences in Copenhagen in 1990 and in Moscow in 1991;
–the Conference on Economic Cooperation in Bonn in 1990;
–the Symposium on Cultural Heritage in Cracow in 1991;
–and last but not least, the next follow-up meeting in Helsinki.

There we should also think about new institutional forms of pan-European cooperation. We can well imagine a common institution for the coordination of East-West economic cooperation, as well as the creation of a pan-European environmental council.

Ninth: Overcoming the division of Europe and the division of Germany requires far-reaching and speedy steps in the field of disarmament and arms control. Disarmament and arms control must keep pace with political developments and, if necessary, be speeded up. . . .

Tenth: With this comprehensive policy we are working toward a state of peace in Europe in which the German people can regain its unity in free self-determination. Reunification–that means reattaining the national unity of Germany–remains the political aim of the government of the Federal Republic.

We are thankful that we received renewed support in this from our friends and partners in the declaration of the NATO summit in Brussels from May of this year.[1] . . .

Today there are many promising signs indicating that the decade of the nineties will bring more chances for peace and freedom in Europe and in Germany. Much depends–and everyone is aware of this–on our, the German contribution. All of us must face this historical challenge.

NOTES

Source: Zanetti, 256-65.

1. On May 30, 1989, the NATO leaders issued a joint communiqué at the end of the summit pledging that the Western alliance, moving into its fifth decade, would meet the challenge of the political and economic realities of the 1990s. It vowed to continue the close partnership between the countries of Europe and North America. The communiqué declared that the allies were committed to maintaining only the minimum number of nuclear weapons necessary to support their strategy of deterrence. For a foreseeable future, it said, NATO's strategy of deterrence would be based on the stationing of adequate and effective nuclear and conventional forces and that these would be updated and modernized whenever necessary.

27
Stefan Heym, "Ash Wednesday in the GDR" (December 1989)

The great, the elevating moments are past—on the belt route around Leipzig, when the crowds suddenly broke into "We are the people!," and on the Alexanderplatz in Berlin, when the people, now a million strong, comprehended that they had learned overnight to stand tall and a kind of collective sigh of relief became audible, and finally at the border crossing as the border opened and the people, still speechless, fell into each others' arms and first one, then another, a third, and then a fourth said: "Incredible!"

Then came Ash Wednesday. This people who, after decades of submissiveness and escape attempts, had pulled themselves together and taken their fate into their own hands, who seemed to be heading toward a promising future, became a raging mob. Pressed shoulder to shoulder they moved toward Hertie and Bilka in the pursuit of glittering plunder.[1] What faces they made as with cannibalistic desire they rummaged through the sale tables intentionally placed in their way by the Western shopkeepers. With what patient humility they had previously stood—orderly and obediently as they had been taught at home—in line for the handout, called "welcome money" by the strategists of the Cold War out of malice and psychological cunning.

But it is understandable. How long did they have to wait, those poor people, before they were allowed to touch, look at, smell, or fondle the colorful stuff piled high on the shelves without any "All gone" and no "Don't have none," just the disdainful smile of the girls at the cash register—the entire western half of Berlin, the whole western half of the country one huge "Intershop" rich in goods and gleaming.

These greedy people are not to blame. At fault are those who directed an economy in that country behind the Wall in which a lack of logic led to a lack of goods and even the best will and the best work yielded inefficiency and shabby fruit.

But that is the least of the new reality. The whole encrusted structure of this state has been broken open, its facade is crumbling, exposing how little solid structure underlay it. A shocking realization, because—and this is the other side of it—people didn't just do sloppy work, play the hypocrite, and defraud others. Some even made an effort with an honest heart; and despite all the handicaps, they brought to light some good things which threaten to land on the historical trash heap along with the dirt and idiocies of these years. A kind of anarchy spreads, because each official tries wherever possible to find a new position in the general melee of musical chairs. Hesitantly, but finally, each of the formerly powerful politicians resigns one after the other, but who is there to take their places? Where is the shadow cabinet that stands ready in the West, where the reserve party that could take over and create a new order?

Now we are paying for the fact that the grand old men eliminated every talent who could have succeeded them. And what use is an opposition that is nothing more than a topsy-turvy of jumbled opinions? And does anyone know whose money is where his mouth is and who really represents meaningful ideas and who just spreads rumors and places half-baked thoughts and vanities before the people?

And where in the devil's name is the new conception that is so badly and urgently needed? More socialism—yes or no? And if yes, then what kind of socialism? With what percentage market economy and what property relationships?

And the people, whether comrades or not, brought into line for so long, have become insecure after the abolition of the guiding thread. Their hearts are more open, and for this reason every charlatan of western or eastern origin will be able to drum his hocus-pocus into their heads.

The people in this GDR, which was raised freshly baptized by the people in the days of October, have set out in search of truth. But what is the truth? And what turmoil will come before it crystallizes?

And how much time do we have left?

For the clock is ticking. Despite all efforts, despite turning-point and transformation, innovation and reform, change, reversal, reorganization, whatever we call it, the sand, whose sifting triggered the whole process, continues to run. Even the freedom to travel, intended as enticement to stay, was hardly effective. How many of them left in November for emergency quarters in the gymnasiums and barracks of the Federal Republic—never to return? A hundred thousand? Or even more?

If this continues, then the day will come when the Republic will have become incapable of functioning: the inner cities ruined, the infrastructure a network riddled with holes; no more doctors or nurses, no postmen and no power plant workers, no street-pavers, carpenters, farmers, salespeople, truckdrivers–just pensioners and administrative officials who have nothing more to administrate and a lost-looking accumulation of secret police and a few artists who hope to find a new audience.

Sound harsh? But it has to sound so harsh if we want to pull ourselves together now, now, now. It has to sound so harsh if clarity is to enter our heads on the cardinal question: Do we want the GDR or do we not want it, do we want it despite the crisis into which it was pushed by an incompetent, unimaginative, dictatorial government?

Sometimes it seems as if there sat in Bonn or Frankfurt or somewhere else in the Federal Republic, in the quiet office of a think tank, a few guys who, according to precise calculations, pull now more loosely, then more tightly on the noose that lies around the donkey's throat, whereby they dangle financial aid, know-how, managerial help, joint ventures, and whatever else before its nose. To make the bundle bounce even higher they say: but first you must do this and change that and guarantee us this, until the poor creature, loaded up and harassed, falls to its knees and begs to be slaughtered.

And what could be opposed to this? Morality–socialist morality even? Love for a country that is only part of a bigger one and was originally nothing more than an arbitrarily demarcated zone of occupation? A feeling of belonging to a community that conspired to establish a new world, a more just world? But look how a party that called itself the leading party played fast and loose with such visions of the future!

But still, and still: something, nine-tenths covered over, has remained in the people of the dreams and ideals that were once–although distorted by the phraseology of Stalinism–handed down to them, and there is a hope, against all probability, to which one could cling. To that one can reply: we hoped all those years, before the Wall existed, and still afterwards; now we want something real, and we want it now, not simply in the distant future. Good, let's talk about it.

Let's talk about unification. It is a fact that two capitalist German states are not necessary. The *raison d'etre* of the German Democratic Republic is socialism, regardless in which form. Its goal is to offer an alternative to the pirate state with the harmless name "Federal Republic." There is no other reason for the existence of a separate East German state. Simply to serve as a military frontier for the marshalls of the Soviet Union is nonsense in the age of atomic annihilation, and whatever pretext one might find for such a status, it would all too soon prove flimsy.

And if you think about it, wasn't the existential crisis of the German Democratic Republic brought on precisely by means of this constellation, back in Reykjavik, in discussions between the American President Ronald Reagan and the Soviet State and Party Leader Michail Gorbachev, when the latter tried to explain to the former that in view of the atomic stalemate peace should reign between the blocs, that even the blocs had become superfluous, Europe–the world–a common house?[2]

Moreover, it's a fact that the Stalinist economy that was in vogue for so long behind the Wall is now bankrupt; the state is bankrupt, and whether it can pull itself up by its own bootstraps is doubtful.

Since the Soviets have their own problems to solve, the only savior remains the West, especially the Federal Republic, which waited so long for just this moment and made its contribution to finally bringing it about. But wouldn't it be more obvious for them to fold their arms and wait with a smile on their faces until the half-dead cadaver lies with all four limbs in the air so that then they can cannibalize it?

Such ideas are being considered; but others too, by different people. Wasn't the stability of Europe what first triggered all the wonderful democratic developments in the East–in Poland, the Soviet Union, Hungary, the GDR and Czechoslovakia–grounded in the existence of two German states? What kind of stability would that likely be with a new combined Germany, a Germany controlled by Daimler-Messerschmitt-Bölkow-Blohm and the German Bank?[3] And how far would it be from there to the demand for a return to the borders of a greater Germany of 1937, and for borders expanded even further beyond that? And all of that with atomic weapons in the bag?

Perhaps the GDR is not just attractive for those who dream of real socialism on German soil, but also for sober-minded business people and politicians. What kind of help would this reeling country actually need? And what kind of reform and new form would be necessary–without mimicking everything that is customary in the West–to get the economy of the GDR in motion again and make it interesting to investors? Is it possible to imagine a confederation of two different kinds of economic systems that could eventually lead to a confederation of two states with different kinds of social systems?

And how much time do we have left? The government, which is provisional, lives from one demonstration to the next and usually simply reacts, instead of showing its own ideas; and the new groups that send their representatives to the assembled masses sense, I fear, only little of the fate that threatens them, as well.

If everything drags on as it has until now, if nothing changes in the areas that really count, in the economy and the currency, then the day will come when the workers will be tired of promises and will leave the factories and say: Let the next best person take over this mess.

Who this next best person will be is clear enough. And then the GDR would not just be sold, but given away.

The clock is ticking.

NOTES

Source: Naumann, 71-78. Translated by Laura Jackson.

1. Hertie and Bilka are inexpensive department stores similar to Woolworth.
2. In October 1986 Ronald Reagan and Michail Gorbachov met in Reykjavik to negotiate an agenda for a summit in the US. Their talks turned surprisingly into intense and detailed negotiations over arms control; the stalemate over the so-called Strategic Defense Initiative came as the superpowers appeared on the verge of reaching an accord that would entail substantial reductions in offensive nuclear weapons.
3. Daimler, Messerschmitt, Bölkow, Blohm, and the German Bank are among the major pillars of West German industrial capitalism.

28
Statement by Günter Schabowski Announcing the Resignation of the Central Committee and the Politburo of the SED
(December 3, 1989)

. . . On the suggestion of the Politburo and as a result of the investigations of the Party Central Control Commission, the Central Committee concluded: "Hans Albrecht, Erich Honecker, Werner Krolikowski, Günter Kleiber, Erich Mielke, Gerhard Müller, Alexander Schalck-Golodkowski, Horst Sindermann, Willi Stoph, Harry Tisch, Herbert Ziegenhahn, and Dieter Müller are to be expelled from the Central Committee. Because of the severe nature of their offences against the statutes of the SED and in light of numerous demands made by councils of district delegates, they will simultaneously be expelled from the SED."

Second, the Central Committee announces its resignation.

And third–please excuse me for a moment–the Central Committee concluded: "The former Central Committee considers it its duty to give an account of the reasons for the crisis in the SED and in our society before the planned special party congress. We will form a committee to do that."

It is my task to announce further a resolution made by the Politburo of the SED. This resolution has the following wording: "The Politburo accepts the criticism made by major parts of the membership that the current party leadership was incapable, in line with the task given it by the ninth and the tenth meetings of the Central Committee, of uncovering the entire extent and severity of the errors made by members of the former Politburo and of drawing from them the necessary conclusions. This statement must be made despite the fact that members of the current Politburo who were in the former leadership of the party were largely responsible for bringing about the personnel and policy decisions that led to the process of renewal within the leadership of the party. In order to counter further threats to the existence of the party, as well as to ensure that the political and organizational preparations of the party congress can go forward, the Politburo deems it necessary to announce its resignation."

I would like to add that work on the political and organizational preparation of the party congress will be continued by a committee that is yet to be formed. . . .

NOTES

Source: Wimmer, 198-99.

29

Egon Krenz's Speech on the Occasion of His Resignation as Chair of the *Staatsrat* and as Chair of the National Defense Council (December 6, 1989)

When the *Volkskammer* elected me chair of the *Staatsrat* on October 24, 1989, I took the oath with the firm intention of investing all my energy in the maintenance of this country as a sovereign socialist republic and in the well-being of its citizens, in a firm alliance with our socialist brother states and the peaceful cooperation of all people and states. Together with political allies I had previously taken the initiative for a reversal of policies among the leadership of the SED. Our actions were motivated by the insight, which grew over a longer period of time, that the old leadership constantly heightened the contradiction between the will of the people and policies that were far removed from reality, and that they were leading our country into a profound crisis.

My long-time membership in the *Staatsrat* and in the Politburo under the leadership of Erich Honecker undermined for many citizens the credibility of the politics of a renewal of socialism for which I stood. The people's trust, however, is the first prerequisite for carrying out the function of the chair of the *Staatsrat*. Meanwhile, events have occurred that were not foreseeable at the time of my election to be chair of the *Staatsrat*.

In the interest of stability in the GDR and of the necessary revolutionary renewal of our country, I resign from my position as chair of the *Staatsrat* and as chair of the National Defense Council of the GDR.

It is my hope that the people of the GDR will make the process of renewal for which they have struggled irreversible. But we must also heed the danger posed to our fatherland by anti-socialist forces. Every revolution holds within it the inherent danger of gathering opposing forces. These anti-socialist forces want to break the pride of our people and put the work of many generations up for sale. We will have to fight together against this. In this hour of supreme danger, all those who care about this country must stand together in patriotic duty.

NOTES

Source: Wimmer, 206-7.

30

Self-Definition of the East German Round Table, Formulated at its First Meeting (December 7-8, 1989)

The participants in the Round Table are meeting out of profound concern for our country, which has fallen into crisis, for its autonomy, and for its long-term development.

They demand open revelations about the ecological, economic, and financial situation of our country.

Although the Round Table cannot serve a parliamentary or governmental function, it wants to provide the public with proposals for overcoming this crisis.

It demands from the *Volkskammer* and the government that it be promptly informed and consulted about important decisions on legal, economic, and fiscal policies.

It defines itself as part of the civil control in our country. It is planned that its activities will continue until free, democratic, and secret elections are held.

NOTES

Source: Herles/Rose, 23.

31
Speech by Gregor Gysi, Chair of the SED, Before the Special Party Congress (December 16, 1989)

. . . As a party that is renewing itself, it is our political duty in the coming months to make an essential contribution to the current discussions about the future of the GDR. We want to inject our position with manifold voices into the debate, so that the two German states can be joined by treaties without endangering European stability by premature and ill-considered actions and inciting fear among the nations of this continent. A unification of the two German states–that would be the decision, for which no politician would be willing to take responsibility, to transform the GDR into an underdeveloped federal state with an uncertain social future for its citizens, in other words, to turn it into the slum of the FRG. That would be an undignified farewell to a country that, after all, bears the dignified name of the German Democratic Republic.

The citizens of the GDR did not live in vain. They always worked with diligence, they lived with anger, but, let's not forget, with pride, as well. They fought on their own for self-determination and we cannot endanger that. With their peaceful, democratic, populist movement they created the unique opportunity to finally establish a humanist, social alternative to the Federal Republic of Germany and thereby to stimulate the democratic competition between the two German states.

. . . According to our records, [the SED] still has 1.7 million members. No other party or democratic movement in our country brings together nearly as much organizational strength. But we must be present everywhere, we must articulate, state clearly what we want, how important it is for our country. And, comrades, with a bowed head one has a very limited perspective. The things that face us can only be mastered if we stand tall. . . . We should never overlook the fact that the break with the Stalinist-oriented thought patterns and organizational structures of the SED is a more or less complicated learning process for every individual comrade, a process that requires tolerance and patience, but also persistence.

. . . We must and will develop together an internal party democracy based on the will of the majority of the party members. The practice of grassroots democracy, the guarantee of common action within the party, do not call for unanimous decisions. It is important, rather, that we support, always and everywhere, the open exchange of ideas and guarantee the right to free expression of ideas in the process of developing them and making decisions. There can no longer be uniformity in the party. . . . The styles, forms, and methods of the actions taken by the party apparatus have to serve the creative, forward-looking work of the party and close ties with the grassroots of the party and the citizens on a daily basis. We can never again allow the apparatus to become autonomous from the elected councils. But it is also clear that the councils need the support of their full-fledged members. The party apparatus must work according to the demands of the upcoming election campaign and, in any case, work more effectively. It will be smaller in the future but–we hope–more efficient.

. . . Let me now turn to the political system of the GDR. The political system of the GDR is becoming more and more pluralistic. It can only function according to the principle of nonviolent political exchanges on the basis of a constitutional consensus. That is, at the same time, a new challenge for our party. We want to work together with the political parties, societal organizations, and political movements toward developing common basic positions for the solution of the severe economic, social, political, and humanitarian problems of our country. The profound crisis in the GDR can only be overcome if all of us work together. . . . We want, out of a sense of patriotic duty, to actively help shape the Round Table as an essential form of dialogue for the development of a broad consensus in questions relevant to the survival of our country. We do not view the Round Table merely as a transitory phenomenon in the political system of the GDR. It represents societal interests. Between the parliamentary and extra-parliamentary forces, the Round Table can attain such a consensus on basic political questions and themes that largely represent the will of the people. With this, the results of its meetings or the opinions formed at the Round Table will assume an immediate significance for the political and governmental decision-making processes. Of course, it cannot replace state decisions and state jurisdiction.

. . . All citizens of the German Democratic Republic have–must have!–equal rights, equal opportunities, regardless of their nationality, their world-view, or their beliefs. That is a fundamental constitutional principle that in the future will have to become more vital.

. . . Our support of the coalition government led by Hans Modrow is of vital significance for our country. We all have to understand one thing clearly: whether or not our ship of state will maneuver around the reefs of anarchy and annexation by the FRG and will be able to have once again free passage in deep waters depends largely on this government. . . . At the same time, we expect prudent but also timely actions from this government.

. . . We must develop a politically new state that is open to Europe and sees its future as a place within the framework of a European confederation. A new constitution should incorporate all the good ideas inherent in our Marxist and bourgeois-democratic constitutional heritage, and it should develop into binding basic rights and basic duties for citizens and communities those demands that emanate from the grassroots. . . . The conservation of the natural environment as well as the free development of the arts and sciences stands as a new dimension of our politics. Part of any democratic constitution is the establishment of civil and control mechanisms. Personal data must be protected under the law. . . . A new pillar of constitutionality should be erected by means of the creation of a constitutional court that must be independent. A completely new position with regard to the separation of powers is necessary. . . . The people's representatives must become the supreme state organizations on all levels. This position guarantees the democratic character of the entire state organization. . . . A new socialist constitution for the GDR must constitutionally and bindingly establish the sovereignty and right of self-determination of the people and demand the right of our citizens to free personal development.

. . . Some thoughts about the shaping of our economy and agrarian politics. The decisions about the future of socialism in our country, about the fate of the GDR, will be made especially in our economy. The space within which politics can maneuver depends on the productivity and effectiveness of the economy. There can be no other intellectual point of departure. Our proposals for radical economic reform are aimed at the reshaping of the demand-side market, which was previously characterized by the administration of lacks, into a supply-side market oriented toward people's needs.

. . . The stated aim of our party is to be represented at the highest levels of the people's representation by a strong, competent faction. Much is at stake; the GDR itself is at stake. We are willing to take responsibility for this country. We are open to forming a coalition with all forces that care about the well-being of this country and the sovereign future of the GDR. We know that no party and no movement can take on the formation of democratic socialism alone. We accept the responsibility for this country, which is our homeland. We must fight so that no political vacuum develops that could be occupied by right-wing forces. By struggling for ourselves, we are fighting for the GDR, for the social security of our workers, indeed, for stability and peace in all of Europe!

NOTES

Source: Wimmer, 229-32.

32
"On the Formation of a Common German State":
Declaration by the "New Forum" (December 18, 1989)

In the past, other nations have experienced German nationalism as state aggression. We must take this, and the fear that results from it, very seriously.

The New Forum supports the recognition of the existing borders in Europe and demands the same from the government of the Federal Republic. The main problems of our world–securing peace, the damaged environment, social and economic misery–cannot be solved at a national level. The nations of the world must move closer together and become aware of their responsibility for each other. We support the principle: One world instead of three!

This should not make us blind to the fact that both German states share a particular relationship with each other–on the levels of culture, history, language, and family.

The revolutionaries of 1848 and 1918, the antifascist resistance, the movement of the worker's councils in the occupation zones, the solidarity of the West Berliners and the West Germans with the uprising on the 17th of June, 1953, and the refugees after the 13th of

August, 1961, are examples of a different German tradition and a community of solidarity from below.[1]

The awakening and the transformations in the GDR are successes on the part of the peaceful mass demonstrations and the self-reliance of the people in this country.

We now have the chance to clean up the Stalinist swamp nonviolently, but thoroughly, and start all over again. We distance ourselves from those who are stirring up hatred, panic, and nationalist sentiments. We are for a reshaping of relations between the two German states.

*Re*unification means a Germany in the borders of 1937! Unification *now* means for some people quick prosperity, but for many people it means unemployment, the abandonment of democratic participation, excessively high rents, and, what is more, the legalization of extreme right-wing and neo-fascist parties and organizations.[2]

A *future unification* can only occur on the basis of the equality of both German states. Prerequisites for this are:
–total demilitarization and neutrality;
–ratification of a peace treaty;
–guarantee of the Oder-Neiße border with Poland;
–social security for all, the right to work, the right to a place to live;
–democratization, participation in the affairs of businesses and communities;
–just economic relations with the countries of the Third World.

Stability in Europe requires first of all a stable GDR. For an economic stabilization we also need aid from outside.

We must not fall from confrontation into confederation. What we now need is cooperation. But the people must be included in that decision and must be able to control how that aid is used: for the partial interests of a few, or for an ecologically oriented economic reform, for the building of a socially just society!

For the Berlin speaker's council of the New Forum:
Ingrid Köppe, Uwe Radloff, Gabriele Kleiner, Reinhard Schult,

Ingrid Brandenburg, Julia Hamburger, Martin Gaber, Bernd Albani, Klaus Brandenburg, Marianne Tietze.

NOTES .

Source: *Die ersten Texte des Neuen Forum,* flyer.

1. On the 17th of June, 1953, the GDR regime sent in tanks to put down a workers' uprising that arose in protest against an increase in the work quota; subsequently this day was celebrated as the "Day of German Unity" in the Federal Republic of Germany.
2. Such right-wing parties and organizations were illegal in the GDR, but they are legal in the FRG.

33
Statement by the Round Table Regarding the Visit of West German Chancellor Helmut Kohl in Dresden (December 18, 1989)

The participants of the Round Table welcome the official working visit of Chancellor Kohl in the GDR. They would like to express the expectation that this visit will contribute to the expansion of relations between the GDR and the FRG and thereby observe the responsibility of both German states for the construction of a peaceful order in Europe that transcends political systems. The common will to peace, which must be characterized by the active cooperation of the GDR and the FRG for peace and disarmament, should be expanded by a set of treaties for the regulation of their relations. The long-term perspective on this relationship can only fit in with a pan-European development that moves toward the overcoming of the division of Europe.

This visit ought to outline the political and economic framework for the further shaping of relations between the GDR and the FRG, as well as prepare concrete steps for closer cooperation. That relates above all to questions of cooperation in the areas of the economy, science and technology, environmental protection, transportation, postal and communications systems, tourism, and legal assistance.

The participants at the Round Table appeal to Prime Minister Modrow and Chancellor Kohl to steer the talks and their results in the direction of cooperation and communication for the good of the citizens in both their states. The sovereignty and political identity of each of the two German states should not be put into question by either side. The governments of both German states are called upon to stress that they are conscious of and will act according to their responsibility for the stability and security of Europe.

No destabilization of Europe, and therefore of the world, should originate on German soil.

We expect clear statements about how a sell-out of the GDR's goods and services and the entry of neo-Nazis and other right-wing radicals into the country can be prevented in the face of the abolition of visa permits and of the requirement for a minimum exchange of currency for Westerners traveling into the GDR.

NOTES

Source: Herles/Rose, 28-29.

34
Helmut Kohl's Speech at the Ruins of the Church of Our Lady in Dresden (December 19, 1989)

Ladies and gentlemen, my dear young friends, dear fellow countrymen and countrywomen!

First of all I would like to thank all of you for such a friendly welcome. My dear friends, hundreds of journalists from all over Europe have come to us and I think that together we should show them how we are able to hold a peaceful rally in the heart of Germany. Hence my most sincere request that—despite all our enthusiasm—we now concentrate together in these few minutes on the business of our meeting.

The first thing I want to pass on to you is a warm greeting from all your fellow citizens in the Federal Republic of Germany.

The second thing I would like to communicate to you is my recognition and admiration for this peaceful revolution in the GDR. We are experiencing for the first time in German history a nonviolent revolution that is taking place with such great seriousness and in a spirit of solidarity. I thank you all very much for that. It is a demonstration for democracy, for peace, for freedom, and for the self-determination of our nation. And self-determination means for us—us in the Federal Republic, as well—that we respect your opinion. We will not and do not want to patronize anyone. We will respect what you decide for the future of this country.

Dear friends, I came here today to the talks with your Prime Minister, Hans Modrow, in order to help the GDR in this difficult situation. We will not abandon our fellow countrymen and countrywomen in the GDR. And we know–allow me to say that here, even in view of this enthusiasm, which delights me greatly–how difficult this road to the future is. But together we will travel this road into the German future! Today was my first meeting with Prime Minister Modrow. Both of us are aware that in this historical hour–regardless of our different political heritages–we must try to do our duty for our people.

It was a first discussion, it was also a serious discussion, and it accomplished positive results. We agreed to work intensely in the next few weeks so that as early as spring we will be able to ratify a treaty about cooperation between the Federal Republic of Germany and the GDR. We seek close cooperation in all areas: in the spheres of economics, transportation, environmental protection, in the domains of social policy and of culture. Above all, we seek in the sphere of economics the closest possible cooperation, with the clear aim of improving living conditions here in the GDR as quickly as possible. We want people to feel comfortable here. We want them to remain in their homeland and be able to find happiness here. It is decisive for the future that people in Germany be able to come together, that free movement in both directions be permanently guaranteed.

We want people in Germany to be able to meet wherever they want to. Dear friends, in the coming year you will have free elections. You will decide freely who will sit in your parliament, provided with your trust. You will have a freely elected government. And then the time will have come for what I have called "confederative structures"–that means: joint governmental committees, joint parliamentary committees–so that in Germany we can live with as many common interests as possible.[1] And let me also say, on this square that is rich in tradition, that my goal is–whenever the historical hour allows it–the unity of our nation.

Dear friends, I know that we can reach this goal and that this hour will come if we work for it together–and if we do it with reason and with good judgment, with a sense for what is possible. It is a difficult road, but it is a good road; our common future is at stake. I also know that this cannot be reached from one day to the next. We Germans do not live alone in Europe and in the world. A glance at the map demonstrates that everything that changes here must have consequences for our neighbors, for our neighbors to the east and for our neighbors to the west. It makes no sense not to acknowledge that many will watch with apprehension, and some even with fear, as we take this road. But no good can come of fears. As

Germans we have to tell our neighbors: Considering the history of this century, we understand some of these fears. We will take them seriously.

Naturally, we want to represent the interests we have as Germans. We affirm the right of self-determination to which all people of this world are entitled—even the Germans. But if we want to realize this right of self-determination for the Germans, we cannot disregard the security needs of others. We want a world with more peace and more freedom, a world that knows more togetherness and no more confrontation. The "German house"—our common house—must be built under a European roof. That must be the aim of our politics. In a few days the nineties will begin, the last decade of this century. It has been a century in which, above all in Europe and also here in Germany, there has been much poverty, much misery, many deaths, much sorrow—a century that laid upon us Germans a special responsibility—in view of the terrible things that happened.

Here at the ruins of the Church of Our Lady in Dresden, a memorial to those killed in Dresden, I laid down a wreath—to commemorate the suffering and remember those who died in this spectacularly beautiful old German city. In 1945—and I say this to the young people here on the square—I was 15 years old, a schoolboy, a child. I then had the chance to grow up "on the other side," in my homeland in the Palatinate, and I belong to that young generation who took an oath after the war—just as you did here—"Never again war, never again violence!"[2] I would like to add to this oath, while standing here in front of you: in the future, only peace should ever have its source on German soil—that is the aim of our commonality!

But, dear friends, true peace is not possible without freedom. That is why you are fighting, that is why you are demonstrating for freedom in the GDR, that is why we support you, and that is why you deserve our solidarity. Dear friends, we are only a couple of days away from Christmas—the celebration of peace. Christmas, that is the holiday for family and friends. Especially in these days, we in Germany feel ourselves to be a German family again. All of us have felt this during these weeks and days. Let me remind us all of the moving images we saw in the middle of Germany in September, in October, in November—of those images that showed how friends and relatives met each other again; we waited for that for over forty years. We are thankful that we can experience this now. All this did not happen by itself. Many people helped bring it about, not least of whom were the citizens on the streets and squares of the GDR. But in the outside world many also helped. And I have good reason for mentioning Michail Gorbachev's politics of perestroika, which also created these possibilities, the Solidarity freedom movement in Poland, the reformers in Hungary.

Dear friends, we are thankful for this. Now it is a matter of continuing peacefully down this road in the time that lies ahead of us, with patience, with good judgment, and together with our neighbors. Let us work together for this goal, let us help each other in a spirit of solidarity. I greet from here in Dresden all our fellow countrymen and countrywomen in the GDR and in the Federal Republic of Germany. I wish all of you and us a peaceful Christmas, a happy 1990.

God bless our German fatherland!

NOTES

Source: Zanetti, 266-69. The Church of Our Lady in Dresden, built from 1726 to 1743 by G. Bähr, was one of the many representative baroque buildings that made this beautiful city along the Elbe into "the Venice of the North." The Church was destroyed by bombs in the Second World War and never rebuilt; it stands as a monument to the war dead.

1. At this point Chancellor Kohl is still referring to the "confederative structures" first outlined in his ten-point program. These structures would regulate the economic, political, and cultural relations between the two German states.
2. The "Rhineland-Palatinate" is one the federal states of the Federal Republic of Germany.

35
Günter de Bruyn, "Pious Wishes, Open Questions"

Pious wishes, *pia desideria*, were indeed such, as long as one was pious, and therefore were not without effect, at least on the wishers themselves. Not until later, in less pious times, when people no longer believed in their power, could they not be fulfilled. Even political wishes have their value in times of transition, quite apart from whether they can be fulfilled at all. They are reality, even when they can't (even partially) be fulfilled. They can lend courage and elan to the oppressed and frighten those in power. Plans for salvation and party programs depend on them, all of which–including the conservative ones, which want what is utterly impossible, namely a standstill–have goals that lie completely out of reach and yet are still useful.

When, in the wake of a double protest movement that manifested itself in flight and revolts, Egon Krenz was permitted to take
his high office, it became clear in his statements of the first days
that he wished to appear as the personification of a transition, yet
one of GDR conservatism. All the changes he wanted to allow were
intended to maintain the status quo and hence were not of a fundamental but of a modifying nature. He attempted to rescue the theory by calling those changes in socialist countries inspired by crises
changes that followed certain set laws. The practice of socialism
he declared sacrosanct: socialism under the leadership of his
party. Since, in Krenz's opinion, all freedoms demanded from below
and granted from above could not change anything in this,
"socialist pluralism" was to become the playground for future creativity: one established by the majority party, on which it is also
allowed to play, but which it can close again at any time.

It was not long before Krenz, reacting to the protest movement,
distanced himself from this initial concept of the "first leader of
the state and the party."[1] But even for him the insight came too
late. And the party? From that point on the leadership role was
not to be abandoned, but not incorporated into the constitution, either. Instead, it was to be won again each day, a concession with
which the SED sacrificed its professed claim to the leadership role
but did not yet lose its dominance. In the beginning, at least, the
party can respond to the wishes of the people by playing the game
of party equality without loss of power, since it still controls the
state. *The* party, as it was colloquially called for decades, and
rightly so, had transformed the state into an administrative and
executive organ of its power, and it is doubly present through the
integration of its people into the state on every level as well as
through the functionaries of its own hierarchy. The replacement of
a few men who made themselves particularly noticeable in an unpleasant way cannot hide the fact that the actual power centers in
Berlin, in the district and county seats, do not reside in the buildings of the state offices, but in those—no less large—of the party officials.

Even the previous bloc parties, which in the past could only
vote "yes" or in the best case remain silent, have at their disposal
the means to make the game serious, although they are modest, if
still functional, in comparison with those of the leadership party.
They possess not only a preserved party apparatus and the rooms
that go along with it, but also presses, publishing houses, and several newspapers with which they could venture not just to fill their

prescribed role in the game, but rather to strive for political power or go into the opposition. The chance for them to participate with a good conscience lies in the different interpretations of the term "socialism." Because their role calls for them not to share the world-view of the majority party, they are also not bound to its doctrine, which prescribes the explanation of politico-economic concepts, and hence could take what is sacrosanct as something for which the term social justice exists. But as a hindrance, Article 1 of the constitution also stood in their way, because it would hardly have been credible if they had presented themselves to the voters as an alternative to those previously in power and at the same time had accepted them as the leading power. In order to be successful, they would need a program that distinguishes itself from the party in power through more than adjectives (like Christian or Liberal) and a membership that is not just–as up until now–simply taken care of or tolerated, but that wants to be politically successful.

The established parties share their lack of a clear-cut agenda with a third group lacking both history and possessions, which has neither political experience nor organizational structures nor meeting rooms nor publishing opportunities, and not even official authorization. They are not the bearers, but rather the product of the democratic people's movement, whose demands they partially helped formulate, and their strength lies–at least for now–in their fresh and untarnished engagement. That their agendas seem so vague results, on the one hand, from the tactic of the established parties of adopting the demands for civil freedoms and ecological improvements as part of their catalog of promises, and on the other hand, however, from the fact that the new movements share the identical democratic starting points and an identical goal, one that is decisive for their future political work. All of them want to transform single-party rule to democratic rule without attacking the socialistic foundations, and only after that do they want to establish priorities–out of caution and insecurity. They have no solutions for the economy that has fallen into crisis, and it is difficult for them to assess which of their demands can be fulfilled by the reforms of the leadership party before the elections and where after that the gaps and deficits are. Because they are all of the opinion that it is not socialism that failed, but rather its particular Stalinist form, and because they have set as their goal the bold and honorable but precarious, never-before-realized experiment of democratic socialism, it is conceivable that the winds of change might not blow in their sails but in those of a reformed leadership party.

In this early stage of rapid development it would be premature to predict more than that the pious wishes will lose their driving force and only be realized partially because they (as, for example, the industrial upswing, including the anticipated flood of cars and–in contradiction with this–the end of environmental pollution) stand in the way of each other. The free elections, in case they ever occur, will bring surprises, and not just because the extent of the economic plight under which they will take place is unknown, but also because for the first time *the* people who belong neither to the old parties nor to the new and who also are not going out into the streets, will express themselves politically. Without drawing premature conclusions, it should be considered that hundreds of thousands brought about the reforms by means of flight or protests, but millions took spontaneous advantage of the opening of the borders to move toward the display windows of the German West, voluntarily, heedless of the exertion, in impressive euphoria. The question as to whether it was primarily the new and previously inaccessible that drew them, a long dreamt-of prosperity that was so attractive, or also (or above all) feelings of national solidarity that set in, cannot be answered today, but it can be decisive for the future. That during the protest demonstrations, which were characterized not only by discipline and peaceableness, but also by political restraint, demands for German unity were initially not heard at all and were later not predominant, should not deceive us into thinking they did not exist.

As it appears, the opposition activists have developed a GDR state consciousness that is stronger than the one previously proscribed. This consciousness is made up of pride in the things achieved by means of democratic protests, of insight into what can be accomplished in Europe today, of the vision of social justice, and of defiance against the rich, patronizing relatives in the West (to whom one must also be grateful). It does not take seriously national feelings, which are often accused of serving as a cover for chauvinism or the drive to prosperity. It must be assumed that the new parties will thus fail to represent large portions of the electorate. These will perhaps lay their stakes on the "safety and security" of the leadership party, which in this respect has proven itself up to now, or else on the unity of the Germans, which promises them the less certain but more tangible prosperity. The unrealistic taboo on the German Question, practiced for two decades, is merely perpetu-

ated when, in the lofty proclamation "For our country," the old slogans of definition, including an enemy in new guise, are offered and
jointly approved by the independent organizations in the style of
the old bloc parties, instead of the reasonable explanation that the
sensitive stability of Europe should, in the name of peace, not be
disturbed by German unity before European unity. But to force all
national concerns to the right could soon prove dangerous. For the
alternative dream of the true, but now really perfected socialism
(no longer hindered by the hunting lodges of the few guilty ones)
has already been dreamt by many for far too long.

NOTES

Source: Naumann, 23-29. Translated by Laura Jackson.

1. According to the principle of democratic centralism followed in the
GDR, the chair of the *Staatsrat* served simultaneously as the leader of the
party.

36
Helmut Kohl's New Year's Television Address to the German People (January 1, 1990)

Dear fellow countrymen and countrywomen!
The past year was a year of great transformation in the history
of Europe. The people in the GDR and in other states of Central,
Eastern, and Southern Europe fought successfully for freedom, human rights, and self-determination after over forty years. The realization of these principal values is a prerequisite for the construction of a common European house. That is why we all hope that the
reforms will be successful.

For us Germans, but also for all our friends in West and East, the
opening of the Berlin Wall—and now of the Brandenburg Gate, as
well—was a fascinating event. For 28 long years the Wall was the
symbol of the inhuman division of Germany and Europe.

The most moving images of the year 1989 came from the border,
which finally opened for everyone. Who could ever forget the joy
and the happiness in the faces of those people who were able to
find their way to each other again?

I was deeply moved by the warm reception the people in Dresden gave me. We can be proud of our fellow countrymen and countrywomen for their courageous engagement for freedom, human

rights, and self-determination. Their prudence, their persistence, and their political judgment are exemplary. . . .

Even after decades of division, the awareness of the unity of our nation is alive. . . .

The past year brought us a good bit closer to the unity of our fatherland. But without the fundamental changes in the Soviet Union, in Hungary, and in Poland, the peaceful revolution in the GDR would not have been possible. We would like to acknowledge this thankfully. . . .

. . . Freedom remains our supreme possession. Without it real peace cannot be secured. Without it there is no prosperity, no social progress, and hence also no chance for real solidarity with the "Third World." . . .

All democratically minded people and nations have to stand together in solidarity. We therefore remain firmly anchored in the community of values shared by the Western democracies. That is the only way to secure and maintain peace and freedom in Germany and Europe. At the same time, we ought not forget the poverty and problems of the people of the "Third World."

In my Ten-Point Plan for German Unity I sketched a road along which the German nation can regain its unity in free self-determination. The authorization of independent political parties and free elections in the GDR are important steps down this road.

We want to do everything possible to improve the economic situation for the people in the GDR quickly and noticeably. They should feel contented in their homeland–in Mecklenburg and Thuringia, in Brandenburg, Sachsen, and Sachsen-Anhalt.

German unity and European unification have to be pursued together. Germany is our fatherland, Europe our future! The European Community ought not end at the Elbe River.[1] . . .

The decade that lies ahead of us can be the happiest for our nation in this century: it affords us the chance for a free and united Germany in a free and united Europe. Our contribution will be decisive in this process.

I greet all Germans. God bless our fatherland.

NOTES

Source: Weiland, 10-12.

1. The Elbe River runs through Central Europe from Czechoslovakia to Dresden, Madgeburg, and then north through Hamburg.

Government Policy Statement by Hans Modrow, Chair of the *Ministerrat* of the GDR, Before the *Volkskammer* (January 11, 1990)

Mr. President, honored delegates!

The government I head has been in office for almost eight weeks now. In spite of the brevity of this time period, I think it is time to give you a first accounting. The people of the GDR and the *Volkskammer* have a right to such information.

Let me first say a word of thanks. It goes out to all those who have supported the activities of this government, assisted us with advice, criticism, and action. It goes out above all to those citizens whose work made the work of this government possible.

If the GDR passed several difficult tests in these days, if it gained a bit of democracy, a bit of freedom and respect, then it is the people, who set down a new, a good path, who deserve the credit for this. Those who work, those who are prudent, and those who are restless in this country deserve the credit; they are the ones in the GDR who turned a new page in the book of German history and began to write a new chapter of this history.

All those who unleashed this democratic renewal and today are participating in it should at the same time understand: we have been afforded a historical opportunity that should be used without hesitation and ought not be undermined or gambled away.

A new politics was initiated, although–let me add this–a great deal of the old politics has to be completed. The time was too short to shape this in such a way and to conclude it. We experienced the opening of the borders to the Federal Republic of Germany and to West Berlin, the millions of human contacts, but also recognized the dangers of this development, which were demonstrated in the acts of vandalism at the Brandenburg Gate.[1] An irreversible process of democratization has begun, a great test for the people of the GDR, a test viewed by the eyes of the entire world. The most important observations I can make about this today are: we have for the most part succeeded in maintaining a peaceful existence. The word "nonviolence" has become the sign of this democratic revolution. We have for the most part succeeded in keeping the economy working and guaranteeing the supply of goods, although services have suffered. We have for the most part succeeded in maintaining social stability. At the same time, we know that it is by no means perfect and that many citizens are worrying about their future. I share these worries, but I also have reason to say optimistically: all of us together, we are the entire republic, we have the power and economic substance to face these problems. We should all have the courage and the will to grapple with them.

Dear legislators! The internal political situation in the GDR is, as you know, still contradictory. Let me mention some significant points that are really quite different in nature. In most of the businesses, people are working responsibly and with great effort. The departure of skilled workers, however, is painfully evident in many places. Of great consequence is also the temporary absence of workers who have traveled to the Federal Republic or to West Berlin and who, through this loss in productivity, magnified a number of economic problems. Our economy currently needs about 250,000 laborers. At the same time, we need to integrate into the workforce tens of thousands of people who lost or will be losing their jobs. To guarantee them the right to work in many instances demands retraining, a complicated process for many of them, especially for older people who are faced with making a new beginning.
. . .

Let me address a completely different aspect of domestic policy. We have registered with great concern acts of violence, acts by neo-Nazis or by people who potentially could become neo-Nazis, as well as hatred of foreigners. The deplorable graffiti at the memorial in Berlin Treptow is merely one symptom of this.[2] On January 1 in Karl-Marx-Stadt you could hear the call "Communists out– Nazis in." From Beeskow we hear that young people in civilian clothing were brutally beaten only because they attend officers' training schools.

The slogans of rowdies, such as "dirty communist pigs" and "We'll beat you all to death," indicate the political position and danger posed by certain extremist groups. Together we will have to mobilize all democratic forces decisively against such phenomena.

It is also necessary to rigorously bring in the organizations of state power. It is high time to guard against the beginnings of an extremism that is obviously starting to have a considerably greater effect from across the border.

International experience teaches us that aside from the army and the police there have to be constitutional mechanisms for guaranteeing justice and security with specific means. This is the task of the intelligence agency of the GDR and the bureau of investigation under civilian leadership. It is a matter of guaranteeing peace, of maintaining our sovereignty, of strengthening the economy, of protecting the population from dangers resulting from terrorism, drug-related crime, extremism, and ecological crime. The work of these new agencies should concentrate on these issues. This must happen on a legal basis and under legislative control, as well as being subject to public scrutiny. . . .

We are working under the assumption that, as early as January 15, the government, represented by the Attorney General, will provide the Round Table with detailed information about the security situation, and that then a way has to be found to protect the safety of the citizens. . . .

The government seeks constructive cooperation with the Round Table and it has demonstrated this in its deeds. On December 22, for example, Professor Luft and other representatives of the government, upon the request of the Round Table, made statements about economic, financial, and social policies. We will continue this practice, since the government needs and seeks the advice of the parties and groups participating at the Round Table. . . .

I would like to call upon the Round Table in particular to make substantive proposals for my next meeting with Chancellor Helmut Kohl. The same is true for suggestions or detailed ideas about the future participation of the GDR in COMECON. The participants at the Round Table were offered the chance to work with the government, in the capacity of civilian control, to dissolve the Office for National Security. At the same time, we proposed assisting the Round Table, upon request, by making governmental experts available.

It should not go unmentioned that the *Ministerrat* decided on December 21 to support the work of the Round Table. This creates significantly better working conditions for the new parties and groups. They will be supported directly by the state in all personnel and financial matters, as well as in other ways, until legislation is passed regulating political parties.

What we are still today lacking from the Round Table, however, are thoroughly discussed proposals for a law governing political parties and elections. Both are urgently needed so that–as planned–elections can be planned for and held on May 6. . . .

Let me add this: attempts to publicly call into question the legitimacy of this government or to control its work by means of a right to veto its resolutions do not serve the establishment of orderly political conditions under which one can work properly, either within the government or at the workplace in the factories.

Every citizen has the right publicly to express his or her criticism, and no one should forego that right. But every citizen should have an interest in the functionable working of the government. Anyone who believes that a prime minister and his cabinet can work under the threat of veto by one political group is ill advised. The same is true for ultimatums about when and where I am supposed to appear within one hour. And where the supposed illegitimacy of this government is concerned, I do not remember having become prime minister by means of a coup! The generally accepted political agreement says that this government–if it does not resign for compelling reasons–will remain in office and be active until a new parliament is elected on May 6 and a new government is formed.

That is no longer a long time. From the very beginning, however, I did not view it as my responsibility to think solely up to May 6 and avoid all decisions that reach beyond that date. One could ruin this country very quickly and thoroughly by acting in such a stupid way. The crisis in our economy and our society that we have to overcome is already profound enough. It would be irresponsible to increase it in any way whatsoever. I took over a bad inheritance, and not because I am presumptuous, but because I feel an obligation primarily toward the people of this country. The same is true for the members of this government. We therefore have to be active and see to it that the citizens have trust in their country, in their government, and in the further shaping of our democratic renewal, and that this trust is deepened.

But we also have to make resolutions that go beyond May 6 if we want to seriously address and realize economic reforms, if it is a matter of protecting the environment; for that, too, requires a long-term view and progressively oriented decisions. We are obliged to be accountable for this, and we will meet this obligation today as well as in the future.

In the incipient election campaign we will surely have to be understanding of emotions, controversial positions, and an altogether different picture of domestic politics, one to which most citizens are not accustomed. There can be no understanding for interference from outside or attempts to hold a sort of pre-election campaign on the part of the Federal Republic at the expense of the GDR. The citizens of our state have the absolute right to make their own decisions without patronization or even well-meant advice. I can only advise against burdening the relationship between the GDR and the Federal Republic in such or similar ways. . . .

What the government constantly needs is constructive criticism and above all energetic and expert help for mastering the tasks that have to be resolved in this country day by day. The *Ministerrat* meets on a weekly basis in order to work rigorously through a tight program, if I may put it this way. And information about these meetings is given continually in press conferences in order to inform the public quickly through the media about the resolutions that, in many cases, go back to their initiatives. The *Ministerrat* has proven to be a workable institution, as can be seen on the example of its resolutions, beginning with the reactions to the decisions of the twelfth meeting of the *Volkskammer*. In the foreground stand questions of production and distribution, social questions, problems with the transportation system, and, last but not least, the health care system. . . .

Please allow me some further explanations of the economic situation. At the beginning of the year, roughly two months after the opening of the borders to the Federal Republic and West Berlin, it has become more serious. The government and leading economic agencies are doing everything possible to continue controlling the economic development. The workers in the factories have a decisive influence on this. Under the given circumstances, even if they are unsatisfactory in many workplaces, everything ultimately boils down to the productivity of the individual. Along with the necessary efforts of the state organs, it creates the prerequisites for economic stability and, building on that, economic progress.

Aid for the GDR from the outside is needed and we call for it, but we have to exploit our own possibilities and means of support as much as possible. In every factory people should ask themselves whether their own span of responsibilities, whether their own ideas, whether their own material and financial possibilities are already being optimally exploited. To wait for directions–we have to say this openly–that time ought to be over by now. And we also have to get used to that. . . .

Honored legislators! Please allow me in conclusion some words about the international aspects of the work of this government.

In matters of foreign policy, the government tried to gain external credibility, to secure and, if possible, further improve the international conditions for the process of renewal in our country. As a result of these efforts, we can say today that the GDR has proven itself reliable in its relations with the East and the West and shown especially its neighbors that its actions are predictable. Outsiders give us credit for the fact that the internal processes in the GDR, which can in part be called stormy, have thus far not threatened European stability. They continue to hope for this, and we aim to justify this hope.

Our relations with those states with which the GDR is allied through the Warsaw Pact Treaty are essentially trouble-free today. That is favorable for the road we have taken toward renewal. We know how valuable it is that the Soviet Union is sympathetically following developments in our country. Michail Gorbachev explicitly stressed this in his talks with me.

The cooperation with the USSR, our most important ally and trading partner, has priority for the foreign policy of this government. It is particularly encouraging for us that our political aims and ideas about the present as well as future development above all here in Europe are for the most part identical. We can begin the year 1990 on the best of terms with the Soviet leadership, a year which, according to Michail Gorbachev, must be a key year in disarmament, a year in which freedom, democracy, and equality will be further spread. The most recent developments in Czechoslovakia, Romania, and Bulgaria have significantly strengthened the positions of renewal in those countries. They will further the democratization of relations among the allies of the Warsaw Pact, a process to which we are also committed. From the further transformation of the Warsaw Pact into a primarily political alliance we expect favorable conditions for the disarmament policy pursued by the Warsaw Pact allies, which takes account of the process of rapprochement between East and West in Europe. . . .

Experienced by millions and visible for the entire world, in these last two months there has been an extraordinary intensification of relations between the GDR and the Federal Republic and West Berlin. It goes far beyond what we were accustomed to. The government of the GDR understands the great interest foreign countries show in these developments. We also have taken note of the fact that in the case of the neighbors of both German states, some concerns and even fears have been expressed that could result from a newly emerging German Question. In the name of the government of the GDR I would like to emphasize: we are well aware of the fact that the existence and the relationship of the two German states to each other has ramifications for fundamental positions of European politics. We are aware of the responsibility connected with that. The GDR stands behind its politics of peace and will not do anything that could threaten stability in Europe. Our position on European borders, namely on the Oder-Neiße border with Poland, is definite. Only in a politically stable Europe can we find answers to the new, vitally important questions of European politics that will be beneficial to all nations.

The government of the GDR–and it is not alone in this–is of the opinion that a unification of the GDR and the FRG is not on the agenda. The prospects of the relationship of both German states with each other is a question of the future. The answer must and can only be given within the context of the pan-European development. We are pursuing the idea of a common European house in the understanding that the step-by-step abolishment of the opposition between East and West will lead to the overcoming of the division of Europe. That necessitates an intensification of European cooperation that goes as far as the dissolution of military alliances and extensive disarmament, whereby we have to say that unilateral concessions made by the Warsaw Pact have not yet been met equally by NATO.[3] The GDR and the FRG can support the European process immensely with their proposed treaty union. This way they will also work together for the interests of Europe.

As you know, Chancellor Kohl and I agreed in Dresden to continue our meetings and to come to further important agreements. It is in the interest of Europe and in the interest of both German states that the economy of the GDR quickly be made capable of operating on a large scale and with high effectiveness in international cooperation. This requires substantial financial aid from the FRG. This will certainly be beneficial for the people in both German states.

In this context let me also point out that one cannot speak of a sell-out of the GDR. Anyone who draws this conclusion, for example, from the agreement between our IFA-conglomerate for automobiles with Volkswagen to develop a modern compact car, is mistaken. The same is true of further plans for cooperation, capital investment, or sales partnerships. The interests of the GDR, above all of the workers, will be protected.

To put it more clearly: it was not too much, but rather too little participation of the GDR in international cooperation that is one factor responsible for the present situation of our economy. We do not need so-called national autonomy, but international cooperation. Everything we are doing today and everything that will be done in the future should serve the purpose of making life easier for the citizens of the GDR and giving them a reason to remain in their traditional homeland. Neither we nor the Federal Republic can be interested in the opposite development, the kind we have experienced over the past year. In this hour all of us should recognize our own responsibility for ourselves and our families, for the further democratic renewal of the GDR, for a cooperative relation of the two German states, and for a peaceful coexistence in Europe.

In these brief eight weeks the government has tried to summon the energy to do justice to the tasks with which it was charged. It dared a new beginning–just like the GDR as a whole. It must answer for this in the judgment of the people and the *Volkskammer*. If and where it has accomplished something, this is the result of cooperation, the result of the coalition. The cooperation in this coalition government was and is constructive. Mutual information and consultation belong just as much to normal relations as do criticism. I am thankful for this cooperative spirit. Above all, I would like to ask the *Volkskammer* and the citizens of our country to place their trust in my government for a further stretch along this road, to lend their support. And in this hour I also call upon the Round Table to work together with us constructively and in full awareness of our responsibility to the people.

NOTES

Source: *Europa-Archiv*, 45 (1990): 99-108.

1. Modrow is referring to a series of vandalizations of official monuments and gravestones that occurred throughout Germany on New Year's Eve 1989; they were presumed to have been committed by neo-Nazi groups and skinheads.
2. On January 3, 1990, the Soviet memorial in Berlin Treptow was covered with racist and xenophobic graffitti; the PDS used this incident to organize an antifascist mass demonstration, despite the fact that the Stasi was rumored to have been involved in this act of vandalism.
3. At that time the Warsaw Pact had already made significant steps toward its dissolution; it was formally dissolved in 1991.

38
Statement by the Chair of the *Ministerrat* of the GDR, Hans Modrow, Addressed to the Participants at the Round Table (January 15, 1990)

Ladies and gentlemen!

It was difficult for me to accept your invitation, and it is unavoidable that I will have to leave after about an hour in order to be present at the New Year's meeting of the diplomatic corps.

Please take my presence today–I will make another proposal to you in a minute–as a sign of good will and, above all, of my great concern about the domestic political situation.

In my most recent government policy statement I addressed the restless people in our country, people who will be needed for a further democratic development. At the same time–and that is not a contradiction–reason and good judgment are necessary so that the GDR will not fall apart. If that were to happen, and some people seem to want that, the citizens of this republic, those of the Federal Republic, and the political stability in Europe would be ill-served, indeed they would see a black day.

All of us have the responsibility for preventing this. Therefore I appeal to the citizens of the GDR to remain prudent. I plead once again to a number of politicians and media in the Federal Republic of Germany not to turn the GDR into a playground for their interference. And I ask the representatives of all parties and groups here at the Round Table not to let the Prime Minister and his government fail at their task but to make sure that they can do the necessary work.

Everyone who lays claim to political responsibility may come to a point at which he or she has to decide between the general welfare and the aims of party politics. When I took office I decided to work for the interests of *all* citizens. It would be a matter of fairness to acknowledge this. For the citizens of the GDR it would be beneficial to support this work.

I hope that the questions on the agenda for today can be answered in a satisfactory manner by the government representatives. I have drawn some consequences from the criticism expressed on January 8.[1] Mr. Koch was relieved of his duties as government official responsible for the dissolution of the Office for National Security.

Let me take this opportunity to thank the representatives of the Protestant and Catholic churches as well as the Task Force of Christian Churches for their efforts in support of the Round Table and of domestic peace in the GDR.

In my statement to the *Volkskammer* on January 11, I already stressed the important, indeed, indispensable work the Round Table is performing in the service of democratic renewal. Let me repeat and emphasize:

The government needs and seeks the advice of the parties and groups participating at the Round Table. Democratization as well as stabilization and economic reform need the consensus of all responsible forces. That it has to be found by way of discussion follows from the political pluralism not merely of those represented at the Round Table, but especially from the complicated situation in the

GDR. I do not and did not have any other understanding of the Round Table.

What I request of you includes three main items:

First, and foremost, we should join in making sure that the further domestic political development proceeds peacefully, that the humanistic slogan of the revolution begun in October, "no violence!," remains valid. Our responsibility for the lives and the health of our citizens as well as our responsibility to the world demands this.

Second, I would like to ask for your assistance so that the work in all areas of the economy can be accomplished undisturbed and as productively as possible, in order that our daily life can run its normal course and the reform processes can be continued. I also consider this a necessary prerequisite for the greater effectiveness of the financial aid promised by the Federal Republic of Germany.

Third, I would like to ask you to use your political influence so that the citizens of the GDR remain in their traditional homelands. No one can expect miracles after only about eight weeks of work by this government. I assure all citizens of the GDR, however: our country has the realistic chance, through our own efforts and through aid from outside, of achieving a stabilization of material production and distribution within this year, which will mark the beginning of prosperity. It is worth staying in the GDR.

On the basis of what I have just said, let me emphasize and expand on the proposals my government has presented to the Round Table. These are in particular:

–the immediate and responsible participation in the work of the government through competent representatives;

–the cooperation in commissions, task forces, and other government committees, as well as in its organizations, including the committee on the economy;

–the contribution of substantial ideas for my next meeting with the Chancellor of the FRG, especially for the content of our treaty agreements;

–the participation of a group of representatives of the Round Table in the meeting with the Chancellor of the FRG;

–the participation in the preparation of laws and measures and other important decisions of the *Ministerrat*, with the aim of making the work of the government more efficient. I have in mind participation in the drafting of necessary reforms, which should take effect before May 6, as well as participation in the work of the GDR in COMECON, but also and especially participation in regulations and more effective methods for the quick redeployment of those energies that have or will become available.

We will provide you with the requested disclosure of information about economic realities and facts upon reaching a timely agreement.

Concerning the dissolution of the Office for National Security and the originally proposed two new offices, I refer to my statements at the last meeting of the *Volkskammer*. As I stated then, no new offices will be formed before May 6. The government will inform the public about the further dissolution of the Office for National Security. Today government representatives will explain to you the details on the basis of resolutions made by the *Ministerrat*. I ask once again for your cooperation in the civil control of the dissolution of said office.

On the basis of these primary requests put to the government and of the proposals of the Round Table, government representatives with professional competence and proper authority will continue to be available to assist the discussions of the Round Table.

In light of the weight and urgency of the pressing problems, I propose to you that my representatives Luft and Moreth, the further members of the *Ministerrat* Fischer, Meyer, and Wünsche, as well as myself, have ample opportunity at the January 22 meeting of the Round Table to hear your views, to express our own opinions, and to answer questions.

Let me repeat: it is my particular concern that the government retain your support in order that it be able to act.
Ladies and gentlemen!

According to the agenda, you will now hear the report of the government on domestic security, delivered by the Minister for Internal Affairs, Mr. Ahrendt, as well as the preliminary report on the state of the dissolution of the Office for National Security. Mr. Manfred Sauer, head of the Secretariat of the *Ministerrat*, will speak to you about that.

If you will permit, I would like to make the following statement with regard to the second report.

1. The materials of which you and, via the media, the citizens have become aware were the object of many deliberations, ultimately even in the *Ministerrat* over the weekend. The primary purpose of these was to heed, during the preparation of the preliminary report, all those justified criticisms about the unsatisfactory revelation of facts that were voiced here at the Round Table as

well as in the *Volkskammer*. That means that we decisively urged that an intensive and thorough examination and investigation take place, a decisive precondition for an effective, accelerated procedure for the dissolution of the Office for National Security and for the elimination of the old structures of the former Office for National Security.

2. At the same time the government commission was and is being reconfigured; it now contains a new head and will be further supported by competent assistants. Thanks to these measures, as well as to the determination of exact dates for the next step in the dissolution of the Office for National Security, it will be possible to conclude this process earlier than originally planned. We will, of course, keep the Round Table and our citizens informed about this.

3. Finally, I would like to stress once more the willingness of my coalition government for cooperation. There should not only be closer cooperation between our government representatives and the Round Table's task force for security, but–I would like to reiterate this–the offer to the Round Table to participate directly in the work of the government for the dissolution of the Office for National Security through civil control still stands. We are also willing, if necessary, to support the Round Table's task force for security by supplying them with the assistance of governmental specialists.

To conclude: I am hoping for close cooperation between the government and the Round Table. It is not only a matter of working through the past in this area as well. Above all, it is a matter of eliminating the reasons for existing fears once and for all and of building mutual trust. Without this mutual trust progress on the road to democratic renewal is not possible. We should all agree on this–and that is my most cherished wish–not only here at the Round Table, but in our country as a whole.

NOTES

Source: Herles/Rose, 54-58.

1. On January 8, the opposition in the GDR decided at the Round Table to annul its cooperation with the government because of disagreements with the way Modrow handled the dissolution of the Office for National Security.

39

Resolutions of the Eighth Meeting of the Round Table Concerning Relations Between the Round Table and the Government of the GDR (January 18, 1990)

I

The Round Table disapproves of the fact that on 11 and 12 January 1990, the government presented legislation regarding constitutional changes for ratification by the *Volkskammer* without prior public discussion.

The Round Table demands that the government make available to the Round Table all draft legislation, in particular laws dealing with the constitution as well as with property rights in the GDR, before their ratification by the *Volkskammer*, and that a proper amount of time be allowed for their public discussion.

II

The Round Table disapproves of the fact that the executive council of the *Volkskammer* refused to give participants of the Round Table the right to speak at the fourteenth meeting of the *Volkskammer* on January 11 and 12, 1990.

The Round Table demands from the executive council of the *Volkskammer* that for all further meetings of the *Volkskammer* until the election, members of all the new parties and groups represented at the Round Table will be invited and supplied with limited parliamentary rights, such as the right to speak before the *Volkskammer* and the right to make inquiries of the government.

III

In reference to the information of the Independent Investigation Committee (IIC), the Round Table demands that the government or the *Volkskammer* reexamine all sales of real estate, businesses, and similar assets of the people's property made since July 10, 1989, as well as sales of contested property of parties and organizations, to determine whether they were legal.

(The following is the information of the Independent Investigation Committee).

We have become members of the IIC. This IIC sees its function as administering the revocation of those privileges that do not rest on the accomplishments and creativity of individual persons, but rather were claimed almost automatically by higher functionaries of the SED and the state apparatus.

While we were trying to investigate the numerous reports from the population which are supposed to uncover the privileges of functionaries, the government passed the following resolutions:

1. A resolution on the sale of single family houses that are the property of the former public assistance agency of the *Ministerrat*.

–In this case the former renters (such as Mr. Krenz) received purchase rights and financing for 75%. These very favorable terms were supposed to be met by January 31, 1990.

2. A resolution on determining the social security benefits for the members of the Office for National Security.

–The members of the Office were offered similarly favorable terms for the purchase rights of homes of the former Ministry for Security.

3. A resolution on the information about vacation homes and guest villas of the *Ministerrat*.

–This resolution only includes a condition of possible use by the population.

At the same time, the SED-PDS retains ownership of the guest villas and recreational homes that are now bringing in money for the party by being used as hotels.

All these resolutions were signed by the Prime Minister on December 12, 1989, and are valid from that date on. There is no public information about them.

Some citizens of the IIC are representatives of the opposition in the *Ministerrat's* Committee for Investigating Misuse of Power and Corruption, under the direction of Professor Dähn, which was demanded by the Round Table. On the basis of numerous civilian protests, Professor Dähn, in his capacity as government representative, and the IIC submitted proposals to the government on January 4, 1990 and on January 9, 1990 for the elimination of all unjustified privileges.

For example, an immediate moratorium on the sale of the above-mentioned properties; the conversion into communal property of those businesses that up to now primarily served the realization of the privileges of functionaries.

In the government policy statement of the *Volkskammer* of January 11, 1990, none of the proposals of the IIC were heeded. Our experience has been that investigations are being obstructed on a massive scale. To this very day there are attempts to conceal structures and cover up connections. We ask whether it is coincidental that all government representatives for the disclosure of official misconduct and corruption in the districts are members of the SED-PDS.

On December 4, 1989, we were willing to enter into a pragmatic alliance with the government to secure the people's property and the elimination of privileges. We have to state for the record that our work as IIC has been and is being exploited to create misgivings among the citizens.

Up to now we have no records about the properties owned by the SED, no information about the revision of all accounts of the Branch for Commercial Coordination, and we do not know whether the money from foreign currency exchanges is indeed flowing into the state budget. We were refused permission to look at the existing documents about real estate, property, and businesses owned by the SED and the *Ministerrat*. The claim to democratization made by the SED and the other old parties will have to be measured by whether of not they are willing to make their assets public and verifiable.

IV

By petition of the task force on the economy and especially in light of the planned economic reform, it was resolved:

The Round Table demands from the government, beginning with the month of January, that the government produce and publicly distribute publications about its resolutions and discussion materials.

V

The Round Table reminds the government once more of the insufficient disclosure of economic facts, in particular of the extent and structure of subsidies.

By petition of the Free German Trade Union Association (*FDGB*) on December 22, 1989 to the acting president of the *Ministerrat*, Professor Luft, it was agreed to present a fundamental concept for changes in policies governing prices and subsidies.

In this context we will have to clarify the difference between the redistribution of subsidies and the elimination of subsidies.

The first price changes have been resolved. We declare unambiguously: we are for price reform. In the cases of further price changes, which must be introduced, however, we have to make sure that in particular citizens and families who have a limited income or who, because of their size, have a very low per capita income, will not be pushed to the limits of a minimal subsistence.

We therefore demand that the government's promise given on December 22, 1989 be honored before further price hikes take effect.

We also expect from the government a breakdown of the price index that reflects the real development in prices, as well as statements about the minimal subsistence level.

NOTES

Source: Herles/Rose, 71-74.

40
Plan for a Unified Germany, Presented by Hans Modrow, Chair of the *Ministerrat* of the GDR (February 1, 1990)

Europe is entering a new phase of its development. The postwar chapter is being finished. The prerequisites for the peaceful and neighborly cooperation of all nations are beginning to take shape. The unification of the two German states is on the agenda.

The German people will find their place in the construction of a new peaceful order, whose result will be the overcoming of the division of Europe into inimical camps as well as the division of the German nation. The hour has come to bring the Second World War to an end, to ratify a German peace treaty.[1] Such a treaty would regulate all the problems related to the aggression of Hitler's Germany and the failure of the "Third Reich."

A final solution of the German Question can only be achieved by free self-determination of Germans in both states, in cooperation with the Four Powers, and in consideration of the interests of all European states. It must further the pan-European process, which aims at ridding our continent once and for all of military threats. The rapprochement of the two German states and their eventual unification must cease to be perceived as a threat to anyone.

In this spirit, I am proposing a responsible national dialogue. Its aim should be the determination of concrete steps leading to a unified Germany that is to be conceived as a new factor of stability, trust, and peace in Europe.

On the basis of such a dialogue and through bilateral negotiations, the representatives of the GDR and the FRG could find the best possible answers to questions concerning the future of the German nation. The steps along the road to German unity could be:

–Ratification of a treaty about cooperation and good neighborly relations under a treaty partnership, which might already include essential confederative elements like an economic, currency, and transportation union, as well as a common legal system.

–Formation of a confederation of the GDR and the FRG with joint agencies and institutions like, for example, a parliamentary committee, a chamber of federal states, joint executive agencies for certain areas.

–Transference of sovereignty rights of both states to authoritative agencies of the confederation.

–Formation of a unified German state in the form of a German Federation or a German League through elections in both parts of the confederation, convocation of a unified parliament to ratify a unified constitution and a unified government with its seat in Berlin.

Necessary prerequisites for this development are:

–Each of the two German states must be careful to make certain that the steps toward German unity are in accord with its obligations toward other countries and groups of countries, as well as with necessary reforms and changes. The transformation of the GDR into a federal organization would be part of this process. Preservation of stability, justice, and domestic order belong just as necessarily among these absolute prerequisites as do the strict fulfillment of previously ratified treaties between the GDR and the FRG which, among other things, stipulate non-interference in each other's internal affairs.

–Preservation of the interests and rights of the Four Powers as well as the interest of all European nations in peace, sovereignty, and secure borders. The Four Powers should declare their intention to resolve once and for all, after formation of a unified German state, all the questions resulting from the Second World War and the postwar period, including the presence of foreign troops on German soil and the membership in military alliances.

–Military neutrality of the GDR and the FRG on the way to a federation.

This process of German unification should be accomplished on the basis of agreements between the parliaments and governments of the GDR and the FRG. All sides should declare their will to democratic and nonviolent forms of political confrontation and create the necessary guarantees for this, including opinion polls.

This conception avows the democratic, patriotic, progressive ideas and movements for the unity of the German nation based on a common history and the recent past. It avows the humanist and antifascist traditions of the German people.

This conception is addressed to the citizens of the GDR and the FRG, to all European nations and states, and to the international public with the plea for support.

NOTES

Source: *Europa-Archiv*, 45 (1990): 119-20.

1. Because of the Cold War and the division of Germany, a peace treaty officially ending the Second World War was never signed and hence there was no international document regulating the boundaries and other political issues of the successor states to Hitler's Third Reich.

41
Martina Krone, "No More Chances for Us?" (Early February, 1990)

I am not as optimistic as Jens Reich was fourteen days ago. For Mr. Modrow has proclaimed it for us: "Germany, united fatherland" is to define our perspective.

I ask myself where they all went, those with whom I cried out in October: "We are the people. We are not leaving." These two sentences, however, stood for a very specific hope, namely: you cannot chase us away; we will exert our energies here in this country for just, better relationships; there are more of us and therefore we are stronger. Whether or not we were aware at that point that we were not fighting simply against a Politburo, but also had risen up against the all-encompassing State-Security-SED corruption, is only tangential here. We are on the best track to win this battle without violence. But are we really using this chance for the construction of solidarity, without the degeneration "into an elbow society," as it was described in the initial appeal of the New Forum?

A steadily growing majority in this country (and unfortunately also in the New Forum) sees the only hope in the introduction of the social market economy–sometimes it is even given an environmental tinge–and in a speedy unification of the two German states. It seems to me as though quite a few of those who support these goals do not know what they are condoning. But can they know? Our state media industry has, in concert with its counterpart in the West, done everything in its power, for a full forty years, to talk the people out of their real needs and their potential for power.

But then why did we rise up in the first place?

The disregard for the interests of the broader levels of the population had become unbearable to us. We were conscious of the problems, but every attempt to correct the prescribed course was seen immediately as a test of power and handled accordingly. Although there were always more and more bodies popping up everywhere who stood up against the authorities, the desired system of repression nonetheless always made sure that they remained isolated and gave up. The last resort for the unteachable, then, was the possibility of flight, because prison was, on account of the ever more courageously practiced solidarity–we recall here the storming of the environmental library in October of 1987 or the events of January of 1988–no longer an option for those defenders of power who were wary of their good reputation as wise national fathers.[1] The circumstances in the corporations as well as in the universities, the condition of national education or of the health care system: we were prevented from carrying out every intervention; we were simply degraded into voiceless marionettes.

We could not put up with it all anymore. And now? Instead of the personal initiative we have been demanding for years, we are pushing for the business people of the FRG to make our businesses profitable as soon as possible, so that we can finally buy everything we want. But these experts could neither prevent the rise in rents in their own country, to the point where a growing segment of the population can no longer pay them, nor the fact that approximately two million welfare recipients are living under the subsistence level. What good is the most booming private economic sector to them? It has also not occurred to them to put the brakes on the process of monopolization, which has forced countless small and medium-sized businesses into bankruptcy. Where does the majority in our country get the hope that we will be spared all of that? And the realists among them: what affords them the hope of not being among those whom these things affect?

I suppose it is the magic invocation "performance principle," together with faith in one's own ability to glean all of the advantages from this principle. Yet why, for example, are domestic teachers in the Federal Republic judged more efficient than domestic tutors, and accordingly paid far better for much less work time? Why does a German worker at VW earn decidedly more than his colleague in South Africa? The answer is obvious: because he works longer and harder! That is what he is told, and who does not like to believe such things, when for exactly the same personal reasons the numerous unemployed can be written off as failed existences.

It is the banks, however, with whose support the business concerns exploit the North-South dichotomy and are able to justify such dangerously unhealthy beliefs. The driving force is, plain and simple, economic rationality. Yet in these calculations I miss a couple of the values that we ought to assert as primary in our society: justice and solidarity. "We want to participate in export and world trade, but we want to become neither the debtor nor the servant of the leading industrial nations, nor the exploiter and creditor of economically weaker countries." This is an article from the founding appeal of the New Forum: have we already filed it away?

And now we are filing in to the election. It too was moved forward, so that no time at all would remain to weigh the developmental options, to question them fundamentally. On account of persistently absent analyses of conditions, concrete concepts cannot be hashed out. Populist slogans are taking the place of considerations for our future. This or that individual person no longer has the ability to influence the course of events. At least within party structures: there the direction is prescribed by the steering committees, or whatever those bodies are calling themselves these days.

And within New Forum? Who is calling the shots here? The structuring impulse has gone so far that there are elected spokescouncils, and that elected delegates could take part in the decision regarding the agenda of unification on January 27-28. But who are these spokesmen and occasional spokeswomen? They are the very individuals who could afford to take time to make the necessary rounds through the country, to participate in discussions that lasted whole days and nights, and to establish organizational ties. Yet all those who were not able to simply leave their jobs and remain away from home for days on end, because they were neither private artisans nor pastors nor something else in that vein–that means of course the majority of people in the country–have seen themselves once again become relatively helpless with regard to political events. And they are also the ones who had to learn, to their horror, that a conference of delegates had, for example, deleted from the agenda the for them all-important right to a veto of their management.

Another example is the removal of quotas for women in all positions in society. Once again the same problem: those affected were underrepresented. In their majority, the women present did not have to enter into an all-out fight over the complexities of children-family-workplace. This is the only feasible explanation for why many of the women delegates (and naturally the majority of men) did not recognize the necessity of quotas. How are the overburdened women described above supposed to find a way to actively involve themselves when the assistance of quotas is taken away from them? As it stands, others will always retain the necessary decision-making powers.

With these two decisions, the New Forum has, in my eyes, forsaken the claim to represent the interests of the domestic (in both senses of the word) citizens. If the experts from the various workgroups muddle along by themselves without giving dialogue with the residential and business groups a higher priority, it will never happen that we, who in full consciousness want to stay here, will be able to arrive at a competent decision-making capability. After all, not all of us are capable of weighing the pros and cons. What good will external appeals to a confrontational political culture do? Who is supposed to do the confronting here? There is no relevant basis. The Berlin Economy Group presents an excellent example: it was in charge of cultivating ties to other economic groups, but did it ever hold discussions with the people, for example, from the group involved in television electronics?[2] Yet these are the very individuals who, should they find majority support in society, have to go to bat for these clever insights.

I can already hear the counter-arguments: we no longer have any time, every day so and so many people are leaving the country, the economy is on the brink of collapse, and so forth and so on. But should the way out really be that we simply join in, out of ignorance, with the slogan that has come to be the majority opinion: "Germany, united fatherland?" The question of German unity cannot, on the contrary, be the primary one. We are staring immense problems in the face. And if always only foreign political conditions are cited among those that would have to be fulfilled–in however many steps it may take–before unification, then the domestic ones are glaringly missing, as I see it. In no way will I allow myself to be spied upon by the Office of Constitutional Protection, after the dissolution of the State Security apparatus, only because I remain firmly convinced that the capitalist form of society is not the most humane. I also do not endorse giving up the free day for household matters that women receive here.[3] On the contrary: men, too, must have this day. In addition, I have no desire to have to put up, in a parliamentary democracy, with the way the German Republicans have become socially acceptable, just because their view must be permitted to have its say as well. And when I view the corruption that functions even better under the partnership of capital and politics, I cannot help but think that the handsome villas of Wandlitz will be dwarfed in comparison.

All those who stood up in October for changes in *this* country are now sitting there like rabbits in front of the snake, hoping that the imminent bite will not be all that painful.

Even in the New Forum we have been unable to stem the tide of this development. The forms established to date are preventing a large portion even here from actually participating in or having input in decisions. We must figure out a way to set up social forms of communication that will not allow decisions affecting whole strata of society to be made hierarchically and under the exclusion of the vast majority of the population. We must lend our support to the premises necessary for this goal.

One such premise is that the general curtailment of employment hours be carried out, so that, whatever else happens, energy and time for cooperation remain present. I cannot imagine that this could not be achievable, as long as it is patently clear that the conversion of the economy will not occur without unemployment.

Furthermore, we must also fight as a citizens' movement to ensure that the right to shelter and to gainful employment be laid out explicitly in our constitution. Every member of our society must be able to depend on this, because otherwise no one will be responsible for searching for a solution to problems of this nature.

We must make sure that there are no more fringe groups among us, because all sectors of the population who differ for whatever reason from the fully productive, heterosexual, white male between twenty and forty-five years old will receive the same rights, material privileges, and opportunities to represent their interests. Then discussions of the performance principle will become discussions of the justice principle.

Maybe we will even be able to once again become a citizens' movement, one that can effectively represent the interests of people dependent on salaries, women, the socially disadvantaged, the single parents, foreigners, and many groups left unmentioned.

NOTES

Source: Blohm, 57-63. Translated by Bill Hutfilz.

1. On 15 December 1987, as part of a general tactic of intimidation, the Stasi stormed the Environmental Library in Berlin and four of its members were accused of solidarity with non-socialist forces; on 17 January 1988, at the yearly rally in commemoration of Rosa Luxemburg, over a hundred people were arrested by Stasi officers; this incident is frequently referred to as the "Luxemburg-affair."
2. The Berlin Economy Group is a group of intellectuals, philosophers, and economists, organized by Rainer Land and Michael Brie, who made recommendations on economic policy to the various oppositional political groups in the GDR prior to and during the revolution.
3. Women in the GDR were entitled to stay home from work one day each month in order to take care of household tasks.

42

Communiqué by Helmut Kohl after his Discussion with Soviet General Secretary Michail Gorbachev in Moscow (February 10, 1990)

Tonight I must convey just one message to all Germans. General Secretary Gorbachev and I are in agreement that it is the sole right of the German people to decide whether or not they want to live together in one state. General Secretary Gorbachev promised me unequivocally that the Soviet Union will respect the decision of the Germans to live in one state and that the Germans themselves are responsible for determining the timing and manner of unification. . . . [The German Question] must be embedded within the pan-European architecture.

NOTES

Source: Weiland, 59.

43

Positions of the Round Table for the Negotiations Between the Two German Heads of State, Helmut Kohl and Hans Modrow, in Bonn (February 12, 1990)

1. *About the Situation*

Those who are in positions of political responsibility in both German states now have to act in accordance with the joint national responsibility.

In the current complicated situation, which is characterized by fast-paced destabilization, they have to exhibit the highest measure of political reason and not be guided by emotions. The political development has to be kept under control and remain transparent for the citizens of both German states.

The Round Table expects that the FRG, as economically and politically stronger partner in the unification process, will now undertake everything possible to hinder a further destabilization of the situation in the GDR and to contribute to its civil order. It is obvious that some forces in the FRG are currently steering a course toward a conscious aggravation of the problems in the GDR. In our opinion this is also not in the interests of the FRG.

At present it is above all a matter of making sure that the citizens of the GDR remain in their country.

Therefore, the Round Table expects the meeting of the two heads of state to send clear signals for improvement of the living conditions in the GDR.

2. Economic Steps Along the Road to Unity

The Round Table is of the opinion that we in the GDR primarily have to live up to our own responsibility for improving the productivity of our economy. That demands the speedy and persistent realization of economic reform. Visible results in the interests of the people, however, can only be achieved if the FRG comes through immediately with the financial aid discussed in Dresden. We view an amount of 10 to 15 billion D-marks as appropriate, and believe it should be offered immediately, independent of any further negotiations. The Round Table supports the creation of a joint German commission that would make proposals for the use of these funds.

As a result of its work so far, the Round Table insists that within a short time a commission of experts from both German states examine and then disclose the possibilities, conditions, and effects of a currency union or a currency alliance. The government is not authorized to negotiate a currency union or a currency alliance at the present moment simply because any hasty regulation would be harmful to both German states. Before such agreements are made, all the modalities, as well as the advantages and disadvantages, have to be thoroughly discussed in a broad societal framework.

The Round Table does not authorize an overhasty surrender of the financial authority of the GDR.

The Round Table demands that all measures for the solution of existing questions about currency and the economy be linked with a social safety-net mechanism for the population of the GDR. This requires the development of a social charter that guarantees social standards for the citizens of our country. It ought to become the basis for supplementing a currency and economic alliance by a social alliance.

The Round Table supports, moreover, the speedy passage of a trade-union law, the creation of legal regulations for worker's councils, a real estate law, and a law regulating cooperatives that safeguards the property and social rights of farmers in particular.

3. *Political Steps for German Unity*

On the basis of the negotiations between Prime Minister Modrow and Chancellor Kohl in Dresden, the Round Table demands that all further political decisions be based on the concept of a step by step consolidation, regulated by treaties, of the two German states.

The Round Table supports the creation of a Joint German Council for the regulation of the unification process. That would be an important step toward German unity, one that could be taken immediately.

4. *German Unity–European Security*

The Round Table is of the opinion that the process of creating German unity must remain integrated in the process of European rapprochement, and that both the interests of the Four Powers as well as those of all European nations have to be considered. This reciprocity must be preserved. The process of German unification ought not be separated by means of artificial overheating from the European process. It must further the creation of a peaceful European order.

The Round Table asks the governments of the two German states to support the convening at the earliest date possible of a conference of the victorious powers of the Second World War with equal participation of the GDR and the FRG. This conference would have to accomplish essential preliminary work for the next CSCE conference, especially regarding the process of German unification.

The Round Table thinks it advisable to preserve what has been achieved in the process of European detente and supports the demand for a second CSCE summit meeting in September of this year, at the latest, in order to speed up the European process. A proposal to this end ought to be made jointly by the two German governments.

The Round Table supports the plans and proposals for a separation of the power blocs, for a demilitarized zone in Central Europe, for a reduction in troop size of the national armies, and for the removal of foreign armed forces from German soil. The Round Table opposes any attempt to extend NATO, directly or indirectly, to the territory of the present GDR. It supports the idea that, after the *Volkskammer* election on March 18, 1990, the governments and parliaments of the two German states should deliver a joint declaration about the acknowledgment and security of the presently existing borders with their European neighbor states.

The Round Table points out that the GDR can contribute important foreign policy experiences, which could be significant as mechanisms for building bridges between East and West. The vast potential of our economic, scientific, and cultural relations with the Eastern European countries ought to be utilized.

Position of the Initiative for Peace and Human Rights, the United Left, the Green Party, the Independent Women's Organization, and Democracy Now about point 3. Elaboration of the positions of the Round Table for the negotiations between Prime Minister Modrow and Chancellor Kohl on February 13-14, 1990:

In the process of rapprochement, the two German states should place themselves at the head of initiatives for military and political detente in Europe. Both states should orient themselves toward a speedy demilitarization of their territories in order to advance the dissolution of power blocs that should follow from European detente and to create the conditions for a union of the two German states.

In this context, the negotiations about a CSCE follow-up conference should take into consideration the proposal by the two German states for a conference of the victorious powers of the Second World War with equal participation of the GDR and the FRG. Its aim ought to be the ratification of a peace treaty that guarantees the present borders of both German states with their neighbors, provides for the removal of all foreign troops from Germany, and makes the unification of both states possible on the basis of international law.

NOTES

Source: Herles/Rose, 115-18.

44
Press Conference after the Meeting between Helmut Kohl and Hans Modrow in Bonn (February 13, 1990)

Statement by Helmut Kohl

Ladies and gentlemen!

Your unusually large number at this press conference indicates how important today's meeting is. It is the first meeting this year between the governments of the Federal Republic of Germany and the GDR. All of us were conscious during these talks of our national responsibility, which follows from our common history. I remind you of the fact that 45 years ago the large-scale bombing of Dresden took place. This date stands for the suffering of our people. I pointed this out with good reason at the very beginning of today's talks–in order to make our total responsibility clear.

The visit of Prime Minister Modrow is taking place on the basis of conditions that no one could have anticipated even a few days ago. We Germans now have the historical opportunity to bring about the unity of our fatherland in free self-determination. Unity is now finally possible. Whether or not we embrace this opportunity wholeheartedly and, at the same time, with prudence, depends primarily on us Germans.

The road to German unity was finally cleared by General Secretary Gorbachev last weekend. This step deserves our respect and our gratitude. I would like to quote here what the Soviet news agency TASS has reported about the results of my talks in Moscow:

> Michail Gorbachev stated–and the Chancellor agreed–that between the USSR, the FRG, and the GDR there are no longer any differences of opinion about the fact that the Germans themselves have to resolve the question of the unity of the German nation, and that they themselves have to decide in what governmental form, in what time-frame, with what tempo, and under what conditions they want to realize this unity.

Let me state here with great emphasis that under no circumstances do we regard this new attitude of the Soviet Union as a carte blanche for unilateral national actions. The unification of Germany must be embedded in the pan-European architecture and in the entire process of East-West relations. No one has a greater interest in this than we Germans.

We want to take into consideration the legitimate interests of our neighbors and friends in Europe and in the world. This way the resolution of the German Question will mean a decisive increase in stability and security for all of Europe. I just talked on the phone with my colleague [Foreign Minister Hans-Dietrich] Genscher, who, as you know, is currently participating in the conference of foreign ministers in Ottawa.[1] I am assuming that the talks among the pertinent foreign ministers will lead to a positive result–that means that the Four Powers, i.e., the Soviet Union, the US, Great Britain, and France, as well as both German states will soon take up negotiations in order to come to agreements along the lines I just outlined.

Until the completion of German unity, we still have a difficult road ahead of us. However, we are not taking a single step into unknown territory, since the light at the end of the tunnel can already be seen clearly today. Without a doubt, we are facing a great challenge. But I am certain that we can master it. The talks with Prime Minister Modrow and his delegation were business-like, open, and on the whole characterized by the mutual wish to send some signs of hope to the people in the GDR. They took place against the background of a situation that, above all as a consequence of the ongoing stream of immigrants, has clearly come to a head. The number of immigrants in 1989 amounted altogether to about 340,000. Since the beginning of this year another 85,000 were added.

For that reason I made two things clear in our talks today.

First, our repeatedly expressed willingness to help on a short-term basis wherever this is urgent and necessary, especially for humanitarian reasons. Our supplementary budget for 1990 includes relevant financial aid packages. Let me just mention certain key words, such as travel funds, an ERP-credit program–above all for small and medium-size businesses–training and transfer of technology, as well as environmental protection and improvement of the transportation systems.[2] We have set aside more than 300 million D-marks for medical instruments and equipment. All in all, we are talking about more than 5 billion D-marks for the GDR. This makes one thing unequivocally clear: we are willing to take on far-reaching commitments for the people in the GDR so that they can remain in their homeland and help shape the new economic beginning there.

Second, we are going a significant step further. I proposed to Prime Minister Modrow that we take up immediate negotiations for the creation of a currency union and an economic community. To this end, a joint committee will be formed, which will begin its negotiations immediately.

What does this offer mean in concrete terms? This offer essentially has two parts.

1. On an established date, the GDR-mark will be replaced by the D-mark as currency.

2. Simultaneous with this, the GDR must create the necessary legal conditions for the introduction of a social market economy.

For the government of the Federal Republic both elements are inseparably intertwined. Let me add: politically and economically this offer by the government of the Federal Republic means that we are willing to give unusual, even revolutionary answers, for our part, to unusual, even revolutionary events and challenges in the GDR. For there can be no doubt about one thing: in a politically and economically normal situation our road would have been a different one–and that would have been one of step by step reforms and adjustments with the introduction of a common currency only at a later date. It is against this background that the critical remarks by experts and specialists must be understood. Yet the increasing severity of the crisis in the GDR makes more extensive and courageous answers necessary.

In this instance, political and social transformations have led to a dramatic shortening of the political timetable, so that there is no longer any basis for step by step plans, no matter how they are defined and economically founded. In such a situation it is a matter of more than just the economy. It is now a matter of giving a clear, unmistakable sign of hope and encouragement to the people in the GDR. That is the reason, and that is the only reason, why we made the decision, which can indeed be called historical, to offer the GDR the immediate creation of a currency union and economic community.

For the Federal Republic of Germany this means that in this offer we will call upon our strongest economic player–the D-mark. With this we allow our fellow countrymen and countrywomen in the GDR to partake immediately and directly of what the citizens of

Erich Honecker and Helmut Kohl meet in
Bonn, May 1987

GDR refugees arriving in West Germany, October 1989

Facing page (top): GDR citizens flee to the West via Hungary and Czechoslovakia, summer 1989

Facing page (bottom): An East German mother and her child share their joy upon receipt of a West German passport, summer 1989

A former GDR citizen celebrates as he crosses the border from Austria to West Germany, fall 1989

Facing page: Citizens from both parts of Berlin climb the Wall, November 9, 1989

Inhabitants of West Berlin break away pieces of the Wall at Friedrichstrasse, November 10, 1989

Facing page: Young East and West Germans occupy the Wall at the Brandenburg Gate, November 10, 1989

Visitors from the GDR are welcomed at one of the newly opened German-German border crossings in Berlin, November 11, 1989

The opening of the Brandenburg Gate is
celebrated with speeches by Hans Modrow,
Helmut Kohl, and others, December 22, 1989

A watchtower along the German-German border is demolished, February 1990

Facing page: Souvenir hunters at the demolished Wall, February 1990

Helmut Kohl and Hans Modrow meet to negotiate the German economic and currency union, February 13, 1990

Demonstrators in Dresden demanding "We want one new Germany," February 1990

Campaign rally for the "Alliance for Germany"
in Magdeburg, March 6, 1990

"German Unity: Freedom, Unemployment?":
Inhabitants of an industrial region of
Brandenburg demonstrate at the chancellory
in Bonn for the retention of industrial jobs,
October 29, 1992

Chancellor Helmut Kohl greets former Soviet President Michail Gorbachev in Bonn, September 8, 1994

the Federal Republic built up and achieved in decades of persistent work. For the D-mark–one of the hardest, most stable, and generally accepted currencies in the world–is the foundation of our prosperity and our economic productivity.

A currency union only makes sense, however, if the GDR, for its part, immediately introduces far-reaching reforms for a market economy. What this means in concrete terms is:

–a complete inventory of financial data and facts;

–the guarantee of the proven policy of stability pursued by the *Bundesbank* for the entire territory in which the currency is used;

–the implementation with speed and conviction of the announced economic reforms, under the headings of free trade, property laws, competition, environmental protection, a price and wage system determined by the market, as well as freedom in foreign trade;

–the reform of state finances, including the system of taxes and duties;

–the necessary social and ecological support of these reforms, for example, by introducing unemployment insurance and adjusting the retirement system.

Let me stress: precisely the social and ecological foundation of this policy of reforms is of central significance for the government of the Federal Republic. Without it, the economic reorientation of the GDR cannot, in our view, be successful. Therefore the former economic difficulties can only be removed with a market-oriented and, at the same time, socially and ecologically supported process of transformation; that is the only way in which the flow of private capital can begin and new businesses and jobs that will be promising in the future can be created.

No doubt, this road demands great adjustments and efforts. However, whenever one acts decisively, the opportunities far outweigh the risks. No small reason for this is the economic situation in the Federal Republic of Germany, which in many respects is unusually favorable. Above all, our extensive surplus in foreign trade attains a new significance in view of the GDR.

To state it more clearly: if we succeed in redirecting a small portion of our trade surplus in the amount of 130 billion D-marks into the GDR, if we succeed in utilizing a small portion of our yearly capital export in the amount of 100 billion D-marks for the GDR–then this will be enough to bring about a strong economic recovery there. In short, there is no fundamental lack of goods and capital that could be used for the new economic beginning in the GDR.

I judge just as positively the great willingness of our businesses to invest in the GDR. I know on the basis of many discussions that there are already today a wealth of concrete projects for investment and cooperation that could be realized within a short time. Let me add: it is obvious that in this context the economic framework in the GDR–which is determined only there and not here–plays a decisive role.

The motto for the coming months is: national solidarity. In this hour solidarity is our self-evident human and national duty. It is a matter of a great joint effort, with which we can guarantee for our thus far divided fatherland a happy future in a free and united Europe–driven by the will to serve peace in the world as an equal partner in a united Europe. I can say on behalf of the Federal Republic of Germany: we accept this responsibility.

The talks were–let me repeat this–characterized by a spirit of responsibility, even if we were by no means in agreement on a whole number of questions, as is understandable, during this meeting. That is why I want to stress: this was not the last set of talks. We will have to continue our meetings–also and, above all, after the new *Volkskammer* has been elected and the new government is in office.

Statement by Hans Modrow

First of all, I would like to thank the media for the attention that they have given for months to the developments in the GDR and with which they followed these developments. Through the media a historical process, with which a new chapter of German history has begun, was made known worldwide: a process of liberation from ossified forms and unusable substance, a process the people alone executed but have not yet by any means completed. I must remind us particularly in this moment that German unity is coming nearer. May we never forget that the people of the GDR bring with themselves into this unification not only the bitter defeat of really-existing socialism, but also that proud statement: we are the people. I deeply hope that this statement and its political content will not get lost. May we never forget that the GDR has values to bring to a future Germany, intellectual and cultural values that grew over decades in spite of everything, and material values of which the workers and engineers, the farmers and craftsmen, even the so-called minor employees need not be ashamed.

Anyone who today speaks quickly and with pleasure about an unstable GDR or its difficult economy will ultimately have to deal with the question of whether we are not artificially lowering the price of unification to the disadvantage of the people. My government knows the substance of the GDR very well, and I am telling you that it provides a very hopeful foundation–diligent people, capable people, indeed, as has often been proven, quite creative people–and on top of this comes an enormous infrastructure, which, to be sure, needs investments, but is by no means outdated. Let me mention a sum: the total national wealth of the GDR is 1.4 trillion marks, among this the state property of 980 billion marks and 6.2 million acres of agricultural land.

There is, therefore, much room for all that Chancellor Kohl emphasized in terms of investment, in terms of future cooperation. Today we had extensive and, in my opinion, constructive talks about the steps that have to be taken now to achieve a single German state. There remains the problem of gradual progress, of balancing things out, of those things Chancellor Kohl repeatedly mentioned in former times; prudence and good judgment will continue to be necessary. It became clear in these negotiations that in my Government of National Responsibility there is a common position where the guarantee of the social possessions of GDR citizens is concerned, and even after yesterday's meeting of the Round Table in the GDR–we also forwarded the advisory material of this meeting of the Round Table to Chancellor Kohl–there is agreement about this. What also became clear is that both governments have to face the necessity:

1. of viewing the steps toward unification within the European process and of embedding them absolutely within this process;

2. of even now doing everything possible so that immediately after the 18th of March, that is, after the *Volkskammer* elections, the process of a relative rapprochement in the direction of an economic and currency union or an economic community can be initiated. As emphasized already, as early as next week experts will already begin their negotiations and their work. We therefore consider it urgently necessary that we avoid all surprises, that information be supplied, that terms that are not yet spelled out not suddenly appear in the media. It is necessary in this regard that joint, professional work be accomplished.

3. And it should be emphasized once more that already at this point we have to make provisions for certain social securities so that pensioners and those on social security and other groups of the

population will be sheltered from problems. That also holds for savings accounts. There is also the guarantee and necessity that the farmers not have to worry about losing their land and soil. There is also the expectation, expressed yesterday by the Round Table, that the Federal Republic will have to show its solidarity with the German Democratic Republic in the form of financial aid.

I continue to view my duty as protecting the citizens of the GDR from harm and looking for common mutual interests with the citizens of the Federal Republic. No one should enter upon a future Germany with fear. For that reason it is also appropriate to repeat the plea that all people remain in their traditional homelands. Everyone will have prospects, everyone will have opportunities.

On February 1 I submitted a step-by-step plan for the unification of the two German states. Today we can certainly discuss how the steps will relate to each other or in what order they will be realized. But it will still be necessary that we continue to proceed with prudence and good judgment. Ideas–even those concerning a future federal structure on the territory of today's GDR–clearly expect and demand that they be thoroughly worked out, and we assume in this regard that a process tied to the work on a constitution must be initiated.

Prior to that, as you know, I had the opportunity on the 30th of January to reach an agreement with Michail Gorbachev in the Soviet Union, in Moscow, to the effect that this unification is the Germans' right and that it belongs on the agenda. The GDR assumes that today and in the future it will be and remain a partner of the Soviet Union, and the Soviet Union for its part has stated as well, as Chancellor Kohl just emphasized, that it will deepen its relations to the presently existing two German states and, at the same time, will in the future also see itself tied to the development of a unified Germany. At the same time it must be stressed that with regard to all these developments and processes, we must always pay attention to the international context. We are pleased that subsequent to this Chancellor Kohl discussed his ideas about the unification of the two German states in Moscow and was informed of the Soviet position.

Now it is indeed a matter of deciding on and initiating concrete steps. My government, as far as that is still possible, will continue to work toward this until March 18 and beyond. After the elections the newly elected parliament, the newly elected government, will surely also continue these steps–that can be concluded from the programs and concepts of the various parties that are currently campaigning for the elections in the German Democratic Republic. Just as it adhered to all the promises made in Dresden, my government will continue in the future to pursue this work and follow these procedures.

In this context, where the borders of the future German state are concerned, I understood the Chancellor to say that in the talks conducted in Moscow and in the concluding statements, the Oder-Neiße border has been accepted and that the unification of the two German states makes no claims for alterations of the borders with neighboring states.

Let me conclude by saying: through the cooperation of both governments more has been achieved for the rapprochement and practical cooperation of the GDR and the FRG in the last three months than previously in decades. Let me also emphasize that there has never been a government in the GDR, and perhaps anywhere else, that created such a far-reaching program of laws and resolutions in such short time, and all this ultimately has the purpose of creating conditions for all that will be accomplished in the following weeks and months. The efforts of the two states should be continued and intensified in this spirit, in order to create favorable conditions for the consolidation of the two German states.

NOTES

Source: *Europa-Archiv*, 45 (1990): 194-199.

1. The foreign ministers of the Four Powers met in Ottawa on February 13 and declared their willingness to conduct talks with the governments of the Federal Republic and the GDR about German unification.
2. A so-called ERP Special Fund was created by the government of the FRG to defray part of the cost of unification.

45

Policy Statement by Chancellor Helmut Kohl Before the *Bundestag* of the FRG (February 15, 1991)

Madame President, dear ladies and gentlemen!

With my official oath of office I accepted the duty, like all my predecessors, to work to the best of my abilities toward the possibility that the German people might be able, in free self-determination, to fulfill the unity and freedom of Germany. Today I can report to the German *Bundestag*: never since our country was divided, never since our constitution was written were we as close as we are today to our aim, the unity of all Germans in freedom. . . .

We owe our gratitude to all those who contributed to this historical turning point. We owe thanks first of all to our friends and allies in the West. They stood by us through dangerous times when blockade, Wall, and barbed wire were supposed to make the division of our country and its capital city permanent.[1] They stood by us in times of despondency when even in this country some people wanted to alter the Basic Law, because it was based on the "lie of this republic."[2] They stood by us in times of conflict, when missile deployment in the East and the Western response threatened also to have an effect on German matters. In the Treaty on Germany they declared their support for the aim of German unity in a free and democratic form, and in letting us join European integration–in the supplementary protocol to the Rome Treaties–they made room for the special case of our relations with the GDR.[3] Today we can build on that. For that we are and remain grateful.

We thank General Secretary Michail Gorbachev, who in conjunction with the far-reaching transformation of his country also led Soviet foreign policy in a new direction and set the standard for a new dynamics and a new way of thinking. . . . In this hour we also thank the Poles and the Hungarians, the Czechs and the Slovaks, who led the way with far-reaching reforms in politics, economics, and society. Without their example the recent developments in the GDR would not have been possible. . . .

Last but not least, we owe hearty thanks to our fellow countrymen and countrywomen in the GDR; to the people in Berlin, in Leipzig, in Dresden, in Halle, in Chemnitz and Plauen, who with their watchwords "We are the people" and "We are one people" did more than anyone else to seize this opportunity for Germany. In this hour our warmest greetings and our thanks go out to them! It is precisely the occurrences of the last six months in the GDR that helped the Soviet leadership come to the recognition that the direction and tempo of developments either in the GDR or in the other reform states of Central and Eastern Europe cannot be determined from above. On the contrary, the people themselves took their fate and their future into their own hands.

General Secretary Gorbachev and I were in agreement about the fact that the *Volkskammer* elections scheduled for March 18 will be a key factor. In light of the campaign platforms with which the clear majority of all the parties and groups in the GDR have established themselves, I would reiterate my firm conviction–and the

General Secretary did not contradict this–that the result of this election will not only be a democratically legitimate and, we hope, effective government, but also a government policy with the clear aim: "unity as soon as possible!"

The General Secretary and I further agreed that not only the campaign and the elections have to take an orderly course, but also that the process of unification must be embedded within a stable European framework. Only on these two tracks can the aim of German unity be achieved with certainty. . . . With these ideas in mind, General Secretary Gorbachev and I–as well as Foreign Minister Genscher and Soviet Foreign Minister Shevardnadze–addressed what is probably the most difficult question: the future of the alliances. I gave voice to my conviction that even when the security interests of the Soviet Union are reasonably met, a future united Germany

–ought not to be neutralized or demilitarized–this is, to put it bluntly, the "old way of thinking";

–but rather that we should, and wish to, remain integrated in the Western alliance.

The history of this century demonstrates: nothing is more threatening to the stability of Europe than a Germany that oscillates between two worlds, between West and East. And vice versa: a Germany firmly allied with free democracies and increasingly integrated into the political and economic structure of the European Community is the indispensable stabilizing factor that Europe needs, especially at its center. With regard to this topic I made clear:

–that our alliance, in adherence with its aims, must concentrate more on its political role; and

–that no units and organizations of the Western alliance will be moved to the territory of the current GDR.

I know that I am in agreement with the President of the United States on this. . . . According to the meetings of the foreign ministers in Ottawa, . . . the following course looks likely: after the elections on March 18, the government of the Federal Republic and a democratically legitimated government of the GDR will talk about the road the Germans will take to arrive at their unity. We Germans will then negotiate with the Americans, the British, the French, and the Soviets about the external aspects of the creation of German unity, including the security questions of neighboring states. . . .

The talks with Prime Minister Modrow and his delegation took place in a business-like and very open atmosphere. For us it was a matter of sending signs of hope to the people in the GDR. The situation has become more critical. The political parties and groups in the GDR at the so-called Round Table passed on to the Federal government a position paper for the talks between the Prime Minister and myself in which they referred to a "situation, which is characterized by fast-paced destabilization." . . .

If the Modrow government, as I expected after the talks held in Dresden before Christmas, had already introduced the necessary laws for the protection of investments before January, as did Hungary, then we would already have a completely different situation in the GDR where investments are concerned. Those in positions of responsibility in the GDR–the government, the Round Table–have the power to send the proper signals so that the economic recovery can begin.

If, for whatever reasons, these decisions are not made, then all financial assistance, even to the tune of billions of marks, will be without the desired effect. Therefore, it remains true: the introduction of the D-mark in the GDR and the inducement of market-oriented reforms in the GDR are one and the same side of the coin of economic success.

But it also seems important to me that the extent of the economic challenges with which we are now dealing be viewed soberly. In population the GDR does not quite reach the number of people in the state of Northrhine-Westphalia. If we take economic strength as the basis, the *Bundesbank* assumes that we are dealing with the power of a medium-sized state in the Federal Republic–let's say, for example, Hesse.

President Pöhl has also pointed to the fact that the capital created within a single year in the Federal Republic of Germany corresponds roughly to the entire savings in the GDR. I am not mentioning these comparisons in order to minimize the problems; that is far from my intent. But they also should not be limitlessly exaggerated. The challenges have to be seen as they really are, namely, anything but simple, but eventually solvable for a country like the Federal Republic of Germany and to be mastered together with the GDR.

I am addressing this mainly to those who once again–as we have experienced often enough–would like to profit from fear. We experienced this in 1983 in connection with the missile deployment, in conjunction with the implementation of the NATO double-track decision, and we are experiencing it now in an especially insidious way, in that the people in the GDR are told to worry about their savings, in that statements are made that are clearly false, and in that here in the Federal Republic some people are making propaganda and acting as if the pensioners or others were threatened in their existence.[4] We have been familiar with this insidious game for years, and we know how to counter it.

With the tasks that lie ahead of us, neither the economic productivity, nor the stability, nor the social security of the Federal Republic of Germany will be endangered. In the GDR, as well, the transformation to a social market economy should not give rise to fears; for a market-oriented order and social security are, according to our understanding and according to our experience in the forty-year history of the Federal Republic of Germany, inseparable from one another.

Our road to success was the road of the social market economy, and in these decades of comparing the systems we have seen that Marxist socialism has failed and that the social market economy is experiencing a renaissance all over the world. The basic principles of our path are:

–productivity and social justice;

–competition and solidarity;

–self-responsibility and social security.

Our material wealth is one of the highest, our social safety-net one of the most tightly woven in the world. For most citizens in the Federal Republic of Germany this has meanwhile become self-evident; not so for our fellow countrymen and countrywomen in the GDR. They worry about whether traveling the road to a currency union and an economic community might not cause them to be pushed off to one side.

I take these concerns, harbored especially by older citizens and by those who are threatened with unemployment, very seriously. However, I can assure the citizens of the GDR: a social market economy always also means social balance. It is our aim that we will soon also achieve social unity.

To achieve this, the government of the Federal Republic is prepared to cooperate immediately in erecting a modern order for the workforce and society. According to our experiences, the first step needs to be the further development of the social security systems for the elderly and the unemployed. . . .

In the Federal Republic of Germany, through hard work and productivity, we successfully overcame the structural transformation brought on by technical progress and international competition. I am also convinced today that together we will shape the further economic and social development in both parts of Germany in a positive way. The citizens of the GDR can count on our solidarity–not only in words, but in deeds.

To the citizens in the Federal Republic of Germany I would like to say this: our social safety-net will remain tightly knit. No pensioner, no one who is unemployed, no war victim, no welfare recipient needs to fear a cut in programs. On the contrary: the dynamics of our economic development will benefit our social security systems in the future, as well.

For that reason, anyone who talks about the totality of economic challenges facing Germany should do this responsibly and with knowledge of the facts. In this context, I want to expressly applaud the fact that the President of the *Bundesbank*, Mr. Pöhl, also addressed this topic in a responsible way. I thank him for that.

What is now important is that we remain on track politically and economically. Steering a clear course toward a social market economy is of central significance for the Federal Republic, but also for Germany as a whole. If in these days we stick to the fundamental principles that brought the Federal Republic of Germany from the economic null point after the Second World War into the leading group of industrial nations in the world, we can master the challenges of the nineties.

The coalition of the Liberal Democrats, the Christian Social Union, and the Christian Democratic Union already accomplished great things in the reconstruction years of the Federal Republic.[5] After taking over the government in 1982, we demonstrated again– in a difficult situation–that we can solve the economic and social problems of our country in a rational manner. We are determined to act even in the coming times on the basis of these experiences and in this spirit.

The guiding principle of the coming months is national solidarity. In this hour, solidarity is our self-evident human and national duty.

NOTES

Source: *Europa-Archiv*, 45 (1990): 199-207.

1. During the blockade of West Berlin, which lasted from 24 June 1948 to 12 May 1949, the Soviets, in response to a deterioration of allied cooperation in postwar Germany and the currency reform in the Western occupation zones, blocked all ground access routes into West Berlin; all food and supplies had to be delivered by air.

2. In the seventies left-wing opposition was voiced against the official policy of the FRG toward the GDR inscribed in the Preamble of the Basic Law.

3. The supplementary protocol to the Rome Treaties establishing the European Economic Community in 1957 deals with West German participation in the community.

4. The Nato double-track decision of 1979 by the Nato Council of Ministers established a policy of simultaneous missile deployment (Pershing II) while working toward the negotiation of disarmament treaties.

5. The coalition of the Liberal Democrats, the Christian Social Union, and the Christian Democratic Union determined postwar West German politics until the late sixties and, after an interim period of alliance between the Social Democrats and the Liberals, took over the government again in 1982.

46
Policy Statement by Prime Minister Hans Modrow Before the *Volkskammer* of the GDR (February 20, 1990)

As you know, on February 13 a meeting of the heads of government of the two German states took place in Bonn. On that day and on February 14, numerous further meetings, as well as discussions with politicians and business representatives, were also held. The main topics were the necessary and possible steps for the unification of the two German states. I would like to inform you about this and draw some conclusions.

That meeting was the first official deliberation by the governments of the two German states about principal questions for the unification of the GDR and the FRG. In this respect this meeting went substantially beyond the meeting in Dresden. It demonstrated that the solution of the German Question has been placed on the agenda. In that context it also made clear the partly divergent, partly convergent positions of both governments.

At the same time, a process for the clarification of the merger of the two states was initiated: today, experts on both sides are beginning to discuss the problems that have to be solved, especially with regard to a currency union. With that, important preliminary work for the period after March 18 should be accomplished. This way the expectations of wide circles of the population in both states can be met.

Our government of national responsibility was represented in Bonn by all member parties. To the delegation of the GDR belonged ministers from all 13 parties that now form the cabinet. They all contributed to the results of this meeting. They were able to accomplish such constructive work because they shared a common position. Those are the positions that the Round Table established on February 12 for the Bonn meeting and that correspond to the fundamental attitude of the government.

I gave this position paper to Chancellor Kohl at the introductory discussion and stressed: there is a remarkable agreement, one that cannot be ignored, among the political forces in the GDR about fundamental questions of unification, something that, by the way, was confirmed again yesterday at the Round Table.

The members of the government delegation made it clear in Bonn, just as I did previously, that preparations for the solution of the German Question can be made immediately and should be made immediately. The actual decisions of the GDR, however, will only be made by the new *Volkskammer*, to be elected on March 18, and by the government it appoints.

In Bonn there was agreement with the government of the FRG on one point concerning matters of foreign policy: the process of unification should not be allowed to go contrary to European interests, it must rather be completed in national and international responsibility. It must be a road to Europe and for Europe, it must serve peace, and it cannot be allowed to harm anyone.

For precisely that reason it is unfortunate that Chancellor Kohl could not decide to make a clear statement recognizing the Oder-Neiße border, although in the press conference he was certainly called upon to do so. In the name of the government of the GDR, I repeat what I said a few days ago in Warsaw: the Oder-Neiße border is the western border of Poland according to international law. It is today's eastern border of the GDR and must be the future eastern border of Germany. This border was established in the Treaty of Görlitz between the GDR and Poland in 1950, and it was recognized in the Warsaw Treaty between the FRG and Poland in 1970.

With the statement "war should never again be launched from German soil," our Polish neighbors refer in particular to the recognition of their western border at the Oder and Neiße rivers.

The plan for a Two-Plus-Four Conference, that is, of the Four Powers and the two German states, was agreed upon last week in Ottawa. This conference has the mandate of discussing the external aspects for the creation of German unity, including the question of the security of the neighboring states. In this way the interests and responsibilities of the Four Powers, as well as of the GDR and the FRG, regarding the process of European integration can be considered. Chancellor Kohl expressly agreed when I said that we have to approach each other rationally. The conference agreed upon in Ottawa could make this significantly easier for the international framework.

On the basis of these observations I therefore propose–and I know that I am going beyond the limit set for my government:

First, experts of both German states should begin as quickly as possible with the preparations for the Two-Plus-Four Conference. In the same short time period, perhaps even parallel to the German-German negotiations, preparations should be made for the CSCE summit in order to synchronize these processes as early as possible. The GDR and the FRG together should make sure that political impulses for the European confederation proposed by French President Mitterrand derive from this meeting. The two German states should inform the other CSCE states on an ongoing basis about all the important steps of further German-German rapprochement.

Second, the governments of the GDR and the FRG together should declare–binding by international law even before the planned CSCE summit–the incontestability of existing borders with their neighbors, especially the western border of Poland.

It doesn't have to be emphasized that the border question is of principal significance for mutual trust, predictability, and therefore for peace and security. I consider it normal and justified for neighboring states like Poland to express the wish to participate in the international process of negotiations about German unification where questions concerning their borders are at issue.[1]

Third, the two German states should commit themselves to the principle that the overcoming of the division of Germany must go hand in hand with radical disarmament. The next steps in that direction have to be agreements in Vienna about conventional disarmament as well as about future limits on the number of Soviet and American troops stationed in Europe.

Also necessary are far-reaching reductions in the armed forces of both German states, as well as further negotiations of the 35 CSCE states about a European security system.

Regardless of what the future military status of a unified Germany might be, it must be guaranteed that no one's security will be threatened in any way. Germany ought not to be in NATO. It is imaginable, therefore, that a demilitarization of a unified Germany could go hand in hand with a step-by-step demilitarization of Europe.

The emphasis of the meeting was on what the two German states had to clarify and agree upon between themselves. I agree with Chancellor Kohl that for unification we do not need an excess of emotions, but rather soberness and good judgment. This was not always the case prior to the Bonn meeting.

The Chancellor's office made the incorrect claim that the GDR will be bankrupt within the next few days, and the same source spread the rumor that the *Volkskammer* elections would take place even before March 18. In the future, German-German negotiations should not be prefaced in this manner.

It also came as a surprise that before the Bonn meeting a new topic for negotiations was announced by the media, namely the topic of a currency union–and with the stipulation, to boot, that it would have to be completed within a few days. Even economic experts in the Federal Republic confirmed that a change of currency in conjunction with a currency union has to be diligently prepared and secured. Ultimately, the interests of over 16 million GDR citizens, and presumably also the interests of the citizens of the FRG, are at stake.

The position of my government must be that the capitulation of the GDR in the matter of currency policy and, successively, in all other areas is not open to debate. That was also the position of the Round Table.

Undoubtedly, the economic and currency union is necessary for the merger of the two states. But I agree completely with the leader of the Social-Democratic Party of the FRG [Hans-Jochen Vogel]: the principle of social justice has to be upheld in the process of unification on both sides. We cannot, he recently said in the *Bundestag*, have one side profit from German unification while the other has to pay for it with the deterioration of their living conditions.

For this reason, we always need to pay attention to the relationship between economic union, currency union, and social security.

That is true for the preliminary work of the experts. That is the attitude of my government and I hope that this will also be the position of the *Volkskammer* and the government after March 18.

Over the last few weeks my government engaged intensively in the preservation of the social issues of our citizens even during politico-economic transitions. That is the aim of the regulations, which just went into effect, for support and social balancing in job placement and training, as well as financially supported measures for workers and employees who want to take early retirement. The task of preparing an unemployment insurance program was begun, for, since temporary joblessness cannot be avoided during times of structural transition, there must be some kind of social security system. The salary increases already passed last year for certain groups of employees will take effect without any restrictions. Over and above that, we included further areas, so that all the financial resources now available for salary increases–this should be made explicit here–will now be exhausted.

I consider it a binding responsibility of every future government, even under conditions of a social market economy, to defend the right to work, to strive for social security for the young and the elderly as well as for families, to guarantee social assistance and protection to pensioners, single parents, and sick or disabled citizens. If the government of the Federal Republic understands the social undergirding of an economic and currency union merely in terms of concrete unemployment insurance and adjudication of the social security system, then that is not enough. If the transition to a social market economy is not to give rise to concerns, as Chancellor Kohl claims, then there has to be more than this. Doesn't the future Germany need a social charter, as well, by means of which inalienable values are preserved and guaranteed for the future? Not the least of what is at issue here is the preservation of the social rights of citizens, especially the right to their own appropriate living space as well as the guarantee of their savings and other things accrued from their individual labor. Interesting thoughts about this–for example, those published yesterday–have even come from scholars in the FRG. The Institute for German Economy in Cologne considers it feasible to realize a conversion of the entire monetary savings in the GDR to D-marks at an exchange rate of 1 : 1 and thinks that this is, economically speaking, the best solution.[2]

In this context I would like to appeal to the citizens of the GDR to have faith that their savings will be preserved. Honestly earned money should remain in your accounts. There it will retain its value. It also doesn't make any sense to open several accounts. A future currency conversion will undoubtedly be tied to persons, and in such a case it does not matter whether that person has his or her money in one or in three accounts.

There are also questions about real estate, about farm land, and about properties. I would like to clarify the position of the government as follows: in principle, the property reforms introduced as a result of the Second World War on the basis of the Potsdam Agreement and the Laws of the Allied Control Board are and remain legally binding. Ownership of land and of homes should not be allowed to be disengaged from the duty to serve the social needs of human beings. That means that land ought not to become the object of speculation. In order to avoid a sell-out of the land, land sales should be strictly regulated in the area of today's GDR during a transitional period of five to ten years, and let me stress: land used for agricultural purposes and the property of farmers must especially be protected. Interference in the ownership and use of land unavoidably has a negative impact on farmers.

The land reform implemented in the GDR following the war ought not be put in question.[3] All legally acquired rights to land, real estate for recreational purposes, and similar acquisitions have to be fully accepted as legal titles. Farmland must remain farmland!

And anyone who built a weekend house with his or her earned money ought not to be stripped of the fruits of his or her labor.

In Bonn I declared, in agreement with the Round Table, that this government is not authorized to negotiate a currency and economic union. Every over-hasty agreement would be harmful to both states.

Security and trust must be built, and insecurity and fear, especially in the area of fiscal policy, must be counteracted, by agreement on a clear succession of steps to be followed. In this spirit I understand it to be the charge of this government–a charge which my cabinet members and I sought to pursue in Bonn–to ward off dangers to the citizens of the GDR. May the next government also be guided by this aim.

Yesterday a motion was introduced at the Round Table to ensure that the property of the state be handled everywhere with care so that, in the end, it will be brought to better use and accumulate. This attitude deserves our full support. . . .

As you know, the government of the Federal Republic could not come to a decision about committing to the GDR the financial aid package that was already discussed in Dresden. We demanded it again in Bonn. My government delegation and I were guided in this by the expectation expressed at the Round Table on February 12 that the FRG, as economically and politically stronger partner in the unification process, should do everything it can to counteract further destabilization of the situation in the GDR and work toward reassurance.

Not the least thing at issue is compensation for those increased economic difficulties and losses caused by the opening of the GDR borders. According to the calculations of the Ministry for Trade and Supply, the sales of goods, including cheap restaurant meals to citizens of the FRG as well as West Berlin, calculated over a year, amount to at least 4 billion marks.

In light of this situation, it was and is a matter of having the possibility of quickly acquiring goods from the FRG that would directly benefit the citizens of the GDR, significantly improve the living conditions of the people in cities and in the country, take into account the urgent needs of the infrastructure, and support measures for the stabilization of industry.

To state it unequivocally: we are not interested in 15 million marks in cash, but in the delivery of consumer goods and materials, machines, urban engineering, and other things in the stated amount.

This financial aid in solidarity with the GDR should, in our opinion, be tied to the currency union, economic union, and social security; in other words, it should support the consolidation of the two German states. Such immediate aid is also necessary, in my mind, to counteract further emigration from the GDR. Precisely this must be a common interest of the GDR and the FRG.

Last but not least, I also want to repeat here what I already said quite clearly in Bonn. The GDR has more than a little to contribute to unification: great intellectual and cultural values, great material values which have been produced by our people over decades.

Please allow me to mention some numbers again. The gross national wealth of the GDR in 1988 amounted to 1.4 trillion marks, including 980 billion in state property which will be integrated into the new unified German state. The cooperative property amounts to 140 million marks. There are 280 billion marks worth of private property. The GDR will bring with it 6.2 million acres of agricultural land and that–as opposed to the farm economies in the Federal Republic–without any debts.

Despite all the difficulties we have at present, these basic facts should not be forgotten. The GDR is not nearly as rich as the Federal Republic, but it does not enter into a united Germany as a beggar or a sinner.

The GDR is a good piece of Germany, a great piece of Germany, as Federal President Weizsäcker observed, upon which one can build and will have to build in the future. And, as I said, it is not all about material values. Indeed, I specifically warn you against leaving the resolution of the German Question to the D-mark.

In spite of all the differences of opinion that existed during the talks in Bonn and will probably not be absent in the future, I would like to characterize the meeting with Chancellor Kohl and the ministers of his cabinet as constructive. It is a good start for further business-like cooperation in many areas. It set the course in the direction toward "Germany, united fatherland." I did not get these words from demonstrators, but rather from the national anthem of the German Democratic Republic.

The further steps of the consolidation of the two states should not be determined by election campaign tactics but by national responsibility as befits this historical process. The politicians, indeed, all the people in East and West, expect that German unity will be brought about rationally and with supreme awareness of our responsibilities. I pointed especially to this necessity in my conception of the road to Germany unity.

What we in the GDR now need is self-confidence, recollection of our own proper values, and, above all, the will to hard, rational, productive labor. We should now roll up our sleeves in order to bring that productivity into play that will overcome all difficulties and make possible a speedy equalization of the standards of living.

Anyone in the GDR who is still sitting on packed suitcases should unpack them.

The next *Volkskammer*, which we will be electing in just less than four weeks, will be called upon to take a historical step, the valid step toward German unity. May only good come of this for our people, for the nations of Europe, and, above all, for our neighbors!

NOTES

Source: *Europa-Archiv*, 45 (1990): 208-12.

1. Poland demanded that it be allowed to participate in the Two-Plus-Four negotiations and was, in fact, later invited to the meetings at which the eastern border of Germany, which is shared with Poland, was discussed.

2. The Institute for German Economy in Cologne is a think tank that makes recommendations concerning economic policy.

3. The land reform implemented in the GDR following the war was the first part of a systematic program of collectivization that was continued later with the collectivization of agriculture and industry.

"Alliance for Germany": Mail Circular of the "Alliance for Germany" in the District of Böhlitz-Ehrenberg in the Vicinity of Leipzig (March 2, 1990)

Dear citizens of Böhlitz-Ehrenberg!
   What do we have left?
   –a degenerate housing infrastructure, two thirds of all units without flush toilets, outdated heating systems, and little comfort;
   –a permanent need for housing;
   –an outdated water supply and waste water system which, in part, is close to breaking down, no central sewage plant;
   –ruined streets;
   –a lowered frequency of runs in public transportation;
   –a culture without performance halls;
   –a young generation without space;
   –the drama of what once was the most beautiful forest spa in Europe;
   –depressing public squares and loveless playgrounds;
   –constant standing in lines for goods needed daily, above all for those who are employed full-time;
   –quality of restaurants–where?
   –a "Barnecker Steg"–as demonstration object;
   –the "2000" milkplant in Gundorf on Gülle, the ideal scenario for animal/human being/nature?
   –the worries and problems connected with housing developments at the outskirts of town–really only a marginal problem?
Dear citizens!
   It is a question of our future, of the future of our children, of the well-being of us all!
   Therefore support the Alliance for Germany and the CDU
   –for a social, ecologically justifiable market economy;
   –for a tight social safety-net and a health care system that lives up to its mission;
   –for the support of trade and business for a stronger middle class as the motor of the economy;
   –for successful local politics on the basis of individual development of financial means.
   Only an effective, functioning economy can save our town from ultimate decay!

With your vote, we will turn our community into one of the strongest and most attractive industrial communities!

With your vote in the first free election you will make a decision about your and our future!

CDU

NOTES

Source: *Aufbrüche*, 135.

48

Wolf Biermann, " 'That was it. Trap Shut. The Monkey lives': An Obituary for the GDR, a Farewell from 131 Chaussee Strasse, and a Few Frank Words about the Perpetrators Who Now View Themselves as Victims." (March 2 , 1990)

Revolution in the GDR. I had already exhausted my hope and was just as surprised as my faithful old enemies, the corrupt old codgers in the Politburo. But now history leaves us, the adversaries of yesterday, off to the left, as it veers off sharply to the right.

Get black with anger, turn red with joy, or become yellow with astonishment, see a rosy future, cry Germany united fatherland and wave the black-red-gold flags, buy yourselves red cherries in winter from New Zealand–I'll pass.[1] I won't swallow another spoonful of this rancid hope. I no longer am moved on behalf of this divided country.

Germany is no tragedy of humanity. The rift is healing itself; other, deeper rifts now gape. The Germans will soon struggle to their feet and find themselves. Five billion human beings vegetate on this earth, and all of us have always belonged to the 500 million who live in prosperity.

These days, the GDR finds itself in a free-fall. "The *Land* of Saxony greets our Chancellor Helmut Kohl," read a banner in Dresden. The Saxons and Mecklenburgers, the Thuringians and Brandenburgers are expeditiously falling flat on the ground of the Basic Law of the Federal Republic of Germany. The West negotiates soberly over the modalities of this collision.

Just as rashly as the Germans rushed into the Thousand-Year Empire, just as drunkenly as they then marched into the war, so they later staggered apart from one another and flailed at one another in a blind rage.[2] But now Gorbachev has raised the Iron Curtain, and now the siblings who previously hated one another are falling upon each other in a loving frenzy. And we, the leftists in East and West, stand to the side with idiotic smiles on our faces.

To be sure, under Ulbricht and Honecker there were always rebels, the occasional rabble-rousers, self-helpers, gripers, and stoically brave refuseniks. And a few have even become a glimmer of hope for the people in this endless night: Pastor Brüsewitz immolated himself on the marketplace, Robert Havemann cheered the disheartened with the inspiring example of his fearlessness.[3] And my banned songs loomed, in the form of bootlegged tape recordings, like glow-worms in the dark.[4]

The internal socialist conflict is last year's business. The "Third Way" of the GDR is over. There remain only two minorities who are still interested in a socialist experiment: the power-holders of yesterday and their preferred victims of yesterday, both leftist Christians and radical leftists. The oppositional minority of the dark ages has long since fallen once again into the minority.

Since the sun has risen in the East, the people are rubbing the sleep out of their eyes. The silent majority finally has the floor. Those who for forty years sucked everything in are now finally coughing up big words. Brave citizens, who swarmed to the so-called "elections" like bees to honey, now roar like lions. Moral titmice, who for good reason were silent their whole lives long, now shout out "Helmut! Helmut!"

On the day of the Chancellor's visit to Dresden, a small crowd hit the streets with this motto: "Directly from Stalinism to capitalism—without me!" They were cursed by about 3,000 citizens, spat upon, and driven through the streets. The standard was held by an old friend of mine, Bernhard T., a blue-collar worker, for years spied on and terrorized, and incarcerated in the Dresden Stasi prison on Bautzener Strasse, because he belonged to the leftist opposition. He, of all people, was now being disparaged by the Germany-Germany mob as a "red Stasi pig" and with the cry: "Get rid of the Reds!" A loony bin.

Those who were still dancing yesterday to the party tune shouted down everyone who, on the square in Leipzig, even expressed the slightest doubt about the collective German suicidal tendencies. The overly patient victims of the totalitarian regime were now demanding total and immediate annexation by the Federal Republic.

Those who had never defended themselves in the past now clamored for revenge. The same person who had never once let out a peep was now foaming at the mouth. The hatred of the Stasi runs deeper than the love of freedom; it has become solidified.

I know of enough people who sat in the Stasi prison and were tortured there. Such people speak with disgust about the Stasi, with bitterness, with caution, and with sad mockery: they speak almost like exhausted therapists. I found the lynch-mob degree of hatred against this operation among those who had never voiced a word of protest.

It is the shame about their own weakness, the horror at their own cowardice, rage over their own deathly patience with these murderers. How often these now raving protesters had bitten their tongues when it was time to protest, how often they had remained silent at congresses or had even calumniated against innocent people, how often they had looked away when they could have lent a hand. How many lovers have left each other in the lurch, how many friends have betrayed one another. In forty years, the everyday shabbiness has come together in a flood. The not-quite-finished joke about Ulbricht, cut short because a stranger took a seat at the table. Almost everyone has gotten their dander up, even if it was only over petty little acts of informers, which nonetheless bordered on denunciations, and often only for the sake of trifling advantages.

This "cover-all" informant system could not have functioned without the occasional compliance of those against whom others were informing. Hatred of the Stasi is the unattested hatred of the miniature Stasi in one's own heart, it is self-hate in all of its manifestations, it is the suppressed shame of the inculcated subservients about their own self-accused irresponsibility. The people are, on the inside, at least as run-down as the houses.

Fine; those are the subservients. But the bigwigs do not come across any better. I am amazed at this sudden astonishment, this childlike shock in the GDR at the wastefulness and luxury living of the old aristocracy. The ten hoarded video recorders in the freezer were not dear to Willi Stoph and Harry Tisch. I have no desire to poke around in the nightstand of Margot Honecker and prove to myself that she had a whole army of Western curlers and ten bottles of very old scotch.[5] That the late-awakening children over there are now exclaiming ooh! and ahh! may yet pass. But the meticulously groomed media gangsters in the West ought to know already what real luxury is in this world.

Spiegel did not restrain itself from the idiocy of printing a Swiss jewelers invoice for (I don't remember exactly anymore) about

9,000 Swiss francs, whatever, which were paid for a whole set of jewelry: bracelet, necklace, ring, brooch, and earrings . . . all for Margot's withered neck. That must be a wonderfully cheap metal, for so little money! It is exactly what every neighborhood dentist here in the West gives to his embittered wife so that she might decide to forgo making him account for his mistress in the house on Mallorca.

And old Honecker himself was supposed to have had a swimming pool twelve meters long, ten times over again . . . and that gets the hens cackling! Every second pharmacist in Altona and every third salesman in Hamburg lives in more luxury.[6] They publicly preached water and privately drank wine? That was copied too late and too badly from Heinrich Heine. I find it much worse when the rulers publicly preach wine and privately guzzle blood.

If I misunderstand Marx correctly, then I can formulate a modified basic political rule of history: in every society, the aim is to distribute the produced wealth as unjustly as possible without getting anyone overly upset. That's the way it will be in the future, as well. In any event, it is tricky to locate this happy medium, because the tolerance of the exploited is a variable quantity.

But the Stalinists did not fail because of this correctable error. It was not the social injustices that were devastating, but something else: the bigwig system led to a situation where there was not even any wealth created that could be distributed with the requisite injustice. Thus, even the luxury that the socialist feudal aristocracy derived from universal poverty was itself paltry and useless. This pauperous wealth is indicative of their failure as the exploitative class. The bigwigs had luxury yachts? And went on hunts? And bathed in Wandlitz with Omo?[7] And passed privilege along to their broods? A weekend house for the pampered daughter? A stylish car for the doltish son? It is as banal as it is comical. The rich and powerful in the West do that too, only a couple of levels higher, with style, and without a bad conscience. They also had more time to unfold their ruling culture; they are not as nouveau riche and newly powerful.

Socialism is no longer a goal. The people are fed up with hearing about a socialism with a human face. With this tautology, Dubcek inflamed our spirits back in 1968.[8] It, too, is now passé. The ambitious animal experiment performed on living human beings is now over.

Yes, it is a pity, but also a stroke of luck. Even the most ordinary annexation by the Federal Republic is still better than everything we had before. Admittedly, I had something else in mind. But it is not, of course, the task of world history to please little old Biermann. What I wanted is patently impossible: a German nation that not only satisfies its short-term needs, but also seeks its own road with all of its demonstrated creative power, a road that circumvents the peaceful self-extinction of the human species.

For this reason, with things standing as they do and developing as they are, my amusements can only be negative. I do not begrudge my old enemies their setbacks, and I wish the Stasi criminals a rough time of it. I gloat without a tinge of pity whenever I think about that moron Mielke and that smart alec Markus Wolf, about that lobotomized Hager and that hypocrite Hermann Kant. I wish the absolute worst for that prematurely reeducated Nazi Günter Mittag and his dreaded collective director Wolfgang Biermann from Zeiss-Jena.

But what will become of the people who tried their hands at choral recitation, in the Saxon dialect, and could only spew out this single really original line: "We are the people!" Ah yes, even the revised version puts a smile on my face: "We are *one* people!" "Germany, Germany," the people were screaming on Cathedral Square in Erfurt; that was my welcome. Yes, we are one people and also want to be one. But what kind of a one–this question now burns brightly.

In my new "Ballad of Jan Gat under the Sky in Rotterdam," the lyrics read: "two half pigs simply do not / make a whole fatherland." I am experiencing reunification like an overwrought soap opera, a histrionic love marriage. Joe Prosperity, an ugly beau, is marrying his wretched, battered little cousin from the poor house.

But whoops, it just doesn't turn out that way! The poor Eastern girl is not so poor after all. Within the socialist bloc, the GDR was to a large extent still the paradise of prosperity. And by any calculation, the GDR belongs to the small, elite club of the super-rich, and that in a world that hungers and thirsts. Anyone who, then, flees with his Trabi into the land of Mercedes is saving himself from the maybe eighth-richest country on earth and heading into the third-richest.

Honecker and his hypocrites were thus lying through their teeth by telling the half-truth: the GDR, a thriving nation. But Chancellor Kohl and his reunification lackeys have been lying even more deceitfully with the other half of the truth: the GDR is a worthless scrap heap that will be beyond salvation without an immediate annexation by the Federal Republic. And Czechoslovakia? Certainly it is far more run-down than the GDR! Therefore, annex it too? Hungary is cheerily going to pot, Poland is a miserable praying mass, and the Soviet Union is gnawing on the hammer and sickle. Is the only salvation for them also to be adopted by Helmut Kohl, indeed as soon as possible? Viewed from Ethiopia, that is all cynical balderdash.

Up until the end of this miraculous year '89, my political fantasy stretched only this far: hunt down the bigwigs–yes!; disempower the Stasi–by all means!; the Wall must be removed–that goes without saying! I could even picture in my mind a revolution without bloodshed and without old-fashioned barricades. That has all been said for ages and has been sung for years. Now reality has hatched our dream. Yet other creatures are crawling out of the eggshells, and they are not the ones I dreamt of–more crocodiles than nightingales.

Reality has once again shown itself to be more fantastic than any poem. The impertinent farce born of the daily political struggle, my merry poison-and-gall songs among the turmoil, all the verses composed out of parody and pain: all are now sinking out of contemporary history and into the void of literary history. The "Ballad of the Working-Class Poet Max Kunkel from the VEB Chemie-Leuna" was still a kick in November.[9] Now, two months later, it is but a cheat sheet of historical consciousness for use against an all too rapid memory loss. Who was Hans Modrow, yeah, and who were Honecker and Ulbricht, Axen and Schnitzler, and what actually was that thing they call "the Stasi"?

"It could be that someday, when everything has been achieved / I will have achieved nothing–apart from a beginning from the top." I began with this song in Leipzig. And so it was supposed to be now in the GDR, a really new beginning. But the beginning from the top has, in the meantime, shown itself to be an annexation from below.

Nevertheless, it is true for me personally. I am beginning from the top. I finally am in a position where I do not need to know any better. I no longer have the crutch of oppositional validity; I am finally no longer correct. The old play is over and done with. The familiar villains and their adversaries are exiting the stage in unison, and the new script is just now being written.

Truly, the revolution has liberated me from always having to play the same role. The voice crying out in the wilderness may once again speak softly, may even stutter or keep silent. I am now taking a spiritual inventory and adding up the last nickels and dimes of the communist utopia. Coins without value, a little pocket change, that's all I have left.

In spite of all that, and to no surprise, I am still of the same opinion. I cannot extinguish the dream inside me, the dream of a more just society. This dream is older than anything that ever called itself communism. It is as old as humanity itself and has been killed off again and again, for the simple reason that it has always resurrected itself.

In the search for a future, I and many others seek, in all of our insecurity, to apply models from the past. In my own helplessness I trotted the Communards out from under the mothballs of history, that hacked-down, brave people from Paris in 1871. This happened totally unawares and yet cannot be an accident: three times in my most recent songs I have made use of this old word of hope. Like a child in the dark, I sing of the Commune de Paris and their radical democracy. Perhaps the Pere Lachaise cemetery has become the last terrain, perhaps only there does my utopia have solid ground underfoot, where that soil is watered with the blood of the Communards.[10] And perhaps a chimney of a crematorium in Auschwitz is the only thing about which a barbarian such as I can still write a poem.

I would really love to have been in the majority for once. In rare historical constellations, there may even be such an appropriate blind luck. Vaclav Havel is enjoying one such constellation these days. When on December 1, after twenty-five years of a GDR ban and after thirteen years in the West, I headed for a concert in Leipzig the aroma of just such a fleeting happiness filled my head.[11] I enjoyed a paralyzing elation.

On December 3, I was driving with my wife across the border crossing at Invaliden Strasse on our way over there. That was all, just to drive around, to take it all in, to compare, to remember.

A captain of the state security force shoved our papers through the slot into the control container, and it took a minute. Half in jest I said: "So then, what will become of you, if things keep proceeding as they are?"

The man spoke like a child: "Mr. Biermann, they have betrayed us sooo . . . indeed . . . I have sacrificed eight years of my life for it . . ."

I asked: "What sort of work did you use to do?"

"Automobile locksmith."

"Well, then. . . ."

"Yes, but as a locksmith. . . ."

"You will have to work more and earn less."

"If only we had listened to you sooner . . ." (At this point I would have gladly socked him in the face.)

And on he whimpered: "Do you know what they used to say to us? Biermann is a criminal. And you know what?" He hemmed and hawed for a while and thought most deeply and finally blurted out, in great agony, the amazingly profound observation: "They themselves were criminals!"

"No!," I laughed.

"Yes!," he said with deadly earnest.

Then I knew that I had in front of me one of those perpetrators who now saw himself as a victim. And that damned "That you are, indeed. But only partially."

The day flew by quickly; in the early evening it was already pitch black outside. Unter den Linden, the Schinkel guardhouse, Marx-Engels square, the Christmas market next to the Alex, then Wilhelm Pieck Strasse, Oranienburger, past the synagogue, Friedrich Strasse, the corner of Chaussee Strasse number 131, my old apartment.[12] The front windows entirely dark. I steered my car in front of the door almost automatically up to the corner of Hannover. In the glass case in front of the Federal German Consulate sat someone in a uniform.

My very pregnant wife said: "Hey, the baby is really pushing on my bladder." So I led her down the old hallway. We groped through the dark for the backyard door. "You can go in here." And so she squatted right there in the courtyard. I turned away and craned my neck up toward the windows at the back of the building: "Meticulous, meticulous." Then the pissing noise suddenly put a little pressure on my bladder, and so I stepped on a little farther and relieved myself. And at just that moment it occurred to me: leaving our scent! Yeah, that's it: my house! My apartment! The dog comes home and lays claim to what is his, he stakes out his old territory. A chuckle shook me, and as a result I tinkled on my shoe.

We never got a hold of ourselves again; it was so funny. The old fears magnified our laughter to the point of silliness. And thus we were finally in the jovial mood we needed: "Come on up with me, let's go clinkle on the bell of my old door." Once again the medicine of laughter–clinkle or tinkle–Mr. Freud, are you there? Two flights up. My door, as always: at eye level a little hand-sized door, covered with reflective glass. A simple name on the bell: Seidel. Once, twice, nothing. Finally the little door within the big door opened: a man, about my age. "Hello!"

He: "Who are you?"

I: "Wolf Biermann . . . you know, the folk singer, thirteen years ago I was forced out of the GDR. . . ."

"I don't know you."

"I lived in this apartment for twenty years."

"How should I know that?"

"I just wanted to see how it has changed over the years. Might we maybe have a look inside?"

"That is out of the question."

"Do you live here?"

"Yes, why not?"

". . . all alone in this large apartment?"

"Yes, why not?"

"Before, Martin Florchinger, the Brechtian actor, and Agnes Kraus, the actress and dancer, and one other woman lived here with me. Is it not a little big for just you?"

"No, why should it be?"

"For whom do you work then?"

"Foreign trade."

"Schalck-Golodkowski?"[13]

That was it. Trap (and door) shut. The monkey lives. Stasi.

We trudged back downstairs in the dim light. I thought: if the Stasi is dismantled, then I really could move back into my old rooms without much trouble. With kith and kin from Hamburg, right back into the second apartment at Chaussee Strasse number 131. Tile stoves and briquettes up out of the cellar; the old neighbors; the nice saleswoman at the produce stand; a couple of friends as well: M. with his rebuilt Wartburg crankshaft;[14] the delightfully deranged Hussel, master cooper and big melon head; Doctor Tsouloukidze, the dear cold specialist; Ilya and Verutschka, the aged Jewish children of the Gulag; and my Weidendam bridge with the Prussian eagle on it;[15] my Huguenot cemetery with Hegel and John Heartfield; the grave with the "Kaiser's Birthday" poet Johannes R. Becher, who stuck us with that god-forsaken line "Germany, united fatherland;"[16] the Brecht Archive around the corner; and, more useful for my purposes: Hans Bunge, the living Brecht Archive.[17] And just a couple of short steps from the Berlin Ensemble.[18] Why not, indeed.

Two full months have passed since then. No one is saying anything about moving over there anymore. Modrow is in decline, Kohl is puffing himself up. If the GDR is soon to be gobbled up, I will do better to remain in my dear hometown of Hamburg. The Soviet

Union is self-destructing anyway; the huge empire is disintegrating into its component parts. Ten or twenty new states will emerge as sworn enemies of one another. Communism is at its end, not only in reality: no, much more real than that–also in one's dreams.

When I came to the GDR in 1953, to the little city of Gadebusch in Mecklenburg, I found a communism that was in sound health and almost already fully realized. Our beloved Stalin had just passed away, and on the seventeenth of June I did not notice anything untoward in this dump. I thought things were great, because I did not yet understand anything.

But once I had lived a couple of years in the workers' and farmers' state, I noticed that communism was ailing. I wrote songs and poems that were intended to make it healthy. But the bigwigs did not appreciate my bitter pills.

When I was finally banned, when the Stasi threatened my neck, I screamed and yelled out the truth: that communism was not merely sick, but deathly ill.

Then came the revocation of my citizenship, which, in my initial state of shock, I did not want to view as an opportunity and good fortune. I went out into the world for the first time, to countries that are both poorer and freer than the GDR. And I grasped the incomprehensible. Richer or poorer, it was all the same: communism was not deathly ill at all; it had been long dead. No tears and lived lies, no infusions of capital and melancholy songs can help it.

The corpse is lying all over the land and contaminating the air.

I do like two of the people among the group that is now thrusting itself before the public eye in the GDR: the rivals Bärbel Bohley and Gregor Gysi. But Bohley has too little grasp of power politics in her heart. And the young lawyer Gysi, in his role as bankruptcy administrator, thinks too much with his heart. If he would only pay attention to his lovely wife, he would not persist in trying to perform mouth-to-mouth resuscitation with his smacker on the cadaver of communism. What is it to me, anyway?

Dig the graves! After the murderers come the gravediggers. Should I maybe shovel with my guitar? Give me a spade. Let's finally bury this giant little cadaver. Even Christ had to lie buried in the ground for three days before he could carry out his master work: the resurrection.

NOTES

Source: *Die Zeit*, 2 March 1990, 65-66. Translated by Bill Hutfilz.

1. Black, red, and gold are the colors of the German flag.

2. Hitler's Third Reich was called the Thousand-Year Empire, since it, like the Holy Roman Empire of German Nations founded by Charlemagne, was supposed to last a thousand years.

3. Brüsewitz and Havemann were well-known critics of the GDR regime.

4. The author is a well-known poet and song-writer who lived in the GDR until his forced emigration to the West in 1976.

5. Margot Honecker was Erich Honecker's wife; she served as GDR secretary of education.

6. Many well-to-do residents of Hamburg live in Altona.

7. Wandlitz was an enclosed development near East Berlin where the former GDR political elite resided in luxurious homes. Omo is the name of a West German detergent.

8. Alexander Dubcek led the Czech revolution that culminated in the Prague Spring in 1968.

9. In the GDR it was customary for writers to have jobs in the VEB (state owned) industries, and factory workers were encouraged to compose literature about their work situations.

10. The Paris Commune was an attempt to establish a revolutionary Marxist government in Paris during the Franco-Prussian War. It was brutally suppressed by both French and Prussian forces. The Paris Commune is often evoked by socialist intellectuals as an attempt to found a utopian society that is snuffed out by the forces of reaction.

11. Biermann's poetry was banned in the GDR in 1965 and his GDR citizenship was revoked in 1976. Forced to leave the GDR, he returned to live in Hamburg, his birthplace.

12. These are names of famous streets, squares, and buildings in central East Berlin.

13. Alexander Schalck-Golodkowski was is charge of "Commercial Coordination," the office that regulated the influx of hard currency into the GDR.

14. "Wartburg" is the name of the GDR luxury auto built in Eisenach near the famous Wartburg.

15. In his song "The Prussian Icarus" Biermann compares himself to the Prussian eagle represented on this bridge.

16. The poet Johannes R. Becher served as cultural minister of the GDR and composed the text of the GDR national anthem.

17. Hans Bunge has co-authored a Brecht biography, edited critical collections on Brecht, and has conducted several interviews with Brecht's collaborators such as Hanns Eisler.

18. This is the theatrical ensemble with which Bertolt Brecht worked following his move to East Berlin after the war.

Preamble of the Social Charter Proposed by the Round Table
(March 5, 1990)

1. The striving for unity of the two German states and the related currency and economic union must include a social charter. This must lead to an improvement in the living and working conditions, to the unity of work, leisure, and family, guarantee the safeguarding of existing social standards, and reduce the threats to our natural environment.

2. German unity has to be completed by means of a reciprocal process of reform of both German social security systems, retaining their positive traits.

Social standards that have evolved historically in both German states should be preserved, further developed, and taken to a higher level of security.

In a unifying Germany a humane existence must be guaranteed to all people by means of a fundamental social security system.

3. The economic, currency, and social union must create preconditions for countering unemployment and improving the well-being of all citizens. Disadvantaged groups such as the disabled, the elderly, families with many children, and single parents require special social protection.

4. We need to create the legal framework for enabling citizens to form associations as well as interest communities and interest groups so that they can help determine and shape their living conditions on an economic and social level.

5. The social development in both German states is tied to the equal treatment and equal rights of men and women, of people of different race, color, nationality, religion, and age.

6. In the process of developing an economic, currency, and social union between the two German states, the social benefits of the GDR citizens must be preserved. In the cases of all variants that are negotiated for the equalization of income and price structures, far-reaching legal protection for personal property must be guaranteed. The stability of the savings of the GDR citizens has to be safeguarded.

7. The development of German unity and the social reforms bound up with it could, by serving as a model, make a contribution to the economic, social, and political integration of a unified Europe.

NOTES

Source: Herles/Rose, 238-39.

50
Election Poster of "Alliance 90" (March 10-11, 1990)

Encouragement
For years we have been committed to peace and justice in the GDR.

Now we are facing an election!

For the first time our votes are being solicited.
We can help determine our future.

Do not be discouraged by the large number of political parties!
Do not stay home, get out and vote!

The party we elect has to encourage peace and justice in our country
and care for the protection of the natural world.

**We have decided to vote for those who have participated from the
beginning:**

"Alliance 90"

–New Forum
–Democracy Now
–Initiative for Peace and Human Rights

NOTES

Source: *Aufbrüche*, 145.

51
**Klaus Hartung, "The Great Changing of the Wheel,
or The Revolution Without Utopia" (March 1990)**

I

The co-founder of the New Forum, the microbiologist Jens
Reich, a Berlin scientist with a rather sarcastic wit, has developed
a penchant for elegiac images: "We have been living in a hut upon a
dam," he said at the beginning of February in Tutzing, where "new

answers to the German Question" are sought in vain. "The dam has broken, we are swept away along with it, we try to swim with the current, we try desperately to keep our heads above water, that is, we are still trapped in the old way of thinking."

Why this image of drowning? We all know that the masses in Leipzig no longer look to East Berlin, but to Bonn instead. The opposition no longer has the power of the street on its side. But it has great political successes to show for itself: it has succeeded in crippling, dismantling, and disarming the largest citizens' army ever to bear arms in Germany, the Stasi. In addition, it has produced effective, democratic organs of control and a government of national consensus. The bitter paradox: successes and defeats are intimately interrelated. The opposition did the dirty work of dismantling the SED state, but it was, probably for that very reason, not visionary.

But would it really have been possible for the utopia of democratization to be more attractive than the push for unity? Twenty-eight years of the Wall: that was clearly the concretized wish for reunification. Since that October, the utopias of another GDR, of another Germany, have been damaged and destroyed from above and below by the pace of the drive for unification: democratic socialism, dialogue, the nation as a "friendly, diverse motherland" (Konrad Weiss), confederation as a forerunner of a Europe without borders, and last but not least the utopia in which the revolutionary people determine their own fate with their own hands.

The alternative has, in the meantime, reached a crisis point in its existence (if it still exists at all): a regulated, that is, cooperative process of unification or the precipitous annexation of the GDR. Chancellor Kohl is creating an ice-cold and decidedly successful politics of greater leverage and is making use of two instruments: the strength of the D-mark and the fear of the masses over there. It is that banal. The existential anxiety of the GDR populace, the fear of being the victims not only of forty years of really-existing socialism but also of its bankruptcy, drives them in optimistic hordes into the future poor house of the Federal Republic.

Flight into unity, therefore, and the end of reflection? One thing is certain: the ways and means by which the GDR populace will become a part of a unified Germany will determine the political relationships and democratic culture of the next decades. The hour of unity: is it the hour of leftist melancholy?

Time and Wasted Time

There has never been so much beginning. But where have they gone, these beginnings? Were they just the beginnings of a long-anticipated end? And the promises of the beginning: were they just fictions, sprung from the ambivalence of the initial hour? These are questions that already exhort to the work of remembrance and the difficulties of reconstructing the past. Anyone who writes today, now, writes in the knowledge that in these months eons lie between today and the day before, writes with his or her back to time, well aware that the next item of news will shatter his or her most recent formulations all over again. Reflection takes time, particularly reflections about Germany, about what is emerging, about what has been. Yet at the same time it is preferable to remain within the spirit of the times, so that one's reflections also remain relevant. That is the dilemma.

Revolutions have a nasty habit of coming too soon and thus taking their protagonists by surprise. But the so-called gentle revolution in the GDR and what occurred after that October came, by contrast, too late; and it was, in an idiosyncratic, incomparable way, at the mercy of the dictates of time, in the dual form of time pressure and of lost time. The thousand-times repeated statement by Gorbachev, "He who arrives too late is punished by life," was fittingly formulated in the GDR.[1] It was a judgment of an elementary nature which, one must admit in hindsight, is true not only for the SED dictatorship.

The stigma of delay adheres to all events. The SED apparatus only fell apart after the forces that had held it together had already worn themselves out. The relationships first had to come to such a crisis point that the totality of society stood opposed to the totality of control and repression. The opposition between weapons and human beings first had to become absolute before the masses could appear on the streets in Leipzig. It was not the opposition who effected the collapse, but rather those who occupied the embassies in Budapest and Prague, the flood of refugees across the Czechoslovakian border, the exodus of young and qualified specialists, the stone-washed-jeans people in their Trabis. In other words: even before the overthrow of the system, the further existence of the nation had been placed in question.

One cannot ignore how much the fate of tardiness directed events after October 9. When 70,000 Leipzigers assembled on Karl-Marx-Platz on that evening, even though they suspected firing orders and even though they knew that emergency wards and supplementary blood supplies had been set up in the hospitals, they presented the regime with the alternatives of either terror or backing down. That was one of the few moments of revolutionary timeliness. Since that point in time the collapse of the apparatuses of political power has rushed on ahead of the mass movements. The radicality of the masses was outdone by the panic of the apparatchiks, in their maneuvers to retain both power and a justification for their existence. Thus the masses were cheated, as it were, out of their own revolutionary symbols, out of their own storming of the Winter Palace. A strange revolution, in which not even a single statue fell. When at the end of January the Stasi headquarters on Normannen Strasse was finally stormed, the on-rushers found only deep-frozen asparagus spears, shark fins and steaks, dust-covered files from the years 1981 and 1982, and emptied offices.

Even the actions of the governments Krenz/Stoph and Modrow followed the logic of delay. The travel law, which could have solidified a framework for social dialogue as early as the beginning of October, could only radicalize the masses on the sixth of November. The decision of the Modrow government to continue paying the salaries of Stasi operatives for three more years could have had a positive effect only a moment sooner, by representing a conception of social reconciliation and by destroying the Stasi. At the beginning of January, however, it became, in the eyes of the masses, evidence for the continued existence of the Stasi, and not only because the government had snuck the decision through over the Christmas recess.

In any event, neither the government nor the SED-PDS has ever succeeded, where the key political question of the destruction of the Stasi is concerned, in breaking out of the force field of delayed reaction. The SED frittered away the time it still had at its disposal with its party congress that was moved up to the beginning of December. The faction of reform and democratization had not carried its internal dissent all the way to fragmentation of the party. An untenable compromise prevailed between democratization and the preservation of ownership rights–ownership of apparatuses, newspapers, publishing houses, real estate–on the basis of which it became clear that the compromise could not last. Thus the party shirked its last and truly historic task, namely to be the pole around which social debates about democratization revolved. Their desperate clinging to forty-year-old property will probably cause them to end up as managers of real estate.

The timing of the government's decisions was pre-determined by the self-destructive tendency of the party. It recognized far too late that this party would not be able to constitute a state until the time of the elections. So everything came too late: the decisions to reform the economy, the recognition of the Round Table as a powerful body, the acceptance of the opposition into the government, and so on right up to Modrow's plan for a "Germany, united fatherland." The government of national emergency hardly has time between now and March 18 to rule, and it can at best be a lame-duck administration of emergency under campaign conditions.

Was the regime of delay and wasted time therefore unavoidable? Were there no hopes against the runaway self-destruction of the GDR? Is what we are now witnessing in the first weeks of February, the reversion of the process of unification into the push for annexation according to the dictates of the Bonn hegemony–which would be tantamount to the liquidation of all the elements of the peaceful revolution–truly unavoidable, truly a preliminary decision for "Germany, united fatherland?"

Pan-German Domestic Politics

The melancholy "could-have-been" that underlies these statements does not derive from the conviction that a more fitting politics could have rescued the regime from the pressure of time. That would be an illusion, and self-righteousness to boot. We have all learned that prophecies are best held back until the next news report. It is therefore not compelling to play the backward-looking prophet. Nevertheless, I maintain that the process of German unification is in no way so cemented that it will from now on be pointless to talk about political missteps.

The German-German dynamic certainly cannot be left out of these considerations about the particular timing that dictates and directs the GDR revolution. On the contrary: it gives renewed force to the maelstrom of delay.

The time to achieve a metamorphosis consistent with the level of its own strength, while absent in the GDR, exists in the FRG. The less time Modrow had, the more time Kohl had to play with in order to drive the GDR toward its own self-destruction. Even more ominous, the government and the protagonists of the democratization of a new GDR have, for all practical purposes, left the question of unification to the politicians in Bonn. Since November 9 at the latest it has been a question of pan-German domestic politics. But the leaders in the GDR even reacted to this development too late. There can be no question that without the utopia of an autonomous road toward the democratization of GDR society the authority of the SED could not have remained intact. However, the illusion of having time to be able to place democracy before unity had to have its ramifications. The ignorance of the national question played right into the hands of politicians in the FRG, who then only had to seek a direct line to the streets in Leipzig, Dresden, and Magdeburg in order to have political developments in the GDR in the palms of their hands. This is an eventuality that, in spite of all its comprehensibility, defies explanation.

The political powers of the GDR acted in the three months of that revolutionary autumn as though the fiction of a national independence were a reality. One could almost speak of a blind spot where the Wall was concerned. It had been, of course, the most important element of GDR domestic policy. In the sense that the Wall allowed the West Germans to ignore the GDR populace, it bound the GDR populace to the Federal Republic. The Wall was a synonym for the national outrage of perpetuating a second-class German existence, for the misery of deprivation, for the worthlessness of money, for the humiliation of absurd restrictions on freedom. Its fall placed the national question before all other questions. The incessant flow of emigrants especially forced a collective German domestic policy. The emigrants basically set the pace of German-German politics. Only a policy that dealt with the exodus could have a chance of becoming master of rapidly fleeting time. Each attempt to defend the achievements of the GDR revolution against the pressure of a unification from below necessarily led to the powerlessness of delay.

Power and Powerlessness of the Masses

The masses make history; the masses have made this history. They have overthrown the GDR state. But not only that. They have upset the division and with it the postwar order of Central Europe, therefore also bringing the postwar era to a close. They have placed the peace treaty on the agenda and accelerated the pace of European unity and shattered the future of the military alliances. The GDR population has transformed itself into an active mass and forced a new epoch.

There can be no doubt as to the historical rank of the mass movement in the GDR. But in the meantime, one asks oneself, rather depressed, whether this movement will also, or should also, be the subject of this new epoch. The enthusiasm of the outset is gone. To put it mildly. In the eyes of Hildegard Hamm-Brücher, the "dream of a revolutionary October" has turned into "the nightmare of nationalism." Politicians both over here and over there view the masses no longer as the heralds of a new era, but as a problem for securing stability, for domestication. Signals to quiet the masses are what are being sought, not clarifications about the reality of the economic misery. The apologia of the "peaceful revolution" changed into a lasting entreaty, because meanwhile mass radicalism had induced fear. The admonishing fantasy and subversive wit of the autumn demonstrations has given way to the shrill resonance of "Germany, united fatherland." The eco-liberal Ulrich Hausmann even sensed in this a growing threat to civil society. Why the disconsolation that led from the radicality of language to radical flag-waving, to the voiceless black-red-gold? Why has so little content, so little of the historical role remained?

One should recall the sigh of relief, the thankfulness with which the first mass demonstrations were greeted at the end of September in Leipzig, in order to recognize the degree of the deflation of emotions in only these few months. The sense of relief sticks in one's memory: finally the spark of democracy in Eastern Europe had been lit. The repression in the GDR had ultimately become, since 1987, as absolute at is was obsolete. Signals of understanding, of solidarity, like the white ribbons of the emigrants around brief cases and car antennas, had been forbidden, and bicycle demonstrations for the rescue of the Pleisse were repressed.[2] The persecution of dissidents became so pervasive that suspicion of complicity had to be endured. In that October the mute GDR finally began to speak, and it was a peculiar voice in the European concert.

What, then, has changed? What has led an emancipation movement into intolerance, into the shouting down of any speaker who sets other priorities than that of reunification? Has the long-dormant inner core of nationalism finally awoken? Is it now the "hollow" mass on the street, whereas in that October it was the courageous ones?

If one examines the short history of this mass movement, one theory is clearly false: that the nationalist element was inherent in the demonstrations from the very beginning. If one views the Monday events in Leipzig, the political barometer of the republic, one thing becomes clear: the mass demonstrations were, at least until the end of 1989, politically quite precise. They were the effective, responsive opposition on the street. It began with the breakthrough of the opposition: "Legalize the New Forum." In the next stage came reactions to the offer of dialogue. One of the most clever slogans from November against the artifice of dialogue went: "Those of us who are hard of hearing need subtitles: freedom and democracy." Egon Krenz's slick manipulations of shifts in power were denounced: "360-degree turn?" "No protection for the species of *Wendehälse*." The mottoes persecuted the apparatus's struggle for survival. "Cut off the branches of power; preserve the trees." "Resignation is progress." International engagement could not be overlooked; solidarity with the Romanian people was exhorted, there were moments of silence on account of Prague police excesses, representatives of students from Czechoslovakia were cheered. The last Monday demonstration in December was a silent vigil in remembrance of the victims of Stalinism.

The persistent theme was, of course, the Stasi. It was not only the chant of Monday happenings in various locations: "Stasi into the national economy," not the whistles and candles in front of Stasi buildings. The demonstrations practiced mass control, reacted to movements of mass flight, secret institutions, and the removal of files. Above all else, though, the masses hindered every attempt to reform or transform the Stasi, to save parts of its apparatus. I do not think anyone could have envisioned the success of a mass movement of this magnitude before that October. It not only dismantled the Stalinist apparatus of power, but in so doing also took over, for all practical purposes, the power of the state.

Why did the experience of power not make the people on the street proud? Why did the contents of the demonstrations not consume them? Why did this experience not incite the people to articulate their interests for a future society? The shift from "We are the people" to "We are one people" is so terrifying not because of its national sentiment, but because of the dramatic disappearance of self-consciousness. "We are the people" is a clear expression of power-consciousness; "We are one people" is at best an appeal to the Federal Republic. Not to mention such idiocies as "Kohl is good for the soul!"

Fear invaded the demonstrations, a new fear. The power collapse of the SED state from above did not change everyday life below. There the functionaries continued to lead, work, and carry out projects. The SED contributed to its own downfall by leaving the impression that it could play a political role even after the first democratic elections. The demonstrations against neo-Nazism after the attacks at the Soviet Memorials in January, conducted in the style of the old struggle demonstrations, could not help but evoke the nightmare of a renewed SED leadership.[3] The call for reunification was always underlaid by this fear. Reunification means for the masses–and here it is not necessary to listen closely to the Monday demonstrations in Leipzig–the best formula for a radical coup de grace after forty years of the GDR and the SED.

Was there another option, a *tertium datur*? Could democratization itself not mean this coup de grace? Why did the masses not see that immediate unification would also annul their first steps toward a democratic society? Did the masses drop the ball, or was it the politicians? Did the pressure of lost time force them into the tacit alternative of reunification or democratization?

Coup de Grace and Moral Lament

The call for a coup de grace is understandable, but not entirely self-evident; it also means an end to decades of one's own life. Why this radicality, which is directed against one's own life history?

Since that revolutionary October, the masses have been not only on the streets; they have also taken stock, in the collectives, the social institutions, in the schools and universities. A mass investigation was set in motion concerning the issues of environmental information, profit and loss calculations, a search for hard facts and for remaining foreign currency. It is a process, carried forward by factory groups of the New Forum, by citizens' committees, and by the many round tables in the republic that have little exposure but great meaning. Except that this flowering of the people's power was overtaken and devalued by the uncovering of "misuse of power" and an economy of privilege. The *Spiegel* cover story on Schalck-

Golodkowski was posted for weeks in the factories.[4] This revelation, dealt with in the minutest detail in the news and aided by the cold professionalism of the Western media, must have negated in a moral sense every thought of a capacity for reform within GDR society. In the moral sense above all others, for the GDR is a very moralistic country.

The primacy of morals over interests was embodied in the state: the founding myth had the GDR originating out of anti-fascism; individual advancement was supposed to spring from "social activity," increases in production from the "historical task"; a peacock's tail of immaterial rewards, of orders and titles, accompanied success; not to mention the fog of forty years of agitprop. Under such a persistent moralistic strain any kind of state would have fallen apart, all the more so an economic system based on lack. This moralizing impulse was not perforated by the revolution, but inherited by it. The first thing attacked was not the bankrupt politics, the structures of Stalinism, or the elimination of freedoms, but the lack of credibility. The people did not observe with elation the trembling of the thousands of tiny, disempowered Stalins; instead, they saw their moral depravity. The unhealthy climate of personal shame, of self-accusations, of public penance–every party chairperson a head penitent–prolongs this same Protestant rigor. This is more likely to promote a new double moral standard than it is to produce an effective relationship between morals and politics.

The universal moralistic lamentation intersects with the individual one. Bringing morals under state control has buried the private person beneath the sediment of official values. One had to be anti-racist, internationalist, and anti-nationalist, from the cradle to the grave. The devastating result of this pedagogical situation? A universally applied local anaesthetic against the canon of the good socialist individual. Tolerance, internationalism, anti-racism: these are virtues that cannot be inculcated by state pedagogy. They are the products of public debate, of a culture that allows for public expressions of prejudice and hate. There never was such a culture here. No wonder, then, that the image of the overly ecstatic Trabi driver, who can only say "Incredible!" and "Irreversible!," is being replaced by the intolerant GDR-ite, who is now finally letting himself go, venting his hatred of Poles and asylum-seekers and busying himself with his Germanness. The people in the GDR are facing the fatal alternative of either being blind to the Wandlitz Republic or having been its accomplices. The consciousness of a universal complicity is in the air, especially since without a shot of

moral double standard neither tiles nor spare parts could be pro-
cured. This is a questionable motive for rushing into unity and, after
forty years of morality, for assimilating oneself all the more im-
personally to victorious capitalism. Added to this is the history of
a forty-year-long subjugation. The problem of working things
through. Everyone in the GDR knows that nothing will be solved by
charges against the SED and rabid criminal proceedings against
the functionaries. It is less a question of how individuals were
wronged than of how they allowed themselves to be wronged. In
contrast to National Socialism, after the defeat of really-existing
socialism priority must be given to coming to terms with the past
rather than to criminal justice; whereas after National Socialism
coming to terms with the past was elevated to the status of an un-
binding political duty only because criminal justice failed.

Delay and decay of values: it is undeniable that among the
GDR populace a demagogic disposition predominates–not only because electoral candidates from the Federal Republic are turning
up–and that a precipitous annexation can also bring a collective
German push toward demagoguery.

November 9 was no day of nationalism. It was one of the most
humane days of German history. That much remains. But that day
and the days that followed were at the same time marked by a
cruel, demoralizing, shocking paradox. The struggle to stand tall
again led the masses to the display windows of the West. Freedom
to receive welcome money. The GDR-ites went straight from depra-
vation into poverty. Just as they had had no goods for their money
in the GDR, so they now had no money for the goods in the West.
What did they see? They saw a frictionless society, they saw a
lifetime spent standing in line, trying to organize. Rip van Winkles
of really-existing socialism, who had lost forty years as though it
were just a day. An eerie, quiet devaluation of their former efforts.

The dynamic of reunification that set in afterwards was intensified by that November. Even here the pressure of time prevailed,
the pressure of the lost lifetime. In front of the display windows of
the West, the masses lost once and for all the strength and conviction that the effort of democratizing the GDR still made sense.

But yet another, a specifically German paradox began on
November 9. With the opening of the Wall, the population of the
GDR came over in multitudes, they clogged the streets, formed mute
lines in front of the banks, crippled the local traffic, and drove, in
their silent social Darwinism, the West German customers out of
their consumer temples. All of this unleashed fear as well as joy.

Reunification for the GDR-ites meant the deliverance from a lost lifetime; for the Westerners, reunification meant the only feasible guarantee that "the people over there" would stay over there. There were not actually any nationalistic motivations, but rather a mixture of a racism of prosperity and the frustration of lack–although probably a demagogic disposition for nationalism.

The Opposition: The Intellectuals as Victims of Unity?

The opposition arose out of the tendentiously illegal culture of the niches of human rights seminars. "We have not coped well with the step from antipolitics to politics," as Ludwig Mehlhorn analyzed the situation. Indeed, the opposition had produced no political authority–with the exception of Bärbel Bohley–before the revolt. Anyone who might have played this role was forced all too soon to take the path to prison or emigration to the West. Most representatives of the opposition held a pessimistic view of the political culture of the country in the first place. Even up to today it has not produced any great speakers. Moreover, there also existed no societal cohesion in which they could have evolved. The separation from the masses became definitive once the opposition no longer dared to confront the masses. While the opposition was fighting for a democratic transformation of the GDR, the street was demanding the liquidation of the republic. The opposition saw itself increasingly as the victim of the popular hatred of intellectuals. One reason why the opposition could not become the protagonist of the mass movement certainly lay in its always fragile national identity. In Eastern Europe, the consensus of national autonomy was the sure precondition for the fact that the people could train the leadership they had. This fundamental consensus was absent.

But even the opposition was controlled by the regimen of delay. They were dissidents, politically committed to a long-term democratization project within the system. The democratic revolt took them by surprise; they were overrun by the reunification dynamic. Their fate can be described perfectly by the example of the New Forum, the strongest organization in October. As long as it was still a phantom, it was politically powerful. As soon as it turned seriously to the task of organizing itself at a grassroots level it lost its influence on the grassroots. Part of the reason for this was certainly because it was a *German* organization that took its time where fundamentals were concerned, although practical politics did not allow it any time. But also the grassroots democratic concept itself,

the cause of endless debates on the order of business despite the
pressure of the election race, was delayed. It was a populist pedagogical program that was supposed to educate the people to independent political actions at a point in time when, as the populace
had recognized for some time, the compulsion to take to the
"streets" was incomparably more effective and economical. That
explains why the SPD-East, which took the lead in transferring
the spectrum of parties from the Federal Republic to the GDR, was
able to be so successful. Characteristic of this defeat of the opposition is the cooptation of the "Democratic Awakening" into an electoral coalition with the CDU.[5] And it is the tragedy of the coming
election on March 18 that the most important organization of the
revolutionary turn, the New Forum, will probably lose the election.

II

An overly dismal picture? It cannot be dismal enough if it helps
to dispel as quickly as possible as many illusions as possible. It is
neither the time for nostalgia for the peaceful revolution nor the
time to endow, as many leftists from the Federal Republic are doing, the revolution with a spiteful question mark, only because the
revolutionaries with the black-red-gold flags are not adhering to
the classical iconography. It was a revolution, and the fact that a
central government armed to the teeth collapsed without bloodshed justifies the assertion that forty years of really-existing socialism had meant more than social regression. In any case, those
mired in failure are the leftist utopians, both over here and over
there: the utopia that democratization here could have triggered a
democratic push over there; the utopia of the plannable displacement of the planned economy by the market economy; the utopia of
an amalgam of society-wide rationality and the market, of free
initiative and poverty-free socialist safeguards. The ideas of Elmar Altvater, Rainer Land, Michael Brie and others are plausible
as abstract sketches, but, to quote the detective novelist Raymond
Chandler, "there is not enough fear in them." Such utopias do not
lend themselves to becoming a dam against the egregious discrep-
ancy in prosperity that could not help but burst forth with the
opening of the Wall.

The revolution and the removal of the German schism have unleashed enormous energies, energies that were necessarily directed,
first and foremost and with astonishing radicality, against the
GDR state and its social foundations. Who in their right mind could

have preached "construction" after forty years of the "construction of socialism?"[6] But the fate of these energies is in no way decided by the political decision for German unity. Unity is much more a code word for a radical displacement of the political power relations in united Germany. In this very year the basic constellation of the relationship between democracy and capital will be established. Anyone who maintains that he or she can already predict the outcome of this struggle, which has just begun, will not be a factor. Leftist analyses and nightmarish visions of the hegemonic power of a nation that is 80 million people strong are nothing but an attempt to legitimate preemptively their own political irrelevance.

The political task is clear enough: it is necessary to derail Kohl's politics of greater leverage. These politics are instituting the primacy of capitalism over democracy. That is to say that the lever itself must be destroyed. This era does not need new visions, utopias, and great projects; none exist that could be developed anyway. The only form of political thought that will be right-thinking is one that combines these forces. For the West German Left, that means that they must jettison long-cherished attitudes, articles of faith, and convictions: their consideredness, their anti-Social-Democratism, the love of principle, and whatever other sorts of sectarianism there is. Who with whom against whom: that will be the question in the 1990 election year. Kohl is practicing a secure, instinctual politics of material compulsion; the fact that he is giving priority to a currency union over economic reform–pushed through against the advice of all the experts–provides the best evidence of this.[7] Thus, it is a matter of asserting the primacy of politics in general over material compulsion. A few principles for this can already be identified:

Buying time. In order to buy time, politics must take the lead with time pressures. You have no time, therefore use it well. The key to buying time lies in the so-called emergency aid measures for the GDR. The necessity of emergency aid has enjoyed the broadest consensus ever since the onset of the GDR revolution, the CDU included. This consensus remained verbal, and it has degenerated into the theme of election-strategic punditry. Around the question of emergency aid the broadest imaginable political alliance must coalesce, an alliance that cuts across party lines and that must in any event be a German-German alliance, an immediate reunification from below. But appeals about and testaments to the dramatic situation in the GDR do not suffice for emergency aid. Programs, agendas, and issues to be addressed are also required. In any case, the open conflict between the GDR authorities and the Bonn government–with the support of the opposition in the Federal Republic–will be a precondition, a conflict that is probably only conceivable after March 18.

A pan-German domestic policy will also be necessary. The attempt on the part of the West German parties to win the GDR election campaign and thereby double their influence is currently putting this goal in jeopardy. Only if an Ibrahim Böhme can stand before the electorate of the Federal Republic and express his demands, and can count on the support of the SPD-West in this, can an opposition against Kohl's politics of greater leverage have any positive prospects. That is, the opposition must act as a pan-German unit, from both sides. The Left must understand unity as a national task and not as a problem for its own identity.

And a discussion of legal matters must begin quickly and concretely: the GDR's option for having all forms of ownership must be assured on a pan-German level. The Basic Law's provisions for a new constitution at the time of a free unification of the Germans have to be approached aggressively. A major theme in this arena will be a provision, unfulfilled by the Basic Law, of an economic constitution. The constitutional discussion has already gone awry in the GDR insofar as it is concerned exclusively with the GDR. It has to serve as a contribution to a constitutional convention; in other words, it must consciously intervene in the Federal Republic.

The 1990 election year will usher in the hardest-fought campaign in the existence of both German states. The degree of stupefaction of demagoguery now manifesting itself is horrifying. The opposition politician who has the courage to lay out honestly what the price of German unification will be can win the election. Can. Kohl will win no matter what if the opposition lacks this courage. Clearly, more political courage is demanded now than has prevailed to date in the political cultures both over here and over there. Very soon, to cite just one criterion, a politician will be needed who has the strength to tell the Monday demonstrators in Leipzig that their marches for reunification and against the SED have become passé.

Illusionary demands? Nevertheless, there is a broad consensus that buying time has to be the primary goal of unification politics. Economic politicians say it, left and right, bankers and social politicians say it. Kohl's coup in announcing the currency union did not unleash any conviction, but only a loud whistling in the wilderness, signifying the assurance that West German economic strength will be sufficient. For the buying of time there are two fundamentally key concepts: 1) the decision for German unity must be put behind us with political expeditiousness in order to disencumber it of the pressure of fear on the street. Should this succeed, then Kohl's lever will already have been shortened. 2) The unification process must be so intimately tied to European unification, to the interests of neighboring states, and to the victorious powers, that the German-German stampede to annexation will be nipped in the bud. Willy Brandt, in spite of all his national rhetoric about German workers' movements, always has at the heart of his speeches the hierarchy peace, Europe, unity. The "Genscher Plan" has also developed these elements into a focal concept: after the GDR elections, a treaty concerning the "roads to German unity within Europe." After this fundamental decision, no more time pressure should remain. The GDR will be tied to a panoply of European and international institutions. Added to that would be the "partnership of stability" with the Soviet Union. Yet here again it is a matter of formulating this consensus effectively against the impetus to annexation. By this I mean that it would be hopeless to set store solely in Europe, in peace politics, and in Germany's neighbors, without coming to grips with the dynamics of German unification itself.

One can only hope for a successful politics of buying time, of course, if areas of interest, conditions, and objective moments that support it are present. I refuse to discuss the costs of unification. The estimates run to an upper limit of one trillion D-marks and the hope for a second economic miracle. The key seems to me to be the question of whether there are conceivable interests that could lure the GDR population away from giving up their self-respect and their fear of being left high and dry. I believe that there are some, even a great number.

1) There is the ability to rely on West German arrogance. One component of the modesty of the GDR-ites over against the West German racism of prosperity has always been hate. The GDR populace is now becoming familiar with the Manchester aspects of capitalism, through the emergence of former property-holders and further still through the dabblings of socialist collective directors with the concept of efficiency; the social market economy is being wholeheartedly embraced. The terrified renters, the workers threatened by unemployment, and the intellectuals on the verge of social marginalization will have no choice but to quickly organize

their interests. It is hard to imagine that the GDR populace, despite all of its yearning for the blessings of the D-mark, will become the defenseless victim of forty years of capitalism in the Federal Republic after having been the victim of forty years of really-existing socialism.

2) The brutal program of currency union, which Kohl has just announced, will not work: the predictable unemployment and pauperization of the masses cannot just simply be "socially cushioned." Even if portions of the GDR population can be transformed into welfare recipients in line with West German standards, they will nonetheless remain welfare recipients in run-down apartments, a neglected infrastructure, and a polluted environment. There will be a German-German two-class poverty. I believe that the experience of real populist power is still too fresh and too real for all of this to transpire without resistance. One can expect instead a second phase of the GDR revolution, a phase of social revolution. At any rate, the threatening pauperization will quickly strengthen its own government as an interest group.

3) It is an out-and-out swindle that the social safety-net can simply be extended to the GDR. The so-called social safety-net is not simply a truckload of money; it is rather a system of rights and institutions. The adjudication of legal differences, according to legal experts, will take at least a decade. Above all, it is a question of whether the concept of a minimum pension will be able to be unceremoniously pushed aside in the GDR; of whether, in the realm of health care, the dominance of private doctors, the pharmaceutical industry, and the West German state insurance nonsense can be slickly transferred. More likely is a fundamental sociopolitical discussion both over here and over there.

4) The new democratic structures have proven to be powerless against the reunification dynamic, the professional election campaign, and the hegemony of the political sphere of the Federal Republic. Nevertheless, the democratic institutions are successful. There exists an organizational process from below, in citizens' committees, in the numerous round tables, in investigative panels, in free trade unions, in citizens' organizations. A party politics driven chiefly by campaign opportunism is principally inferior to this grassroots democratic process. This is especially evident in the experiences of the Federal Republic over the last decade. It is inferior above all when it is a matter of political questions that are simply not resolvable without the input of those concerned because they are not recognizable: this applies to all questions of ecology, urban

redevelopment, and the change-over of agriculture. The more quickly the demagoguery of German unity is reined in, the more clear it will be that the process of democratization in the GDR is in no way over.

5) This brings me to the most important point: the sum total of societal tasks in the GDR is so great that without a pan-societal vision, without the concept of an all-inclusive, GDR-specific reform, nothing can really be changed. The disintegration of the cities is so systematic, touches housing and infrastructure, that money, materials, and credits for the middle class alone will bring no salvation. The independent actions of the residents will be crucial. For its part, this requires more hope and more conviction than the mere supremacy of the D-mark can offer, and new rights to boot. It would be absurd to have faith that onrushing capitalism will have a studied, pan-societal competence, the likes of which it certainly has proven that it did not have in the Federal Republic. An investor such as Hoechst AG will not practice in the GDR that renunciation of environmentally hazardous production that it notoriously circumvents in the FRG.[8]

The GDR will become a land of social reforms even if the demonstrators in Leipzig cried out with conviction: "Never again experiments with us." Experimentation will be in the best interests of the people. As a result of his, a GDR identity will emerge, even once the GDR state has disappeared. The salary levels and standard of living in the GDR will remain lower for a long time, expressed in net figures. Those who want to emigrate will emigrate. Anyone who remains will do so because of the opportunity for a self-determined future. A country for youth, then: the young East.

The regimen of time destroyed many promises of new beginnings from the days of October. But it also destroyed world visions–especially leftist ones–convictions, and articles of faith. Jens Reich called the opportunity of the GDR a tabula rasa. The mind has truly been liberated. The overcoming of the division of Germany has created the opportunity for mingling cultures, languages, experiences, and observations that were separate for forty years. The energy for a new, richer culture can spring from such a mingling.

NOTES

Source: Blohm, 164-86. Translated by Bill Hutfilz. Hartung's title alludes to Bertolt Brecht's poem "Der Radwechsel" (The Changing of the Wheel).

1. Soviet leader Michail Gorbachev made this statement while attending the celebrations of the GDR's fortieth anniversary.

2. The Pleisse is the river that runs through Leipzig.

3. In January of 1990, the Soviet memorial in Berlin Treptow was vandalized by fascist demonstrators.

4. The prominent West German weekly *Der Spiegel* ran a much-publicized cover story on the GDR head of Commercial Coordination, Alexander Schalck-Golodkowski, who fled to West Germany after the peaceful revolution and is now residing in a luxurious home at the Tegernsee in Bavaria.

5. The oppositional group "Democratic Awakening" joined an electoral alliance with the CDU for the March 1990 *Volkskammer* elections and was, for all practical purposes, swallowed up by the larger party.

6. Hartung argues that the opposition's rhetoric of "construction" backfired because of the negative experiences the people had with forty years of "construction of socialism," a propaganda slogan employed by the SED regime.

7. The decision to push for a currency union with the GDR was taken single-handedly by Chancellor Kohl against the advice of many economic experts, such as the president of the *Bundesbank* and major representatives of West German economic think tanks.

8. The Hoechst AG is a well-known West German pharmaceutical conglomerate.

52
Jürgen Habermas, "D-Mark Nationalism" (March 30, 1990)

Three months after the democratic revolution "over there," they are shaking each others' hands "over here"–the politicians have become businessmen, the intellectuals have metamorphosed into bards of German unity. Günter Grass is castigated in the literary supplements, and in the talk shows the very sight of a leftist economics professor is enough to transform friendly ladies and gentlemen of the middle class into a mob. Today the self-torturing, superfluous question is finally justified: What will become of the identity of the Germans? Will economic problems guide the process of unification onto sober pathways? Or will the D-mark become the object of libido, emotionally revalued so that a kind of economic nationalism will overwhelm republican consciousness? The question is open, but it demands to be answered in view of the psychic damage already caused by the conquest of Western political parties in the East.

It is difficult not to write a satire about the first flowerings of chubby-faced D-mark nationalism. The triumphant Chancellor let the thin but honest Prime Minister know the conditions under which he was willing to buy up the GDR; in terms of monetary policy he pumped up the voters of an "Alliance for Germany" blackmailed into existence by himself; in terms of constitutional policy he set the course for annexation via Article 23 of the Basic Law, and in terms of foreign policy he protested against the phrase "victorious powers" and left open the question of Poland's western border. When it finally dawned on him that Mr. Schönhuber would be able to hold high the long-since collapsed legal fictions far longer than he would, he wanted at the very least to take away from Schönhuber an issue that could prove powerful among radical right-wingers: the "reparations," whatever that might mean. The shamelessness of his nationalism, supported by the stock market trends, set up a cold-blooded comparison between, on the one hand, the historically justified moral rights of Polish forced laborers to compensation (and the rights of neighboring countries to a guarantee of the existing borders) and on the other the fiscal-political "wiggle room" and the liquidity of the third great industrial power, which found itself in the process of swallowing up the leading industrial power of the COMECON and wanted to keep itself fit for this transaction. Only *one* unit of currency for *all* transactions. German interests are weighed and forced through in German marks. True, the language of the Stukas was even worse.[1] But the sight of this German muscle game is obscene nevertheless.

I

To understand how it could come to this, one must remember the inner situation of the Federal Republic at the moment when—and let us admit it in the jargon of youth—it was caught with its pants down by the stream of refugees over the Hungarian border and by the subsequent reaction to that stream: the opening of the Wall. All rhetoric aside, who had really still counted on anything like reunification—and who had even really still wanted it all? Willy Brandt, at any rate, had declared at the Munich Chamber Theater in 1984 that the German Question was no longer open; and the audience had applauded. Outside the theater, in the country at large, the mood cannot have been very different.

In 1960 Karl Jaspers had spoken clearly: "The history of the German nation-state is at an end. What we . . . can achieve as a great nation is insight into the world's situation: that today the idea of the nation-state is a calamity for Europe and all the continents."[2] This credo was shared at the time not only by the liberals and the leftist intellectuals. In a study published in 1983, Wolfgang Mommsen paints a complex picture of the "transformations of national identity of the Germans" in the Federal Republic. While the politicians of the first generation, the "fathers of the Basic Law," still believed that they would be able to continue the nation-state tradition of the Weimar Republic and thus also of the "small-German" Bismarck Reich without a thorough-going process of questioning and reform, the general public in the fifties and sixties had developed a more pragmatic self-understanding which put the question of national identity on the back burner.[3] According to Mommsen, this consciousness is characterized by four elements: the dethematization of Germany's most recent past and a rather ahistorical definition of the current situation; furthermore, an aggressive separation from the systems of Eastern Europe, particularly the GDR, that is, a continuation of the historically rooted anticommunist syndrome; an orientation toward the values and behavior patterns of Western civilization, especially the "protective power" USA; and, last but not least, pride in West Germany's own economic accomplishments. Mommsen is probably correct in suspecting that this last element, the self-confidence of a successful economic nation, forms the core of the political self-understanding of the population of the Federal Republic–and a substitute for a national pride that is widely lacking. This also explains why the high level of acceptance for the constitution and the institutions of democratic rule of law are not really anchored in normative convictions.

> Among the citizens of the Federal Republic there is a very strong tendency ... to view the parliamentary system not first and foremost as a democratic framework for the continuous development of social relations, but rather to confound the constitutional system with the social order and view them as one thing.[4]

Although Mommsen still touches on discussions that had begun in the 1970s about the alternative between a Federal-Republican national consciousness on the one hand and an all-German national consciousness on the other hand, he comes to a surprisingly clear conclusion:

> If I am not completely mistaken, then the history of the German Question has today returned to its normal state ... that is, the exis-

tence of a German cultural nation in the center of Europe which is divided into several German state-nations. Everything suggests that the phase of consolidated nation-statehood from 1871-1933 was merely an episode in German history, and that we have once again, though at a higher level, reached the state of affairs that existed in Germany after 1815: a plurality of German states with mutual cultural-national identity.[5]

This argument from 1983 puts Wolfgang Mommsen, in hindsight, into the group of those fighting for a constitutional patriotism oriented toward the civic state-nation of the Federal Republic. Since the end of the 1960s, all the elements of self-understanding for the citizens of the Federal Republic have been put into question except one: the self-confidence of the economic nation. The student protest movement put an end to the shoving aside of a Nazi past that was sweepingly condemned but generally bracketed out. The Eastern treaties (with the recognition of the GDR) and the initial successes of detente at the very least destabilized the anti-communism so typical of Germany. The Vietnam War, the growing strength of the European Community, and the recognition of diverging interests between Europe and the USA all increased the distance between the Federal Republic and the United States. Since then "national identity" has become the topic of public discussions. The liberal consensus, characterized by the slogan "two states—one nation," now had to be spelled out explicitly and defended not only against leftist nationalists on the margins of the Green spectrum but also, and above all, against the neo-conservatives.

In a climate of economic crises and debates on security policy, these neo-conservatives suspected legitimational weaknesses in the political system, ascribing them to a "loss of history" and inadequate national self-confidence. Such neo-conservative attempts at compensatory creation of meaning had different accents, however, depending on whether the longed-for "return to the nation" was tailored to a Federal-Republican or an all-German identity; the "fatherland Federal-Republic" was the position of a minority.

The new conceptions would have been capable of finding support solely from the still unquestioned element of pride in the rebuilding achievements and economic power of the Federal Republic. The "Model Germany," brought into play for a while by the Social Democrats, contained traces of such pride, but it never had any significance beyond the realm of campaign strategy. However, the attempts to renew a traditional patriotism necessarily had to seek a connection with the identity of the entire nation, on the left and on the right; for this reason they were unable to use a value ascribed only to the Federal Republic as the basis for an economic-national-ist-based self-understanding. And the proponents of a Federal-Re-publican constitutional patriotism, of course, had to pursue a strat-egy of strengthening the normative value of identification with the civic state-nation founded in 1949 in order to differentiate that value from *prepolitical* values: the *Volk* as a historic community of fate, the nation as a linguistic and cultural community, or, now, the social and economic system as a performance community.

On the basis of the statistical data available in 1987, H. Hon-olka showed that the transformations in mentality of the citizens of the Federal Republic were, in fact, moving in this direction. While opinion polls up into the 1970s had shown a rising curve for economic pride, the most recent polls have shown that pride in democracy is now more important:

> In the well-known international study of political culture done in 1959 by American political scientists Gabriel A. Almond and Sidney Verba, national pride still rested chiefly on *Volk* characteristics and the economic system, while the political identity of other Western nations like the USA and Great Britain was based above all on political institutions. By now the citizens of the Federal Republic have also come closer to the normal kind of Western national identity. Pride in aspects of the political system has pushed far ahead.[6]

The data which show that the national pride of the Germans is comparatively weak do not contradict this. It was precisely in the course of the 1980s that evidence was growing for the position an-nounced by M. R. Lepsius at the twenty-fourth conference of sociolo-gists:

> An essential transformation in the political culture of the Federal Republic lies precisely in the acceptance of a political order which determines and legitimates itself in constitutionally concrete forms through rights of individual participation. In contrast to this, the idea that political order is bound to the collective values of a nation separated from other nations as a "community of fate" with ethnic, historic, and cultural categories has faded. The crystallization of "constitutional patriotism," the acceptance of a political order constituted by rights of self-determination, and the separation of such an order from the idea of an ethnic, cultural, collective "community of fate" are the central result of the delegitimization of German nationalism.[7]

These thoughts give voice to the pride of an entire generation of postwar West German intellectuals. They are only a year older than the opening of the Wall, with which, suddenly, the unification of two of the three successor states to the "Greater German Reich" has come into view.[8] Will this unification throw the Federal Republic, which Lepsius and many others of us believed only a short while ago to be a "post-nation-state political commonwealth," back into a nationalist past that its own citizens had believed was over?

How this question will be decided depends to some extent on the way in which the process of political unification is presented and invoked–that is, on the mobilization of emotions "back there" and "over here." Now, from an all-German perspective, the resistance which previously prevented the inclusion of the repressed components of Federal-Republican economic pride into national identity as a whole has disappeared. With a view toward the German-German currency union, all Germans might now be able to identify themselves with the potency of an expanded empire of the D-mark. The "Alliance for Germany" already seems to have opened up this fallow emotional field, and already the arrogance of economic power has caused nationalist weeds to sprout.

Classical imperialism had channelled similar emotions in a different way. Back then territorial conquest and military protection of domestic industries were supposed to open up markets. In the sensitive web of an interdependent world economy which knows no national boundaries, market power itself becomes the national clarion. A new economic nationalism would trade in its militarist face for the philistine attitudes of the friendly, supercilious development helper. Thus even the compensatory ideas of the neo-conservatives would be outdated. The renewed national consciousness would no longer make up for the burdens of a capitalist modernization that is nevertheless also cushioned by social-welfare measures; a national consciousness that found its symbolic expression in the strength of the D-mark would, on the contrary, be forced to ignore the voice of enlightened self-interest, pushing the skeptical economic burgher to collective efforts and sacrifices *in his own language*.

II

These are reflections on a transformation in the identity of the reunified Germans that has become *possible* in the current constellation. I am not asserting that anyone is actually *working for* an economic nationalism of this sort. Nevertheless, the German policies which the Chancellor's office has been following in a very goal-oriented way after its initial hesitations pave the way for such a transformation in mentality.

As early as his Ten-Point Plan, the Federal Chancellor showed a certain impatience to push forward on the path to nation-state unity–less in the contents of the plan itself than in the fact that stages were operationalized at all on the way to the goal. But the rhetoric of these first weeks after November 9 left open the alternative between a seriously European solution to the German Question and a German solo effort. Viewed more closely, the alternative remained unclear. The invocation of a European solution offered an empty formula which anyone could fill up as he or she wished. In those first weeks it was not just the European neighbors and the two superpowers but also spokespeople for the GDR opposition and the majority of the West German population who viewed the process of unification in a chronological framework which seemed of necessity to give European unification a certain procedural priority. At any rate, there seemed to exist an option to plan operative steps for a period in which the independence of the GDR would be guaranteed–even after the process of confederation–so that the difficult process of economic equalization would take place in a European framework.

What interests me above all in this scenario, which reserves an important role for the European Community, is the unencumbered role that the Federal Republic could have taken on as the proponent of coordinated European economic assistance *for all* the countries of Central and Eastern Europe currently undergoing a process of transformation. Far from the heave-ho tactic of dragging their German fellow countrymen and countrywomen onto their ship via constitutional law and an over-hasty German-German currency union, the Federal Republic, as the strongest power within the European Community, could have appealed to the solidarity of *all* Europeans and to the historical indebtedness of Western Europe vis-à-vis *all* its Central- and Eastern-European neighbors. In spite of this, the Federal Republic could have carried out its specific German-German duties via a transfer of capital (to date rejected) for building up the infrastructure of the GDR. This reflection is written in the historical subjunctive and is intended merely to recall an option which would have been immune to normative objections. Such a policy would certainly have privileged our fellow countrymen and countrywomen with respect to the citizens of other Eastern neighbors who found themselves in the same situation–but only to the obvious extent normal for states belonging to the same nation; and it would have been understood by others. The most basic political wisdom teaches us that simply shoving the living standard gap from the Elbe to the Oder and Neiße rivers is bound to arouse nationalist distrust vis-à-vis the reunited Germany among the neighboring states unfortunate enough to wind up on the wrong side of the gap. Above all, however, the European alternative recommended itself by taking the rhetoric of non-paternalism and non-interference seriously. Without a breathing spell and without freedom to maneuver and for an independent political public sphere to crystallize, however, the first free election degenerated into a "battle of the parties of the Federal Republic for the GDR."[9]

After his visit to Dresden, the Chancellor quickly decided on a double strategy of undisguised destabilization and quick annexation of the GDR, in order to make the Federal Republic master of the situation and at the same time preempt international friction. Evidently, the government of the Federal Republic wants to enter once more into the difficult negotiations about distributing the burdens among the EC partners, about a transformed security system, and about decisions on a peace treaty from a position of strength provided by an economic and political annexation that is already a *fait accompli*. Hence, on the one hand, the government of the Federal Republic stepped on the gas pedal; it effectively dramatized the number of refugees, even though no one knew how to influence their motives. On the other hand, it could reach the goal of annexation–that is, unification according to the Federal Republic's terms–only by breaking down the GDR's resistance and creating the necessary majority for unification via Article 23 of the Basic Law.

The destabilization, which took on a macabre twist in Telschik's rumors, was directed not just at the remnants of the old regime, but also at the very opposition that had toppled the regime and was now primarily interested in changing structures from within–that is, in self-stabilization and self-reflection.[10] Only this fact can explain the silent delegitimization of the Round Table and the rudeness to Modrow's government, which, as two

Federal constitutional judges determined, had gained a certain legitimacy even according to our own standards to the extent

> . . . that it is supported by the Round Table and the oppositional groups represented in the government. This means: the old system is already liquidated–in fact, only the execution of liquidation still remains to be accomplished. It is no longer necessary to withhold "success" from this government, if time is of the essence.[11]

But "withhold success" is precisely what the federal government did. It opposed the very financial assistance for the infrastructure that it will have to put forward anyway to improve for private capital now pushing into the GDR.

The CDU/CSU campaigned for the support of GDR voters with its wonted charm. If it had simply been a question of disempowering the old regime, the Chancellor would certainly not personally have taken the trouble to force an oppositional group like Democratic Awakening into an alliance with a discredited bloc party, only to turn around and lead an election campaign which flew in the face of historical truth by putting the newly-founded SPD into the same boat with the successors to the SED. In this way it mobilized the masses, who (according to a report in the *Süddeutsche Zeitung* of 7 March 1990) beat up student counter-demonstrators at a DSU rally in front of the Leipzig Opera House, shouting slogans like "red fascists–leftist terrorists," "red pack" and "reds go home." Whatever else was necessary was accomplished by people like Schnur and Ebeling, and by the promise of an economic miracle attested to with refrains from Ludwig Erhard, a miracle which was supposed to be inaugurated by the currency union dangled all-powerfully in front of the people's eyes. For forty long years the population of the GDR had been forced to vote for the ruling elite. Kohl made it clear that this time it was also wiser to do the same thing.

The role of the SPD was hardly any more honorable. If things should go badly, the SPD will have to ask itself if it did not make a historic mistake at its convention in Berlin out of fear of a replay of the role of "unpatriotic so-and-so's." I will not say anything about Willy Brandt; it was the party, after all, which sent him to the marketplaces of the GDR. It is understandable that the SPD did not want to hand over their most famous name to the young founders of the SPD, whose mentality recalls precisely the all-German party of Heinemann in the early 1950s, without taking a hand in molding the new party.[12] And the emotions which overcame old comrades in the historic triangle of Gotha, Erfurt and

Leipzig are certainly understandable. Moreover, it is naive to accuse a political party that wants to win a majority of opportunism.
Nevertheless, these honorable motivations do not suffice to justify
ignoring other considerations–or refusing to make any decisions at
all and singing hymns of praise to both Willy Brandt and Oskar
Lafontaine at the same volume. When the SPD decided to fight
with the CDU/CSU for the laurels of the first all-German party
and to fill its sails with national emotions, it was not just betraying
its better traditions; it was also helping to create the very smoke-
screen behind which any alternative to the German policies of the
federal government disappeared. The SPD, too, ignored the recom-
mendation of the Round Table to restrict election campaign imports
from the West. Even worse, it advised its comrades to reject electoral alliances which were the only chance for leftist opposition
groups to establish themselves throughout the country. It is true
that this, too, conforms to the ordinary rules of the party power
politics. But these ordinary rules assume an ordinary situation in
which the rules do not have to be dictated from the outside and do
not discriminate against the very same people who created the
revolution in the first place.

The policies of *faits accomplis* have not yet reached their goal;
the mentality they count upon, and which they reward, has not yet
triumphed; the election campaign in the Federal Republic has not
yet begun.

As far as we citizens of the Federal Republic are concerned, it
seems that we can still count on that mixture of enlightened egotism
of economic burghers and *gratis* altruism of *citoyens*, which gives
Ralf Dahrendorf cause to rejoice:

> The self-satisfied think it's very good that things are getting better in
> the East, but those folks ought really to stay where they are. And if
> there really isn't a Wall anymore, then we'll just have to reunify.
> Perhaps then even a few of those people will go back to where they
> came from, the ones who got an inspection sticker for their Trabis
> without being punished and who, to make matters worse, are filling
> up the local youth hostel during school vacations. . . . Under these
> conditions nationalism is entirely the wrong word. Whatever has
> become of the Germans?[13]

I do not want to pour water into the wine with references to a climate that has, in the meantime, become noticeably more severe, especially in and around the "local youth hostels." But the economic
burgher's premise that the citizen's altruism can be had for nothing
is true only in times of calm. In times of uproar, what will become of

a mentality which the citizens of the Federal Republic had actually gained after forty years? It is usually the others who are concerned with ordinary citizens' identity problems: the politicians on
Sunday and the intellectuals even during the week. The citizens of
the Federal Republic *had developed* a non-nationalist self-understanding, as well as a sober view of what the political process produces for every individual in terms of cash and useful things. What
will become of these attitudes under the pressure of a policy which
hides its own insecurity under arrogance, and which is steering directly toward an all-German nation-state?

This has already achieved one thing: the national question has
once again been opposed to questions of republican equality and social justice. If prepolitical values like nationality are not kept in
strict convergence with the universalist spirit of civil rights, dangerous collisions can ensue. Now, before the local elections in
Bavaria, the CSU has to cut back on social programs for refugees
with its left hand at the same time that, with its right hand, it
continues to denounce the unpatriotic Lafontaine, who has long since
been suggesting the very same thing, but for different reasons. Lafontaine had shown an early sensitivity to normative confusion
when he warned of German jingoism and demanded equal treatment
for non-German asylum seekers and German immigrants from the
GDR and other countries. The policy of the German one-man show
threatens to throw citizens into a value dilemma which has a sad
prehistory in Germany. Once the economic burgher's premise of cost
neutrality can no longer be adhered to, the very large "Alliance for
Germany" might well look for the wrong way out of the dilemma.
With easy variations, it could continue its election campaign
within the Federal Republic and demand of citizens here collective
efforts in the spirit of nationalist identification with the expansion of the D-mark empire from which they have lived well up to
now.

III

The alternative to this vision of economic nationalism is the
strengthening of those components of our self-understanding with
which, in the 1980s, "the citizens of the Federal Republic have
also come closer to the normal kind of Western identity."[14] Identification with the principles and the institutions of our constitution demands, however, an agenda for reunification which gives
priority to the freely exercised right of the citizens to determine

their own future by direct vote, within the framework of a non-occupied public sphere that has not already been willed away. This means, concretely, that the will of the voting public is given precedence over an annexation cleverly initiated but in the final analysis carried through only at the administrative level–an annexation which dishonestly evades one of the essential conditions for the founding of any nation of state-citizens: the public act of a carefully considered democratic decision taken in both parts of Germany. This act of foundation can only be carried out consciously and intentionally if we agree not to accomplish unification via Article 23 of our Basic Law (which governs the annexation "of other parts of Germany").

I do not ignore the weight of the arguments in favor of conserving a proven constitution. But reflections on stability cannot replace normative considerations. It is strange to see how those who base their arguments on Article 23 are the very same people who insisted for decades on the call for reunification in the preamble of the Basic Law. The preamble makes it unmistakably clear why the Basic Law is called a "Basic Law" and not a "constitution": it is intended to give the political life of the federal states "a new order for a transitional period," that is, until the time comes "to realize the unity and freedom of Germany in free self-determination." If, now, the GDR, like the Saarland, accedes according to Article 23, without any further changes in the Basic Law, the chosen method of unification will implicitly underline what the irredentists have always confirmed: that the conditions for Article 146 have not yet been fulfilled. That Article states: "This Basic Law loses its validity on the day that a new constitution takes effect, chosen by the German people in free determination." And it is quite true: an "annexation" of the GDR could not be the same thing as a free decision of the *entire* German people; because the citizens of the Federal Republic would have to leave the decision to the representatives of the GDR. When, then, if not now, will that day foreseen in Article 146 ever come? Are we still waiting for East Prussia and Silesia?[15] If one wants to exclude this misinterpretation–as I do, after the *Bundestag*'s decision on Poland's western border–the last article and the preamble of the Basic Law would have to be cut, and the Basic Law itself would have to be stripped of its temporary nature. Such changes, however, would simply prove that the "annexation" of the GDR cannot fulfill what it is supposed to fulfill: the unification of two parts to one *whole*. An annexation via Article 23 would let Article 146 "run itself empty," and that would run counter to the methodological premise of interpreting every rule with a view to the unity of the constitution.

Manipulations ahead and behind and a problematic interpretation of Article 23 of the Basic Law would simply be the juridical price for a policy of speed. The political price would be even greater; we might wind up paying it for several generations. We would not just lose the chance of improving a good constitution–which, at the time, of course, was not legitimized by a popular referendum–we would also lose the historic chance of carrying out the process of state unification with the clear political understanding of constituting a nation of state-citizens.

If we do not free ourselves from the diffuse notions about the nation-state, if we do not rid ourselves of the prepolitical crutches of nationality and community of fate, we will be unable to continue unburdened on the very path that we have long since chosen: the path to a multicultural society, the path to a federal state with wide regional differences and strong federal power, and above all the path to a unified European state of many nationalities. A national identity which is not based predominantly on republican self-understanding and constitutional patriotism necessarily collides with the universalist rules of mutual coexistence for human beings; it collides with the fact that state integration is now happening simultaneously on three levels–the state, the federation, and the European Community. Via Article 23, citizens can merely *suffer* the process of unification. The path via a constitutional convention, on the other hand, prevents a policy of *faits accomplis* and might wind up giving the citizens of the GDR room to breathe after all, allowing time for a discussion about the priority of European viewpoints.

Only a popular referendum on the constitution–that is, on the alternative between an all-German federal state and a federation that would allow the Federal Republic to keep the Basic Law–gives *all* citizens the chance to say no. It makes possible a quantified minority vote; it is only then that the decision of the majority becomes an act consciously carried out, around which the republican self-understanding of future generations can crystallize. It is only in view of freedom to choose between alternatives that the consciousness that is already widespread among the younger generation can be made clear to all: that the founding of a single nation of state-citizens on the territories of what, until now, were the Federal Republic and the GDR, is not already a foregone conclusion because of prepolitical imponderables like linguistic community, culture, or history. For that reason one would at least like to be asked.

My friend Ulrich Oevermann argues that "with the revolutionary events in the GDR the *unaccomplished* task of constituting a political nation-state has once again posed itself practically."[16] I consider this argument entirely false. It is supposed to be a revolution "to make up for lost time," but not with respect to society or the democratic state of law; rather, with respect to a nation that arrived too late, which is finally coming to self-realization in the nation-state. If, as Oevermann does, one decisively rejects the "transposition of the political onto the level of culture and spirit," it is inconsistent to blur the distinction between a nation of state-citizens and a nation of *Volk* developed by M. R. Lepsius. In contrast to the classical nation-states of the West, the successor states to the old German Reich and the small-German Reich of Bismarck never succeeded in intertwining the political incorporation of state-citizens with the pre-political conditions of the "historically and materially given unitary nation" to which Oevermann refers. In Germany, as Lepsius notes, there were strong tensions between the "political level of the people as bearers of political sovereignty" and the prepolitical "level of the *Volk* as an ethnic, cultural, socioeconomic unity":

> The recognition of these tensions is the basis for a civil society of democratic self-legitimation. Any confusion between the "demos" as bearer of political sovereignty with a specific "ethnos" leads ultimately to the repression of forced assimilation of other ethnic, cultural, religious, and socioeconomic groups of the population within a political union. Thus an effort was made in the German Reich after 1871 to Germanize the Poles in Germany's eastern provinces, as well as the citizens of Alsace and Lorraine; and Catholics and Social Democrats were discriminated against as unpatriotic and unreliable–ultramontane or internationalist. . . . Depending on the characteristics that are chosen to fill up the nominal category of the state-citizens, a whole range of highly differentiated possibilities for discrimination emerges, because the law of equality among state-citizens can be vitiated via additional categories: ethnic sameness, religious sameness, cultural sameness, or racial sameness. The most extreme example of such vitiation of the norm of equality for state-citizens via the addition of a further criterion to ensure political sameness were the National-Socialist laws concerning the Jews, according to which German state-citizens of Jewish origin were deprived of their rights to equality.[17]

It is only in this connection that the subject Auschwitz gains its relevance for the consciousness in which the process of political unification is being carried out. It is entirely erroneous to bring Auschwitz into play as a metaphysical guilt which is concretely paid off by the loss of East Prussia and Silesia, as Karl Heinz

Bohrer suggests. It is just as false to use Auschwitz as the axis for the negative nationalism of a community of fate, which Oevermann would like to make the basis of a nation-state subject which can (now for the first time?) be held responsible. Auschwitz can and should remind the Germans, no matter in what state territories they may find themselves, of something else: that they cannot count on the continuities of their history. Because of that horrible break in continuity the Germans have given up the possibility of constituting their identity on something other than universalist principles of state citizenship, in the light of which national traditions can no longer remain unexamined, but can only be critically and self-critically appropriated. Post-traditional identity loses its substantial, its unproblematic character; it *exists* only in the method of the public, discursive battle around the interpretation of a constitutional patriotism made concrete under particular historical circumstances.[18]

In an essay on "The Insanity of the Nation," Reinhard Merkel hits the nail on the head:

> German nationalist intellectuals still reject the lesson of the Enlightenment, the French Revolution, and Ernest Renan: that the "nation" in democratic states–if it is anything at all–cannot be the protection of the particularity of the *Volk* against outside forces. It must, rather, be the symbol of a "daily plebiscite" within society itself on democratic participation in political self-organization.[19]

IV

Karl Heinz Bohrer may well suspect that the self-understanding of constitutional patriotism is guided by a moralism which robs artworks of their uncanniness, and which brings us to the point of repressing entire categories of the psychic and cultural tradition which used to form part of German identity, because these categories supposedly helped prepare the consciousness that ultimately made the Holocaust possible. Here he may have been thinking of the sources of new French inspirations: Carl Schmitt, Martin Heidegger, or Ernst Jünger. But the very prestige of the newspaper in which Bohrer gives voice to his concerns gives the lie to his fears. It is news to me, at any rate, that the critical investigation of our young-conservative tradition has led to a taboo or even to a marginalization of the tradition. Bohrer himself mentions the " 'irrational' tradition" of Friedrich Schlegel, Novalis, and Nietzsche. I have to wonder who on earth might come up with the daring idea of *not* hooking up with the tradition of *early* Romanticism and the criticism of the Enlightenment carried out by our greatest Enlightener. This is a fight against paper tigers. At most what has been forgotten is the tradition of anti-Enlightenment and German nationalist intellectuals who, starting with Franz Baader and Adam Müller, Ernst Moritz Arndt and J. F. Fried, were able to mold the German bourgeoisie politically.[20] This tradition, which was mocked so brilliantly by Hegel and Heine, Engels and Marx, is a constant in German intellectual life right up through Werner Sombart's *Merchants and Heroes*.[21] During every national wave–after 1813, 1848, 1871, and 1914, not to mention other dates–there were always new generations of intellectuals who joined this tradition, moved by the storms of German fate. This stream of energy, which was crystallized in the "ideas of 1914," ought not to be regenerated in the new national wave. This is a matter of intellectual hygiene, not repression. Bohrer complains about the colonization of our consciousness, the epidemic of a notorious loss of memory, spiritual provincialization. But is it not in the Federal Republic that, for the first time, we have brought our spiritual traditions to play *in all their forms*, including Heine and Marx, Freud and Mach, Bloch and Benjamin, Lukács and Wittgenstein?[22] Is it not here that, for the first time, this tradition has operated in its more radical dimensions? The spiritual sparks of a German-Jewish culture that was preserved in the emigration are responsible for the fact that the Federal Republic "has become connected not just economically, but also culturally with the West. In other words, its strength lies precisely in the fact that here a culture characterized by international thought was able to develop, nevertheless structured by Germans."[23]

We ought not to establish any short-circuited connections between large-scale national growth and intellectual productivity. Karl Heinz Bohrer is a brilliant essayist and an excellent literary critic. With remarkable intransigence, he likes to follow the traces of the ecstatic abysses of aesthetic experience. He is fascinated by the grand gestures of the amoral. These gestures signal the autonomy of an art which has broken off communication with the good and the true. But Bohrer also knows that this transgression can only be born "in the head." Why should a cerebralized art–it can be studied via Gottfried Benn–dive into the belly of the nation?[24] The aestheticization of the political is one of the worst arguments for us "becoming a nation again." And intellectuals will be among the first to suffer if they once again get a national podium from the top of which they can hold their speeches.

Inasmuch as German intellectuals have become spiritually provincial, they ought to blame themselves first and foremost; they certainly ought not to hope that the longed-for symbolism of a resurrected Reich will make them more productive. The "aesthetics of the state"–which have been a thing of the past since Louis Philippe, and for good reasons–will not experience a renaissance simply because Kohl and Waigel will soon be joined by Thuringians and Saxons in raising the flag of a new economic nationalism above the ruins of the Reichstag.[25]

Fear of making what is most particular in our national cultural tradition taboo takes on another meaning with certain other intellectuals. Such intellectuals first equate the Stasi past with the Nazi past, and then they throw both onto the trash heap of a covered-up, silent history. "Without Trial Courts" is the title of one lead article in which retroactive melancholy reveals an unsuspected generosity:

> This time we ought not to speak of "coming to terms" with the past. Even the semantic cudgel "repression" . . . ought not to be used. And especially the shabby assertion of an "inability to mourn" as the supposed spiritually constitutive cause for obduracy and repression . . . The insistence on that kind of "coming to terms" transformed a moral intention into immorality. It became clearer and clearer that such terms were essentially being used in order to produce a political submissiveness intended to further claims to power.[26]

What that meant was explained earlier by the *Rheinische Merkur* (in a guest column of 24 November 1989).[27] With the help of bankrupt state socialism, it was finally time to draw a line under the past: "Is the emotion of anti-fascism ('antifa'), this brooding on coming to terms with the past, losing its privileged position, shoved aside by the power of the present?" Anti-fascism, the spirit which alone gave birth to the democratic state of law in Germany after 1945, is now supposed to belong finally to the past, along with the hollowly propagandistic antifa organizations of state socialism.

It is not a coincidence that this obscene debate is being revived at a moment when Gorbachev is robbing anti-communism of its *raison d'être*. The facade of that anti-totalitarian consensus, always strangely asymmetrical, which seemed to unite the population of the Federal Republic, has been broken irreversibly. Under these circumstances the bankruptcy lawyers of anti-communism are making one last effort and offering a deal: discretion is supposed to reign "back here" and "over there." As if the non-communist left in the

Federal Republic could have any interest in spreading the cover of communicative silence over the part of Stalinism which has, via the GDR, become an element of German history!

In his speech on his own country Peter Sloterdijk looks at "German silence" as well as the great Silent Ones, the "former bearers of the Reich's word," the powerful speech-makers of yesterday, now relieved of their positions. Then he turns to his own generation: "Those born in Germany after 1945 ought to realize clearly that the later-born, in order to come into the world, will have to break the silence of their ancestors after the fact at the decisive points."28

NOTES

Source: *Die Zeit* (March 30, 1990). English translation in *New German Critique* 52 (1991): 84-101; translation modified. Habermas's notes are marked AN (Author's Notes).

1. "Stukas" is the name of a German war plane used during the Second World War.

2. AN: Karl Jaspers, *Freiheit und Wiedervereinigung* (Munich: Piper, 1960), p. 53.

3. German Chancellor Otto von Bismarck's Second German Reich, founded in 1871, is usually referred to a the "small-German solution" since it did not include other German-speaking areas of Central Europe, such as Austria, in the German nation.

4. AN: Wolfgang Mommsen, "Wandlungen der nationalen Identität der Deutschen" (1983), *Nation und Geschichte* (Munich: Piper, 1990), p. 62.

5. AN: Mommsen, p. 76; see Siegrid Meuschel, "Kulturnation oder Staatsnation," *Leviathan* 3 (1988): 406-35.

6. AN: H. Honolka, *Die Bundesrepublik auf der Suche nach ihrer Identität* (Munich: C.H. Beck, 1987), p. 104. Cf. also D. P. Conradt, "Changing German Political Culture," *The Civic Culture Revisited*, eds. G.A. Almond, S. Verba (Boston: Little, Brown, 1980), pp. 212-72.

7. AN: M. R. Lepsius, "Das Erbe des Nationalsozialismus und die politische Kultur der Nachfolgestaaten des 'Großdeutschen Reiches,' " *Kultur und Nation*, ed. M. Haller (Frankfurt: Suhrkamp, 1989), pp. 254ff.

8. The FRG and the GDR are, de facto, the two successor states to Hitler's Germany.

9. AN: H. Rudolph in the *Süddeutsche Zeitung* of 8 March 1990.

10. Horst Telschik was a leading staff member in the *Bundeskanzleramt*, the office of the West German Chancellor, until 1991.

11. AN: *Der Spiegel* 10 (1990).

12. Gustav Heinemann, who would become the so-called "people's" president of the Federal Republic in the seventies, started out as a popular CDU politician, later left the party in reaction to their policy of rearmament, joined the SPD in 1957, and was attorney general for the SPD from 1966 to 1969.

13. AN: Ralf Dahrendorf, "Politik. Eine Kolumne: 'Eine deutsche Identität,' " *Merkur* 44 (March 1990): 231.

14. AN: See Honolka, *Die Bundesrepublik auf der Suche nach ihrer Identität*, p. 104.

15. East Prussia and Silesia are parts of Poland that were annexed by Hitler in 1937.

16. AN: Ulrich Oevermann, "Zwei Staaten oder Einheit?," *Merkur* (February 1990): 92.

17. AN: M. R. Lepsius, "Ethnos und Demos," *Kölner Zeitschrift für Soziologie und Sozialpsychologie* 4 (1986): 753; for a critique of the concept of a nation of state-citizens see B. Estel, "Gesellschaft ohne Nation?," *Sociologia Internationalis* 2 (1988): 197ff.

18. AN: See Jürgen Habermas, "Geschichtsbewußtsein und postrationale Identität," *Eine Art Schadensabwicklung* (Frankfurt: Suhrkamp, 1987), pp. 159-79.

19. AN: Reinhard Merkel, "The Insanity of the Nation," *Die Zeit* (9 May 1990): 52.

20. Franz Baader (1765-1841) was a critic of the doctrine of economic liberalism who had been influenced by the teachings of the Catholic church; Ernst Moritz Arndt (1769-1860) fought all his life for the founding of a German national state in his various political functions as professor, parliamentary representative, etc.; Adam Müller (1779-1829) was a political philosopher and one of the most important representatives of the Romantic theory of state and society; he argued for an organic, catholic-universalist concept of the state and against a rational order of society, individualism, and a free market; Heinrich Jakob F. Fried (1802-1870) was a Romantic painter and poet.

21. AN: See D. Losurdo, *Hegel und das deutsche Erbe* (Cologne: Pahl-Rugenstein, 1989).

22. These are the names of famous Jewish German/Austrian intellectuals who contributed in significant ways to the German philosophical and literary tradition but who were excluded from the center of cultural politics because of their radicalism.

23. AN: Mommsen, "Wandlungen der nationalen Identität der Deutschen," p. 83.

24. Gottfried Benn is one of the most important German poets of the twentieth century; his early expressionist poetry, influenced by the ideas of Friedrich Nietzsche, describes the experience of cerebralized art in which life is negated. He was the most influential poet in West Germany in the immediate postwar years.

25. Louis Phillippe is the bourgeois name of King Louis XI of France.
26. AN: *Frankfurter Allgemeine Zeitung* (6 February 1990).
27. The *Rheinische Merkur* is one of the leading dailies in the Federal Republic of Germany.
28. AN: Peter Sloterdijk, *Versprechen auf Deutsch* (Frankfurt: Suhrkamp, 1990), p. 52.

53
Government Policy Statement by Lothar de Maizière, First Freely Elected Prime Minister of the GDR, Before the *Volkskammer* (April 19, 1990)

The renewal of our society took place under the motto "We are the people!" The nation became conscious of itself. For the first time in many decades human beings in the GDR constituted themselves as a people. The elections that produced this parliament were elections by the people. For the first time the *Volkskammer*, the people's chamber, rightfully bears this name.[1]

And the motto "We are the people!" turned into the motto "We are one people!" The people of the GDR constituted itself as part of a people, as part of the one German people that is supposed to grow together again. Our electorate clearly expressed this, their political will, in the elections of March 18. This will binds us. To fulfill it as well as possible is our common responsibility.

The new beginning of our society is a deeply democratic new beginning. We have a democratic task. . . . We have the first freely elected parliament and the first freely elected government for two generations. And it is a broad majority of the parliament and the electorate that supports the coalition. All political forces in Europe are participating today in the process of German unification. We represent in this process the interests of the GDR citizens. The "yes" for unity has been spoken. We will have a decisive say about the road we take to get there.

The new beginning of our society should also be an honest new beginning; in the great historical process of our liberation we have one politician to thank for effectively pulling together many positive impulses: Michail Gorbachev. We sense the heavy burden he has to bear in the Soviet Union. We ask the citizens of the Soviet Union not to view the politics of the GDR and its striving for German unity as threatening. We are aware of our historical guilt toward the Soviet Union, and as a free state we would like to cooperate on friendly terms with the Soviet Union, a state in which the new way of thinking was victorious. Glasnost and perestroika opened new historical horizons for the world, horizons that for a long time were not thought possible. They also promoted a citizens' movement in the GDR that extended into all social sectors.

A decisive force in this process was the new democratic groups in which people came together and burst the chains of the past.

The bearers of the peaceful revolution in the fall of 1989 have earned an outstanding place in German history. That should always remain present and vivid in this chamber.

If at this point I express my thanks for our freedom, I also think of the freedom movement in our neighbor states to the east. The Solidarity movement in Poland had lasting effects on all of Eastern Europe. Neither martial law nor hate propaganda were able to forestall democracy. Names like that of Lech Walesa, or that of the great proponent for civil rights and today's president of Czechoslovakia, Vaclav Havel, will be recorded in the history books forever and move the hearts of freedom-loving people.

We think of the Hungarian nation and its citizens who tore down the Iron Curtain and, with that, also a piece of the Berlin Wall. Already in the next months this inhumane monument to disgrace will be torn down.

In the name of the government of the GDR, I would like to thank the citizens of the Federal Republic of Germany. They stood by us, they encouraged and helped us wherever possible. And let's not forget: for decades the Western media–although not entirely without self-serving motives–were the most important source of information for many GDR citizens. Frequently they were the only mouthpiece for the oppressed and the political dissidents of this country.

The unrestricted affirmation of the self-determination and unity of the German people by responsible politicians in the Federal Republic–let me name only Richard von Weizsäcker, Helmut Kohl, Willy Brandt, and Hans-Dietrich Genscher–puts us in the position of being able to realize unity now.

At this point I would like to thank Hans Modrow once again for his commitment. Because of his cautious politics, I am sure, we were spared many things. During the difficult times of the last half year he, as a true democrat, remained above party politics and, in cooperation with the Round Table, stabilized this country.

Dear delegates, one more word of thanks ought not to be forgotten today. That is the thanks to the churches. We owe it to them for providing protection for political dissidents and defending those who were denied their rights. Their prudence and affirmation of nonviolence preserved the peacefulness of our revolution. It could have been quite different. We have reason for deep gratitude for having been spared those experiences that, for example, the Romanians had to have.[2]

But our history does not only cover the last five years. As a free government and a free parliament we pay our respect to the victims of fascism. We think of the victims of the concentration camps and of the war. But we also think of the victims of Stalinism, of the victims of the 17th of June, 1953, and of the victims of the Wall. War and postwar, the interwovenness of infinitely many people with guilt and reconciliation and historical guilt once more, has left its traces on the face of our people.

We would like to learn from those who in those dark times dared to put up political resistance. These human beings are the pride of our nation, and their accomplishments are the moral treasure of our nation.

The people who took part in the resistance remind us of our responsibility for our history. It is not the PDS alone that is responsible for our past in the GDR. My party, too, is responsible for it. All of us are responsible for it. It was always only a tiny minority who dared to vote against the official candidates at the elections or who stayed away altogether. Each of us has to ask himself or herself whether he or she always did the right thing and what he or she learned from all this. It is not always the courageous people of yesterday who demand the punishment of others today. . . .

In these weeks we experienced once again how our young democracy got entangled anew in the spiderweb of the former Ministry for State Security (Stasi). We will establish a governmental commission that will work on uncovering and dissolving the entire organization of the Ministry for State Security, or the Office for National Security. This commission will see to it that the deserving work of the citizens' committees will come to a legally codified conclusion. The mastery of the Stasi past needs the urgent attention of constitutional justice. To protect the citizens from being spied on in the future, we will present a far-reaching law for the protection of information. In Germany there should never again be a central agency that uncontrollably gathers information about the private lives and private thoughts of its citizens. . . .

State Security was not the actual illness of the GDR, it was only one of its symptoms. The actual hereditary illness of socialist society was the dictatorial centralism that, due to a Stalinist delusion, was put in the place of democracy, in the place of the self-determination of the people. This centralism created an atmosphere of pressure that poisoned all social life. Coercion and pressure wipe out initiative, the willingness to assume responsibility, individual convictions, and make it difficult to follow one's own conscience.

For this reason, today it is not enough to take up a problem; rather, we have to start much earlier. We have to make ourselves aware of the damage done to our psyches, which expresses itself in hatred, impatience, in a new, now anti-socialist opportunism, in exhaustion and desperation. We have to help each other become free human beings.

The quality of our road will be able to be measured by the preservation of basic values in our society. Four things are at issue:
    –the freedom to dissent;
    –justice for all;
    –peace as the aim of domestic and foreign affairs;
    –responsibility for life in all its forms.

These values indicate the direction I–and, I believe, all of us–want to take. . . .

We by no means view the free market economy to which we aspire as an end in itself; rather, we see in it a natural, internationally tested, effective economic form, one that, at the same time, gives us the chance to finally conform to our moral duties in our own society and in the world to the necessary degree.

We want to work, live, and reside in an ecologically responsible social market economy. We will now develop it step by step. . . . In the next eight to ten weeks we want to lay the foundation for the economic, currency, and social union so that it can take effect before the summer break. We consider 1 : 1 the basic exchange rate. Part of this must also be the safeguarding of the property rights based on the land reform and transfers of property that, according to the laws applicable at the time, were legally binding and, hence, should remain legally binding. It is further necessary that, before the change to the new currency, the amount of the previous subsidies be added on a differential basis to wages and pensions. Only after this has happened can prices and rents be deregulated step by step so that they can follow the development of wages.

One of our most important duties vis-à-vis our own people and humanity in general is the guarantee of an environment in which we want and are able to live. We cannot remove our deficiencies in this area from one day to the next. But with the help of the Federal Republic, we will introduce a well-conceived and financially feasible program for environmental protection that preserves existing jobs and creates new ones.

The third dimension of this quality of life, after the socioeconomic and the ecological aspects, is our intellectual life. Education, culture, and the media should be an expression of our freedom. Their manifoldness, their plurality, will be part of our social wealth. It is the task of the government as well as of the parliament to watch over this wealth and work against renewed deformations.

The mandate given this government demands the development of German unity in an undivided, peaceful Europe. This demand includes conditions regarding pace and quality.

Unity must come as quickly as possible, but its framework must be as good, as rational, and as durable as necessary.

The debate about the currency exchange rate of 1 : 1 or 1 : 2 made it perfectly clear to us that there is a connection here, and that we have to negotiate conditions that guarantee that GDR citizens do not get the feeling that they will become second-class citizens of the Federal Republic.

Both, pace and quality, can best be guaranteed if we achieve unity along a path, set forth in treaties, that follows the route established by Article 23 of the Basic Law.

Since the summer of last year we have seen many wonderful signs of the friendship, helpfulness, and openness of the citizens of the Federal Republic. But we also view with concern tendencies toward a dwindling willingness to share and offer solidarity.

Therefore, one heart-felt request to the citizens of the Federal Republic:

Please remember that for 40 years we had to carry the heavy burden of German history. The GDR, as you know, did not receive any Marshall Plan assistance; on the contrary, we had to pay reparations.[3] We do not expect you to make any sacrifices. We expect a communal spirit and solidarity. The division can, in fact, only be overcome by sharing. We will work hard and well, but we will need your compassion and solidarity in the future just as we felt it last fall.

People ask us: Don't we have anything to contribute to German unity? And our answer is: Yes, we do!

We are contributing our land and our people, we are contributing created values and our diligence, our training and our gift for improvising. Necessity is the mother of invention.

We are contributing the experiences of the last decades, which we share with the countries of Eastern Europe.

We are contributing our sense of social justice, for solidarity and tolerance. In the GDR we had an education against racism and xenophobia, even if in reality we were not able to practice it very much. We should not and do not want to make room for xenophobia.

We are contributing our bitter and proud experiences at the threshold between conformity and opposition. We are contributing our identity and our dignity.

Our identity, that is our history and culture, our failures and our accomplishments, our ideals and our sufferings. Our dignity, that is our freedom and our human right to self-determination.

But it is not only a matter of the last forty years. In Germany a lot of history has to be worked through, above all that history that we pushed more to the side and, therefore, did not connect often enough with ourselves. But anyone who reclaims the positive aspects of German history also has to take account of its guilt, regardless of when he or she was born and entered into this history as an active agent.

Germany is our inheritance of historical accomplishment and historical guilt. If we avow our faith in Germany, we must also avow this double heritage.

Yet, we do not stop with Germany. It is a matter of Europe. We know the current weakness of the GDR. But we also know: in its economic potential it is not a poor country.

The real problems in our world–we all know that–are not the German-German or the East-West problems. The real problems lie in the structurally manifest injustice between North and South.

If this is not to result in a deadly threat for the existence of human beings, we will have to participate in the overcoming of this injustice. The establishment of a juster international economic order is not only a thing for the great powers or the UN, rather it is the task of every member of the world community.

Even the peaceful coexistence of Germans and foreigners in our country can be a contribution to a new quality of coexistence among different peoples.

The clarification of the legal situation of foreign citizens and the creation of deputies for foreigners on different levels will be just as necessary as the support of initiatives that encourage us to experience cultural diversity as a form of wealth.

The liberation of Nelson Mandela and the lifting of apartheid in South Africa, the fate of the tropical rain forest and aid for the Third World move us in the same way as do our own problems–indeed, not only "in the same way as": they are our own problems.

We know that our capacity to solve our own problems depends upon our willingness to perceive the problems of others.

The coalition government we have formed faces great, difficult, and very concrete tasks, which necessitate clear and strategic decisions.

The economic policy aim of this coalition government is to convert the former state-guided command economy into an ecologically oriented social market economy.

The conversion of state-run plan guidance to a social market economy must occur at a quick pace but also in orderly steps. In the coming months both will have to exist side by side, whereby we will have to operate according to the motto "as much market as possible and only as much state as is necessary.". . .

The task of the government regarding the establishment and implementation of a federal budget for 1990 is guided by the need to stabilize state finances and by the necessities of large-scale economic balance.

A concrete statement will only be possible when the new government has in front of it a complete assessment of the financial and economic situation. We will try to make this information public as quickly as possible and draw the necessary consequences. Today I can only say this much.

The presently existing budget plan for 1990 has to be streamlined in adherence to the conditions of a social market economy. . . .

Our citizens attach, for very good reasons, high expectations to our energy and environmental policies.

In energy policy we will follow the aim of producing and using energy that is friendly to the environment and efficient. . . .

Special attention and support will be given to the redirection of jobs that come available into other important areas, especially into the infrastructure, into trade and service areas, and into construction.

Through the construction of a productive environmental industry our quality of life can be decisively improved. Many new jobs will be created in this way.

The government will take appropriate measures for stimulating the economic use of natural resources, recycling, and recyclable products. . . .

The complicated economic situation in our country is also mirrored in an underdeveloped infrastructure, especially in the area of transportation, mail, and telephone service, as well as in construction.

The construction of an effective transportation system is one of the basic preconditions for the development of a free-market structure, for economic growth, and for the well-being of our country. . . .

The government faces up to its social responsibility for guaranteeing appropriate housing conditions for all citizens. This necessitates a new housing policy that guarantees rent control and the protection of renters, and that makes possible the preservation, renewal, and addition of housing units. A rent ceiling for housing, which is self-adjusting depending on the general development of wages, is absolutely necessary. The socially needy will receive a housing allowance. Protection of renters against eviction is among the social principles defended by the coalition. . . .

In the name of the government let me state: the results of the land reform on the territory of the GDR are not on the table. But we assume that in the future all forms of property will have to be placed on the same footing.

A completely new land law will guarantee the availability of real estate under consideration of the general good and the exclusion of possibilities for speculation. . . .

The economy is no end in itself, rather it is a means for guaranteeing that everyone has the necessities of life, for making human development possible, and for promoting the realization of human dignity.

Creating work and jobs, especially for women, single parents, for parents of families with a large number of children, and for the disabled, is the aim of this government.

The struggle against the anticipated unemployment requires the following immediate measures:
  –the retraining and re-qualification of workers;
  –the establishment of effective employment offices;
  –financial security in case of unemployment;
  –the protection of employees by means of a law protecting them against unfair termination, a law governing working conditions, and a law regulating wages.

Our concern must always first be for those who cannot partake of our prosperity due to reasons beyond their control.

We have to lend our support to the weak in our society. We have to make sure that the fruits of communal work are distributed fairly, and we have to stand up for the principle that those who bear the burden will also get some relief from it. Especially in a society in which the free play of all forces can develop, it is important that the strongest force, that is, the state, assert itself as the defender of the weak. It should not only be a matter of redirecting material assistance to, among others, the disabled, but of creating a legal framework so that no one needs to ask for charity but only need demand what is owed him by right. . . .

We need a comprehensive system of daycare centers and an adjudication of work time and family time, which will benefit the family and especially the children. Therefore, we need more flexible working hours, a shorter work day, and more part-time work. But we also want to help those who for a certain amount of time wish to dedicate themselves to the education of their children, to a disabled child, or to the care of their own parents. We will help these men and women so that after this time period dedicated to education or care of the elderly they will be able to find their way back into the work force. It is the aim of the government that compensation in salary will be made for such time periods and that they will be included in the time counted toward social security benefits.

The distribution of responsibilities in this society, and that means within the family, as well, is frequently unequal. If the basic value of equality is to become meaningful, then it is not enough that so many women are in the work force and derive a higher level of self-assurance from that; rather, our women must have the same chances for promotion, the same pay, altogether the same chances in all professions. Equality in the workplace should not be realized at the expense of the women themselves. To ensure the equality of women in the workplace and in society we will appoint representatives on all levels of society, that is, in the districts, in the *Länder*, and in the *Ministerrat*, who make sure that equality becomes a reality in the everyday life within businesses and administration, as well. . . .

The crisis in our health care system is well known. We need more doctors, more nurses and certified caregivers. We need medical assistance for the disabled and the elderly, and a reform of medical rehabilitation. We need to improve the medical equipment in our hospitals and rebuild many hospitals, nursing homes, and homes for the elderly. We also have to bring about definite improvements in their social and economic-technical infrastructure. . . .

We are also inheriting a catastrophic situation from the years of SED rule in the education sector. Especially in the last few years great problems and errors have piled up.

We have to get rid of the bureaucratic-centralistic system of state guidance and develop a balanced relation between the responsibility of the state and social initiative. The uniformity cemented in the last decades has to be replaced by a differentiated and flexible educational system that does not exclude alternative models. The government has set itself the goal of creating, by means of structural changes, those free spaces in which the responsible cooperation of all those active in education will be able to develop. . . .

In the realm of culture, we will pursue a policy that guarantees unrestricted cultural-artistic creation, free of any form of regulation, that is open to all the intellectual treasures of our people, of Europe, and of the world.

The government considers it its duty to protect and promote culture and art. It acknowledges the necessity of subsidies for culture and art. For the support of cultural tasks of supra-regional significance, we suggest a central cultural fund through a cultural foundation for a united Germany.

The government will create the preconditions for the decentralization and federalization of culture and cultural politics and pave the way for the establishment of the cultural sovereignty of the *Länder*. . . .

Madame President, dear delegates, I am personally particularly interested in the issue of the constitutional state. The previous legal system essentially served as the guarantor of the existing power structure and made sure that any oppositional sentiment was criminalized and exterminated at its roots. Thousands of citizens experienced themselves the degree of relentlessness and inflexibility with which this was pursued.

The rehabilitation of citizens who, for political reasons, were persecuted by the criminal justice system and disadvantaged in the workplace or who unjustly experienced other disadvantages will be an important concern of a new legal policy.

The government will make sure that the justice system is reconstructed according to constitutional principles and that the principle of the division of powers will be instituted.

We consider the following measures to be necessary:

1. the establishment of a constitutional court;
2. the step-by-step creation of separate courts for administrative law, labor law, and civil law, within the framework of an ordered justice system;
3. the transformation of contractual courts into regular courts;

4. the incorporation of the military courts as well as the military district attorneys into the civilian justice system;

5. the strengthening of the bar association. . . .

Aside from constitutionality, democracy requires a further condition: the decentralization of power. Formerly, all power originated in Berlin. Decisions were made in Berlin. . . .

We will decentralize power. In 1991 there will be *Länder* again. Elections for these *Länder* are planned for late fall of this year.

This federal structure is one of the basic conditions for German unity, a basic condition for democracy, and a condition for the successful restructuring of our economy. . . .

I am now coming to the last major point of my government policy statement.

Our future lies in German unity in the context of an undivided, peaceful Europe. We in the government are responsible for 16 million people, and that will determine the actions of this government. All Germans have a shared history that was only apparently interrupted at the end of the Second World War by the division of Europe. Both German governments agree that the aim of our negotiations cannot be a business partnership, but must rather be a true community. That will determine the spirit of our negotiations. Unification must develop out of the will of the people and not out of the interests of governments.

Germany lies at the center of Europe, but it should never again seek to elevate itself to being the center of power in Europe. We do not want to fall between the cracks of the nations of Europe, but wish instead to be a pillar for a bridge of reconciliation. Germany must be a factor for peace. The unification of Germany ought to strengthen stability in Europe and promote the creation of a peaceful, democratic, and cooperative European order.

We want to contribute to German unity our experiences of the significance of inner peace in society. We know that first of all we must come to terms with our history. There can no longer be one part of Germany that is guilty for everything and another that supposedly preserved its innocence. We, too, have to accept the communal responsibility for the crimes of the National-Socialist dictatorship.[4]

The unity of Germany ought to strengthen the community of Europeans. The essential precondition for this is the guarantee of all existing borders in Europe. It is also essential that our neighbors feel secure about their borders with Germany.

The internationally binding recognition of the Polish western border, as it is described in the Görlitz Treaty between the GDR and Poland and in the Warsaw Treaty between the Federal Republic of Germany and Poland, is indispensable.

With the completion of the unification of the two German states, the future German constitution should, among other things, no longer contain Article 23 of the Basic Law. Germany has no claims to territory in other countries and will not raise any such claims in the future.

Unification has become possible in connection with detente across the globe and the end of the East-West conflict. The division of Germany was an expression of this conflict. Detente stands under the banner of human rights and disarmament. In this phase of the politics of detente, defense policies and disarmament policies go hand in hand. In this regard, as well, we recall the roots of the democratic renewal in our country. An essential foundation of this renewal is the peace movement.

It is the task of the GDR government to pursue a policy that, as the beginning of a European security system, supports the process of dissolving the military alliances by means of structures that transcend alliances. A European security system with fewer and fewer military functions is the aim of our negotiations. We consider the extension of the concept of security to include the areas of the economy, environment, culture, science, and technology, a sign of the times.

On the present territory of the GDR there will, for a transitional period, be a radically reduced and strictly defense-oriented National People's Army, in addition to the Soviet Army, whose task is the protection of this territory. Loyalty to the Warsaw Pact Treaty Organization will mean for us, among other things, that in our negotiations we always consider the security interests of the Soviet Union and those of the other states who signed the Warsaw Pact Treaty.

The government of the GDR seeks a drastic reduction of all German military forces. The GDR renounces the production, distribution, ownership, and stationing of atomic, biological, and chemical weapons and seeks the same for a united Germany. We furthermore also support a global ban on all chemical weapons as early as this year.

The nuclear disarmament process has to be continued. By the end of this year we hope for a positive conclusion of the START negotiations between the Soviet Union and the United States promising a fifty percent reduction of strategic nuclear weapons.[5]

With a peaceful and secure European order, we can create the preconditions for the suspension of the allied rights after the Second World War over Berlin and Germany as a whole. The government of the GDR is committed to seeing that this suspension take place within the framework of the Two-Plus-Four Talks. They also belong to the general framework of the CSCE process for the creation of a peaceful European order.

For us, the CSCE has special significance. The government of the GDR particularly supports the idea of creating a CSCE security agency for the verification of disarmament and restructuring agreements. We also favor forming a CSCE commission for the settling of disputes and for the establishment of a permanent joint council of the foreign and defense ministers.

The government of the GDR wants to play a leading role in the process of disarmament. We will introduce immediate measures first to limit, and then, within a foreseeable time frame, to totally stop the production and the export of weapons of war. We will introduce a restructuring of the People's Army and a step-by-step suspension of the military responsibilities of the GDR. Political cooperation within the framework of the Warsaw Pact Treaty, however, should be intensified. To this end, the government will contact the governments of the signatory states to the Warsaw Pact Treaty in the very near future.

The GDR wants to develop and deepen its special relations to the nations of Eastern Europe in the areas of economics, politics, and culture. The relations to the European Community will play an important role in this regard. The government of the GDR would welcome a quick, gradual expansion of the EC.

The creation of German unity is tied to the realization of human rights. The new patriotism should thus be an expression of the fact that we support basic and human rights. For that reason, we will join the European Human Rights Commission. We will also ask for the participation of the GDR in sessions of the European Council.

Until German unification, the GDR government will negotiate about the extension of the EC to the present-day GDR. It will be our aim in these negotiations to arrive at the stipulation of deadlines for the full assumption of treaty duties and rights. That is particularly important for our agriculture, for the tax system, and in the areas of social and ecological norms.

For the existing foreign trade commitments of the GDR, especially with the Soviet Union, we will have to find solutions that guarantee the treaty loyalty of the GDR and that, above all, will contribute to the stabilization and strengthening of the situation in Central and Eastern Europe. I want to stress this expressly once more: our foreign trade commitments with the Soviet Union will be strictly met and will be honored by a united Germany in the spirit of honoring a treaty.

A unified Europe has to promote peace and consolidation in the world. An appropriate means for this are the deliberations in the context of European political cooperation. We will submit a proposal to be allowed to participate in these deliberations.

We want to contribute to a peace process in the Middle East that pays attention to the right to self-determination of all people living there.

The end of the East-West conflict is making considerable progress. This obliges us to dedicate our full attention to the North-South conflict. To be sure, we have our problems, but they are small in comparison with the concerns and needs of the people in the developing countries. We feel solidarity with the people of the Third World and hope for a cooperative partnership. Especially after the events that lie behind us, it is particularly significant for us to support the message of social justice and democracy even in those countries with which we are already cooperating. Therefore, economic, medical, and social projects will take precedence for us.

The economic cooperation of the GDR will develop everywhere in the world into an increasing cooperation with similar projects and positions of the Federal Republic of Germany. Parallel to the unification process of the two states in Germany, there will be a consolidation of the German-German engagement in the countries of the Third World. Our long-term aim must be a just economic order that affords all human beings an economic future and social prospects.

This government of the democratic center has a demanding platform. We know that we have a difficult road ahead of us. No government can work wonders, but we will strive to accomplish all that is possible with all our means. If we acknowledge what is possible for us and realize it soberly, gradually, and with prudence, we can lay the foundation for a better future for the people in our country. For that we rely on the support, the courage, and the energy of all citizens.

NOTES

Source: Zanetti, 272-97.

1. "People's Chamber" is the literal translation of *Volkskammer*, the German designation for the East German parliament, which now, for the first time in its history, consisted of freely elected representatives. During the days of SED rule the outcome of elections was predetermined.

2. In Romania, the leading Communist politician, Nicolas Ceausescu ordered the Timisoara slayings by the Securitate in December 1989, which resulted in many thousands of deaths; after his flight from Bucharest, however, he was captured on December 22, tried, and executed on December 25 by an extraordinary military tribunal that sided with the rebellion.

3. As opposed to the Federal Republic and other European Countries which received financial and other assistance from the US after the war for the reconstruction of their economies, the GDR had to pay stiff reparations to the Soviet Union, and this hampered its economic growth considerably.

4. The official GDR policy toward German history was that the GDR was founded by antifascist forces and hence did not have to accept responsibility for such crimes of National Socialism as the Holocaust.

5. Strategic Arms Reduction Treaty negotiations between the Soviet Union and the United States were begun on 29 June 1982.

54
"Article 23 of the Basic Law: No Connection at this Number": Pamphlet of the Green Party of Lower Saxony (Spring 1990)

FRGDR

The majority of the electorate in the GDR decided on March 18: for Helmut Kohl and his promise of a quick currency and economic union. Including an economic miracle. With this, the chances for an independent development in the GDR have further decreased. It seems as if only a broad mobilization against the predictable results of the chaotic unification for the two German states could prevent the sheer annexation of the GDR according to Article 23 of the Basic Law.

The quicker the currency, economic, and social union comes, the worse the consequences for the people in the GDR. Women, in particular, will be affected by it when jobs will have to be eliminated in masses and their social securities dismantled. The cost for a–

completely inadequate–cushioning of this process will have to be borne mainly by the socially weak in the FRG. For the foreseeable future, therefore–even with regard to the processes of pan-European unification–the development of confederative structures is a better alternative than the unification of states.

Bonn Dictates

The events since November 1989, above all the systematic destabilization campaign pursued by the government of the Federal Republic, killed the hopes of many people for an independent development in the GDR. After forty years of SED politics, which left a society without hope, the people in the GDR see the solution to their problems only in speedy annexation. A currency and economic union entered the discussion very quickly–however, only along the lines of the terms dictated by Bonn.

The Bonn officials never entered into negotiations on equal terms with the Modrow government and the Round Table. And even the government that was freely elected on March 18 is derogatorily referred to as a "transitional government."

Courting its right-wing electorate, the government of the Federal Republic is trying to sneak its way out of recognizing, in accordance with international law, the Oder-Neiße border as the western border of Poland. This is only the most obvious expression of nationalism and pan-German delusions that are increased by the annexation of the GDR by the FRG.

Growing Together Instead of Chaotic Unification

The path toward the unification of the two German states must consider the existential rights of the citizens of the GDR and of all people in Europe. Without an open, democratic process with the equal inclusion of the people and the government of the GDR, this is impossible. A constitutional convention with an equal representation of male and female delegates should propose a new constitution on the basis of the constitution of the GDR and the Basic Law of the FRG. Separate referendums in the GDR and the FRG must decide about its ratification.

The new state cannot be a centralized state of the old sort. On the contrary, it must support the re-establishment of genuine federal structures and district self-administration.

Above all, the foreign citizens in both German states are feeling the negative effects of the national frenzy. We oppose their further exclusion. The right of political asylum must apply without any exceptions.

The immediate creation of a currency and economic union must be rejected. The anticipated mass unemployment has already begun. We already know now that, above all, women will lose their jobs and will experience great difficulties. Businesses are laying off female workers. Social services such as daycare centers will be cut back. The right to work and comprehensive, state-financed childcare, as well as all-day school hours and the continuation of abortion rights must absolutely be maintained. The assumption of existing regulations from the FRG would mean a decrease in social services.

The wish of GDR citizens for a hard currency and for social security can only be realized by means of stable, staggered exchange rates and comprehensive, immediate aid packages.

Rights Instead of Charity

There is a danger that women will be the losers of annexation. Therefore, a participation of women on all levels of politics and society according to minimal quota requirements is just as necessary as a social charter that above all secures the rights and interests of the female population.

No further incitements for emigrating to the FRG should be retained. As long as there are emergency shelters, people will leave the GDR as refugees. The shelters should, therefore, be closed immediately. We want the sociopolitical equality of emigrants and refugees with the citizens of the FRG, and no more.

Ecological Reason Instead of a Sell-Out

We need an ecological reconstruction of the societies in the FRG and the GDR, not a copy of the FRG in the GDR. The fact that the ecological development in the GDR in many instances is far more catastrophic than in the FRG should not obscure the insight that it is our form of economy that produces ecological catastrophe on a global scale.

The growing together of the two German states should not become a pretext for the massive extension of the highway system, in particular along the border. On the contrary, today we have the opportunity to hinder the environmentally destructive consequences of our Western transportation policy by developing a modern public transportation system. A massive subsidy for the modernization of rail traffic is necessary and possible.

Environmental Cooperation

We GREENS in Lower Saxony want above all to promote ecological district and regional partnerships in a future state of Sachsen-Anhalt, with comprehensive means coming from the state government.

1. The export of refuse to the GDR must be stopped immediately. Joint future concepts of refuse management should be geared toward prevention and recycling.

2. The generating of nuclear energy should be stopped immediately. This includes the closing of all currently operating plants, as well as the suspension or abandonment of further projects such as Schacht Konrad, Asse, Gorleben, and Bartensleben.[1] Particularly in Buschhaus and Harbke the mining and use of coal has to be reduced and clean-up should be considered.[2] Energy saving and the exploitation of regenerative energy sources should have precedence.

3. Cleaning up our water by replacing the sewage system and establishing effective purification plants, as well as the cleaning up of the Werra, Weser, and Elbe rivers, are urgent tasks.

4. Instead of building new highways, public transportation along the border region should be increased and financially supported. Before we start digging for a new light rail connection between Hannover and Berlin, an environmental impact study should be completed.

5. The entire border area and major parts of the Harz mountains should be made into a protected natural area. The plans for the

drainage of the swamp near Drömling should be dropped. Those parts of the Lüneburger Heide that today are used for military purposes should be reforested and returned to nature.[3]

6. The conversion of industrialized agriculture into extensive agrarian use, above all ecological methods of working the land, should be financially supported.

Demilitarization Instead of NATO-Germany

We reject unification without the binding recognition of today's existing borders. The firm embedding of unification in the CSCE process is just as indispensable as is the inclusion of the allies of the Second World War and all neighboring countries, especially Poland.

After two world wars, Germany historically lost the right to decide on its own discretion about its size and its role in world politics.

That is another reason why the former bloc politics has to be abandoned in favor of a new peaceful European order that embraces Western and Eastern Europe. The complete demilitarization of Germany is necessary. The strains caused by the military, by troop exercise areas, maneuvers, and low-level flights, must be stopped immediately.

We reject models for a factual inclusion of all of Germany in NATO as they have been brought forward in different versions by people like Dregger, Genscher, and Brandt.

Let's make use of the opportunity for a complete demilitarization of the Federal Republic and the GDR by the year 2000 as the beginning of an irreversible worldwide disarmament process whose aim is the complete overcoming of the illusion of military security and the bloc system, as well as the sensible use of economic resources for surmounting the immense costs of the process of peaceful European unification.

Waffles, not Weapons!

The Greens

NOTES

Source: Pamphlet of the Green Party, Landesverband Niedersachsen.

1. These names refer to sites in Lower Saxony where nuclear energy plants were either operating or were in the planning stage.

2. Buschhausen and Harbke are sites in Lower Saxony where the landscape has been destroyed by coal mining.

3. The Lüneburger Heide is an area in Lower Saxony named after its native plant, heather.

55
Statements by West German Foreign Minister Hans-Dietrich Genscher at the Opening of the Two-Plus-Four Talks in Bonn (May 5, 1990)

Opening Statement

Forty-five years ago almost to the day, a war that claimed innumerable victims and caused immeasurable pain ended in Europe. We honor the victims of the war and the violent regime when we express–as we did in the first sentence of the Helsinki Final Act– once again our common will to contribute "to peace, security, justice, and cooperation in Europe."

We are beginning our talks today in that spirit. We want to create preconditions for a new chapter, for a peaceful and happy period of German and European history.

The horrors of the Second World War and the Holocaust have not been forgotten. After the war people died due to expulsion and flight. Others lost their lives and their freedom because they cried out for freedom. An Iron Curtain divided Europe, it divided the German people.

We know what feelings and memories other nations associate with what was done to them then in the name of Germany. President Richard von Weizsäcker spoke for all Germans in the speech he gave on May 8, 1985.[1]

Since the end of the war we have succeeded, despite all the tensions and confrontations, in preserving peace. Forty-five years without war, that is a new experience for our continent.

All nations should be able to consider a united Germany a contribution to a better Europe. That is the will of all Germans, who do not tie the unification of the two German states to any claims for land from any of their neighbors. With the participation of Poland in negotiations about border questions, the road will be paved for the recognition of the Polish western border by unified Germany according to international law.

Clear-sighted statesmen and courageous nations have given us the chance to get rid of the last debts of the war years and postwar years of European history and to create the architecture of a common European house, the structure of a peaceful European order.

I think that our sense that we are taking part in a historical turning point is not deceptive. Europe–and the world–are no longer characterized by the confrontation between East and West.

The transformation that is changing Europe is the result of intelligent politics and peaceful revolutions. Europe is finding its way back to itself and to its unity not through power politics but rather under the sign of human rights and basic freedoms.

The human being with his or her dignity and rights, concern for the survival of humankind, are at the center of the politics of all states whose representatives are gathered at this table.

That is the task with which history has charged our generation. We are now called upon to shape Europe. We bear a great responsibility for our children and our grandchildren.

The establishment of German unity is inseparably bound up with the European process. The president of the Czechoslovak Republic, Vaclav Havel, expressed this in January before the Polish parliament in Warsaw with the following words: "It is difficult to imagine a unified Europe with a divided Germany. It is just as difficult to imagine a unified Germany in a divided Europe."

On February 13, 1990 in Ottawa, we agreed that the foreign ministers of the Federal Republic of Germany and the German Democratic Republic would meet with the foreign ministers of France, the United Kingdom, the Soviet Union, and the United States in order to discuss the external aspects of the establishment of German unity, including questions regarding the security of the neighboring states.

We have to resolve difficult questions. But if we are all willing not only to assert our own interests but also to respect the interests of our partners, then we will arrive at resolutions.

Our responsibility for the future of Europe demands decisiveness and good judgment.

Dear colleagues, I would like to extend a warm welcome to you and your delegations.

As the chair of this first round of ministerial discussions, I would like herewith to formally open our talks.

Introductory Statement

For the Federal Republic of Germany I would like to make a few fundamental remarks.

German unification, which is desired by the people in both German states and by their democratically elected governments and parliaments, will be the result of a politics of responsibility.

A unified Germany is emerging on the basis of the right to self-determination that is laid down in international law as well as in the principles of the Helsinki Final Act.

Self-determination also means that the Germans themselves decide in what type of state, at what time, at what tempo, and under what conditions they want to realize their unity. This is how President Gorbachev stated it on February 10, 1990 in Moscow, and I think that this is the understanding shared by all of us at this table.

The modalities and the time-frame according to which German unity will take place are beginning to take shape.

The Federal Republic of Germany and the German Democratic Republic are equal participants in the process of unification. We are working from the standpoint of the still existing rights and duties of the Four Powers with regard to Germany as a whole and for Berlin; we want to transfer these rights and duties in an orderly fashion. Those are the central concerns of the discussions that will take place at this table.

The position the Federal Republic of Germany hopes to achieve for unified Germany is preordained by the Basic Law. Its preamble expresses the wish of the German people to serve peace in the world as an equal partner in a unified Europe.

Germany's geographical position in the heart of Europe inseparably ties our fate to the fate of Europe. For forty years we endured the division of Europe in the form of a bitter division of the Germans.

We wish to contribute the energy that develops out of our peaceful unification to a single Europe–whole and free. We do not want to create a German Europe, but rather a European Germany.

Both German states see in national unity not only an aim of German politics, but rather a contribution to a new Europe, as well. That is why we associate our road to unity and our politics after unity as closely as possible with the European process.

German unification does not create new problems for Europe; on the contrary, it will contribute to new and lasting stability. To translate this knowledge derived from European history into a politics for Germany and for a unifying Europe is what we conceive as the European calling of Germany at the end of this century.

Democracy has taken root and been preserved for over forty years in the Federal Republic of Germany. The people in the GDR struggled for their democracy themselves in a peaceful revolution for freedom.

United Germany will be a free, constitutional democracy. Such a state should not give anyone cause for concern or, worse, for fear. We are embedded in the European Community. For all of its members, it is the guarantee of internal and external stability, and in its will to political union it is a stabilizing anchor for all of Europe.

We are members of the NATO Alliance. In the future we will remain committed to its goal of creating a lasting, just, and peaceful European order.

German unification is taking place within the framework of the CSCE process. The Helsinki Final Act helped pave the way for unity. Just as we draw upon the CSCE principles for the chance for German unity, we feel ourselves bound to the principles of the Helsinki Acts as a measuring stick for the internal and external aspects of the establishment of unity.

We know that German unity is a concern of our neighbors and of all Europeans. For that reason, we want the results of the Two-Plus-Four Talks to be presented to the special summit of the CSCE states this fall.

Principle VII of the Helsinki Final Act established a connection between the right for self-determination and the equality of all nations. Self-determination and equal rights are indispensable foundations for lasting peace; they prevent revenge and revisionism.

The Federal Republic of Germany has proven that, in the interest of a peaceful and lasting order in Europe, it is willing to renounce sovereign privileges, as our Basic Law (Article 24, Paragraph 2) expressly stipulates.[2]

This will also be true for unified Germany. It is important that equal things be treated equally, and that neither discrimination nor singularization take place.

The list of principles in the Helsinki Final Act can also point the way toward resolving difficult questions. The Helsinki Final Act expressly stresses that all its principles are of fundamental significance. In this context I want to remind you of the principle of sovereign equality, which gives all participating states the right "to be or not to be a treaty party in an alliance."

Because we are aware that the effect of the Western alliance, which is adapting to the changes in Europe, was to create peace and security, an unallied unified Germany would be no gain for Europe.

The CSCE talks and the multilateral disarmament talks constitute the framework for new structures for securing peace in Europe. Both German states are of the opinion that this framework is capable of and in need of being expanded.

The Germans would like to support this jointly, even before they are united in one state. It is in this framework that the German nation, together with the other nations participating in the CSCE process, will find its place and develop its potentials.

This framework offers new answers to the questions of security in Europe. Disarmament will play a central role in this.

The establishment of German unity not only changes European structures, it also affects the bilateral interests of numerous partners of the Federal Republic of Germany and of the German Democratic Republic.

We do not want to create German unity at the expense or to the disadvantage of other states. We believe that a unified Germany will not diminish the possibilities of intensive, mutually beneficial cooperation, but instead will significantly improve them.

That is especially true for the relationship of unified Germany with the Soviet Union, which will also be of central importance for unified Germany.

We are aware that we will have to find answers to a series of difficult questions. But we would like to hold these talks without delay.

We cannot let events move ahead faster than our discussions. And we have to live up to people's expectations in both parts of Germany.

Closing Declaration

The six foreign ministers agreed on the agenda of the Two-Plus-Four Talks.

First item: Border questions.

Second item: Political-military questions, with consideration of initial steps for appropriate security structures in Europe.

Third item: Problems of Berlin.

Fourth item: Conclusive regulation and settlement of the rights and duties of the Four Powers according to international law.

The foreign ministers expressed their fundamental positions about the external aspects of the establishment of German unity. It gave me great satisfaction to take note of agreement on the following points.

The will of the Germans to realize their unification in an ordered fashion and without delay was acknowledged by all participants. German unity should become a gain for all states. It is the purpose of the talks to reach a conclusive regulation, according to international law, that transfers the rights and duties of the Four Powers.

There was notable agreement on the assessment of the significance of the CSCE process and the necessity of expanding and intensifying it.

The next meetings of the foreign ministers are planned for June in Berlin, July in Paris, and the beginning of September in Moscow. The exact dates for the next two meetings will be settled in the next few days through diplomatic channels.

We agreed on inviting the Polish foreign minister to the third meeting of the foreign ministers in July in Paris if questions concerning borders are discussed. The Polish foreign minister will be permitted to speak to all questions that are related to border questions.

As chair of this conference I will send a letter of invitation to the Polish foreign minister today. The Polish political advisor will be invited to the last meeting of lower officials before the Paris foreign-ministers meeting.

The political advisors (of the foreign ministries) were charged with the task of further preparing, on the basis of the deliberations of the ministers, the questions regarding the agreed-upon agenda that need to be resolved before the next meeting of the ministers. To accomplish this they are permitted to consult experts or even form subcommittees. The political advisors should meet regularly and, if necessary, hold conferences over several days.

I can conclude that the talks took place in a business-like, constructive, and trusting atmosphere, and that they were characterized by the will to understanding.

NOTES

Source: Zanetti, 298-303.

1. FRG President Richard von Weizsäcker gave a speech on the occasion of the fortieth anniversary of Germany's capitulation in which he reminded all Germans of their responsibilities for the crimes of the Hitler era and the Second World War.

2. Article 24, paragraph 2 of the Basic Law regulates the FRG's possibility of joining a "system of collective security" in order to maintain peace within the context of a permanent peaceful European or world order.

56
Preamble to the Treaty Creating a Currency, Economic, and Social Union Between the FRG and the GDR (May 18, 1990)

The High Signatories to this Treaty–

THANKS TO THE FACT that in the German Democratic Republic a peaceful and democratic revolution took place in the fall of 1989,

HAVING DECIDED to realize as soon as possible, in freedom, German unity within a peaceful European order,

WITH THE COMMON WILL to introduce a social market economy as the basis for further economic and social development, with social balance and social security and responsibility toward the environment in the German Democratic Republic, as well, and thereby gradually improve the living and working conditions of its population,

BEGINNING WITH THE MUTUAL WISH to take a first significant step in the direction of establishing state unity according to Article 23 of the Basic Law of the Federal Republic of Germany by means of the creation of a currency, economic, and social union as a contribution to European unification, with consideration of the fact that the external aspects of the establishment of unity are subject to the talks with the governments of the French Republic, the Union of Soviet Socialist Republics, the United Kingdom of Great Britain and Northern Ireland, and the United States of America,

IN THE KNOWLEDGE that the establishment of state unity goes hand in hand with the development of federative structures in the German Democratic Republic,

IN FULL AWARENESS that the regulations of this treaty are supposed to guarantee the application of the laws of the European Community after the establishment of state unity–

HAVE AGREED to conclude a treaty about the creation of a currency, economic, and social union according to the following provisions.

NOTES

Source: *Europa-Archiv*, 45 (1990): 327-28.

57
Summary of the Most Important Points of the Treaty Creating a Currency, Economic, and Social Union

Currency Union: The only valid currency is the D-mark. The German *Bundesbank* will become the only central bank. The following regulations are in place for the exchange rate of the GDR-mark for the D-mark: 1 : 1 for salaries and wages, pensions, rents, leases, fellowships. Likewise 1 : 1 for savings of natural persons up to certain limits. For all other demands and obligations a rate of 2 : 1 will apply.

Economic Union: The GDR is creating the preconditions for a social market economy with the introduction of private property, free determination of prices, competition, free trade, free traffic of goods, capital, and labor. The GDR promises to create a taxation, financial, and fiscal system that is compatible with a market economy and to introduce GDR agriculture into the EC agrarian system.

Social Union: The GDR takes over the pension, health, unemployment, and accident insurance, as well as the welfare system, along lines of the said agencies in the Federal Republic of Germany. It promises to create autonomous wage negotiations, freedom of coalitions, the right to strike, co-partnership, protection from termination, and the legal basis for an industrial constitution according to the model of the Federal Republic. For the initial financing of social systems, the Federal Republic guarantees funds from the federal budget and for balancing the GDR budget from the "Special Fund for German Unity" in the amount of 115 billion D-marks.

NOTES

Source: *Europa-Archiv*, 45 (1990): 327-28.

58
Speeches on the Occasion of the Signing of the State Treaty Creating a Currency, Economic, and Social Union (May 18, 1990)

Speech by Helmut Kohl

This is a historical hour in the existence of the German nation. We have come together after 45 years of painful division in order to sign a treaty with which we will complete the first significant step toward re-establishing the unity of the German state. It is a happy hour in which the hopes and longings of the people in Germany are being fulfilled. After decades, a dream begins to become reality: the dream of the unity of Germany and Europe.

Last fall in a peaceful revolution, the people of the GDR burst the chains of their unjust regime through the power of their love for freedom. We are proud and happy with them about the success of this revolution, and we owe thanks to the hundreds of thousands of people who, under great pressure, brought about these changes with their courage.

With this revolution a phase of German history came to an end that brought many people sorrow, misery, and desperation, and cost some of them their lives. An age came to an end during which in the middle of Germany human beings were tortured and killed in Stalinist camps, in prisons, and in correctional facilities–or lost their lives in the attempt to get past the Wall and barbed wire.

Just like the victims of June 17, 1953, they wanted to live a life in freedom and with dignity. They fought for truth and wanted to be free from lies, from repression by a regime that was forced upon them from outside. They gave their lives for our most precious possession, for freedom. We should never forget, repress, or play down their fate. The crimes that were committed–even after the Second World War–in Germany against Germans are a warning to all of us and should never be repeated.

The signing of the State Treaty is a memorable event for all Germans and Europeans. What we are experiencing here is the birth of a free and united Germany: before the eyes of the world, the representatives of freely elected governments in both parts of Germany are expressing their will to jointly shape their future in a free and democratic state as one nation.

With this historic day of the signing of the treaty creating an economic, currency, and social union, a new chapter of European history is also beginning. At the same time, we have taken on a great task. Its success is of the greatest significance well beyond the borders of Germany for the future of Europe.

With the conversion from a socialist command economy to a social market economy in the GDR, we truly did not take on an easy task. We are entering uncharted territory in many ways, and we had to search as equal partners for solutions to a number of new problems; indeed, we had to take on a hitherto unprecedented challenge.

I would like to thank both delegations responsible for the negotiations and their leaders, Deputy Secretary Günther Krause, and Hans Tietmeyer, a member of the executive board of the *Bundesbank*, as well as all the other participants for their committed work, which they untiringly accomplished during the last few weeks. Without their excellent professional knowledge, their great personal commitment, and their cooperation characterized by the spirit of true partnership, this treaty would not have been able to be written. We can all be satisfied with the result.

The State Treaty creating a currency, economic, and social union is a first decisive step on the way to unity. For people in Germany, unity will become a reality that can be experienced–in important areas of their daily lives. For our countrymen and countrywomen in the GDR the chance for a rapid, comprehensive improvement of their living conditions will begin–after a transitional period that will surely not be easy. In this sense, as well, today is a day of hope and joy for them.

At the same time, another message is connected with the signing of the State Treaty: it is a strong sign of solidarity among the Germans. The fate of the Germans in the Federal Republic and in the GDR will thereby be indissolubly interwoven. From now on one thing is clear: we are entering upon a common future, in a united and free Germany.

National solidarity will also be called for in the future. I am certain that the federal government and the *Länder* have found a good solution with their agreement on the fund for financing German unification. I realize that the road will be a difficult one–but the goal is worth our efforts. To complete the unity and freedom of Germany, that is a great piece of work in which all have to participate. I know that in these days on this side of the border as well as on the other side many people are asking themselves what this unprecedented process means for them personally–for their job, their social security, for their families. I have understanding for such concerns. Yet I would like to ask my countrymen and countrywomen in the Federal Republic: When were we ever economically better equipped than we are today for this joint national effort of German unity?

And to my countrymen and countrywomen in the GDR let me say this: the introduction of a social market economy gives you all the chances, indeed, the guarantee that Mecklenburg-Vorpommern and Sachsen-Anhalt, that Brandenburg, Saxony, and Thuringia will soon again become flourishing landscapes in Germany, where everyone will find it worthwhile to live and work. We Germans now have to stand together and shape a common future with confidence. I am therefore asking the people in the Federal Republic to continue showing solidarity with our countrymen and countrywomen in the GDR. Let us always remember that the people in the GDR were forcefully prevented for forty years from living like the Germans in the Federal Republic.

I also have a request for the people in the GDR: please keep in mind that the prosperity of the Federal Republic had to be achieved through hard work. Millions of people contributed to it over many years with their diligence and their willingness to work. Nothing was given to them. In the GDR, too, this is not a time of gifts; it is a matter of helping as self-help. In that process we should not demand too much from each other. And no one should be left behind on the way to unity. The people in East and West can count on that. No one will be asked to suffer undue hardships.

Part of German unity is also that people come together in mutual understanding. Everyone has to contribute something. The Germans in the Federal Republic, over and above their hard currency and their successful economic system, have to contribute something more: above all, a tested constitution that embraces freedom and the ideals of a democracy with which we were able to gather experiences for forty years.

The GDR, on the other hand, contributes the diligence, ideas, and hopes of its people, as well as, last but not least, the self-confidence of those who courageously triumphed against dictatorship in a peaceful revolution. And perhaps our countrymen and countrywomen in the GDR, with their unspoiled sense of the value of freedom, can sharpen the vision of one or another of us here and help us perceive what a precious value freedom is: a German democracy in a united fatherland.

Germany is continuing to grow together. The unity of the state has come closer–and now is the time to complete it soon. With that we are fulfilling the longing of the people in Germany. They never ceased to believe in unity–and they always knew that unity meant more than is reflected in the phrase "cultural nation." In these forty-five years the wish for a united state remained firmly in the hearts of the Germans. Now it can become reality.

At the end of this century, which brought so much sorrow to the people, we Germans have been given a unique opportunity–the opportunity "to complete the unity and freedom of Germany in free self-determination" and "to serve peace in the world in a unified Europe." That is the mandate as stated in the Basic Law. That is what our neighbors expect of us. We want to be German Europeans and European Germans.

Let us use this opportunity; let us face our duty. I call upon the Germans in East and West: let us create a unified Germany in a unified Europe. Let us walk together into a happier future–for all Germans. Today is a milestone along this road.

Speech by Lothar de Maizière

This is an important day for us. The actual realization of German unity begins today. The currency, economic, and social union makes the process of unification irreversible. What we are accomplishing today is a decisive step toward our aim: the realization of German unity in freedom within a peaceful European order.

The State Treaty is a treaty between the two governments in Germany. In its substance it demonstrates that both governments are willing to shape the process of unification not from above. Instead, the growing together of divided Germany begins with the people and their living conditions. For us the interests of the people in both German states were the yardstick for our talks and negotiations of the last few weeks.

The spirit in which this treaty was created corresponds to the aims and wishes of the people in the GDR for freedom, prosperity, and social justice. In this instance it was not foreign governments that were negotiating with each other, but fellow countrymen and countrywomen and friends who no longer want to be estranged from one another.

Since my government policy statement one month ago, we have worked energetically on this treaty day and night. I owe my thanks to the hundreds of participants who accomplished this work. The treaty is a great piece of work. I would like to express my personal thanks to the two leaders of the delegations, Mr. Tietmeyer and Dr. Krause. At the same time, I would like to thank their staffs.

This treaty is a compromise. Yet it is not the result of bargaining for advantages, but rather a good and balanced whole. It is a solid guidebook for the introduction of an ecologically oriented social market economy.

In this hour I would like to turn first to the citizens of the GDR.

The introduction of the D-mark, the introduction of a dynamic social security system and unemployment insurance as well as financial assistance for the GDR state budget, are a generous political gesture on the part of the Federal Republic of Germany. No one should forget what the GDR-mark would really be worth in a free market today. And no one should harbor any illusions about the deep crises of the GDR economy. We could not and cannot continue on as before.

Not all the hopeful dreams that some of us associated with the State Treaty could be fulfilled. But no one will be worse off than before. On the contrary. What other country has gotten a start-up position as favorable as the one we have gotten with this treaty?

Now it is up to us in the GDR to make the best of it. Beginning with a realistic picture of the situation, we will have to go to work with a new founder's spirit, with commitment, with confidence, and with faith in our own energy. In this work social justice will never be out of sight. In our social commitment we will not let ourselves be easily outdone by anyone.

To the citizens of the Federal Republic of Germany I would like to say:

My government bears responsibility first and foremost for the Germans in the GDR and their interests. That is tied to the electoral mandate in our newly established democracy.

At the same time, however, we are sharing a joint responsibility with the Federal Republic for an undivided future. The stability of the D-mark and the preservation of economic balance in the Federal Republic and in the GDR, that is, in the newly joined economic area, are our aims in the GDR, as well. I promise that we will make sure with all our energies that the capital of the Federal Republic of Germany will be wisely invested here.

We understand the help provided by you in the West as help for self-help. In the long run we should not receive any gifts. We want to work for our future ourselves.

Considering the size of the project of a currency, economic, and social union, it is natural that there are discussions in both states in Germany. I find it amazing, however, that in some places in Germany there are more worries than that there is hope. Too many people are becoming faint-hearted in face of the indubitably high mountain of problems that confront us.

Perhaps where this question is concerned we Germans should not be so self-absorbed, but should look to Europe, instead. I am convinced that as a result of this unification process no German will be poorer, but that we will all thrive together. And this will not occur at the expense of Europe, but for the benefit of a European development toward peace, freedom, prosperity, and social justice.

For that reason, German unity should not evolve in a jealous atmosphere of opposition, but rather in a fruitful spirit of cooperation. We and you, on this side of the border and on that side, Wessis and Ossis: these and similar terms should disappear from our vocabulary soon.

The government of the GDR will now present this treaty to the freely elected *Volkskammer*. I want to emphasize our firm determination to meet the deadline so that the currency, economic, and social union will be able to take effect on July 2, 1990. The results of the negotiations for the State Treaty are courageous, of singular quality, and give reason for hope.

It is courageous, since after forty years of a socialist planned economy this treaty, which directly concerns the existence and the future of all Germans in the GDR, was negotiated in only four weeks. It is of singular quality, since never before was there such a conversion of a command economy into a social market economy on an established day. And it gives reason for hope. We will be successful because both sides are committed to success; indeed, we are practically condemned to it.

We stand before a really great and singular opportunity. History usually does not offer its good opportunities more than once. We want to decisively use the opportunity for freedom, peace, and social justice in the service of Europe to build a better world for our children.

NOTES

Source: Zanetti, 304-10.

"No to the State Treaty": Declaration of Opposition to the State Treaty by Renegade West German Social-Democratic Parliamentarians (June 22, 1990)

During the vote on the State Treaty in the *Bundestag*, the following SPD parliamentarians voted "no": Brigitte Adler, Robert Antretter, Lieselotte Blunck, Andreas von Bülow, Edelgard Bulmahn, Peter Conradi, Gernot Erler, Freimut Duve, Katrin Fuchs, Monika Ganssforth, Konrad Gilges, Peter Glotz, Gerd Häuser, Michael Müller, Günter Oesinghaus, Horst Peter, Bernd Reuter, Günter Rixe, Wilhelm Schmidt, Sigrid Skarpelis-Sperk, Günter Verheugen, Gert Weisskirchen, Norbert Wieczorek, Heidemarie Wieczorek-Zeul. They gave the following explanatory statement.

We are for the unification of the two German states. But we reject the road the government of the Federal Republic is following to reach this goal. We point explicitly to the resolution of June 14, 1990 made by the leadership committees of our party, the Social-Democratic Party, which reads: "The political discussion about the State Treaty between the Federal Republic of Germany and the German Democratic Republic is not a discussion about a yes or no to German unity, but about the proper road and about the politics for which the Chancellor is responsible." We strongly believe that the Kohl government has chosen the wrong road to the unification of the two German states.

We know that the majority of our parliamentary faction decided in the end to vote yes, after long, serious deliberations. We respect that decision just as that majority respects our decision. We will not let ourselves be played off against each other. Our rejection is founded on three sets of motives:

1. This State Treaty prescribes shock-therapy for the economy of the GDR. We know that there are no models for the conversion of a planned economy into a market economy and that the transformation process will not be free of risks. We fear, however, that the State Treaty in its existing form could worsen already critical economic developments and cause dramatic mass unemployment, whose social consequences could endanger democracy in both parts of Germany. The companies in the GDR will be abruptly exposed to the competition of the world market without having been given the chance to adapt to the new conditions; and this in a situation in which the infrastructure of the GDR–especially the railway system, the highway system, and the communications network–is com-

pletely inadequate. What is still lacking is a conception for a planned, ecologically oriented extension of the infrastructure, something that should have been begun already at the end of last year. Without such an infrastructure, private investments will remain a pious wish. Experts are predicting that economic breakdowns will spread like wildfire. The stubborn efforts on the part of the SPD have improved the survival chances for companies in the GDR. However, if today, at the end of this process, we weigh the chances and risks associated with the State Treaty, we arrive at the following results: the government of the Federal Republic did not sufficiently work to counter the danger of mass unemployment with all its immeasurable political and human consequences. This is especially true for women in the GDR, a high percentage of whom are employed and whose working and living conditions will deteriorate more severely than those of men as a result of this State Treaty. Because of the financial situation of the businesses and the communities, it is to be feared that daycare facilities will be closed in large numbers and that the employment possibilities of women, therefore, will be drastically limited. A distinct drop in family income would be the unavoidable consequence.

The road the government of the Federal Republic is taking will lead to an explosion of the consumptive expenditures in the budget of the Federal Republic. Future investments in a new infrastructure for the GDR are being grossly neglected. The result of this will be that the part of Germany that today we still call the GDR will become a "second-rate economic area": a mere market for the sale of our products, a country of dependent branch offices. We deem it irresponsible that German industrial areas so rich in tradition will be downgraded to such an extent. An independent economic development in the "region of the GDR" will be made irresponsibly more difficult.

The State Treaty makes provisions, furthermore, for a careless treatment of land in the GDR. The necessary provisions against land speculation are lacking. Prohibitions of resale, public planning instruments, rights for purchase options by the communities are lacking. There is a real danger that under such conditions a prudent and responsible urban development will be made unreasonably difficult.

With our concerns about the economic effects of this State Treaty we are representing both the interests of the people in the Federal Republic as well as the interests of the people in the GDR. We have in mind the high costs with which this State Treaty will burden especially the average wage earner in the Federal Republic. Today we already have the highest interest rates in the history of the Federal Republic; and the mortgage rates climbed by almost two percentage points. The government of the Federal Republic is misleading our citizens when it plays down this fact with all its grave effects on housing construction and rents. But we also have in mind the GDR citizens, among whom many will be affected, without the chance for a transition, by unemployment, rent increases, and a deterioration of their living conditions. We do not want to support a unification of the two German states that in its first decisive phase is executed by burdening the average wage earners in both parts of Germany, because we are convinced that German unity could have been arranged in a more just and socially endurable manner.

2. In its existing form, the State Treaty, in our opinion, contains serious dangers for the European and international ties of the Federal Republic and greater Germany. The reason for this lies particularly in the dynamics that will be unleashed by this treaty. We assume that it is consistent with the logic of this treaty that the GDR will be obliged within a relatively short time to declare its union with the Federal Republic according to Article 23 of the Basic Law. At the same time, international negotiations about a new European security system have by no means led to a recognizable result. We consider it more than questionable to unleash an almost unstoppable dynamic with economic instruments while at the same time on an international level the future interests of our state have by no means been served.

We are not denying that within a couple of months questions of security policies that are still open today could be solved. But we note that on the day of the vote for the State Treaty, central problems concerning the security of the Federal Republic remain completely unresolved. Among these are the future European security system, the degree of united Germany's sovereignty, the removal of nuclear and chemical weapons, as well as the number and length of the presence of foreign troops on German soil.

At the same time, the State Treaty creates facts that could heighten the impression of our neighbors in the East, especially the Soviet Union, that their security interests are not being preserved. We want neither to forget nor to repress the fact that Hitler's Germany attacked the Soviet Union in the Second World War and that in the course of this attack 27 million citizens of the Soviet Union lost their lives. For this reason we consider it irresponsible that the government of the Federal Republic is further heightening the political upheavals and conflicts in the Soviet Union by irrevocably accelerating the pace of the unification process. The government of the Federal Republic is allowing the rhythm and pace of German unification to be established without regard for the rhythm and pace of the international agreements about a European security system. The foundations for a Europe with a new face are currently being laid. The early phases of a new age have a constitutive character. Upheavals that occur during such early phases can never be totally repaired.

We do not want to bear part of the responsibility for the incalculable risks of such a policy.

3. In preparing this State Treaty, the government of the Federal Republic chose a procedure that disregards the rights of the *Bundestag* and the *Bundesrat*. It tried to exclude the parliament from shaping the State Treaty. The appointment of a committee on "German Unity," which finally was convened on May 13 of this year after the constant urging of the opposition, occurred at a time when a number of decisions were no longer reversible. The unprecedented time pressure prevented the federal *Länder* from engaging in a responsible examination of the State Treaty; the manner in which the government of the Federal Republic proceeded represents a serious violation of democratic and federalist principles. The historical aura of the moment was exploited to eliminate the sober operation of the democratic exchange between government and opposition, between the federal government and the *Länder*. Our rejection of the State Treaty is hence also a criticism of the procedure chosen by the Chancellor and the government of the Federal Republic in preparing the State Treaty.

The unification of the two German states as it is begun by this State Treaty is not a merger but a collision. Nothing demonstrates this better than the fact that the men and women in the GDR who started the revolution are being pushed aside. German unity has to be shaped by the people themselves. We want unity; but we do not want unity in the form of annexation. For all of these reasons, after serious deliberation, we decided to say "no" to this State Treaty.

NOTES

Source: *Frankfurter Rundschau*, 142 (22 June 1990): 4.

60
Television Address by Hans-Jochen Vogel, Leader of the West German Social-Democratic Party, on the Enactment of the Treaty Creating a Currency, Economic, and Social Union
(July 1, 1990)

The Social-Democratic Party of Germany in both parts of Germany affirms German unity. We want to realize it now in freedom. For us, German unity is not an end in itself. Not a value that takes precedence over other values–like peace or freedom–and, for that reason, needs no further justification. We want unity for the people's sake. We want it because it makes the peaceful coexistence not only of us Germans, but also of our neighbors, indeed, of all Europeans, easier and serves their well-being, because a unified Germany within a unified Europe can contribute more to master the great tasks that confront humanity. It is on this basis that we are quarrelling about German unification. But we are not quarrelling about the question "whether," we are quarrelling about "how." Not about the goal, but about the best road to this goal. That is also true for the State Treaty. . . . Here, too, it is about "how." It is reasonable to start with the realization of unity in those areas that are essential for people's daily lives. That means in the areas of the economy, of social security, and of the environment. Also in the area of currency.

The conversion of a command economy into a socially and ecologically attuned market economy is not possible without far-reaching processes of transformation and without risks. But we have clearly warned against the abrupt, unprepared conversion from one system to the other. Whether it is correct to open the locks all the way from one day to the next. Whether the measures for protection and adjustment are sufficient. Whether deep social breaches and shocks in the GDR will not develop as a consequence of the chosen road. Whether more businesses will collapse and more people will lose their jobs than is inevitable anyway. That is why, after becoming familiar with the first draft of the State Treaty, we, in close consultation with the Social Democrats in the GDR, immediately did everything possible to minimize these risks. Thanks to this cooperation, measures that the government of the Federal Republic first merely considered to be individual social adjustments as supplements to the currency union evolved into a social union worthy of this name.

The wage supplements for low wage earners, the guarantees of a minimum social security rate, the obligation to provide social measures in case of massive layoffs, the enactment of the laws protecting against layoffs–all that was lacking in the draft presented by the government of the Federal Republic; it was added only in retrospect. We demanded even further improvements.

First, we must prevent businesses that can survive and are competitive from breaking down because they do not receive any assistance in the critical early phases. Each business saved means fewer unemployed and more hope for the people in the GDR–and, by the way, lower costs for us.

Second, the catastrophic environmental conditions in the GDR must be drastically improved. That will help people in both parts of Germany. That is why the environmental union should have the same rank as the other unions. It should not merely be an addendum.

Third, the billions of marks in the treasuries of the SED, the East German CDU, the other bloc parties, and the so-called mass organizations have to be confiscated for general use. The citizens of the Federal Republic should not have to pay more simply because Mr. Gysi wants to continue employing 10,000 party members or because he does not want to give up the Schalck-Golodkowski firms in Liechtenstein, Portugal, or even in the Federal Republic. Or that the East German CDU retains a fortune that its general secretary estimates at several hundred million marks.

Fourth, furthermore, we have to stop the speculators. The currency speculators as well as the land speculators, who are already at work in the GDR.

There has been some movement in all four areas. The party fortunes have been confiscated. The environmental regulations have been supplemented and improved. Four reactors at the nuclear plant in Greifswald have been shut down, the fifth will soon follow. And for the salvaging of businesses that can survive and the prevention of unemployment, additional measures have also been taken. For example, measures that provide tax advantages for GDR products in certain branches for a transitional period. And a regulation for short-time work, which as a transitional measure also makes possible the establishment of employment offices. That alone could minimize the risks. Even the text of the Treaty itself was changed at the last minute. It was explicitly agreed with the GDR that the realization of the economic union, among other things, has to take into account the social responsibilities of ownership, a social system for housing and rents, consumer protection, the improvement of the infrastructure, the preference of an active employment policy over mere unemployment benefits.

Not all our demands have been met. For example, it would have been better if a more comprehensive solution had been found for the debts of those businesses that can survive, possibly by covering large parts of that debt with the assets of the Treuhand Foundation. The interests of women in the GDR, too, were insufficiently protected. Everywhere they are the first to be laid off and are being ignored where it would have been possible to help them. And whether the speculators really have been effectively stopped remains to be seen. The government of the Federal Republic is responsible for these and other lacks. We cannot be held responsible for the wrong decisions that were made against our explicit opposition. But a failure of the Treaty, after all that had already been accomplished, would have come as a shock in the GDR and presumably unleashed uncontrollable developments. We did not want that. For that reason, and in light of the improvements we achieved, a broad majority of the Social Democrats in the *Bundestag* voted "yes."

Now we are looking to the future. It will make evident whether the warnings were legitimate and whether our fears are confirmed. We hope that this will not be the case. If the situation develops dramatically, however, then the people in the GDR will have to suffer from it. And they will ask: What do we do now? We will not run away from this question, if only because otherwise we will be threatened with a new wave of immigrants. And then we will have to make up for everything that was turned down today. Not in order to prevent damage, but to repair the damage that ensued. And that will be many more times more expensive than sufficient precaution today. It would be good, therefore, if the long road to German unity could be traveled with more cooperation and less opposition from the responsible powers than has hitherto been the case. For that phase of the process of German unity that lies ahead of us we need heart-felt solidarity as well as sober circumspection. Especially in the Federal Republic, we also need more intellectual commitment than was demonstrated so far. For the Federal Republic has to form a better idea about the transformations and changes that unity will demand of it–and not only of the GDR. We should not merely understand ourselves as an enlarged Federal Republic, we must give ourselves a European identity. An identity that lets us work in the heart of Europe toward peace, understanding, and balance.

NOTES

Source: Zanetti, 334-36.

61
Chancellor Helmut Kohl's Report on His Discussions with Michail Gorbachev in the Soviet Union (July 17, 1990)

... Yesterday, as you know–many of you accompanied me–I returned from my second trip to the Soviet Union this year. After my first visit in February I was able to report that we Germans were given a "green light" for our road to unity by the Soviet leadership, that we could also decide ourselves about its form, timetable, and conditions.

Today I have brought with me the news, which is good news for all Germans, that meanwhile between us and the Soviet Union we have also reached an agreement about all the external aspects of German unity. We want forward-looking treaties, comprehensive cooperation, trust, and, last but not least, a broad exchange between our peoples, especially the younger generation. With this we hope simultaneously to make a contribution to a permanent and peaceful development in Europe. All this will be the leitmotif–and I am in agreement with President Gorbachev on this–of a comprehensive treaty of cooperation between united Germany and the Soviet Union to be ratified as soon as possible after unification.

This treaty will be completed on the firm basis and in the clear mutual understanding that German-Soviet cooperation, as well as the firm anchoring of united Germany in the West, will make an indispensable contribution to stability in the center of Europe and beyond. On the basis of this shared philosophy, as President Gorbachev also called it, we resolved the practical problems still lying ahead of us on the road to German unity. Let me, once again, cite the most important points:

First: German unity includes the Federal Republic of Germany, the GDR, and all of Berlin.

Second: With the establishment of German unity, the rights and responsibilities of the Four Powers in relation to Germany as a whole and Berlin cease to be in force. United Germany will obtain its complete and unlimited sovereignty at the time of its unification.

Third: United Germany, exercising its complete and unlimited sovereignty, can decide freely and for itself whether and to which alliance it wishes to belong. This is in keeping with the wording of the CSCE final accords.

I explained the opinion of the government of the Federal Republic that unified Germany wishes to be a member of the NATO alliance, and I know that this also corresponds to the wishes of the GDR. Prime Minister de Maizière made that perfectly clear yesterday in his commentary. In our talks this morning we clearly affirmed this once more.

Fourth: United Germany will complete a bilateral treaty with the Soviet Union dealing with the demobilization of Soviet troops stationed in the GDR, a process that, as the Soviet leadership has stated, will be completed within three to four years.

What I have so simply stated here, "three to four years," ladies and gentlemen, means that the Soviet troops will leave German territory by 1994 at the latest. And let me point out once again: that means that fifty years after the day on which Soviet troops set foot on then German territory for the first time during the fighting in the Second World War, the last Soviet soldiers will withdraw from Germany. . . .

Fifth: As long as Soviet troops are present on the territory of today's GDR, no NATO structures will be extended to that territory.

Articles V and VI of the NATO treaty will become valid for the entire territory of united Germany upon unification.[1]

Sixth: Units of the *Bundeswehr* not integrated into NATO, that means territorial defense units, can be stationed on the territory of today's GDR and in Berlin immediately after German unification.

Seventh: As long as Soviet troops are present on the territory of today's GDR, the troops of the three Western powers, in our opinion, should remain in Berlin. The government of the Federal Republic will ask the three Western powers about this and propose an appropriate treaty. We will have to create a legal basis for this stationing of Western military forces by means of a treaty between the government of united Germany and the three powers. We are working under the assumption that the number and the armaments of these troops will clearly not be stronger than they are today.

Eighth: After the withdrawal of Soviet troops from the territory of today's GDR and from Berlin, troops integrated into NATO can also be stationed in that part of Germany, to be sure, without equipment for the launching of nuclear weapons. Foreign troops and nuclear weapons shall not be moved there.

Ninth: The government of the Federal Republic declares its willingness to make a promise during the ongoing negotiations in Vienna to reduce the military forces of a unified Germany to 370,000 troops within three to four years. This reduction should begin with the enactment of the first Viennese Agreement. That means that if we take into account the former strengths of the *Bundeswehr* and the National People's Army, the military forces of the future united Germany will be reduced by 45 percent.

Tenth: United Germany will renounce the production, possession, and control of atomic, biological, and chemical weapons and remain a signatory to the Non-Proliferation Treaty.

I assume . . . that the three Western powers, as well as the government of the GDR, with which I already spoke today in the person of the Prime Minister, will support these ideas about unification.

Ladies and gentlemen, another area stressed in my talks with President Gorbachev, but also in the talks between Treasury Secretary Waigel with his Soviet partners, was our forward-looking economic-fiscal cooperation. On the basis of the three Western summits in Dublin, London, and Houston, I could make clear to the Soviet leadership and, above all, to President Gorbachev, that the West is counting on the success of perestroika and wants to support him as best it can.[2] According to the many discussions I have had, this is the wish and aim of our Western friends and partners. Already at the end of this week the President of the EC Commission, Jacques Delors, will travel to Moscow and continue these discussions on the basis of the mandate given him by the European Council in Dublin.

President Gorbachev told me that before he goes on vacation he intends to take up discussions on this matter with the current President of the European Community, the Prime Minister of Italy, Giulio Andreotti. The primary work, however–and the two of us completely agree on this–has to be accomplished in the Soviet Union itself. President Gorbachev and his staff are preparing a comprehensive market-oriented reform program, which he hopes to present to the Supreme Soviet in September and which, if all goes well, will take effect as soon as possible. This–and we agreed on that–is the decisive condition for actual and effective Western support of these policies.

Ladies and gentlemen, this short survey of some essential themes and question areas of the next months demonstrates that we are already in the midst of laying the fundamental groundwork for our common European future. For this reason I would like to point out that alone the timetable until December indicates the speed with which this whole thing is rolling along.

–My meeting with the current President of the European Council, Prime Minister Andreotti, on September 10 is the first event in this series.

–I should also mention the German-French summit consultations on 17 and 18 September in Munich.

–The special meeting of the European Council on November 3, 1990 in Rome.

–The CSCE summit meeting from 19 to 21 November 1990 in Paris–that is particularly important to us, since the concluding document of the "Two-Plus-Four" talks should be presented on this occasion.

–Let me mention further the European Council from 13 to 15 December 1990 in Rome–that is a very important date, since the two governmental conferences will be begun on this occasion: the governmental conference about the establishment of the economic and currency union in the European Community and the governmental conference–let me call it that–for the further development of political unity in Europe.

I hope that in this way we can bring this year to a good conclusion and that what was begun in the first half of the year can be continued. I for my part, and the government of the Federal Republic which I head, will do everything possible to make a contribution to this. As you may have noticed, I did not mention another, very important date: the elections of the *Bundestag*, the all-German elections, in December. I assume that they will probably take place on the first Sunday in December, based on the dates under discussion right now. I am certain you understand if in conclusion I express my intention to win this election.

NOTES

Source: Zanetti, 337-43.

1. The wording of Article V of the NATO treaty is as follows: "The Parties agree that an armed attack against one or more of them in Europe or North America shall be considered an attack against them all and consequently they agree that, if such an attack occurs, each of them, in exercise of

the right of individual or collective self-defence recognized by Article 51 of the Charter of the United Nations, will assist the Party or Parties so attacked by taking forthwith, individually and in contact with the other Parties, such action as it deems necessary, including the use of armed force, to restore and maintain the security of the North Atlantic area.

Any such armed attack and all measureas taken as a result thereof shall immediately be reported to the Security Council. Such measures shall be terminated when the Security Council has taken the measures necessary to restore and maintain international peace and security."

Article VI reads: "For the purpose of Article V an armed attack on one or more of the Parties is deemed to include an armed attack on the territory of any of the Parties in Europe or North America, on the Algerian Departments of France, on the occupation forces of any Party in Europe, on the islands under the jurisdiction of any Party in the North Atlantic area north of the Tropic of Cancer or on the vessels or aircraft in this area of any of the Parties."

2. On 6 July 1990 at the NATO summit in London, the Soviet Union articulated its expectation that NATO would reorganize from a military to a political alliance, a transformation that would make it easier for the Soviet Union to accept membership of united Germany in NATO.

62
"The Remains of Approximately 15,000 Days of a Socialist Planned Economy": GDR Prime Minister Lothar de Maizière's Speech on the Occasion of the Signing of the German Unification Treaty (August 31, 1990)

Today we are fulfilling an important prerequisite on the road to German unity. The Unification Treaty which will be signed in a few moments is a painstakingly negotiated work, shaped by a constructive spirit, which keeps the annexation of the GDR and related questions in an even balance. This Treaty is certainly one of the most significant ones in the history of postwar Germany. It creates certainty and clarity about many questions that will arise during the establishment of unity. The Treaty regulates what we consider to be important and correct. Please allow me to mention seven points that I would like particularly to stress.

1. The Treaty clarifies questions pertaining to property. For the people in the GDR and for domestic peace in unified Germany, the affirmation of the results of the land reform from 1945 to 1949 is of central importance. The Unification Treaty creates an appropriate balance between the right to own property and the fact that you cannot simply undo history. It allows for expeditious investment

decisions even where questions of ownership could not ultimately be settled–a regulation that will shape the future of our economic development.

2. The Unification Treaty creates the preconditions for investments in the GDR and, hence, also for jobs. It will introduce a comprehensive program for the advancement of the regions in the GDR. With this, important groundwork has been laid. 1.2 million jobs alone can in this way be saved or newly created.

3. The social security system that is in effect in the Federal Republic will be transferred. This means great advantages for the people in our country. This social security safety-net is exemplary among the great industrial nations. Transitional regulations assure social justice in the few cases where the GDR laws were more beneficial. Precisely here it becomes apparent that in a social market economy, economic and social policy are closely bound up with one another.

4. Among the most difficult topics of our negotiations were questions about the financial outfitting of the future *Länder* and districts. Here we had to find compromise solutions. The current government is creating conditions so that the new *Länder* will be able to participate adequately in the economic power of united Germany.

5. The Unification Treaty reaches far beyond economic and social policies. Protection of the natural basis for human existence and the improvement of the environmental situation on the territory of the present GDR take up an important position in the Treaty. We need clean air to breath, the protection of lakes, rivers, and water reservoirs, and we want to preserve and take care of our beautiful natural landscapes–be it the Schorfheide, the Thuringian Forest, or the Little Switzerland in Saxony, the flat country covered with lakes in Mecklenburg, or the Harz with its Brocken.[1] Environmental protection is protection of human lives. We know what we are talking about.

6. With the establishment of German unity it is not only two states that are growing together. With the dissolution of the centrally governed GDR, five new federal *Länder* are simultaneously being created. They will join with the great federalist tradition in Germany that was suppressed here for a long time. Saxony and Thuringia, Saxony-Anhalt and Brandenburg, as well as Mecklenburg-Vorpommern: a bit of German history is connected with these names, and the people who live there connect them with the feeling of a homeland. This transformation in the basic structure will create many transitional problems that will have to be resolved.

The Treaty provides reasonable and constructive regulations for bridging these problems.

7. With its wealth of variations, culture belongs to our most elemental necessities of life. Its future existence, its care and promotion, means greater self-respect for human beings. The Treaty prescribes that the inherited and newly created cultural substance on the territory of the former GDR should not suffer harm.

The continued validity of educational degrees and their equal evaluation is not only of great psychological significance for the citizens of the former GDR, but also creates the best preconditions for their integration into a common Germany. By adopting the support mechanisms for science and research we have made certain that the freedom of research will be guaranteed in the future and that the whole range of science and research will be able to stand up to international standards. Only a Unification Treaty could make certain that the guaranteed rights of each of the five *Länder* of today's GDR will still be valid when the GDR ceases to exist. The Unification Treaty represents a great success for the future united Germany. Because the governments and parties struggled in joint effort to accomplish it, it also represents a success of democracy. In the name of the citizens of the GDR, I would like to thank the two delegations and their leaders, Federal Minister Dr. Wolfgang Schäuble and Assistant Secretary Dr. Günther Krause, as well as all who took part, for their hard work. What you accomplished in the last few weeks was exemplary. Because of Günther Krause's rigorous and responsible negotiations, we succeeded in accomplishing what is most important for the people in the GDR. We have made sufficient provisions for overcoming the problems that will arise from the transition. I would also like to thank all those who helped to bring about this success with their willingness for consensus and compromise, especially in the difficult phases of the negotiations. I want explicitly to thank our staff, who accomplished the substantial and technical groundwork "at a very fast pace." Without them the work would not have been completed so quickly.

Some people in our country are dissatisfied because the economic boom is not happening fast enough for them. In spite of all the assessments and predictions, they believed that within a few days of the currency union everything on the territory of the GDR would be just like it is in the West. In light of the situation and considering forty years of a failed socialist economy, this simply could not happen. The economic and social problems with which we are currently struggling are not the result of 143 days of social market economy, but the remains of approximately 15,000 days of a socialist planned economy.

Even after the Unification Treaty, not all dreams will be immediately fulfilled. But we are on the right track. The prospects for the future are realistic and more favorable than they have been since the end of the war. Let us not forget that. We should always feel satisfaction about the fact that we put the old system behind us, a system whose distinguishing characteristics were the Wall and the order to shoot, state security and slave trade, lack and privileges, the prohibition to travel, leading people around by the nose, and external determination of every individual. Despite all the help we are receiving, we have to take account of our own energies. The realization of freedom and democracy should not be overshadowed by the warnings of Cassandra.[2] I hope that the Unification Treaty will be ratified by both parties with a great majority. If it is carried by a broad base, it will serve judicial peace in united Germany.

NOTES

Source: *Spiegel: Dokument*, December 1990: 5-6.

1. Beautiful landscapes in the GDR whose environments were nearly destroyed by the economic policies of the SED.
2. Cassandra was the Trojan seer in Classical mythology who predicted the fall of the city to the Greeks but whose warnings were never heeded.

63
The Wording of the Two-Plus-Four Treaty, Signed by the Foreign Ministers of the USA, the Soviet Union, Great Britain, France, the GDR, and the FRG (September 12, 1990)

The Federal Republic of Germany, the German Democratic Republic, the French Republic, the Union of Soviet Socialist Republics, the United Kingdom of Great Britain and Northern Ireland and the United States of America,

Conscious of the fact that their peoples have been living together in peace since 1945;

Mindful of the recent historic changes in Europe which make it possible to overcome the division of the continent;

Having regard to the rights and responsibilities of the Four Powers relating to Berlin and Germany as a whole, and the corresponding wartime and postwar agreements and decisions of the Four Powers;

Resolved in accordance with their obligations set under the Charter of the United Nations to develop friendly relations among nations based on respect for the principle of equal rights and self-determination of peoples, and to take other appropriate measures to strengthen universal peace;

Recalling the principles of the Final Act of the Conference on Security and Cooperation in Europe, signed in Helsinki;

Recognizing that those principles laid firm foundations for the establishment of a just and lasting peaceful order in Europe;

Determined to take account of everyone's security interests;

Convinced of the need finally to overcome antagonism and to develop cooperation in Europe;

Confirming their readiness to reinforce security, in particular by adopting effective arms control, disarmament, and confidence-building measures; their willingness not to regard each other as adversaries but to work for a relationship of trust and cooperation and accordingly their readiness to consider positively setting up appropriate institutional arrangements within the framework of the Conference on Security and Cooperation in Europe;

Welcoming the fact that the German people, freely exercising their right of self-determination, have expressed their will to bring about the unity of Germany as a state so that they will be able to serve the peace of the world as an equal and sovereign partner in a united Europe;

Convinced that the unification of Germany as a state with definitive borders is a significant contribution to peace and stability in Europe;

Intending to conclude the final settlement with respect to Germany;

Recognizing that thereby, and with the unification of Germany as a democratic and peaceful state, the rights and responsibilities of the Four Powers relating to Berlin and Germany as a whole lose their function;

Represented by their Ministers for Foreign Affairs who, in accordance with the Ottawa declaration of 13 February 1990, met in Bonn on 5 May 1990, in Berlin on 22 June 1990, in Paris on 17 July 1990 with the participation of the Minister for Foreign Affairs of the Republic of Poland, and in Moscow on 12 September 1990;

Have agreed as follows:

Article 1

1. The united Germany shall comprise the territory of the Federal Republic of Germany, the German Democratic Republic and the whole of Berlin. Its external borders shall be the borders of the Federal Republic of Germany and the German Democratic Republic and shall be definitive from the date on which the present Treaty comes into force. The confirmation of the definitive nature of the borders of the united Germany is an essential element of the peaceful order in Europe.

2. The united Germany and the Republic of Poland shall confirm the existing border between them in a treaty that is binding under international law.

3. The united Germany has no territorial claims whatsoever against other states and will not assert any in the future.

4. The Governments of the Federal Republic of Germany and the German Democratic Republic shall ensure that the constitution of the united Germany does not contain any provision incompatible with these principles. This applies accordingly to the provisions laid down in the preamble, the second paragraph of Article 23, and Article 146 of the Basic Law for the Federal Republic of Germany.[1]

5. The Governments of the French Republic, the Union of Soviet Socialist Republics, the United Kingdom of Great Britain and Northern Ireland and the United States of America take formal note of the corresponding commitments and declarations by the Governments of the Federal Republic of Germany and the German Democratic Republic and declare that their implementation will confirm the definitive nature of the united Germany's borders.

Article 2

The Governments of the Federal Republic of Germany and the German Democratic Republic reaffirm their declarations that only peace will emanate from German soil. According to the constitution of the unified Germany, acts tending to and undertaken with the intent to disturb the peaceful relations between nations, especially to prepare for aggressive war, are unconstitutional and a punishable offence. The Governments of the Federal Republic of Germany and the German Democratic Republic declare that the united Germany will never employ any of its weapons except in accordance with its constitution and the Charter of the United Nations.

Article 3

1. The Governments of the Federal Republic of Germany and the German Democratic Republic reaffirm their renunciation of the manufacture and possession of and control over nuclear, biological and chemical weapons. They declare that the united Germany, too, will abide by these commitments. In particular, rights and obligations arising from the Treaty on the Non-Proliferation of Nuclear Weapons of 1 July 1968 will continue to apply to the united Germany.

2. The Government of the Federal Republic of Germany, acting in full agreement with the Government of the German Democratic Republic, made the following statement on 30 August 1990 in Vienna at the Negotiations on Conventional Armed Forces in Europe:

"The Government of the Federal Republic of Germany undertakes to reduce the personnel strength of the armed forces of the united Germany to 370,000 (ground, air and naval forces) within three to four years. This reduction will commence on the entry into force of the first CSCE agreement. Within the scope of this overall ceiling no more than 345,000 will belong to the ground and air forces which, pursuant to the agreed mandate, alone are the subject of the Negotiations on Conventional Armed Forces in Europe. The Federal Government regards its commitment to reduce ground and air forces as a significant German contribution to the reduction of conventional armed forces in Europe. It assumes that in follow-on negotiations the other participants in the negotiations, too, will render their contribution to enhancing security and stability in Europe, including measures to limit personnel strengths."

The Government of the German Democratic Republic has expressly associated itself with this statement.

3. The Governments of the French Republic, the Union of Soviet Socialist Republics, the United Kingdom of Great Britain and Northern Ireland and the United States of America take note of these statements by the Governments of the Federal Republic of Germany and the German Democratic Republic.

Article 4

1. The Governments of the Federal Republic of Germany, the German Democratic Republic and the Union of Soviet Socialist Republics state that the united Germany and the Union of Soviet Socialist Republics will settle by treaty the conditions for and the du-

ration of the presence of Soviet armed forces on the territory of the present German Democratic Republic and of Berlin, as well as the conduct of the withdrawal of these armed forces which will be completed by the end of 1994, in connection with the implementation of the undertaking of the Federal Republic of Germany and the German Democratic Republic referred to in paragraph 2 of Article 3 of the present Treaty.

2. The Governments of the French Republic, the United Kingdom of Great Britain and Northern Ireland and the United States of America take note of this statement.

Article 5

1. Until the completion of the withdrawal of the Soviet armed forces from the territory of the present German Democratic Republic and of Berlin in accordance with Article 4 of the present Treaty, only German territorial defense units which are not integrated into the alliance structures to which German armed forces in the rest of German territory are assigned will be stationed in that territory as armed forces of the united Germany. During that period and subject to the provisions of paragraph 2 of this Article, armed forces of other states will not be stationed in that territory or carry out any other military activity there.

2. For the duration of the presence of Soviet armed forces in the territory of the present German Democratic Republic and of Berlin, armed forces of the French Republic, the United Kingdom of Great Britain and Northern Ireland and the United States of America will, upon German request, remain stationed in Berlin by agreement to this effect between the Government of the unified Germany and the Governments of the states concerned. The number of troops and the amount of equipment of all non-German armed forces stationed in Berlin will not be greater than at the time of signature of the present Treaty. New categories of weapons will not be introduced there by non-German armed forces. The Government of the united Germany will conclude with the Governments of those states which have armed forces stationed in Berlin treaties with conditions which are fair, taking account of the relations existing with the states concerned.

3. Following the completion of the withdrawal of the Soviet armed forces from the territory of the present German Democratic Republic and of Berlin, units of German armed forces assigned to military alliance structures in the same way as those in the rest of

German territory may also be stationed in that part of Germany, but without nuclear weapon carriers. This does not apply to conventional weapon systems which may have other capabilities in addition to conventional ones but which in that part of Germany are equipped for a conventional role and designated only for such. Foreign armed forces and nuclear weapons or their carriers will not be stationed in that part of Germany or deployed there.

Article 6

The right of the united Germany to belong to alliances, with all the rights and responsibilities arising therefrom, shall not be affected by the present Treaty.

Article 7

1. The French Republic, the Union of Soviet Socialist Republics, the United Kingdom of Great Britain and Northern Ireland and the United States of America hereby terminate their rights and responsibilities relating to Berlin and to Germany as a whole. As a result, the corresponding, related quadripartite agreements, decisions and practices are terminated and all related Four Powers institutions are dissolved.
2. The united Germany shall have accordingly full sovereignty over its internal and external affairs.

Article 8

(1) The present Treaty is subject to ratification or acceptance as soon as possible. On the German side it will be ratified by the united Germany. The Treaty will therefore apply to the united Germany.
(2) The instruments of ratification or acceptance shall be deposited with the Government of the united Germany. That Government shall inform the Governments of the other Contracting Parties of the deposit of each instrument of ratification or acceptance.

Article 9

The present Treaty shall enter into force for the united Germany, the French Republic, the Union of Soviet Socialist Republics, the United Kingdom of Great Britain and Northern Ireland and the

United States of America on the date of deposit of the last instrument of ratification or acceptance by these states.

Article 10

The original of the present Treaty, of which the English, French, German and Russian texts are equally authentic, shall be deposited with the Government of the Federal Republic of Germany, which shall transmit certified copies to the Governments of the other Contracting Parties.

Source: US Government Publications.

1. Article 23 and Article 146 of the Basic Law describe different options for unification, either through accession or through a constitutional assembly.

64
The Unification Treaty (September 20, 1990)

Preamble

The Federal Republic of Germany and the German Democratic Republic, determined

to establish in free self-determination German unity in peace and freedom as an equal member of the international community;

beginning with the wish of the people in both parts of Germany to live together in peace and freedom in a constitutionally ordered, democratic, and social federal state;

with thankful respect for those who helped freedom break through peacefully, who unswervingly held fast to the task of constructing German unity and who are establishing it;

in the knowledge of the continuity of German history and mindful of the resulting special responsibility for a democratic development in Germany that remains committed to the preservation of human rights and peace;

in the effort by means of German unification to make a contribution to the unification of Europe and to the constitution of a peaceful European order in which borders no longer separate and which guarantees all European nations a trusting coexistence in the knowledge that the invulnerability of the borders and the territorial integrity and sovereignty of all states in Europe is a fundamental condition for peace;

have agreed to conclude a treaty about the establishment of German unity with the following provisions:

Chapter 1: Effect of the Affiliation

Article 1 (Länder)

With the enactment of the affiliation of the German Democratic Republic with the Federal Republic of Germany according to Article 23 of the Basic Law on October 3, 1990, the *Länder* Brandenburg, Mecklenburg-Vorpommern, Saxony, Saxony-Anhalt, and Thuringia will become *Länder* of the Federal Republic. For the formation of and the borders separating these *Länder*, the provisions of the constitutional law for the formation of *Länder* in the German Democratic Republic of July 22, 1990 apply. The 23 districts of Berlin will form the *Land* of Berlin.

Article 2 (Capital City)

The capital city of Germany is Berlin. The question of the location of parliament and government will be decided after the establishment of German unity.

Chapter II (Basic Law)

Article 3 (Enactment of the Basic Law)

With enactment of the affiliation, the Basic Law of the Federal Republic of Germany from May 23, 1949, in the version of December 21, 1983, will take effect in the *Länder* Brandenburg, Mecklenburg-Vorpommern, Saxony, Saxony-Anhalt, and Thuringia, as well as in that part of the *Land* Berlin in which it was not previously valid, with the resulting changes in accordance with Article 4, unless this treaty does not make other provisions.

Article 4 (Amendments to the Basic Law Resulting from Affiliation)

The Basic Law . . . will be amended as follows:

1. The Preamble will read as follows: "In the knowledge of its responsibility before God and human beings, inspired by the will to serve world peace as an equal partner in a unified Europe, the German people adopted this Basic Law according to its constitutional power. The Germans in the *Länder* Baden-Würtemberg, Bavaria, Berlin, Brandenburg, Bremen, Hamburg, Hesse, Mecklenburg-Vorpommern, Lower Saxony, Northrhine-Westphalia, Rhineland-Palatinate, Saarland, Saxony, Saxony-Anhalt, Schleswig-Holstein, and Thuringia have established the unity and freedom of Germany in free self-determination. The Basic Law therewith is valid for the entire German people."

2. Article 23 (Jurisdiction of the Basic Law) is annulled.

3. Article 51, Paragraph 2, of the Basic Law will read as follows: "Each *Land* has at least three votes, *Länder* with more than two million inhabitants have four, *Länder* with more than three million have five, *Länder* with more than five million inhabitants have six, *Länder* with more than seven million inhabitants have seven, and *Länder* with more than twelve million inhabitants have eight votes."

4. The former wording of Article 135a (Old Obligations) will become Paragraph 1. After Paragraph 1 the following paragraph will be added: "Paragraph 1 is also applicable in the case of obligations of the German Democratic Republic and its legal representatives, as well as obligations of the government of the Federal Republic or other bodies and institutions of public jurisdiction that are associated with the transference of properties from the German Democratic Republic to the government of the Federal Republic, the *Länder*, and districts, and obligations resulting from measures of the German Democratic Republic and its legal representatives."

5. The following new Article 143 will be added to the Basic Law: "Legal regulations in the newly affiliated part of Germany can only deviate from the provisions of the Basic Law until December 31, 1995 at the latest, insofar and as long as, because of the differing conditions, complete conformity with the provisions of the Basic Law cannot be achieved. Deviations may not violate Article 19 (Limitation of Basic Rights), Paragraph 2, and must be compatible with the principles set out in Article 79 (Amendments to the Basic Law), Paragraph 3. Article 41 of the Unification Treaty and regulations for its realization also apply to the extent that they determine that expropriations made in the territory referred to in Article 3 of this treaty are not reversible."

6. Article 146 (Period of Validity of the Basic Law) will read as follows: "This Basic Law, which becomes valid for the entire German people after the establishment of unity and freedom in Germany, loses its validity on the day in which a new constitution, agreed on freely by the German people, takes effect."

Article 5 (Future Amendments to the Constitution)

The governments of both parties to this treaty recommend to the legislative bodies of unified Germany that they concern themselves within two years with questions about amendments or additions to the Basic Law that result from German unity. . . .

NOTES

Source: Weiland, 265-68.

65
Television Addresses on the Eve of the Day of German Unity
(October 2, 1990)

Speech by Lothar de Maizière

It is unusual for a state to voluntarily withdraw from history. But the division of our country was just as unusual and unnatural. In a few hours the German Democratic Republic will join the Federal Republic of Germany. We Germans are achieving unity in freedom.

I believe that all of us have reason to be happy and thankful. We are leaving behind us a system that called itself democratic without being democratic. Its distinguishing traits were lack of intellectual freedom and thought on command, the Wall and barbed wire, the bankruptcy of our economy and the destruction of the environment, ideologically calculated tyranny and incited mistrust.

Constitutionality, democracy, and human dignity are taking the place of this tyranny. Our road to freedom was not without dangers and was not without controversy. We thank those who unswervingly followed their road and fearlessly expressed their democratic will. Because they freed themselves from fear, they could wrest freedom for themselves. We know that we could not have taken this road without the new thinking in the Soviet Union and without the support of our neighbors in the East. For this day we also have to thank the understanding of the Four Powers and their receptiveness, which was a condition for German unity.

We are now citizens of a common German state, and with the formation of the *Länder*, which will be completed in a few days, we will simultaneously be citizens of Thuringia and Saxony, of Brandenburg, Saxony-Anhalt, and Mecklenburg-Vorpommern again. We can recall the strengths that stem from the history and the traditions of these *Länder*. The dictates of centralism with its decisions from afar and its ravaging of the rest of the country is finally coming to an end. And, as the Unification Treaty stipulates, united Berlin will be the capital of Germany. With unity in freedom, something that many would not have considered possible is becoming a reality. The forty-year division of our country has been overcome and all of Europe can come together again.

Despite all the contradictions and strains, the history of the last four decades is a part of our personal biography, a part of the identity we developed. It conditioned us and it extracted great exertions from almost all of us. This also created a feeling of identity, and in those who consciously remained here, it created a community that many of us will find difficult to leave behind. We want unity, even if all of us do not experience this transformation today with a light heart.

I know that not all of us are looking into the future without worries. The new currency, the reorganization of the economy, and the introduction of new political structures naturally also bring with them many difficulties. But we have the great advantage of knowing that we have a strong partner at our side. With its help the restructuring of the economy will be completed faster and more favorably than in our neighboring countries. The Unification Treaty offers a secure foundation for the future. We are beginning our future under the sign of hope. I am sure that together we will master the great tasks that lie ahead of us. This depends on the active commitment of every single one of us.

German unity is not complete once affiliation has occurred. It is and remains a common task of all Germans. It is not only a material question, but a question of a lived communal sensibility. Unity is not merely something that can be bought, rather it is something that we must desire with all our hearts. The abandonment of global judgments on both sides is also necessary if we are to overcome division. They are grounded in mutual ignorance and frequently in a lack of empathy. We know very well what the past did to us. We want to put it behind us. We do not want to repress the past, and we will work through it honestly and responsibly. But it ought not to divide our future, as well. We are standing at the beginning of a new age. We have every reason to approach German unity with joy and confidence. Our problems are comparably minor if we call to mind the living conditions of our neighbors in Eastern Europe and events in the rest of the world.

I was Prime Minister of the GDR for almost six months. It was not always simple. Unprecedented problems had to be resolved. The encouragement I was fortunate enough to receive and the support I got from many sides made things easier. I would also like to express my thanks explicitly for the criticism I received. Together we took a difficult road. We put this segment of our journey behind us in an orderly and civilized fashion. Only through the good will of all could the peaceful road of fall 1989 be continued. Throughout history we Germans have set out in many wrong directions. This often occurred out of conscious confrontation with our neighbors. It is a fortune of history that today we can establish German unity peacefully and on the best of terms with our partners and neighbors.

We want to use freedom and unity for the good of all.

Speech by Helmut Kohl

Dear fellow countrymen and countrywomen!

In a few hours a dream will become reality. After forty years of bitter division, Germany, our fatherland, will be united again. For me this moment is one of the happiest in my life; and from many letters and conversations I know what great joy most of you are also experiencing. On such a day we train our gaze into the future. Yet despite all our joy we first want to remember those who particularly suffered under the division of Germany. Families were brutally separated. Political prisoners were incarcerated in the detention centers. People died at the Wall. Fortunately, all this belongs to the past. It should never be repeated. That is the reason why we should never forget it. We owe it to the victims to remember them. And we owe it to our children and grandchildren. They should always be spared such experiences.

For the same reason we should also not forget to whom we owe the unity of our fatherland. We would never have achieved it by ourselves. Many contributed to it. When did a country ever have the chance to overcome decades of painful division in such a peaceful fashion? We are reconstituting the unity of Germany in freedom and on the best of terms with our neighbors. We thank our partners, we thank our friends. In particular, we thank the United States of America, above all President George Bush. We thank our friends in France and Great Britain. In difficult times they always stood by us. They protected the freedom of the Western part of Berlin for decades. They supported our goal of attaining unity in freedom. We will continue to have close, friendly ties with them in the future. We also owe thanks to the reform movements in Central, Eastern, and Southeastern Europe. A little over a year ago Hungary let the refugees cross the border. That was when the first stone was knocked out of the Wall. The freedom movements in Poland and Czechoslovakia gave the people in the GDR the courage to demand their right of self-determination. Now we are about to effect a permanent reconciliation between the German and the Polish people. We thank President Gorbachev. He recognized the right of nations to choose their own course. Without this decision we would not have experienced the Day of German Unity so soon. It is thanks to those Germans who overcame the SED dictatorship with the strength of their love for freedom that this day is already upon us. Their peacefulness and their prudence remain exemplary.

We Germans have learned from history. We are a peace-loving, a freedom-loving people and we will never abandon our democracy to the enemies of peace and freedom without a fight. For us, the love of our fatherland, the love of freedom, and the spirit of good neighborliness always belong together. We want to be reliable partners, we want to be good friends. For us there is only one place in the world to do this: at the side of the free nations. We also want to be good neighbors in our domestic lives. Openness to our neighbors, respect for those who think differently, and solidarity with our fellow citizens from foreign countries are also part of that. Our free democracy must be characterized by variety, by tolerance, by solidarity. Above all, as Germans we now have to demonstrate our solidarity with one another. A difficult segment of our road lies ahead of us–everyone knows that. We want to travel this road together. If we stick together and are also willing to make sacrifices, we have every chance for joint success.

The economic conditions in the Federal Republic of Germany are excellent today. Never were we better prepared than we are today to master the economic challenges of reunification. In addition to this, there is the diligence and productive capacity of the people in the former GDR. By means of our joint efforts, by means of the policies of a social market economy, Brandenburg, Mecklenburg-Vorpommern, Saxony, Saxony-Anhalt, and Thuringia will be turned within a few years into flourishing areas. I am certain that we will be able to solve the economic problems: probably not overnight, but within a foreseeable period. However, it is even more important that we be understanding of one another, that we move closer to one another. We have to overcome that kind of thinking that still divides Germany into a "here" and a "there."

More than forty years of SED dictatorship have left deep scars precisely in people's hearts. The constitutional state has the task of creating justice and domestic peace. In this all of us are facing a difficult test. Severe injustice has to be expiated, but we also need the strength for internal reconciliation. I ask all Germans: Let us prove ourselves worthy of our common freedom. The 3rd of October is a day of joy, of gratitude, and of hope. The young generation in Germany–unlike almost any previous generation–now has every opportunity for a whole life in freedom and peace. We know that our joy is shared by many people in the world. They ought to know what moves us in this moment: Germany is our fatherland, united Europe our future.

God bless our German fatherland!

NOTES

Source: Zanetti, 353-58.

66
Günter Grass, "A 'Steal' Called the GDR":
Speech Given at the Reichstag on October 2, 1990, Before the
Delegations of the Greens and Alliance 90 (October 2, 1990)

The zone, SOZ,[1] the other part of Germany, the illegal state in quotation marks, not recognized, then recognized, the German Democratic Republic, after tomorrow the ex-GDR, East Elbia,[2] the land of Luther, in which, at the time of the peasant wars, another reformer answered the enemy of the rebellious masses belligerently and protested what is still an existing injustice: "The lords themselves ensure that the poor man will be their enemy. They do not want to do away with the cause of the rebellion. How can things get better in the long run?"

With this appeal to and citation of Thomas Müntzer, I come to the present German quagmire: the unity without unanimity to which a date has been assigned.[3] On October 2 the ringing of bells was ordained as a substitute for happiness, which has expired; unless the television, the inventor of new reality, succeeds in cutting to a few scenes of jubilation. This is how history is made.

And yet everything began favorably. For more than a decade the freedom movement Solidarity had paved the way not only for Poland. Vaclav Havel and his dissidents did not allow themselves to be shut up. In Hungary even the Communists helped to uproot the detested system: they were the first to open the Iron Curtain. And thanks to Michail Gorbachev's politics, that incomparably bold undertaking, even the ruling fortress of the SED displayed some cracks. There, where decades of silence had become equal in value to the proverbial gold and complaints were voiced at best behind closed doors, the people, or more exactly, the more courageous element among them, took to the streets and proclaimed, not to be overheard, "We are the people!"

That was an error, as soon became clear, because since November of last year the street has belonged to that part of the populace that had previously been silent. That was the majority. It called out: "We are one people!," and never again, in keeping with the violent intolerance it had learned, did it let the minority have a voice.

In Western Germany the call for unity was embraced, if not by the populace, then at least by the politicians. Amid renunciation of common reflectiveness it was supposed to happen quickly and still more quickly, so that no opportunity would be lost, they said. The piece of furniture called the "Round Table" was too cumbersome. Who knows how long Gorbachev will last. Reservations were anachronistic.

As the last trace of wisdom, a train station announcement was recycled: "The train has departed!" And the very people who otherwise are in the habit of waiting out such problems thought they heard the cloak of history rushing past them, jumped up and grabbed hold. However, because the double power composed of a discord that is now supposed to become a union still lacks a unifying concept, the material aspect of the wish of those who called for national unity was made tangible by means of a promise; finally, in the middle of March–that's how quickly it transpired–elections were on the agenda.

The promised D-mark. The hard currency. The lucky charm. The substitute for thought and the general panacea. The miracle in a new edition.

Since that moment the only thing talked about is money, even though we experienced a short interlude filled with consolational clap-trap and the two-horse team of "dignity and decency" had to pull the cart. But German unity and its coach could not have been whipped and spurred on with any less dignity and decency. What had been declared junk became junk.

All in all it nevertheless remains an asset that the West German franchises have succeeded in expanding their market, in exploiting the opportunities of the moment, in driving out the indigenous, by any measure inferior and poorly-marketed product from "over there" and–without having to invest–buying up a real steal, a steal called the GDR.

This word, quite common in the new German vernacular, stands for endless opportunity. The things you get for a good price, incidentally, at end-of-summer clearances, at the flea market, in the quick exploitation of legal loopholes, in cash transactions that avoid the taxman, legally at compulsory auctions, or by chance, in passing. In short: a steal is always favorable and a favorable steal is always a pale horse. Something that no one had counted on; for who in West German small and big business, a year before this market expansion that is also known as reunification, would have included it in his or her calculations?

No, not only the small and big businesspeople, but also the parties, trade unions, churches, the high and mighty boards of directors and humble stockholders, indeed, the entire West German populace in its diverse simplicity had nothing else in mind but a currency union with "the people over there"–and haphazardly saddled to it the unified state. Although at first, on television, happiness could be documented and the oft-heard cry "This is incredible!" lent the happiness a catch phrase, now in the West displeasure prevails just as fears do in the East. Quarrels are entering the double household. Today people only speak of the additional billions. There is already a lack of space for further corpses in the pan-German cellar. The steal called the GDR is turning out to be expensive.

Of course, I realize that this song sounds bitter. To the old German cry: "But where are the positive aspects?" my reply: "Yes, what ever happened to them?," hardly softens the threatening undertones. But even when it was still possible to waste thoughts on reunification that had nothing to do with money, when it came to me to suggest a confederation of the two German states that could, five or seven years down the road and in deference to the popular will, have been transformed into a "Federation of German States"; and when I thought, in addition, that such a circumspect, and hence cautious and deliberate path to German unity would have been more bearable for us Germans and our neighbors than the impending headlong sprint with its predictable pitfalls; I was called a pessimist, a spoilsport, and discredited as being a "rootless cosmopolitan," if not pegged as such for good.

Now the child lies in the well and on top of that is just scolded from above: It's your own fault! You brought this upon yourself! You were the ones who wanted the D-mark, come what may! Now you've got it!

So the little child in the well is guilty and not Messrs. Kohl, Waigel, Haussmann, accompanied by the chorus of well-read coaxers from Rudolf Augstein to Robert Leicht. They already know the best advice: Only for a few more years will the crying child who fell into the well have to flail about way down there; after that, just as promised, the instruments of the market economy will kick in and investments, which have only trickled so far, will finally begin to flow. Then the child who fell into the well will once again be allowed to crawl out of that hole.

A short while ago, at a conference in Oslo sponsored by the Elie Wiesel Foundation, the discussion centered around hatred. The worldwide increase in hatred was actually the theme of the conference. Nelson Mandela and Vaclav Havel, Yelena Bonner and Adam Michnik, John Kenneth Galbraith and Elie Wiesel–to mention only a few–gave reports from each of their respective areas of experience: how the groundwork for hatred is laid, how it breaks out.

Since I lack insights sophisticated enough to be able to judge in detail all of the conflicts between nationalities that have broken out in the Soviet Union or in the Balkans, I spoke in Oslo about my experiences at home, trying to pinpoint the causes for the still bottled-up, the newly resurfacing, and even the freshly arisen hatred between Germans and Germans on the one hand and Poles and Germans on the other. I said: Because the Germans, in a headlong rush, thoughtlessly and single-mindedly putting their faith in the fetish of currency, are reunifying, a process meanwhile void of all pleasure, whereby the larger part of Germany is determining the pace and the gait, the smaller part, whose populace was a short while ago just happy finally to be able to believe it had broken free of state patronization, is now being subjected to the dictates of profit-oriented colonialists who help themselves here, wait things out over there, and are only prepared to invest once the bankrupt estate of the GDR has fallen to what seems to them rock-bottom prices: and if possible, free of prior debts.

In such lands, stripped to the bone, hatred thrives. One can already observe that there have for a long time been first- and second-class Germans. The new injustice, which rests upon the old injustice, strikes a population that was subjected to such incessant injustice for a whole forty-five years even after the twelve years of National-Socialist rule. It was these seventeen million East Germans who received the brunt of the burden resulting from the war that all Germans started and lost. Weakened from the outset by dismantling and reparations payments in the billions, they never had a free choice; by contrast, the victors presented the West Germans with freedom and granted them the Marshall Plan. The populace of the SOZ, of the state in quotation marks, remained "the poor brothers and sisters" about whom one troubled oneself to think on solemn occasions. Decades of condescension and noncommittal reunification rhetoric were insulting enough. The second-class Germans donned all too happily the hand-me-downs of their rich relatives.

And now they are once again second-class. In place of a communist economy of lack they are offered crass exploitation under the heading "Social Market Economy." This unity looks ugly. The requisite to-do list of the Chancellor of all Germans has grown to mammoth proportions and has begun to cast a shadow. He has succeeded in ensuring the persistence of the division of Germany, even though the Wall has fallen. Unity on his terms is divisive. It adds insult to injury and plays hardball with the weak. Not only proliferating unemployment, but also the growing recognition that later, when work will once again be available at minimum wage, the ownership conditions will all be clearly arranged for the benefit of West German capital. This already well-worn fact stokes the fires of social envy, which as a rule blossom into hatred. To those who once again have come up short, to the downtrodden, to the perennial underdogs, hatred expressed in emotional outbursts at least promises strength.

The still barely organized West German right-wing radicals have already unified with their East German counterparts: they are about to experience a boom. And since hatred only consumes itself as self-hatred in extraordinary circumstances (which may lead to great literature), it will seek targets outside of its own national milieu: west of the Oder River hatred of Poles is already an everyday occurrence.

I have travelled there quite a bit during the last few months. Whether in Cottbus, Guben or in the northern Uckermark, everywhere in the areas close to the border hatred of foreigners is concentrated–otherwise directed more toward Vietnamese or Africans–directly against Polish guest workers and against Poland in general, particularly Polish merchants who, on their way to Berlin, pour over the border in busloads and seem to reinforce traditional stereotypes. Added to this is the fact that many refugees from Silesia and Pomerania living in the immediate border region since 1945 view the recognized western borders of Poland, agreed to by both German parliaments, as a betrayal. The refugee organizations are thus experiencing a commensurate increase in membership, since Poland's economic weakness gives them hope: they really need us.[4] They will come begging on their hands and knees. The Poles will never be able to accomplish anything on their own. Polish economy! We know all about that.

A stay in Poznan and Gdansk proved to me that the growing insecurity there is developing into a fear of the Germans that even in the extent of its irrationality exposes a rational core:[5] the Oder-Neiße line, after all, will constitute the prosperity border between Eastern and Western Europe, visible in the form of German currency, whose power to expand is from the Polish perspective as awe-inspiring as it is terrifying. And surely they have to fear that the former eastern provinces of Germany, Silesia and Pomerania (and above all the border city Stettin), will be at the mercy of the onrush of hard currency; for Poland's weakness and political instability could easily become once again a permanent condition and signal a need for help that would find a captive audience in its western neighbor.[6] Such help would hardly come without a price. Offered in a business-like manner, it would not have to be a trump card. Totally unmilitarily this time, with only the D-mark on the march, it would cross the border.

One might ask oneself these days, east of the Oder: If the rich West Germans are treating their countrymen so mercilessly, how will the reunified Germans then pay back us Poles?

And paybacks are already taking place, if at first only in small sums: for repeated insults and unforgotten disrespect, because the Poles disdained the GDR-Germans during the decades of Communist rule, because the "Descendant of the Prussian State" was considered the loyal vassal of the hated Russians, and because the Poles regarded this state's citizens–in contrast to the West Germans whom they admired from a distance–as second-class and frequently treated them as such.

This is how hatred has always been and always will be brought about, until it progresses unaided: autonomous.

When, in the course of the conference in Oslo, Vaclav Havel spoke, I took note of a few of his definitions: "Hatred itself is more important to the hater than is the object of his hate." In his continually renewed analysis he concerned himself with the particular predisposition of the Eastern European nations for collective hate, since they, as he explained it, were young, inexperienced, and not yet mature. And Adam Michnik, alarmed by Polish anti-Semitism in a country without Jews, spoke of "magical anti-Semitism."

A pat formulation for German xenophobia, which both seeks and finds fertile motives even among Germans, eludes me, because in this country it is rarely hatred, but instead frequently bureaucratic indifference that is the decisive cause of inhumane excess. (And in contrast to this, the German-Polish relationship also distinguishes itself with examples of friendly-conciliatory behavior, which could inspire hope.) Still, I fear that the economic disparity between East and West, exacerbated by ingrained nationalism, will have consequences that will not stop at violence, even though the room for practiced hatred between rich and poor Germans as well as between poor Germans and even poorer Poles is relatively small in comparison with the causes for hatred that are presently arising in complex variety between the industrial nations and the nations of the Third World.

However cynically and pettily we Germans may be involved with ourselves, however epidemically the worry may proliferate that the steal called the GDR could become more expensive, far more expensive than originally envisioned, however more bombastically October 3 as a historically significant date is supposed to illustrate the Chancellor's agenda—other events take priority: the battle over raw materials and their ownership has begun.

Today the danger looms that the latent North-South conflict will explode in the Gulf region as a war with unforeseeable consequences. The only things reacting to this eventuality in this country are gas prices and the stock market. With the price of German unity roughly estimated at three hundred billion marks, the few additional billions as a show of solidarity with America's Desert Army does not seem very substantial. In general we act as though we should keep out of such things; although it has been well known for years that it is through West German support that Iraq was given the capability to produce poison gas and deliver it to its target.

To be sure, the Soviet Union, China, and almost every European nation, by supplying weapons, have made Iraq into a military power of the first order, but the most telling threat does not lie in the so-called conventional realm. It is with chemical weapons that these threats are being made, and Israel's cities have been ominously designated the primary target. For years, more than a hundred West German firms, including such world leaders as Klockner, Buderus, AEG and Siemens, Preussag and MBB, Thyssen, Mannesmann, Carl Zeiss and Degussa, have created the preconditions for a continuation of the genocide of the Jews that is not only imaginable, but becomes more possible with each passing day.[7] Meanwhile, investigations are ongoing against about thirty or more firms–too late!–by the Justice Department. By its inaction and toleration the government of the Federal Republic has already made itself an accomplice in the prior poison gas murder of thousands of Kurds: a crime that apparently invokes common law in its defense, since criminals in the highest governmental and economic positions remain unindicted. No, it was not hatred, about which the discussion at Oslo had to concern itself, that was the identifiable impetus for those transactions, but the drive for profit. This could have terrible further consequences by making present the past German guilt and by causing us Germans once again to be despised. I wrest this premonition from myself with horror. (Even as I write this, reality could have caught up with me, it could already have come true.)

Therefore back to profit–this value in itself–and to the drive for profit that knows no scruples and grabs at anything it can get its hands on, since criminal acts based upon the drive for profit are blessed under the laws of the market economy. I am sure that the gentlemen running the above-named firms of international repute have adjudged all the appropriate deals in crisis zones in that colloquial German, to be steals, an expression that is also in use among the management of all the commercial firms that are divvying up the GDR market among themselves. And if the ministries of Lambsdorff and de Maizière are presently merging in order to take care of the business of the Treuhand Organization in a well-informed manner, this action also adheres to the crooked morals so common today. As one says: Yes, it is not pretty, but it is the accepted modus operandi of international business. The market looks for holes, it wants to grow. Growth is its credo. Are the Germans now somehow to be considered dangerous, simply because they are expanding their market a little?

Are the Germans once again a force to be feared? This question is posed quite often these days, usually with a rhetorical undertone, because stock answers lie at the ready: We have learned from history. We have our good points and bad points just like any other nation. The Europeanization of Germany will banish all suspected dangers. No one has to be afraid of us any more.

Really? Is the completed installation of fully functional poison gas factories, or further still the thoughtlessness with which the government of the Federal Republic accepted these criminal transactions–that is, covered them up–not evidence to the contrary? And are there not even reversions to horrifying behavior where caution belongs to the work routine?

When the foreign ministers of the Soviet Union and the Federal Republic met a few months ago in the once Polish, since 1939 Belorussian city of Brest, that was just one meeting among many. This location did not bother the world in the slightest. Only the Poles reacted with horror that Schevardnadze and Genscher could be tactless enough to meet each other there, where in 1939 the Wehrmacht and the Red Army celebrated their military alliance and held their victory parade. A disgrace, especially because this time it was not, as usual, Chancellor Kohl who showed his boorishness toward Poland, but a politician displaying insensitivity who generally is known as clever, careful, even cautious.

And yet again I hear the prayer-wheel of objections: all of the Poles' fears, while of course understandable, are nonetheless exaggerated; Germany has become penitent and has with great diligence improved itself in the grade-school subject of democracy, earning resounding A-plusses; please do not lend more significance to this meeting of foreign ministers or to any other faux pas than they deserve. . . .

I would love to allow myself to be appeased and conceive us as basically harmless. Yet as soon as I draw the summation of the German unification process all of my fears are reawakened once again. It is horrifying to see how the D-mark has been elevated to an article of faith, as though bankrupt thought could be made up for with money. Alarmingly, the debate about the future capital was conducted over loudspeakers at full volume. The univocality of public opinion from *Spiegel* to *FAZ* to the weekly *Die Zeit* exerts an oppressive effect. The first State Treaty was rammed through both parliaments in a frivolous way. And it was terrifying to read reports of success according to which the strategy of blitzkrieg proves its peacetime effectiveness in the form of politico-financial pincer-offensives.

Who would not be scared when the German tendency to backslide is demonstrated daily, when painstakingly internalized democratic virtues lose their value overnight, when unification is carried out even in the realm of state security, when–already once more–the largest opposition party ducks because they have to fear that at the slightest disagreement they will be branded as "rootless"? And not only ridiculous, but also terrifying are those stupidity-inspired victory poses, according to whose instructions every utopia is to be refused a seat and the right of way is to be denied to every "Third Way." Just as previously the now failed planned economy, the market economy is now being elevated to the status of an ideology. And the Chancellor's relationship to power can be compared with Bismarck's, as though the blood-and-iron politics of the Prussian junker had been a blessing for Germany and its neighbors.

Now, one could say that all of the fears listed here will be relativized, because at the latest after the December elections the politics of the Bismarckian Chancellor will have to declare their own bankruptcy. Even to the notoriously good-willed and indomitably faithful it will not remain a secret that Kohl and his finance minister have made sixteen million Germans socially déclassé. How could the admittedly dilapidated economy between the Elbe and the Oder rivers ever survive the sudden competitive pressure of Western goods? The collapse of agriculture, the skyrocketing unemployment, the new centralism of the Treuhand Organization, the empty coffers of the communes, the Stasi syndrome everywhere, the so often promised investment that stubbornly fails to appear, the used car business that merely increases automobile accidents,[8] the renewed exodus of specialists to the West, the depressed mood–after so much forced optimism–and the predictable economic and social chaos are obvious: the con artist's horses are coming up lame.

Hence they really are not so dangerous after all, the Germans. With all their happiness and the trust of their neighbors they have still only succeeded in making a singular mess of things: they will have to pay for it, continuously have to keep paying for it. Demagogues and dilettantes were at work; even the guardian of the West German currency himself, Karl Otto Pöhl, who had expressed reservations at the outset, finally gave his approval to "unity on credit" and now shares the responsibility.

But since it is not just any mistaken decisions that are to be deplored, but rather a brutally imposed state action that is showing its effects, the overly hurried and ill-prepared introduction of the D-mark–called a currency union–proves from day to day more explicitly its merciless treatment of human beings who have been turned over unprotected to the methods of early capitalism. After decades of ideological indoctrination, leashed in by the communist economy of lack, yet nevertheless hoping for the promised miraculous effect, they are now experiencing the very exploitation whose ugliness the disciplinarians of the Leninist school had previously painted as a terrifying specter.

It is the violence of this politics, devoid of all humanity, that is so horrifying and that spreads fear. Outside our borders (and not only in Poland) people will ask themselves: How much will the Germans–now approximately eighty million strong–soon want to lend a hand here, make a killing there, and be looking for their steals everywhere in the common European house? For the suspected threat no longer lies in the military arena–just as for the Japanese, for the Germans, too, the desire for war has passed–but lies instead in the force of economic expansion inherent in the once-defeated Axis powers, who show little restraint in once again consolidating their power, as recently Daimler-Benz and Mitsubishi have done, and for whom a technological Axis between Germany and Japan merits investigation.[9] Such a "strategic alliance" is already a manifestation of an aggressive will for growth, market control, and the very lack of restraint that have all been demonstrated in the exported poison gas factories.

It is horrifying, in addition, that public opinion in Germany, which just a year ago was so infused with contradictions, has now become so monolithic. Anyone who does not pledge a Yes to unity is considered "out." A unified will is being formed. Even in the intellectual sphere, the virtue of the naysayer has become a rarity. Once carefully cultivated havens–called feuilletons–have been made into places of execution. No picture that was painted in the GDR or–as it is generally termed–in unfree conditions, can from this day on be considered art or shown in a museum. Now only Western art above all else. And when Christa Wolf was dragged before the executioner, it was not only she who was condemned, properly interpreted, but the better part of GDR literature, as well: the time of leniency has passed.[10] From good to evil. What is "cultural identity" supposed to mean here? There is nothing about that either in the State Treaty or the Unification Treaty. It's all rubbish!, claims the common diagnosis. Your cultural association and whatever else you had, you can just forget it.

German unity has adopted the methods of clear-cutting. Anyone who as painter, author, musician, as theater or film director, as circus director, editor, archivist or librarian, dares to complain a little, to whisper the word loss, or worse, to warn of cultural colonization, is denounced as overly plaintive, suspected of leftist scheming, or inundated with suggestions like the following: You have got to stop this whining. In the free market, the only things that make it are those things that gain acceptance. Even in art only productivity counts. Everything has its price. You did want it, after all, this freedom—or am I exaggerating?

The development up to now in the process of German market expansion has proven that my worst exaggerations have been outdone by reality. Thus I allow myself to continue seeing black. From whence should enlightening gray tones spring? That left-liberal power of resistance against state violence, illegality, and corruption among government officials, which had oriented itself in the Federal Republic since the end of the sixties around Jürgen Habermas's concept of "constitutional patriotism," has been more than just made ineffectual.[11] The Greens and Alliance 90 are experiencing in a correspondingly ineffectual way the late celebration of their marriage of convenience. Far too in love with the grassroots democratic sand box games, their ineffectuality was at the same time proof of their fundamental disgust with political power. It was enough to have oneself.

Yet now come the more difficult days; bells are ringing them in. All of the information has been recorded and from now on will be easily accessible to pan-German misuse. The civil servants will take care of the rest: out of the Diestel of today, the Diestel of tomorrow already speaks. Now we have it, the class society: socially divided, the Germans are assured of experiencing domestic strife. Even before it had called itself into existence, the new state broke the Basic Law and denied the people a constitution. No diverse "Confederation of German States," whose citizen I would be proud to be, is in the offing; a monstrosity wants to be a superpower. My No is placed on its doorstep.

Until today I considered myself—often with passion, critically approvingly, and for decades indefatigably—a constitutional patriot. In its overabundance of power the new state will hardly miss such a patriot.

NOTES

Source: *Ein Schnäppchen namens DDR: Letzte Reden vorm Glockengeläut* (Darmstadt: Luchterhand, 1990), pp. 39-60. Translated by Bill Hutfilz.

1. SOZ is an abbreviation for Soviet Occupational Zone; in the years after the war this was the official Western designation of that part of Germany that in 1949 would become the GDR; it frequently remained the name for the GDR in the everyday language of the FRG.

2. Grass is making this sound like the name of a German province.

3. Thomas Müntzer was Martin Luther's counterplayer in the political struggle of the peasant revolt in Germany in 1525; he was a social revolutionary who, contrary to Luther, sided with the peasants and was executed for his radical beliefs.

4. The refugee organizations, i.e., associations formed by the refugees from Silesia and Pomerania who were forcefully resettled in Germany after the war, are frequently the core of conservative chauvinistic politics in West Germany.

5. Poznan and Gdansk are now Polish cities; they became part of Germany after Hitler's annexation of the Eastern provinces in 1937.

6. Stettin is a city in the GDR near the border with Poland.

7. These names include the most well-known West German firms that made substantial profits by illegally selling to Iraq some of the equipment and technology that made possible the targetting of Israeli cities with Scud missiles during the Persian Gulf War.

8. One of the first status symbols GDR citizens bought with their newly-won hard currency after the Currency Union took effect in July 1990 was a used Western automobile.

9. Grass is alluding to the political alliance between Germany and Japan in the Second World War, which, according to him, is repeated in the postwar world in the new German-Japanese economic and technological alliance.

10. The GDR writer Christa Wolf was harshly criticized in the Western media for speaking out during the fall of 1989 for an independent political development in the GDR.

11. Jürgen Habermas coined the concept of constitutional patriotism, which he used to describe the political sentiments of postwar Germans who no longer could identify their patriotism with a German nation- state.

67
Speech by Sabine Bergmann-Pohl, Former President of the GDR *Volkskammer*, at the State Ceremony on the Day of German Unity (October 3, 1990)

Dear Mr. President, dear President of the *Bundestag*, dear Mr. Chancellor, dear President of the *Bundesrat*, dear assembled guests!

This is a day of fulfillment for those Germans who had to live for a long time in the shadow of dictatorship, of division, and of moral alienation. The geography of the Second World War, and after that the divisions of the Cold War, dealt us a bad hand. Now a wound is healing. The freedom for which we fought has given us back our dignity and self-respect. But the past remains preserved in our memory. It will take some time before repression, collaboration, fellow-traveling, and accommodation are overcome and our lives are free of the grip of dictatorship.

But today is the time to ask where we have come from and where we are going, what we bring with us and what we expect. It was not nationalist enthusiasm that motivated those people who caused the revolution of the summer and the fall of 1989 in the eastern part of Central Europe. They demanded their . . . right to be themselves, the right . . . to a free development of their personalities.

But the peaceful revolution in the eastern part of our fatherland did not stand alone. In the West it found its prerequisites in European unity and the security of the NATO alliance, in the politics of detente, and in the insistence on human rights; in the East it was prepared by the Polish struggle for freedom, by the moral courage of the Hungarians, and by perestroika, which reshaped and is continuing to reshape the Soviet Union into a responsible leading power. Many people had ceased to hope for what is being realized today, German unity in peace and freedom. For the Germans it is a gift of history. The Christians among us will see in it God's mercy. But this unity in freedom does not stand in opposition to the interests of our neighbors. It is integrated into greater Europe. We feel this with gratitude, and we promise to be just as much Europeans as we are Germans. Our painful experience, our historical situation, our political hopes come together in this European confidence.

The material wealth we were lacking was less important than the denial of freedom and of justice. The experiences we bear within us and the experiences that haunt us cannot simply be put aside, rather they have to be overcome in a creative way; and nothing will help more in this than the living experience of freedom, faith in justice and the law, and feeling at home in a free Europe. Time, as well as the capacity for empathy and the courage to make unpopular decisions, will be necessary for the two parts of Germany to grow together. Let us respect one another, let us be considerate of the mentality and sensitivity of other people! Let us stand together in order to construct with combined energies that united, peaceful, and democratic Germany that offers social justice to all of its citizens!

What do we from the GDR have to contribute? Aside from all our bitterness, the experience that human beings do not live by bread alone, gratitude for warmth, humanness, family, neighborliness, which proved themselves in difficult times. But above all pride in a gentle revolution that won us democracy. We will bring these experiences with us into the future Germany. But we will also bring with us other things: last, but not least, the difficult experience that one does not live under dictatorships for forty, sixty years without being damaged in body and soul. Freedom, therefore, is also a precious treasure because it protects against such experiences.

What we will have to learn is to make responsible use of our newly won freedom, to attend anew to the meaning of our own work, to realize the way of life of a free society. We do not expect a country where milk and honey flow, but a country in which we can develop our strengths, a country of justice, a country, as well, in which people share out of solidarity, a country that stands on its own culture and, at the same time, participates voluntarily in greater Europe. A country that is not fleeing from its older or more recent history, but instead a country that faces up to this history and draws conclusions from it with heart and mind. Today we have every reason to celebrate the first Day of German Unity; but we also have every reason to recognize the errors of German history. Auschwitz will remain for us an everlasting warning.

Yesterday we belonged to that part of Europe that was denied freedom and in which lies and violence governed. Today we belong to a new Europe without borders, and the unity and freedom of the Germans stand in the center of this new Europe. However, at the end of this century no one will ask about the rate of growth and the gross national product; rather, they will ask whether in the end we Germans developed a life in freedom and permanent peace from the wars and crises of our century. This day means taking leave and moving on–taking leave of a burdensome and burdening past, moving on to a Germany that is reconciled with itself and seeks reconciliation with its neighbors.

It is the happiest of days for the Germans!

NOTES

Source: Zanetti, 359-61.

68
Address by President Richard von Weizsäcker at the State Ceremony on the Day of German Unity (October 3, 1990)

The preamble to our constitution, as it is valid for all Germans as of today, states the decisive thing that moves us on this day:

In free self-determination we are establishing the unity and freedom of Germany. We want to serve world peace in a unified Europe. For our tasks we are aware of our responsibility before God and all human beings.

We feel with all our hearts gratitude and joy—and at the same time our great and serious obligation. History in Europe and in Germany is now offering us an opportunity that has never been known before. We are experiencing one of those extremely seldom historical phases in which something can be changed for the better. Let us not forget for a single moment what this means for us.

Inside as well as outside there are pressing concerns; we are not overlooking this. We take seriously the reservations of our neighbors. We also sense how difficult it will be to live up to the expectations that are directed at us from all sides. But we do not want to be, and will not be guided by fears and doubts, but instead by confidence. What is decisive is the firm will to clearly recognize our tasks and to address them jointly. This will gives us the energy to put our everyday problems in perspective with our tradition and the future of Europe.

For the first time we Germans do not constitute a point of contention on the European agenda. Our unity was not forced on anyone, but rather peacefully negotiated. It is part of a pan-European historical process whose aim is the freedom of all nations and a new peaceful order for our continent. We Germans want to serve this aim. Our unity is dedicated to it. We now have a state that we ourselves no longer view as provisional and whose identity and integrity is no longer questioned by our neighbors. Today the unified German nation finds its acknowledged place in Europe.

We recognize what that means in the significance of borders. No European country has as many neighbors as we do. Throughout the centuries, force has been used because of these borders and much blood has been shed. Now all our neighbors and we ourselves live in secure borders. They are not only protected by the renunciation of the use of force, but by the profound insight into their altered function. The forced loss of homeland was incredibly hard. Disputes over borders, however, are losing all meaning. All the more stirring is the desire to take away their character as things that separate. All the borders of Germany should become bridges to our neighbors. That is our wish.

The ideas of the French Revolution, together with the constitutional developments in America and in Great Britain, created the foundation for Western democracy. A concept of constitutional human freedom, which more and more turned into a yardstick, was formed. It is not applicable everywhere on the first go. But wherever the urge for political freedom, for productivity and a social constitutionality worthy of human beings breaks out–even in the heart of Beijing–the values and regulations of Western democracies constitute the standard against which everything is measured.

We Germans participated early in this democratic development. And yet we only pursued it halfheartedly in our political practice. Constitutionality here grew out of our own traditions. In the Prussian reforms of the Napoleonic era, communal self-rule became the source of a democratic sensibility. Under the symbol of the Paulskirche the people sought unity and justice and freedom.[1] They definitely wanted the unity that was finally achieved in 1871, but they were not a part of the decision-making process. Over and over again there was the Romantic search for a third path for the internal order of Germany and for its place in Europe. But these were illusions. Even the Weimar Republic did not succeed in realizing a viable democracy.

Bound up with the foundation of the Federal Republic of Germany was the fear of heightening the division of Germany from the West. This road, however, did not arrive at a dead-end. At first, only a part of the Germans were allowed to follow it, but today we can make a new beginning together. The unification of Germany is something more than just a mere expansion of the Federal Republic of Germany. The day has come on which for the first time in history the whole of Germany has found a permanent place in the circle of Western democracies.

This is a process of fundamental significance for us as well as for all our neighbors. It will change the center of Europe. We will participate substantially in this, in joint action with our Western partners and firmly bound up with them in our values and aims. Fate divided us during the last forty years in the midst of our European neighbors. It favored the one side and placed burdens on the other. But it was and remains our common German fate. History and responsibility for its consequences are part of this. The SED attempted to prescribe a division. It thought it would be enough to proclaim itself the socialist society of the future in order to free itself from the burden of history.

But in the GDR people experienced things and felt about them completely differently. The people there had to bear much worse consequences of the war than their countrymen and countrywomen in the West. And they always felt that the responsible memory of the past is an indispensable force of liberation for the future. As soon as the forced language disappeared, they openly faced up to the questions of history. The world registered with great respect how honestly the free forces and especially the younger generation in the GDR considered it their task to make up for the historical responsibility the old regime had failed to demonstrate. The visit of the presidents of both freely elected German parliaments to Israel a few months ago to commemorate the Holocaust left a deep impression there. It symbolizes the communal spirit of the Germans especially with regard to their historical responsibility, as well. The National-Socialist dictatorship and the war it initiated caused immeasurable injustice and pain to people in almost all of Europe and here in Germany. We will always remember the victims. And we are thankful for the growing signs of reconciliation among human beings and nations.

The hope for freedom and for overcoming the division in Europe, in Germany, and, above all, in Berlin, never perished in the postwar era. And yet, no one had enough imagination to predict the course of events. Thus we experience the present day as a gift. This time history meant well with us Germans. This gives us all the more reason for conscientious self-reflection.

After the end of World War II, the division of Germany became the central metaphor for the division of Europe. It did not derive from the unified will of the victors, rather it was the consequence of their disputes. The heightened East-West conflict consolidated this division. But let us not make excuses for ourselves. No one here will forget that without the war begun by Germany under Hitler it would never have come to division. In the context of the Cold War and under the protection of the nuclear stalemate, the competition between the social systems of East and West unfolded over forty years. This phase is now reaching its conclusion. The Soviet leadership under President Gorbachev has understood that reforms in the direction of democracy and a market economy have become unavoidable. Without freedom, however, these reforms would be doomed to fail. . . . The success of the reform course followed by the Soviet leadership is still threatened on many fronts. But it has already proven its historical merit. And many people, among them we Germans, have reason for gratitude.

We owe thanks to the citizens' movements and people in Hungary, in Poland, and in Czechoslovakia. The people in Warsaw, Budapest, and Prague set examples. They viewed and encouraged the path toward internal freedom in the GDR as part of a shared historical process. Also unforgotten is their help for the refugees and thus their direct contribution to the overcoming of the Wall and its barbed wire. United Germany will seek an open and close friendship with them in the future. To stand up for freedom and human rights is the central commitment of our Western allies and friends, above all the Americans, the French, and the British. Their protection, their willingness to act, and their cooperation helped us decisively. They placed their trust in us. We wholeheartedly thank them for that today.

How significant the understanding of these partners was for German unification was demonstrated in the unequivocal and constructive attitude of the European Community. It gives me great pleasure to welcome the President of the European Commission, Jacques Delors, and his colleagues and declare our respect and gratitude for their farsightedness.

Above all, we have to thank today those Germans who mustered the courage to rise up against repression and arbitrariness in the GDR. For over ten years, gatherings and prayers for peace in the churches prepared, deepened, and disseminated the ideas of the peaceful revolution. But the power of the state security remained omnipresent. The use of force was an immediate threat long into the fall of 1989. To give in and withdraw would have been quite understandable. Yet the hopes in the hearts of people could no longer be repressed.

We are the people: with these four simple and great words an entire system was shaken and brought down. They symbolize the will of the people to take the community, the *res publica*, into their own hands. In this way the peaceful revolution in Germany became truly republican. That it occurred after almost sixty years of bitter repression makes it all the more amazing and credible. Democrats came together with the goal of attaining freedom and solidarity, both taken together a task for us all. But today we also have to thank the citizens in the West. Without the trust of the people in us Germans we would not have been able to unify. It grew with life in the Federal Republic over forty years. Our population is rooted in free democracy and in European consciousness. The Germans have become predictable, reliable, and respected partners. That decisively promoted the internal consent of our neighbors and the entire world to our unity. Now, however, those four words have given way to many thousands. In a purely incredible effort, agreements and treaties were brought about which today let us put the seal on both our internal and external unity. These matters were often difficult to penetrate. There was no lack of conflicts. The time pressure repeatedly became enormous. People worked day and night.

In the future there will be more than one confusion that has to be cleared up, more than one fight that has to be settled. All in all, however, one can only be amazed at the finished work. I would like to thank the political leadership responsible for this in both former German states, the legislatures, and, last but not least, the numerous excellent staff members in the offices for their work. Their commitment to the cause was exemplary. The accomplished work is reward enough in itself.

The form for unity has been found. Now it is our task to fill it with content and life. Parliaments, governments, and parties have to help with this. But unity can only be established through the sovereign people, through the heads and hearts of human beings themselves. . . . It would be neither honest nor helpful if in this hour we were to keep quiet about the extent to which we are still divided from each other. The external means that forced division upon us did not achieve their aim of alienating us from each other. As inhuman as the Wall and the barbed wire were, they only let us experience all the more profoundly the will to come together. We experience it above all in Berlin, that city of central significance for the past and for the future. To see and feel the Wall daily did not stop us from believing in the other side and counting on them. Now the Wall is gone and that is the important thing.

But now that we have freedom, we must live up to it. We recognize the consequences of the different developments more clearly now than before. The material gap is the first thing that strikes the eye. Even though the people in the GDR were confronted with the economy of lack on a daily basis, made the best of it, and worked hard, the extent of the problems and the degree to which they lagged behind the West only became clear within the last few months. If we are supposed to succeed in overcoming this gap, then this requires not only assistance but, above all, mutual respect, as well.

For the Germans in the former GDR, unification is a daily process of existential readjustment that touches them immediately and personally. That frequently brings with it superhuman demands. A woman wrote to me that they were deeply grateful for freedom and yet had not anticipated the extent to which the transformation would grate on their nerves since it literally meant taking leave of oneself. Indeed, they did not desire anything more passionately than getting rid of their regime. But to be expected to replace simultaneously from one day to the next almost all the elements of their own lives with something new and unknown, that goes beyond all human capacities.

For the people in the West the joy about the fall of the Wall was immeasurably great. However, that unification is supposed to have something to do with their own personal life is either not clear or even highly unwelcome to many. It cannot remain like this. We first have to learn to understand each other better. We will only be on the right path when we truly recognize that both sides have had precious experiences and acquired important characteristics that are worth preserving in unity.

First regarding the West. Here one development must especially be stressed. Over the years the people developed a love for their commonwealth that is free of artificial feelings and nationalist pathos. To be sure, in the forty-year history of the Federal Republic there were many deep conflicts between the generations, social groups, and political directions. They were frequently carried out with great harshness but without that tendency to be destructive that placed great stress on the Weimar Republic. The youth rebellions in the late sixties contributed to a deepening of the democratic commitment in our society, despite all the wounds they caused. Along with the experience that we were able to settle conflicts, there also emerged a common faith in our constitution. . . .

Some people in the West are just now really discovering the advantages of their own state. Some who in the past belonged to the harshest critics of the internal affairs of the Federal Republic now say with concern that liberalism, federalism, and the connection with Europe might suffer in a unified Germany. I do not share such concerns. But it is at least gratifying when especially young people identify with their commonwealth in the West and feel in this context that the Bonn Republic has acquired a good reputation. As humans they grew up in an international and liberal civilization. They do not want to lose the acquired openness to the world. Why should they?

Now regarding the GDR. From its perspective, in the hour of unification distress on the one side is meeting up with prosperity on the other side. But it would be just as senseless as it would be inhuman if we believed that this meeting of East and West were the meeting of unsuccessful and successful forms of existence or even of bad and good ones. It is the systems whose success differs, not that of the people. . . . Every life has its meaning and its own dignity. No segment of life is futile, especially not one that is marked by distress. The Germans in the GDR accomplished humanly significant things under the most difficult circumstances, and we can only hope that these things will become a part of the substance of unified Germany. To overlook this would mean to fall victim to the deposed system one last time. Its design was to determine the thoughts and aims of people by means of absolute rules in state and society, indeed, to form a new, socialist unitary being. Had it succeeded in this, then this human being would indeed have to make an exit together with its system. But communism failed due to the futility of this project. The intellectual freedom of human beings prevailed against the presumptuousness of the system: the individual against the collective. The first beginnings of liberation were formed under this dictatorship. It is precisely lack of political freedom that sharpens our gaze for where the limits of legitimate politics lie and for the fact that there is a freedom of human beings outside of public affairs. Lack of freedom teaches freedom. Life in the GDR made people experienced in this regard.

The state, on the other hand, cared for its citizens according to the definitions of the system. But it did not acknowledge the human being in his or her need and dignity. Thus, people could frequently only survive if they helped each other silently. Need became the foundation of community. Solidarity did not remain an abstract word in grassroots platforms, but became a wholly personal reality. Courage and self-denial were necessary for people to participate in religious congregations and diaconal institutions. But it brought blessings. It supplied internal energy. And it was there that disabled citizens who were neglected by the state were cared for. In this way respect for life was practiced.

To be sure, the regime tried especially hard to make art and culture servile. Today people are vehemently debating the conduct of artists and the quality of their works. Nothing is being repressed here, and that is good. An ethical rigor in retrospect, however, is only persuasive and helpful when it serves self-evaluation. Art in the GDR often did not function as a political demonstration but rather as a force for changing life and making it more meaningful. The regime produced intellectual sterility. Art often nurtured the soul. For its part it also helped achieve the main objective pursued in the religious circles, namely, to extend the realm of inner freedom. From it gradually grew the liberation from the enforced lie, this most noxious of all poisons of the past decades, which undermined trust in the state, in society, between neighbors and, in the end, in oneself. Thus the freedom of truth became the most precious good that the people, with their own courage, achieved through their revolt.

We in the West were spared such tests. We can only show our respect and demonstrate it in the process of unification.

Since the fall of 1989, the human substance of the GDR became visible in a new way under incredibly difficult external conditions, in the citizens' movements, at the Round Table, and in the rebirth of the communities. In the *Volkskammer* people took on responsibilities, without being prepared for them, that could not have been greater. They occasionally were called amateur politicians. Is that supposed to be a criticism? They worked with commitment to resolve the most difficult problems, transcending party politics without nurturing a ritual of confrontations between parties. Over and over again they sought and found necessary compromises. They showed more than once how valuable it is "not always to expect or even hope for the worst from other people so that one's own picture of the world will be confirmed" (Richard Schröder).[2] When amateurs set such an example for professional politicians, that bodes well for democracy.

Now we are in the midst of the work. A particularly heavy and burdening chapter is the tradition of mistrust that the state security service left us. The power of the system is broken. But the trauma lives on. This cannot be worked through from the outside. In this matter there is no external Solomonic authority.[3] Those who were exposed to the contamination can best contribute to decontamination. . . . Wounds to the soul will only heal slowly. The dismantling of mistrust will take some time. It is an existential necessity. It would fail if we attempted to prosecute everyone; we would merely run the danger of ourselves becoming dangerous moralists. Our aim is a justice that has nothing to do with retribution but with reconciliation and internal peace. The concerns about our economic and social existence are now the top priority. Not the least of the reasons for the failure of the old system is its economic crises. It is all the more important that the people in the former GDR do not experience their realized freedom as a new form of need. They have opted for the social market economy that has proven itself in the West. The currency union paved the way for freedom of movement and economic initiative. The legal conditions for competition and social security were advanced. And yet, an orderly system alone does not produce economic productivity. It is the work of human beings. The social market economy does not come to pass in legal codes but rather in the thought and actions of human beings. Part of this is the experience that there can be no freedom without demands being made, that the boom will not come overnight. Those who are affected know this best. The caesura is deep and hard for many people: to retrain, adjust, move, search, begin anew. But experience teaches us that one's own initiative pays off.

No less important is our cooperation in this unified country. We have to act in solidarity now. . . . We now share the responsibility for the economic build-up in the new federal *Länder*, and we are jointly interested in its success. For what does not succeed will be just as much of a burden for the Germans in the West as it will be for the Germans in the East. Our constitutional task is to guarantee comparable living conditions and developmental opportunities for all Germans. Part of this is also an open and fair attitude toward our fellow citizens from foreign countries. One frequently hears today that nothing should be taken from anyone, that it is only a matter of distributing all that accrues. That is stated nicely in the marketing language of current political discourse. Looking at it soberly, however, this would mean nothing other than postponing sharing for the future. That could be too late for many people.

According to a Chinese proverb, mountains are turned into gold when brothers work together. It does not have to be gold, and it will not happen without sisters, either. But there is no road that leads around the recognition: to unite means to learn to share. German unity will not be able to be financed by high-yield loans alone. Publicly and privately we will have to plan differently, cooperate, lend a hand, and give. Many good examples demonstrate that this is possible, in the cases of hospitals, schools and universities, businesses and associations, clubs and families. Even town partnerships can develop into very solid cornerstones of our community. No theory, no matter how clever, no calculation, no matter how exact, can replace the fundamental experience made by human beings of all cultures and religions that human beings only really attend to each other when they share something. We will only be truly unified when we are willing to attend to each other in this way. We can do it. And many, I believe most of us, want to do it, as well.

The nation-state has not come to an end. But anyone who believes he is capable of mastering the future with it alone is living in a past age. No nation can resolve the most important tasks alone. Modern systems do not think and function nationally. That is true for security and ecology, for the economy and energy, for transportation and telecommunications, for research and science. Sovereignty in our age means cooperation in the community of states.

The European Community has created a convincing model for this. It coordinated national powers that are of decisive significance for peaceful relations on a supranational level. In the competition of the systems of East and West, the most important impulses for reforms in the East were derived from it. The Cold War has been overcome. Freedom and democracy will soon have been realized in all states. Not under pressure from superpowers, but voluntarily they can now deepen and institutionally guarantee their relations so that for the first time a common organization of life and peace can be created. A fundamentally new chapter is beginning in the history of the people of Europe. Its aim is pan-European unity. It is an enormous aim. We can achieve it, but also pass it by. We stand before the clear alternative of uniting Europe or falling back again into nationalist oppositions in the tradition of sorrowful historical examples.

Priority must now be given to concrete prospects for the economic and social development of the countries in Central, Eastern, and Southern Europe. The newly won freedom must be able to take root. That is why it should not be permitted to perish in need. The European Community can help in decisive ways in this. Above all, how Europe will progress will depend on it. We Germans have a key role to play in this. We are raising our voice for a constructive and joint Eastern policy for the entire West. Now that all Germans have become immediate neighbors of the Poles again, this nation which is so important for us, it is our task to urge that there be an association between the Community and Poland not in the distant future but in the near future. Similar measures apply to Czechoslovakia and to Hungary. The Soviet Union, to mention another example of central importance, needs close European cooperation as it travels its incomparably difficult road. It wants to overcome the old distance from Europe. It has recognized that the unification of Germany is not an obstacle to that, but, on the contrary, a condition for it.

That is the most important message of the truly significant Two-Plus-Four Conference. And we all know that the future stability in Europe depends on a significant contribution by Moscow. The western border of the Soviet Union should not become the eastern border of Europe. If we Germans send such signals, this happens in the long connection with the West, which has characterized our life in the Federal Republic, mobilized our energies, and brought forth fresh energies. Under no circumstances will we put our Atlantic and European partnership at risk. This is demanded by our own interests, which our fellow countrymen and countrywomen in the new federal *Länder* share. They know the significance our friendship above all with France will also have in the future and are themselves looking forward to the direct relations.

We will only make progress if we work together with our Western partners, above all in the Community and through it. Everything the member countries do through the Community for the whole of Europe strengthens the Community and its members. We Germans will serve our interests best and most quickly dispel the concerns of our neighbors if we do not let ourselves be surpassed in strengthening the Community and if we continue without any delay on our road toward economic and currency union, as well as to political union, just as we promised we would. The faster we Europeans solve our own problems, the better we will be able to fulfill our global obligations. In the context of the Cold War, Europeans continued to export tensions and weapons into the Southern hemisphere. Now it is time to support the CSCE process, to reduce armaments, and to emphatically increase our assistance for the South. Swords to plowshares, this great Biblical expression used during the peaceful revolution does not mean that we should renounce a reasonable, sufficient defensive capability; it means that we must still the hunger in the world and fight against need. The many young voices from all parts of unified Germany provide the encouragement for that.

Our shared responsibility among nations applies particularly to the environment. Not everything people can technically and economically accomplish should be foisted upon nature. More is at stake than the liveability of the earth for human beings, more than their own basis for life. Human beings can destroy something they did not create and something over which they should not have power: natural creation. They stripped themselves of this freedom. In the responsibility of freedom will be demonstrated whether they are ethically and, ultimately, biologically fit for survival. This task is global in the truest sense of the word. It presents itself worldwide to every country, to states, to communities, and to the individual.

The Basic Law now applies to all Germans. In the Unification Treaty we agreed that we will engage in determining the objectives of the state. It is a matter of constitutional tasks that should not be restricted by other laws, but that formulate duties for the lawgivers as well as for us all. Is there anything more urgent as an addendum to our goals than the protection of nature in its lack of rights? Do we have a greater task than the preservation of creation and, hence, the protection of coming generations? I know of none.

Today we are founding our common state. How well we succeed with unity on a human level will not be decided by governmental treaties, a constitution, or legislative decisions. That will be determined by the way all of us conduct ourselves, by our own openness and kindness for each other. . . . I am certain that we will succeed in bridging old and new divisions. We can combine the nurtured constitutional patriotism of the one side with the experienced human solidarity of the other to form a strong whole. We have the common will to accomplish the great tasks that our neighbors expect of us. We know how much more difficult other nations on earth have it at this time. The more convincingly we in united Germany succeed in living up to our responsibility for peace in Europe and in the world, the better our future at home will be, as well. History is giving us this opportunity. Let us make use of it with confidence and with faith.

NOTES

Source: Zanetti, 362-73.

1. The Paulskirche is the church in Frankfurt where the first German democratic national assembly met after the revolution of 1848; it was charged with formulating the first all-German constitution. It stands as a symbol of republicanism, tolerance, and democracy.

2. Richard Schröder is a protestant minister who actively called for reform during the political events in 1989/1990.

3. The Biblical King Solomon was known for his wisdom and good
judgment.

69

Stefan Heym, "Built on Sand"

"And everything will change here," says my Elizabeth with a
twinkle in her eye: her Intershop-look, as I call it, which always
appears on her face as soon as she steps into the Shop and sees the
selection of colorful Western goods, only obtainable for hard currency; but now no one needs the Shop any more, one simply heads
across the border; of course, the currency issue is still problematic.
"Change a lot," she says, "and particularly in real estate–it will
rise astronomically in value." I flinch: real estate. How in the
world does she even know that term?

"We can be truly happy," she continues, "that we bought a
house from the Communal Housing Administration at a time when
no one else was thinking of such things, and for only 35,000 marks,
peanuts; before long, the house will be worth a half a million, if not
a whole million, in hard D-marks, while our dear neighbors still
just pay their rent to the CHA and thus can be evicted at any time,
once the German reunification is in place with its new laws; but possessions are possessions, no one can challenge them, not now or in the
future. And who was it who pounded it into your head that you
should buy, until you finally hired a lawyer and legalized the purchase?"

"Elizabeth," I say, "you are a genius."

She loves to hear that, my Elizabeth, and the conversation
might actually have continued on in this way, full of joy and harmony, had the gravel not crunched in front of the house: a car, and
obviously a very heavy one. "Company?," I say. "In the middle of
the week?"

She goes to the window: "But that's the guy . . ."

"Who?"

"The guy who was here before," she says, "twice, even."

"And why," I ask, "didn't I know of this until today?"

"I didn't want to upset you," she says. And adds: "He parked
across the street, got out, and crept around the house a few times.
He also stood still from time to time, looking around as if he had
lost something, and I wanted to go out and ask him if he were

maybe from the Stasi, but of course, it's been dismantled, and before I could decide what to do, he was gone."

"You're sure that he is the one," I say, "because I see two of them."

She gulps. "He's multiplied."

"And which was your guy then," I ask, "the one with the small-brimmed little hat, the little rotund fellow, or the gaunt one with the corpse-like disposition?"

"The short one," she says.

"The short one," I say, "so so." But before I can ask why she had thought someone like that could have unsettled me, the doorbell already begins to ring.

*

Since a short time ago we are using a Chinese gong as a doorbell, and its deep ding-dong-dang was a delight every time; only in this particular instance does the foreign ringing get on my nerves. My Elizabeth, too, stands there like an oak tree and bites her lower lip.

"Go ahead, open it," I say. "The gentlemen would like something from us, and I for one would like to know just what it is." We both go to the door, hand in hand, together is better. The short one takes off his little hat and makes some sort of bow; the gaunt one flashes his pearly teeth: "Mr. and Mrs. Bodelschwingh, I presume?"

My name is indeed Bodelschwingh, as in the famous Pastor Bodelschwingh, although I and my family are in no way related to him; my Elizabeth took the name in marriage.

"May we?," said the gaunt one.

The twinkle has reappeared in my Elizabeth's eye, but it is quite a different glimmer than before, dark and threatening, her "in-spite-of-all-that" look, as I call it.

The short one wipes his shoe soles back and forth across the doormat, carefully and meticulously: as if the house belonged to him, it occurred to me, although I don't know why. And as he takes off his light, dust-colored overcoat, he introduces himself: "Prottwedel, Elmar, if you please." – "Nice to meet you," I say.

"Schwiebus," says the other one, and offers me his card: "Schwiebus von Schwiebus, LLD, Schwiebus and Krings, consultations in real estate."

"We," says my Elizabeth, "require no consultations."

In the meantime Mr. Prottwedel has conducted himself, with a determination one could only characterize as somnambulistic, through the open sliding door into our living room, and steers his way to the Biedermeier chair we had just taken great pains to have restored–just try to find a master re-upholsterer and such a gold-and-floret-striped fabric, so true to the style, around here–and sinks with a sigh into the seat that seems to be constructed for a posterior like his, and says: "This was my grandpa's favorite chair. Only it was upholstered in green back then, the chair, that is, green with lavender rosettes. My grandpa died in this chair: heart failure."

My Elizabeth pales. Not because of the death scene, she's not that sensitive, but because of the possibility that the chair actually could have belonged to Mr. Prottwedel's grandpa; we had not actually purchased it ourselves, but had instead inherited it from our predecessor, comrade Watzlick. When we took over the house from him, it fell to me as department head. Watzlick said: I am leaving the chair to you, comrade Bodelschwingh, we will be decorating in a modern style in the capital.

"Perhaps," Dr. Schwiebus has a very polished accent, probably from around Lubeck, "perhaps," he says to Mr. Prottwedel, "we ought to divulge the purpose of our visit."

"It seems to me," says my Elizabeth, "about time."

Mr. Prottwedel purses his lips into something resembling a buttonhole. "Surely, Mrs. Bodelschwingh, you noticed my previous appearances in front of your property."

"Twice," nods my Elizabeth, "twice."

"I didn't alarm you, I hope," says Mr. Prottwedel. "It only has to do with memories. A happy youth, which I spent here, with one of the dearest fathers ever, who at that time, you should note, acquired this house and the ground upon which it stands."

"Mr. Prottwedel," says Dr. Schwiebus, "lives, thank goodness, in good circumstances. He is the owner of a brewery, not unknown among us in the West, as well as other interests that fund him sufficiently. In other words, he has no dire need that could make it seem appropriate for him to trouble himself over the re-acquisition of real estate that rightfully belongs to him."

"Re-acquisition!" The slight redness arising in my Elizabeth's face: I know it well, a warning signal. "Re-acquisition," she says, "what do you mean by that?"

"It certainly pleases me," says Mr. Prottwedel, "to be able to observe in what good condition the two of you, Mr. and Mrs. Bodelschwingh, have kept the property."

"How could it be otherwise," nods Dr. Schwiebus. "After all, the Bodelschwinghs, described to us as trustworthy, tidy people, live on the property themselves."

The pink tint in my Elizabeth's face has become a definitive red. "We don't just live in the house," she says, "it belongs to us. Just so you know, Mr. Prottwedel, and you too, Dr. Schwiebus: we bought it and paid for it with our own money, the chair included. There is a sales contract, a valid one, and everything has been recorded in the land register, everything quite legal; you can look it up yourselves."

"Dr. Schwiebus has already looked it up in the land register," says Mr. Prottwedel. "Still, may one not simply visit the house and look around?"

"We understand, Mr. Prottwedel," says my Elizabeth, "your need to pursue your memories." And she adds, almost as an afterthought, "particularly since it doesn't cost you anything, not any more as it did just a short while ago, no twenty-five marks to cross the border."[1]

"Now," says Mr. Prottwedel, "I would very much like to see the upper floor."

*

The steps, first from the one side, then from the other, resound in my brain: it's enough to drive you crazy.

"Why," I say, "don't I just throw these guys out?"

"It's not their house," says my Elizabeth, "for them to stroll around in as they please."

"They're behaving themselves," I say, "like conquerors."

"And the bathroom," says my Elizabeth, "isn't even clean." The outburst, prefigured so long ago by her reddening face, arrives. "And we in the East," she cries out, "brought this upon ourselves!"

"Get a hold of yourself," I admonish her, "they're not deaf."

But she can't be controlled. "It's our house! In my own house I can scream just as much as I want to!"

Then silence. Then Mr. Prottwedel's voice. "Well, here we are again!"

"And how was your tour?," asks my Elizabeth.

Mr. Prottwedel steps behind the period chair, as if seeking protection from her scowl. "The layout of the rooms," he says, "exactly as I remember it."

"Memory," says Dr. Schwiebus, "is half of life."–"And the furnishings," says Mr. Prottwedel, "so traditional!"

After a reflective pause Dr. Schwiebus remarks that he doesn't quite understand our defensive attitude, to say nothing of our resentment: aside form refreshing his memory, Mr. Prottwedel's sole intention is to clear up the ownership questions regarding the house and the lot–at this point he takes a small piece of paper out from behind the kerchief in the outer breast pocket of his jacket–at Marshall Konyev Strasse, previously Hindenburg Strasse number 27, as soon as possible.

"What is there to clear up?!" My Elizabeth stamps her foot. "The house and the lot belong to us, and possessions fall under state protection, always and everywhere, in the East as well as in the West."

"That's the point," says Dr. Schwiebus, "exactly the point: or is it not also in our best interests to avoid the eventual confrontations that might arise once the two German states are happily reunified, with the appropriate legal consequences?" And he takes out of his attache case, black Moroccan leather, a pile of papers, which he spreads out on the table in front of me. On the basis of these papers, he instructs us, it is clear that Mr. Dietmar Prottwedel, the late father of his friend and client Elmar Prottwedel, had legally purchased both the house and the lot at what was formerly Hindenburg Strasse number 27 from a certain Mr. Siegfried Rothmund, who had left Germany shortly thereafter for an unknown destination; and moreover, by an odd twist of fate, had acquired them at the same low price, 35,000 marks, at which we, the Bodelschwinghs, had obtained the property from our Communal Housing Administration; and here is the sales contract.

"Not," says Mr. Prottwedel, "not that we would even dream of throwing you out in the street."

My Elizabeth's lips are quivering. "Out in the street in front of our own house!"

"Or," smiles Mr. Prottwedel, "of making any other demands on you at the present time."

"What are we supposed to do," I say, "pay all over again for something we have already paid for once?"

"Money," interposes Dr. Schwiebus, "no one has said anything about that." And he instructs us again that he and Mr. Prottwedel are far more concerned about title and legal matters, in which case our, the family Bodelschwingh's, claims to the house and lot at the current Marshall Konyev Strasse number 27 were clearly not in question. Only that Mr. Prottwedel also had claims, and it is a question of whose claims were the older ones and, what was even more important considering the changing legal situation, what sort of people it was from whom we had acquired the property in question, and how these individuals had acquired it, and whether or not the nature of that acquisition, according to the laws that would probably soon be in effect in our part of Germany as well, had been legal and otherwise in order.

"You see, my parents' house," explains Mr. Prottwedel, "was expropriated." And he rolls his eyes with pleasure, "Without compensation."

*

This damned waiting. We knew they would come back. Only we didn't know when, and I often found myself, after returning home from my long-since senseless job at my long-since senseless office, sitting in my room and straining to detect any noise from outside. We would wake up in the middle of the night, you sense it when the other person is lying awake next to you; a breath that is too short, a sudden movement, and you begin to think: that just can't be true, you think, life runs its course just fine and then something that seems like it is forever, and if not forever then at least for a considerable amount of time, collapses in an instant; but nevertheless, the house still stood, still belonged to us, with a roof under which we could crawl.

"No," says my Elizabeth, "it just can't happen the way they think it will. One state or two, possessions are possessions, and especially those people over there, what would happen to them if they simply allowed someone to waltz in and say that this was his grandpa's favorite chair."

Silence doesn't help; the fear has to be expressed, otherwise you go crazy. "But they are the victors, after all," I say. "And we ourselves invited them over here. The Wall torn down and then Germany! Germany! Sure, it was no cup of tea before, year after year that eternal Yes and the eternal obedience and some mere trifle in exchange, a little preferential treatment here and there, but at least the house they let you have was yours, and you could sleep peacefully at night."

"You are giving up," she says, "even before the first shot has been fired. Who is this Mr. Prottwedel, anyway? A lousy little businessman; there are thousands of them just like him running around over there. And what about you? How many people were you in charge of in your position? If you had really been such a nobody, they would have fired you a long time ago. And do you think that those people over there, the Ministers and State Secretaries and Chief Executives, don't have need for someone like you, who knows the ropes and how they are laid out and the relationships between the departments. Just wait, before long you'll be showing Prottwedel and Schwiebus the hole the carpenter left in the house for them."

That's my Elizabeth, quite a character, and always pouncing on every opportunity that presents itself. And I realize: the rules according to which things operated in this republic really aren't all that different from the rules according to which superiors and subordinates approach each other over there, and I honestly feel moved and say: "Once again, Elizabeth, you're right. We're not going to let ourselves be intimidated by people the likes of them."

*

Nevertheless we were startled by the renewed crunching of the gravel and the ensuing ding-dong-dang.

"It must be the mailman," I say, and think how funny it would be if it really were. The twinkle returns to my Elizabeth's eyes and she grabs my hand, which she never would have done had she thought it really were the mailman, and we support each other, morally that is, on the way to the front door. But it is neither the mailman nor Mr. Prottwedel nor his friend Dr. Schwiebus; it is a woman who is standing in the doorway, a dark woman who has peculiar facial features and who, as we step aside in amazement, enters and heads for the period chair with exactly the same somnambulistic determination Mr. Prottwedel had displayed just a short while ago.

"I assume," I said, "that that was your grandpa's favorite chair." She is taken aback. "How did you know?"

"And your name is Rothmund?"

"Eva Rothmund," she confirms, "from Tel Aviv," and lets herself fall into the chair in which she appears appreciably more trim than Mr. Prottwedel.

"And you, too, are chasing your memories," I say, "now that it doesn't cost anything anymore, not even the twenty-five marks to cross the border."

"I don't have any memories," she says. "Not of this house, not even of Germany, except for an indirect one: of this chair, about which my grandfather told me so often."

"And what do you want?," I say.

"I am his heir."

"Oh, you are," I say, and then, as a thought occurs to me, a nasty one, "well, that certainly changes things!"

"Why?," she asks. "And how?"

"With your help, Ms. Rothmund," I announce, "I'll stick it to Prottwedel and Schwiebus."

My Elizabeth, though, doesn't seem to think much of the idea. "But, Ms. Rothmund," she asks, "didn't your grandfather sell this property to a certain Mr. Prottwedel?"

"Sell it?" Ms. Rothmund stands up from her grandfather's former favorite chair and takes out of her handbag, cheap brown leather, a pile of papers, which she spreads out on the table. "On the basis of these papers it is clear," she says, "that I am the sole and rightful heir of my grandfather Siegfried Rothmund, and that he, on February 23, 1936, threatened by the SS Stormtrooper Dietmar Prottwedel with arrest and deportation to a concentration camp, signed over his house and lot, Hindenburg Strasse number 27, to the aforementioned SS Stormtrooper Prottwedel."

"What do you mean, threatened?," says my Elizabeth. "What is decisive regarding the ownership of real estate is not the discussions that took place during negotiations, but whether your grandfather received the purchase price of 35,000 marks or not." And I can see what she has in mind: to her, the young lady from Israel, to the extent that she might have the prior claim to our property, presented the greater danger; surely with Prottwedel and Schwiebus, particularly after the appearance of Ms. Rothmund, some sort of settlement could be worked out; West or East, at least the matter would be kept among Germans.

"Decisive, you said," says Ms. Rothmund, "decisive for ownership is the receipt of the purchase price?"

"We have," says my Elizabeth, "already seen the contract your grandfather worked out with Mr. Dietmar Prottwedel."

"Here," says Ms. Rothmund as she grabs one of the papers, "is an affidavit, signed in my grandfather's own hand, composed on the day before his death in the presence of a notary public, stating that the sale of the house and property at Hindenburg Strasse number 27 as well as the attendant sales contract are null and void, since the buyer, SS Stormtrooper Dietmar Prottwedel, withheld the contractually agreed upon sum of 35,000 marks, which in any case only represented a fraction of the true value of the real estate in question."

My Elizabeth gasps for breath. "But where do we stand in all of this?," she finally says, and adds, after a long minute, "you also have to think of us, Ms. Rothmund!"

I'm not so sure that was quite the right thing to say to Ms. Rothmund, who had made a special trip from Israel; but what is one supposed to say in such a situation, now that everything is changing here?

NOTES

Source: *Auf Sand gebaut: Sieben Geschichten aus der unmittelbaren Vergangenheit* (Munich: C. Bertelsmann, 1990), pp. 34-48. Translated by Bill Hutfilz.

1. Twenty-five German marks was the minimum daily sum every West German visitor had to exchange at the border when entering the GDR.

Glossary

Alexanderplatz Main public square in East Berlin.

Alliance 90 Founded on 30 January 1990 as an alliance of six oppositional parties and political groups for the March *Volkskammer*
elections. Their platform supported a gradual rapprochement
of the two Germanies and rejected a speedy currency union between the two German states.

Alliance for Germany Three of the more conservative GDR parties
and initiative groups (Democratic Awakening, the German Social
Union, and the East German CDU) formed the "Alliance for
Germany" in the race for the March 1990 *Volkskammer* elections.

Article 23 of the Basic Law Defines the geographical domain to which
the Basic Law applies. According to its first paragraph, the Basic
Law is in force "initially" in the former western occupation
zones. The second paragraph specifies: "It will also go into force
in the other parts of Germany after their accession." Most political parties and groups supported unification according to the
model offered by Article 23; the PDS and many intellectuals
spoke up against this model and supported a confederation of
the two German states.

Basic Law Provisional constitution of the FRG, put into effect in 1949
in order "to give a new order to the state for a transitional period." Its preamble expresses the wish "to complete the unity
and freedom of Germany in free self-determination." The Basic Law set the framework for two paths toward unification:
Article 23 provided for a fast unification of the two German
states in the form of accession, whereas Article 146 included the
possibility of unification on the basis of a wholly new German
state with a new constitution ratified by a constitutional committee.

Basic Treaty 1972 Treaty regulating relations between the GDR and
the FRG, a product of the early years of detente and Chancellor
Willy Brandt's *Ostpolitik* ("Eastern Policy").

Beeskow Small GDR town along the river Spree in the vicinity of
Frankfurt/Oder.

Berlin Charité Well-known Berlin hospital where the famous German
surgeon Dr. Sauerbruch practiced.

Bloc parties Christian Democrats, Liberal Democrats, National
Democrats, Farmers' Party, SED, and other political organizations such as the trade unions that were represented in the GDR

Volkskammer and always voted as a unified "bloc," affirming resolutions brought to parliament by the Politburo.

Bonn Declaration Joint statement by the governments of the FRG and Soviet Union from 13 June 1989 acknowledging every people's right to self-determination.

Branch of Commercial Coordination Branch of the GDR government directed by Alexander Schalck-Golodkowski and responsible for handling the exchange of foreign currency.

Brandenburg One of the five new *Länder* of the FRG after unification.

Brandenburg Gate Commissioned in 1788 by the Prussian king Friedrich Wilhelm II, this monument was built in Greek style with six Dorian colums carrying the goddess of peace in a chariot; it was badly damaged in the Second World War and reconstructed from 1956 to 1958. After the erection of the Berlin Wall in 1961 it became the symbol of divided Berlin and the German will to unity. On 12 December 1989 it was reopened after 28 years.

Bundesbank West German Federal Bank.

Bundesrat The upper house of the West German parliament, composed of representatives from the governments of the *Länder*, or federal states.

Bundestag The lower house of the West German parliament, composed of elected representatives from individual districts.

Bundeswehr West German army.

Cadre politics East German name for politics decided by a small group ("cadre") of insiders who have exclusive access to power and the decision-making process.

CDU The Christian Democratic Union.

Central Committee Formally the highest party organ in communist parties.

Checkpoint Charlie Famous Berlin border crossing between the American and Soviet occupation zones; dismantled in June 1990.

Christian Democratic Union Christian conservative party that dominated West German politics throughout most of the postwar era; under the leadership of Konrad Adenauer it helped shape West Germany in the immediate postwar years; Helmut Kohl has headed the party since the early 1980s.

Christian Social Union Bavarian Catholic party of regional significance; it is a sister party of the CDU and part of Kohl's ruling coalition.

COMECON International economic organization of the socialist states (Bulgaria, Czechoslovakia, the GDR, Cuba, Mongolia, Poland, Romania, the Soviet Union, Hungary, and Vietnam) founded in Moscow in 1949. Its most important task was the co-ordination of production and trade among individual member states.

Committee for Investigating Misuse of Power and Corruption Official committee of the *Ministerrat* of the GDR.

Communal Housing Administration GDR agency that administered state-owned property.

CPSU Communist Party of the Soviet Union.

CSCE Conference for Security and Cooperation in Europe; the first meeting was held in Helsinki in 1973 with the participation of 33 European countries including the Soviet Union, Canada and the US. In the Final Act of Helsinki all signatory nations agreed to a set of 10 binding principles as the future foundation for coexistence. The CSCE process played an important part in the overcoming of the Cold War.

CSU Christian Social Union.

D-mark West German hard currency which was introduced in the GDR on July 1, 1990 according to the terms of the currency union with West Germany.

DA Democratic Awakening.

Day of German Unity Originally celebrated in West Germany on June 17, in commemoration of the workers' uprising in the GDR on that date in 1953; after unification, celebrated on October 3, in recognition of German unification on 3 October 1990.

Democracy Now One of the citizens' movements that called for political reforms in the GDR in the fall of 1989.

Democratic Awakening Initiative group made up mostly of church activists. It was founded in July 1989, officially established as an oppositional group on 1 October 1989, and formed itself as a political party in December 1989. In its "Leipzig Program" it supported the "right of Germans for unity" and the establishment of a social-ecological market economy. It later became a member of the "Alliance for Germany."

Democratic restructuring Demand for a democratic restructuring of the GDR formulated by several oppositional groups who believed in democratizing all areas of life and building a society of solidarity. It is coined in analogy to Gorbachev's concept of perestroika.

Der Spiegel Bi-weekly West German news magazine.

Die Zeit German weekly newspaper.

DSU German Social Union.

EC European Community.

Elbow society Negative designation used by GDR left-wing intellectuals to refer to capitalist societies, especially the FRG. The implication is that in such a society you have to use your elbows to push your way through the competition.

European Common Market Economic union of the member states of the European Community; free trade agreement and open customs in effect as of 1992. A joint currency is planned to be phased in over the coming years.

European Community Political and economic community of twelve European states with its legislative seat, the European Parliament, in Brussels; its aim is eventually to incorporate these individual states into a political and currency union whose government, the European Council, would act as a unified body regarding foreign and domestic policy matters.

European Council The Council was established in 1949 after an agreement was reached among the European nations to protect the principles of European heritage and to support economic and social programs; it has only an advisory function for the European governments.

European Human Rights Commission Central agency for processing claims against human rights violations; established in 1954, each member country of the European Council sends a representative to this agency.

FAZ Frankfurter Allgemeine Zeitung.

FDP Free Democratic Party.

Five-percent clause Clause in the Basic Law of the FRG that prevents parties receiving less than five percent of the total vote in an election from being represented in parliament. This clause did not apply to the area of the former GDR in the first all-German elections in December 1990.

Four-Powers Agreement Agreement from 3 September 1971 between the four Allied powers and the two German states regulating traffic between the FRG and West Berlin, economic relations between the FRG and West Berlin, communications between East and West Berlin, as well as the exchange of small territories and the diplomatic representation of Berlin by the FRG.

Frankfurter Allgemeine Zeitung One of the two Frankfurt newspapers distributed nationally in Germany; it generally tends to support a more conservative political and cultural agenda.

Free Democratic Party Liberal democratic Party in the FRG. West German Foreign Minister Hans-Dietrich Genscher was this party's leading politician during the 1980's, and he was one of the architects of German unification.

Free German Trade Union Association (FGTUA) East German trade union confederation (German acronym: *FDGB*).

FRG The Federal Republic of Germany.

GDR The German Democratic Republic.

GDR-mark GDR currency. The international exchange rate before the fall of 1989 was four GDR-marks for one West German D-mark, but the GDR regime forced West Germans to exchange currency at a rate of one to one.

Genscher Plan West German Foreign Minister Hans-Dietrich Genscher's plan for unification, which called for a gradual, step-by-step process of unification once East German *Volkskammer* elections had taken place.

German Farmers' Party One of the GDR bloc parties that supported the leadership role of the SED. It left the bloc on 12 December 1989. Its political agenda included support of a social market economy, German unity in the form of a gradual process of rapprochement, and economic restructuring in the GDR.

German Social Union (DSU) Founded January 20, 1990 as a union of 12 different oppositional groups of conservative persuasion, it later became a member of the "Alliance for Germany." It was chaired by the Protestant minister Hans-Wilhelm Ebeling.

German Unity Fund Fund established in May 1990 by Chancellor Kohl and the leaders of the West German *Länder* to finance German unification.

GFP German Farmer's Party (DBP).

Government of national responsibility Designation for the GDR government under Prime Minister Hans Modrow. The SED and the opposition agreed to form a government that included all parties and, for the first time in GDR history, was made up primarily by non-communists.

Grand coalition Coalition between the two largest parties in the GDR (CDU and SPD) after the March 1990 *Volkskammer* election.

Green border On May 4, 1989, Hungary opened its border to Austria, and many GDR citizens used this crossing to flee to the West.

Green Party (East) Newly founded party in the GDR that demanded political change and a far-reaching ecological reconstruction of the GDR.

Group of Democratic Socialists One of the smaller initiative groups from the early months of political resistance in the GDR.

Helsinki Final Act Final agreement reached between the participating nations at the first CSCE conference in Helsinki in 1973.

Hesse One of the original *Länder* of the FRG.

IFA-conglomerate for automobiles In the GDR major industries and factories were owned collectively by the people and organized in so-called "conglomerates." The IFA-conglomerate produced automobiles, trucks, and agricultural equipment. IFA stands for "Industrieller Fahrzeugbau" (industrial automobile production).

Independent Investigation Committee (IIC) Independent committee formed by the Round Table to investigate cases of government abuse under the SED regime.

Independent Women's Organization Founded 17 February 1990 to represent the political interests of women in the GDR independent of the existing parties and citizens' movements; it was represented at the Round Table and filled one cabinet post in the Modrow administration; it formed an alliance with the East German Green Party for the *Volkskammer* elections of 18 March 1990.

Initiative for Peace and Human Rights Citizens' initiative founded in 1985; it was the oldest independent oppositional group in the GDR. Its political mission included demilitarization in East and West and the protection of minorities and foreigners. It joined together with the New Forum and Democracy Now to form the "Alliance 90" for the March 1990 *Volkskammer* elections.

Initiative Group Social-Democratic Party of the GDR Inititative group for the foundation of a Social-Democratic Party in the GDR; signed the joint declaration of oppositional groups in the GDR in October 1989.

Intershop Duty-free shops along the Western transit routes through the GDR; Western luxury products such as television sets, computers, radios, clothing, etc. were available here for those who could pay in hard Western currencies.

Kurfürstendamm The main shopping artery in West Berlin; many theaters and clubs are located nearby.

Länder German federal states. In East Germany, *Länder* referred to the twelve states that made up the GDR; these were converted to five states plus Berlin in the unification treaty with the FRG.

Laws of the Allied Control Board The Allied Control Board established the laws for occupied Germany after the war. By 1948, the allies increasingly disagreed over joint Allied policy for Germany, and this caused the Soviet Union to leave the Allied Control Board.

LDPG Liberal Democratic Party of Germany (FDPD).

Leadership role of the SED The SED was the leading party in the GDR and claimed its leadership role in all realms of society.

League of Free Democrats Alliance of the three liberal parties in the GDR, the Free Democratic Party, the German Forum Party, and the Liberal Democratic Party of Germany for the March 1990 *Volkskammer* elections. It supported speedy unification and an economic and currency union with the FRG by the end of 1990.

Liberal Democratic Party of Germany Founded in 1945, it was one of the four bloc parties in the GDR. It left the bloc on 5 December 1989 and changed its name to the Liberal Democratic Party. It later fused with the West German Free Democratic Party.

London Declaration Declaration made by NATO on 6 July 1990 stating that it will never launch a first strike against the Warsaw Pact nations.

Marshall Plan US Plan for economic and financial reconstruction of postwar Europe.

Mass organizations GDR mass organizations such as the trade unions, the Young Pioneers, etc.

Mecklenburg-Vorpommern One of the five new *Länder* of the FRG after unification.

Ministerrat Council of 23 ministers that made up the GDR cabinet and constituted the leadership of the government; its chair filled the role of prime minister.

Ministry for Trade and Supply GDR ministry overseeing commerce.

Monday demonstrations Beginning in October 1989, Protestant church leaders in Leipzig and other GDR cities called for peaceful demonstrations against the political regime on Monday evenings. By November, hundreds of thousands of people participated in these weekly demonstrations in Leipzig alone.

Moscow Treaty Treaty signed on 20 September 1955 by West German Chancellor Konrad Adenauer regulating the reopening of diplomatic relations between the government of the FRG and the Soviet Union. It reflected the so-called Hallstein-doctrine, which claimed that the FRG should be the sole diplomatic representative of all of Germany.

National Defense Council of the GDR Formed in 1960, it was responsible for the coordination of national defense. The General Secretary of the Central Committee of the SED served as chair of the National Defense Council, thus securing for the party full control over the army.

National Democratic Party of Germany Founded in 1948 and since 1949 one of the four bloc parties in the GDR; it left the bloc on 7 December 1989; the NDPG ceased to exist as an independent party after the March 1990 *Volkskammer* elections.

National Front Alliance of all political parties and mass organizations of the GDR under the leadership of the SED, it constituted all the organizations represented in the *Volkskammer.*

National People's Army GDR army; founding member of the Warsaw Pact.

NATO North Atlantic Treaty Organization; military alliance of North American and European countries (Belgium, Canada, Denmark, France, Great Britain, Ireland, Italy, Luxemburg, the Netherlands, Norway, Portugal, and the US) established in 1949; Greece and Turkey joined in 1952, the FRG in 1955, and Spain in 1982.

NDPG National Democratic Party of Germany.

Negotiations on Conventional Armed Forces in Europe Vienna negotiations, 30 August 1990 (and subsequent dates).

Neue Berliner Illustrierte (NBI) East-Berlin news magazine.

Neues Deutschland Formerly the official newspaper of the SED, now connected with the PDS.

New Forum The largest and most prominent of the citizens' movements in the GDR that demanded political reforms in the fall of 1989.

Nomenclature cadre Group ("cadre") of the most prominent GDR leaders of the inner political circle who had access to bank accounts, hard currency, luxury items, vacation homes, etc.

Northrhine-Westphalia One of the original *Länder* of the FRG.

Oder-Neiße border Eastern border of the GDR with Poland.

Office for National Security Otherwise known as the "Stasi," the State Security Agency, this agency was founded in 1950 and disssolved in 1990 by citizens' committees under the direction of the Round Table. It was responsible for the gathering of intelligence as well as for national security questions. Increasingly it came to focus on the surveillance of the GDR population, and by 1989 the office had swollen to a size of 85,000 regular staff members and about 109,000 unofficial collaborators. By February 1990 the citizens' committees secured about five million files that had been held in the Office for National Security.

Office of Constitutional Protection   The West German intelligence agency.

Ossis   Derogatory name for people from East Germany.

Patronization   The GDR citizens often criticized the SED and its leaders for treating the GDR electorate in a patronizing manner.

PDS   Party of Democratic Socialism; the name adopted by the Socialist Unity Party after the beginning of democratization in the GDR; it gave up the SED's claim to a leadership position and reorganized under its new chair, Gregor Gysi.

Peace circles   Loose circles of citizens in the GDR, usually connected with the Protestant Church, working for world peace.

People's Police   GDR civil police force responsible for non-criminal activities such as directing traffic, etc.

People's property   In socialist societies, major businesses and property are collectively owned by the people, that is, by the state.

Politbureaucracy   A derogatory term, formed by the fusion of the words Politburo and bureaucracy, for that type of political administration typical of state-centralized socialism.

Politburo   Executive Committee of the Central Committee of the SED.

Potsdam Agreement   After the defeat of the Third Reich, the US, Great Britain, France, and the Soviet Union settled on a policy of occupation for all occupation zones as well as Germany's provisional Eastern borders, thereby determining the de facto division of the country.

Power monopoly   In the GDR the cadre politicians and the SED constituted the sole political power in the state and opposition was not permitted.

Really-existing socialism   Designation for the brand of socialism, including Stalinism, that was realized in the Eastern European countries and the Soviet Union in the postwar era.

Reichstag   Berlin building that housed the German parliament after 1871. It was set on fire by the Nazis in 1933, who then placed the blame on communist agitators. After World War II it served as an exhibition hall and it is now designated to be the future house of the all-German parliament.

Republicans   Right-wing West German political party that has led a campaign against foreigners in Germany; its leader is Franz Schönhuber.

Restructuring See democratic restructuring.

Rome Treaties The Rome Treaties of 1957 are the foundation that established the European Economic Community.

Round Table Formed on 7 December 1989 as an instrument of democratic control over the Modrow government; the Round Table included representatives from the SED/PDS, the bloc parties, Democratic Awakening, the Independent Women's Organization, the Initiative for Peace and Human Rights, the Green Party, the New Forum, Democracy Now, the Social Democratic Party, the Unified Left, as well as the trade unions; it held weekly meetings under the observation of Protestant church leaders until the *Volkskammer* elections on March 18, 1990; the most important political body in the GDR until the elections, it presided over the dissolution of the Office for National Security.

Sachsen-Anhalt One of the five new *Länder* of the FRG after unification.

Saxony One of the five new *Länder* of the FRG after unification.

Schalck-Golodkowski firms Firms etsablished by Alexander Schalck-Golodkowski, who was in charge of the Bureau of Commercial Coordination in the GDR.

SED The Socialist Unity Party of the GDR.

Social Charta Set of guidelines proposed by the Round Table and passed into law by the *Volkskammer* in which the social security of all GDR citizens was established as the basis for negotiations about unification with the FRG.

Social-Democratic Party West German social democratic party; under the leadership of Willy Brandt and Helmut Schmidt it controlled the West German parliament in the seventies and initiated the first rapprochement with the GDR (*Ostpolitik*); otherwise it was relegated in the postwar period to the role of the major opposition party in West Germany; its leaders during the process of unification were Hans-Jochen Vogel and Oskar Lafontaine.

Socialist Unity Party Formed in 1946 following the alliance of the German Communist Party and the Social-Democratic Party, it was the dominant political organization of the GDR. The SED claimed the leadership role in GDR politics. After the democratic turn in 1989, it changed its name to the Party of Democratic Socialism (PDS).

Sorbian citizens of the GDR Ethnic minority of Slavic origin in the GDR.

Soviet-German Declaration Joint West German and Soviet Declaration of friendship and cooperation, signed June 1989.

SPD The German Social-Democratic Party.

Sputnik Russian newspaper written in German and available in the GDR. Because it reported on the democratic changes in the Soviet Union, it was banned by the SED.

Staatsrat GDR council of state, a collective head of state elected by the *Volkskammer;* its chair served the function of ceremonial head of state.

Stasi Acronym for *Staatssicherheit,* "State Security," or the GDR Office for National Security.

State Security Force Surveillance network controlled by the Office for National Security.

State Treaty The first State Treaty between the FRG and the GDR, establishing an economic, currency, and social union. This treaty went into effect on 1 July 1990.

Surpreme Soviet Collective leadership of the Soviet Union, established in 1936.

Task Force on Christian Churches Informal task force during the peaceful revolution comprised of representatives of the various Christian churches in the GDR.

Third way The political alternative of democratic socialism, thought of as an alternative to the choice between state socialism and consumer capitalism. This option was preferred by many left-wing intellectuals over the decision to unify Germany as a capitalist country.

Thuringia One of the five new *Länder* of the FRG after unification.

Trabi Abbreviation for "Trabant," the name of the economy car most widely owned by citizens of the GDR, the equivalent of the Volkswagen in the West.

Transit Treaty Treaty regulating passage between West Germany and East Germany, it was one of the agreements negotiated with the GDR in the early seventies.

Treaty of Görlitz Treaty between the GDR and Poland to put an end to border disputes between Germany and Poland. It was signed in 1950.

Treaty on Germany Treaty singed on 23 October 1954 in which the Western allies agreed to end the occupation of Germany and support the integration of West Germany into the Western alliance. This treaty also expressed the Allies' support for a future reunification of Germany.

Treaty on the Non-Proliferation of Nuclear Weapons Treaty signed on 1 July 1968 to prevent the spread of nuclear arms.

Treuhand Organization Institute in Berlin established to privatize all formerly socialized industries and state property of the GDR.

Turn, turn-around, radical turn Translation of the German term *Wende*, which was applied throughout the peaceful revolution to designate the political turning point in the GDR. It refers to the changes demanded by the democratic movements in the fall of 1989 and the subsequent process of democratic restructuring.

Two-Plus-Four Talks Officials of the two German governments and representatives of the governments of Great Britain, France, the Soviet Union, and the United States (the victorious Allied powers of World War II) negotiated at these talks the legal framework for the process of German unification.

Unification Treaty Also called the "Second State Treaty," this second treaty between the FRG and the GDR established the parameters for the unification of the two German states according to Article 23 of the West German Basic Law. It went into effect on 3 October 1990, the Day of German Unity.

United Left Union of individual initiative groups from the Left who supported the "third way" of democratic socialism. Many groups were also ecologically oriented.

Viennese Agreement Negotiations on conventional armed forces in Europe conducted in Vienna in August 1990. They resulted in an agreement about limitations on the conventional military forces of a unified Germany.

Volkskammer The GDR parliament.

Wandlitz The development near Berlin in which the GDR bigwigs had their villas.

Wandlitz Republic Derogatory name for the GDR, referring to the fact that this state was ruled by a small political elite who had access to expensive properties in the exclusive development near East Berlin called Wandlitz.

Warsaw Pact Military alliance of East European countries (Bulgaria, the GDR, Poland, Romania, Czechoslovakia, the Soviet Union, and Hungary) to secure friendship, cooperation, and mutual support, signed in Warsaw on 14 May 1955.

Warsaw Treaty Treaty between the FRG and Poland, signed 7 December 1970, determining Poland's western border as the Oder-Neiße-line.

Welcome money (Begrüßungsgeld) Every GDR citizen was entitled to receive 100 D-marks per year as welcome money upon entering the Federal Republic; this program was discontinued on 1 January 1990.

Wendehälse "Turn necks," derogatory term used in the GDR during the peaceful revolution to designate those political opportunists who constantly shifted positions according to the prevailing political winds.

Wessis Derogatory name for people from West Germany.

Workers' and farmers' state Part of the self-understanding of the socialist state; the workers and farmers, that is, the proletariat, are the constituents represented by the state; this designation formed an important part of socialist rhetoric in the GDR.

Young Pioneers Mass youth organization of the GDR.

Bibliography

Aufbrüche: Dokumentation zur Wende in der DDR, Oktober 1989 bis März 1990. Munich: Goethe-Institut, 1991.

Blätter für deutsche und internationale Politik 34 (1989).

Blohm, Frank and Wolfgang Herzberg, eds. *"Nichts wird mehr so sein, wie es war": Zur Zukunft der beiden deutschen Republiken.* Frankfurt: Luchterhand, 1990.

Deutschland Archiv 22 (1989).

Die ersten Texte des Neuen Forum: Erschienen in der Zeit vom 9. September bis 18. Dezember 1989. (Political Pamphlet)

Europa-Archiv 45 (1990).

Frankfurter Rundschau (1989).

Grass, Günter. *Ein Schnäppchen namens DDR: Letzte Reden vorm Glockengeläut.* Frankfurt: Luchterhand, 1990.

Habermas, Jürgen, "Der DM-Nationalismus," *Die Zeit* (30 March 1990).

Heym, Stefan. *Auf Sand gebaut: Sieben Geschichten aus der unmittelbaren Vergangenheit.* Munich: Bertelsmann, 1990.

Naumann, Michael, ed. *"Die Geschichte ist offen." DDR 1990: Hoffnung auf eine neue Republik.* Reinbek bei Hamburg: Rowohlt, 1990.

Schüddekopf, Charles, ed. *"Wir sind das Volk!": Flugschriften, Aufrufe und Texte einer deutschen Revolution.* Reinbek bei Hamburg: Rowohlt, 1990.

Der Spiegel: Dokument (Dezember 1990).

Süddeutsche Zeitung (1990).

Herles, Helmut and Ewald Rose, eds. *Vom Runden Tisch zum Parlament.* Bonn: Bouvier, 1990.

Weiland, Severin, Michaela Wimmer, and Bernhard Michalowski, eds. *9. November. Das Jahr danach: Vom Fall der Mauer bis zur ersten gesamtdeutschen Wahl.* Munich: Heyne, 1990.

Wimmer, Michaela, Christine Proske, Sabine Braun, and Bernhard Michalowski, eds. *"Wir sind das Volk!": Die DDR im Aufbruch.* Munich: Heyne, 1990.

Zanetti, Benno, ed. *Der Weg zur deutschen Einheit: 9. November 1989 – 3. Oktober 1990.* Munich: Goldmann, 1991.

Die Zeit (1989-1990).

Index of Persons

Adenauer, Konrad West German chancellor (CDU) from 1949-63, xiv, xvi

Adler, Brigitte West German SPD parliamentarian, 238

Ahrendt, Lothar GDR minister for internal affairs and member of the Modrow government, 118

Albani, Bernd Member of the New Forum, 98

Albrecht, Hans Member of the Central Committee of the SED, 90

Almond, Gabriel A. American political scientist, 190, 204

Altvater, Elmar Professor of economics at the Free University in West Berlin, 180

Andreotti, Giulio Prime minister of Italy and president of the European Community at the time of German unification, 247, 248

Antretter, Robert West German SPD parliamentarian, 238

Arndt, Ernst Moritz German politician, 201, 204

Augstein, Rudolf Publisher of the bi-weekly West German news magazine *Der Spiegel*, 268

Axen, Hermann SED politician and co-founder of the Free German Youth, 161

Baader, Franz German political theorist and economist, 201, 204

Bähr, Georg German Baroque architect, 102

Baker, James US secretary of state in office during the political events in 1989 and 1990, xxxviii, xli

Barbe, Angelika Member of the initiative group Social-Democratic Party of the GDR, 13

Becher, Johannes R. GDR poet, 165, 167

Beier, Frank GDR theater director, 81

Benjamin,Walter German philosopher, 201

Benn, Gottfried German expressionist poet, 202, 205

Berger, Götz GDR lawyer, 81

Berghof, Wolfgang SED mayor of Dresden at the time of the demonstrations, xxxiii

Bergmann-Pohl, Sabine President of the first freely elected GDR *Volkskammer*, xliv, xlv, xlviii, 278-80

Biermann, Wolf German song writer and poet who was expelled from the GDR in 1976, 156-67

Biermann, Wolfgang Director of the Zeiss Collective in Jena; close to Stasi head Günter Mittag, 156, 160

Birthler, Marianne Member of the Initiative for Freedom and Human Rights, 13

German Unification and Its Discontents
Documents from the Peaceful Revolution
Richard T. Gray and Sabine Wilke, Editors and Translators

This volume collects in English translation a selection of the most significant historical documents relevant to the "peaceful revolution" in the German Democratic Republic in the fall of 1989 and the subsequent events
leading to the unification of the two German states on October 3, 1990.
Included are speeches by major politicians from East and West Germany,
materials on alternative political programs from the East German reform
movement, and critical perspectives on unification, all chronologically arranged. An introductory essay by the editors examines the historical moments that led to unification, in the context of alternative sociopolitical
models for Germany and Central Europe. A detailed chronicle of significant events begins with the opening of the Hungarian border to Austria
on May 2, 1989, and the mass emigration of East German citizens that fall,
pursues the political course day by day, and ends with the day of German
unification. The book concludes with a glossary of German terms and political associations, as well as an index of proper names that includes biographical information.

ABOUT THE EDITORS

Richard T. Gray is professor of German and **Sabine Wilke** is associate
professor of German, both at the University of Washington. They previously collaborated on the translation of Manfred Frank's *What Is Neostruc-
turalism?* Gray is the author of *Constructive Destruction: Kafka's Aphorisms*
and *Stations of the Divided Subject: Contestation and Ideological Legitimation
in German Bourgeois Literature, 1770-1914.* He is the editor of *Approaches to
Teaching Kafka's Short Fiction,* and translator of *Nietzsche's Unfashionable
Observations.* Wilke is the author of *Zur Dialektik von Exposition und
Darstellung: Beitrag zu einer Kritik der Arbeiten Martin Heideggers, Jacques
Derridas und Theodor W. Adornos, Poetische Strukturen der Moderne:
Zeitgenössische Literatur zwischen alter und neuer Mythologie,* and a volume
of essays on Christa Wolf.